The Brittany Affair
and
the Crisis of the Ancien Régime

EDITED BY

JOHN ROTHNEY
University of Missouri

New York
OXFORD UNIVERSITY PRESS
London   Toronto   1969

FOREWORD

Problems in European History: A Documentary Collection has arisen out of a collective teaching experience. The series seeks to overcome a shortcoming which the authors believe persists in college history instruction. Certainly the restricting confines of the traditional textbook have been expanded as numerous collections of "readings" have appeared. But the undergraduate still remains at a distance from the historian's workshop. A compilation of heavily edited "significant documents" does not make for the sense of contact with the past that the study of history ought to promote. And the predigested selections from contending historians, neatly arrayed on either side of "classic" controversies, do not get the student to probe the underlying evidence; in fact, these academic disputations often leave him bewildered.

The conviction that students learned little of the way in which historians actually worked prompted a group of young Harvard historians five years ago to develop a new approach. The course that resulted—Social Sciences 3: Problems in Modern European History—represented an attempt to focus intensively on a small number of problems. Each problem would involve careful analysis of a wide variety of original source material. The student could develop the skills and understanding of historical explanation. In learning to compare evidence, make and test hypotheses, and judge critically earlier accounts, he would encounter some of the problems of historical research as experienced by the working historian.

In Social Sciences 3 eight studies in historical analysis are presented in a year. Our intention here is to make these documentary collections available, not necessarily as a series except in their underlying aim, but as separate problems that can be studied individually in connection with courses in European history. Each book has been edited and introduced with that purpose in mind. Thus the student can wrestle with the problems inherent in historical writing and judgment while he studies intensively a segment of history of the country or period being taught.

Social Sciences 3 has developed over the past four years through the efforts of our collaborators, who share in the creation of these books beyond what we can gratefully acknowledge. Individual problems were prepared or substantially recast by the respective authors, but each case study was discussed and scrutinized by the entire staff of Social Sciences 3. To all of them, to the Committee on General Education of Harvard College, which has generously given of its time and efforts, and to our students—whose criticisms and suggestions were a fundamental guideline—we extend our thanks.

Cambridge, Mass.   **RICHARD BIENVENU**
August, 1967   **JOHN F. NAYLOR**

PREFACE

The idea of focusing a documentary collection depicting the institutional, social, and intellectual conflicts of the last decades of the *Ancien Régime* upon the problem of the Brittany Affair first occurred to me as I read Robert R. Palmer's *The Age of Democratic Revolution*.[1] For placing the Affair in thought-provoking perspective as a French example of the struggles that centered around "constituted bodies" throughout the Atlantic world in the second half of the eighteenth century, I am much indebted to that stimulating work of synthesis.

In its original form, this problem was called simply "The Brittany Affair." By retitling it for publication I have not meant to imply that the Affair provoked "the crisis of the *Ancien Régime*." Not every historian would agree, indeed, that the fate of the eighteenth-century French monarchy was decided by the outcome of Maupeou's assault on the parlements. Perhaps the "crisis" began in 1715 and was resolved only by the events of 1789. Rather the new title is intended to reflect the prime purpose of this collection of sources, which is not to have the student adjudicate the rights and wrongs of the Breton imbroglio, but to acquaint him at first hand with key aspects of a society on the verge of revolution. The Brittany Affair itself, intriguing as it is, serves primarily as a means of cutting a cross-section through that society and thus making it accessible to analysis. Because what must really be analyzed is the direction the

1. 2 vols. (Princeton: Princeton University Press, 1959–64), Vol. I: The Challenge.

life of a whole nation was taking for more than a decade, I have made a deliberate effort, in my introductions to the six chapters of documents, not to impose my own interpretive concepts too heavily upon the reader. The purpose of the collection will have been satisfied if the reader emerges from it with an understanding of the life of the Old Regime that will enable him to construct a persuasive interpretation of his own.

I received much help in the work of compiling and translating documents from fellow members of the staff of Social Sciences 3 at Harvard, most particularly from Richard Bienvenu, but also from Paul R. Duggan, John Naylor, and Fritz K. Ringer. I am obliged to the Research Council of the University of Missouri for its assistance in the preparation of the manuscript.

Columbia, Missouri   J. R.
October 1968

CONTENTS

IV   The Brittany Affair in Rennes and Paris, 1766–1770, 165

Ministers of France, 1758–1774

1758–1770

Chief Minister and Minister of Foreign Affairs:
>Étienne-François, Duke de CHOISEUL-AMBOISE (1758–1770)

Internal Affairs and Government of Paris:
>Louis Phélypeaux, Count de SAINT-FLORENTIN, named
>Duke de La Vrillière in 1770 (1757–1775)

Comptrollers-General:
>Étienne de SILHOUETTE (March–November 1759)
>Henri-Léonard-Jean-Baptiste BERTIN (1759–1763)
>Clément-Charles-François de L'AVERDY (1763–1768)
>MAYNON D'INVAU (1768–1769)

1770–1774: The "Triumvirate"

Minister of Foreign Affairs:
>Armand Vignerol-Duplessis-Richelieu, Duke D'AIGUILLON
>(1770–1774)

Chancellor:
>René-Nicolas-Charles-Augustin de MAUPEOU (1768–1774)

Comptroller-General:
>Abbé Joseph-Marie TERRAY (1769–August 24, 1774)

Ministers named at the accession of Louis XVI in 1774

Chief Minister:
>Jean-Frédéric Phélippeaux, Count de MAUREPAS (1774–1781)

Foreign Affairs:
>Charles Gravier, Count de VERGENNES (1774–1787)

Comptroller-General:
>Anne-Robert-Jacques TURGOT, Baron de l'Aulne (1774–1776)

First Presidents, Advocates-General, and Attorneys-General* of the Parlements of Paris and of Rennes, 1763–1776

F. P. signifies First President; At. G., Attorney-General; Ad. G., Advocate-General

	Paris	Rennes
	1757 Nolé, F. P.	1734 De la Brisse d'Amilly, F. P.
	1746 Joly de Fleury, Ad. G.	1740 Du Parcq-Porée, Ad. G.
1763	1740 Joly de Fleury, At. G.	1753 De Caradeuc de la Chalotais, At. G.
	1755 Séguier, Ad. G.	1753 Le Prestre de Château-Giron, Ad. G.
	1757 Le Peletier de Saint-Fargeau, Ad. G.	
	1763 De Maupeou, F. P.	1734 De la Brisse d'Amilly, F. P.
	1746 Joly de Fleury, Ad. G.	1740 Du Parcq-Porée, Ad. G.
1765	1740 Joly de Fleury, At. G.	1764 De Caradeuc de la Chalotais, At. G.
	1755 Séguier, Ad. G.	1753 Le Prestre de Château-Giron, Ad. G.
	1764 Barentin, Ad. G.	
	1768 D'Aligne, F. P.	1734 De la Brisse d'Amilly, F. P.
	1755 Séguier, Ad. G.	1740 Du Parcq-Porée, Ad. G.
1771	1740 Joly de Fleury, At. G.	1764 De Caradeuc de la Chalotais, At. G.
	1764 Barentin, Ad. G.	1753 Le Prestre de Château-Giron, Ad. G.
	1767 Joly de Fleury, Ad. G.	
	1771 Bertier de Sauvigny, F. P.	1771 De la Brisse d'Amilly, F. P.
1772	1771 De Verges, Ad. G.	1771 Menardeau, Ad. G.
	1771 Joly de Fleury, At. G.	1771 Grimaudet, At. G.
	1771 De Vaucresson, Ad. G.	1771 Silgny, Ad. G.
	1768 D'Aligne, F. P.	1771 De la Brisse d'Amilly, F. P.
	1755 Séguier, Ad. G.	1740 Du Parcq-Porée, Ad. G.
1776	1740 Joly de Fleury, At. G.	1764 De Caradeuc de la Chalotais, At. G.
	1774 D'Aguesseau, Ad. G.	17.. De la Chalotais, in survivorship
	1775 Joly de Fleury, Ad. G.	1775 Du Bourg Blanc, Ad. G.

Source: the *Almanach royal* of 1763, 1765, 1771, 1772, and 1776.
[* In French, these titles are *Premier Président, Avocat-général,* and *Procureur-général.*—Ed.]

The Brittany Affair
and the Crisis of the Ancien Régime

INTRODUCTION

Almost from the moment on July 14, 1789, when the people of Paris stormed the royal prison called the Bastille and began a new chapter in world history, men have debated the causes of the fall of the thousand-year-old French monarchy. Was the French Revolution, as defenders of the *Ancien Régime* charged from the beginning, the consequence of the subversive ideas of a coterie of destructive theorists? Or was the Revolution, as its supporters insisted, the uprising of a united nation against a tyrannical monarchy supported by a haughty and grasping aristocracy? Historians today usually reject both of these explanations as oversimplifications. Instead they depict the Revolution as developing almost unavoidably from fiscal, political, and social problems that the Old Regime finally proved incapable of solving.

According to Georges Lefebvre, the most distinguished of recent historians of the Revolution, the upheaval really began in 1787, when the nobility rebelled against the bankrupt monarchy's last attempt to compel them to pay their proportionate share of the costs of government. The nobility, seeking once and for all to curb royal power in order to defend their privileges, set an example of insubordination that other groups within French society, with quite different goals, were quick to follow. When a national representative body—the Estates-General—convened in the spring of 1789, deputies of the third estate, middle-class politicians hostile alike to a royal absolutism and to a noble claim to privilege that seemed to have become inseparable, boldly asserted their right to impose a written constitution upon France. Their parliamentary tactics were threatened by royal recalcitrance, but the storming of the Bastille demonstrated that ordinary Parisians would support the third estate's constitutional demands with irresistible violence. A few weeks later, widespread peasant revolts compelled the abolition of many of those very exploitative privileges that the nobility in 1787 had defended by their own acts of revolt. Thus the French Revolution, according to Lefebvre, was in reality not one but a series of distinct if interrelated revolutions, in which groups whose grievances against the Old Regime were different or even opposed momentarily combined to destroy it.

However its origins are to be explained, the Revolution and the convulsive generation that followed it produced by 1815 a France whose political and social organization was very different from what it had been in 1789. True, the growth of large-scale industry, the crowding of the population into large cities had hardly begun when the French monarchy was restored after Napoleon's defeat at Waterloo. But it can be convincingly argued that the Revolutionary and Napoleonic generation created the indispensable political, social, and intellectual preconditions for the dramatic industrialization and urbanization of the mid-nineteenth century. France after 1815 was a fiscally stable nation of citizens equal before the law, governed by representative institutions in which issues were judged not on the basis of tradition or custom, but by the pragmatic criterion of utility. The centralized bureaucracy of Prefects created by Napoleon applied uniform legal codes throughout the country without the slightest concession to geographical distinctions, encouraging the citizens to think of themselves as members of a national, not a peculiar local, community.

Much blood would still be shed in the nineteenth century, to be sure, in conflicts over the proper application of the new political and social principles. It was only after a new revolution in 1848, for example, that the idea became current that the already accepted principle of equality implied political democracy, with a vote for every man. Nonetheless, after 1815 a return to divine-right absolutism, to a hierarchical social structure based on distinctions of birth, to a state hamstrung by historic provincial immunities, was quite inconceivable. It is for this reason that students of the process by which traditional agrarian societies develop into the industrialized, urbanized, mobile societies that dominate the twentieth-century world have identified the Revolutionary generation 1789–1815 as a crucial step in France's "modernization."

As the front page of any recent newspaper clearly reveals, the "modernization" of traditional societies in our own day is frequently a violent process of assassinations, *coups d'état,* rioting, and even of full-scale revolution. The headlines make us wonder, in fact, whether violence must not inevitably accompany at least some episodes of the emergence of new political and social ideals. This is not a new question, but one that was perhaps first posed by the French Revolution. Defenders of the *Ancien Régime* have insisted that violence was *not* necessary: that the French monarchy was peacefully effecting necessary transformations in the nation's life when its efforts were wrecked by an outburst of needless violence.

Historians are now more reluctant than they have sometimes been to postulate "laws" of human behavior, and few would be willing to predict that violence must be an inevitable accompaniment to the process of "modernization." But it may not be impossible to make an informed judgment about the likelihood of violence in late eighteenth-century France. The question is, if the various groups Lefebvre discusses resorted to defiance of the established government and ultimately to violence, was it because they were wantonly reckless or because the existing system prevented them from achieving their goals by any other means? Assuming, as we must, that change was becoming inescapable by

the end of the eighteenth century, could the French state and
French society transform themselves peacefully, or did modernization have to be forced upon them?

To answer these questions really requires us to assess the potential of the *Ancien Régime* for non-violent change. We must
decide whether its institutions and traditions were flexible enough
to adjust to new political, social, and intellectual realities. These
are not easy judgments to make because the "politics" of the
Ancien Régime are so elusive. First of all, we know hardly anything about what the infinite majority of Frenchmen—those illiterate peasants who lived out a toil-filled existence and died all
within hearing of their village church-bell—were thinking. (Indeed, their voices—and the voices of the even more wretched
hordes of indigent vagabonds—are scarcely to be heard in the
following pages.) And even when we admit that we can know
the opinions of only a handful of the population, our difficulties
are not over, because in pre-Revolutionary France there was no
political life as we know it today. There was no parliament: the
Estates-General, the consultative assembly that the king, before
1614, had occasionally summoned to approve taxes, was not convened again until 1789. Among the provinces that made up the
incredible patchwork map of France under the Old Regime,
some of the peripheral ones—*pays d'États*—regularly convoked
local estates, but their abbreviated proceedings were usually confined to purely local questions. A press of sorts there was, reinforced by a growing pamphlet literature, but both were subject
to the caprices of a frequently indulgent but always dangerous
official censorship.

Thus there are formidable obstacles to tracing the political
evolution of the Old Regime and therefore to analyzing its capacity for adaptation to new challenges. Yet these are not such
difficult tasks as to require treating pre-Revolutionary France, as
textbooks sometimes describe it, as an unchanging monolith. Conflicts between social groups, struggles for political supremacy,

clashes of innovation with tradition all must find an outlet some-place, and the historian must study them where they do come to the surface.

This is the reason for a twentieth-century student to interest himself in the Brittany Affair. For a long time its significance was overlooked. This decade-long battle through the French courts that began in 1765 with royal troops arresting Attorney-General La Chalotais of Brittany, with its bewildering series of trials and retrials, was thought to be a subject of only antiquarian interest. More recently, however, historians have recognized that the issues at stake in the Brittany Affair were precisely the issues upon which the fate of the *Ancien Régime* depended. In fact, the Affair can be regarded as a sort of microcosm of the life of France in the late eighteenth century, and anyone who has understood its origins, development, and outcome should be able to make an informed judgment of the adaptability of the *Ancien Régime* to the pres-sures of change. This does not mean that if the historian diagnoses a severe case of institutional paralysis in 1774, when Louis XVI mounted the throne, he must therefore arrive at a prognosis of revolution fifteen years later. "Inevitable" is an adjective that no historian employs lightly. At the very least, however, the Brittany Affair reveals sufficient symptoms of governmental malfunction, social trauma, and intellectual fever to suggest why the reign of that well-intentioned but obtuse and lethargic king would bring on the final crisis of the regime. Indeed, some historians would contend that its condition was already beyond cure when the new reign began.

In order to understand the gravity of this crisis, it must be considered in the perspective of the political, social, and intellec-tual history of the preceding century. In 1665 the ideals of divine-right absolutism, rigid social stratification, and religious orthodoxy personified by the Grand Monarch, Louis XIV (1643–1715), dominated the minds of Frenchmen. By 1765 all three were be-ing seriously questioned. The events of these hundred years can be summarized as the gradual but inexorable decline of a system.

Under Louis XIV, political theorists pushed the doctrine of the limitlessness of royal power to its farthest conceivable extent, justifying their arguments with precedents from all the epochs of French history. The king, it was said, enjoyed all the sovereign authority of the Roman emperors and made law of his own will "by our full power and royal authority," as the form of royal decrees expressed it. As supreme suzerain, overlord of all feudal relationships, the king was declared to be the real owner of all the land in the kingdom: France was actually his personal property. And, according to the most irresistible of arguments in an age of universal religious faith, the king, as the Lord's anointed representative, derived his power directly from Heaven and was answerable for his actions only to divine judgment.

Louis XIV took these staggering descriptions of his own role quite literally. He set out to make them realities with the conscientiousness of a man who relished his royal work. As a child, he had been a terrified spectator of an invasion of the palace by the riotous rebels of the Fronde; his reign was a patient, painstaking, only partly successful effort to ensure that royal authority could never again be so challenged. To convert absolutist theory into practice was not an easy task in a kingdom where, during his boyhood, many noblemen had not hesitated to make war upon their sovereign like their ancestors, the unruly vassals of the Middle Ages. Moreover, France in the mid-seventeenth century was a veritable museum of corporate privileges that had been upheld from time immemorial as barriers to the encroachments of central authority. Even a king who believed that he ruled by delegation from God could not, had he wanted to, have leveled at one blow the customary framework of a whole society; only a revolution could accomplish that, as was demonstrated between 1789 and 1815. Louis XIV proceeded more circumspectly, increasing his power by methods both direct and indirect. He strengthened and developed those already existing monarchical institutions that were under his immediate control, while at the same time he sought to neutralize those potential opponents he could not over-awe by cleverly luring them into dependency upon him.

This double-edged stratagem of rule is what explains the curious variety of Louis's daily royal routine, in which the hard, detailed paperwork of government business alternated with an elaborate and vacuous ceremonial ritual that seems scarcely credible to twentieth-century students. In one or another of his regular councils, after listening to the recommendations of ministers who were usually his creatures and instruments, Louis XIV made the decisions by which the kingdom was governed. To implement his policies throughout France, he relied upon his provincial intendants. These officials, first employed by Cardinal Richelieu, Louis's great predecessor in the work of consolidating royal power, he invested with sweeping administrative authority within their local jurisdictions. With their subordinates, the subdelegates, they formed a vast bureaucratic network for the transmission of reports to Versailles and of orders to the provinces.

From these key ministerial and administrative posts Louis carefully excluded the powerful nobility. This was a conscious and deliberate policy. As Louis explained for the benefit of his successor: It was not in my interest to take people of a more eminent quality. . . . It mattered to me that they should not conceive higher hopes than those that it would please me to give them; this is difficult with people of high birth." No doubt he anticipated that noblemen would resent his confiding the real political power to career-minded commoners while the older offices the nobility were permitted to retain—such as the governorships of provinces—became purely honorary. In order to distract them he created the most ceremonious court Europe had yet known. Its elaborate etiquette was intended not only to glorify Louis, but to disarm the nobility. Absorbed by the game of intrigue for royal honors and stipends at Versailles, many noblemen failed to perceive that the king had skillfully enticed them into a gilded cage. For, jostling

one another to catch the royal eye as the Sun King rose and retired, the nobility could hardly organize the kind of resistance
to the royal will their ancestors had kept up for centuries. Moreover, the competition for royal favor was often ruinously expensive, and a ruined nobleman could hope to recoup his losses only
if the king gratified him with one of the innumerable royal pensions
or sinecures; the need for one of these made many noblemen all
the more dutiful.

This subtly indirect manner in which Louis XIV undermined
the nobility's political strength was characteristic of. the methods
he chose to make his absolute rule real. Seldom did he decree the
abolition of an institution or corporate body whose privileges posed
a threat to his authority. He preferred instead, when ignoring such
a group's claims did not suffice, to subvert it by some form of
corruption. This was often his way of dealing, for example, with
the assemblies of the *pays d'États*. Rather than abrogate their more
or less genuine historic rights to regulate the local collection of
taxes, he was inclined to bribe or intimidate a majority into acquiescence in the royal demands. Or he might change the procedural rules to ensure the victory of his supporters. Though he
often emasculated French institutions, he hardly altered them.

For Louis XIV was no royal revolutionary; his social outlook
was entirely conventional. He deprived the nobility of political
power because power in their hands threatened his own, but like
most of his contemporaries he saw nothing unnatural in their
separate existence as a highly privileged caste.

So profound and lasting has been the impact of the French
Revolution and its related movements upon our Western world
that we find it difficult today to imagine a society like that of
seventeenth-century France, a society whose ideal was not mobility
but immobility, in which prestige derived not from wealth or
achievement, but from birth and blood. Under the Old Regime,
however, the medieval doctrine that God had divided men among
the clergy who prayed, the nobility who fought, and the "third"

estate who labored to support the lofty deeds of the first two remained the legal foundation upon which society was organized.

It was by virtue of their God-given and hereditary function as defenders of the kingdom that noblemen claimed their collective right to stand apart, as a corporate body, from the mass of ordinary Frenchmen. It did not matter that this claim was largely spurious, now that the age of chivalry was long dead. Relatively few of the nobility of the seventeenth and eighteenth centuries could trace noble ancestry back more than a few generations, and fewer still could prove descent from one of those Frankish warriors whose victories, aristocratic apologists declared, had given their heirs permanent superiority over the mere Gauls. Yet the nobility insisted no less firmly on their symbolic privileges: the right to wear a sword, to display a coat of arms, to occupy the principal pew in the parish church. And they clung as obstinately to prerogatives of their birth that were of more practical value: exemption from service in the militia, for example, as well as from the *taille* (the land tax) and the *corvée,* the compulsory labor service by which the Old Regime carried out its programs of public works.

Though they constituted an infinitely small proportion of the population (three or four hundred thousand out of twenty-five million in 1789, or less than 2 per cent), the French nobility were a highly diverse group, and the fifth of the land of the kingdom they owned was shared most unequally among them. They ranged in dignity from the princes of the blood—jealous royal relatives, like the Duke of Orleans—and the "dukes and peers" only a little less grand down to the thousands of obscure provincial squires. Some were great feudal lords who not only collected manorial fees from their peasant tenants but sat in judgment over them in seigneurial courts, maintaining their private gallows at some nearby crossroads as a reminder of their possession of the right of high justice. Many more, however, particularly in the less developed regions of France, were so poverty-stricken that they could be

seen, swords at their sides, themselves plowing the fields that provided them with a marginal subsistence. A hierarchy of so many
gradations naturally created numberless opportunities for snobbery
and envious resentment. The few thousand great noblemen who
had been presented at court scorned the miserable provincials who
had not. Above all, at the end of the seventeenth century there
was still outspoken antagonism between the "nobility of the sword,"
whose titles derived from the military service of some ancestor,
and the "nobility of the robe," who had bought the ennobling
offices sold by the French kings in their perpetual quest for money.
In the eyes of noblemen whose titles had been granted in return
for something other than cash, the "nobility of the robe" remained
mere vile bourgeoisie despite their wealth and pretensions. The
nobles of the robe, however, having purchased with their offices
the right to transmit their titles to successive generations, vehe-
mently insisted that birth separated them as widely from ordinary
commoners as it did their rivals of the sword. Though their family
fortunes had in most cases originally been built up in business,
they warmly embraced the convention that any nobleman who
stooped to engage in some form of productive work thereby for-
feited his quality of nobility.

It would thus be inaccurate to regard the French nobility of
1700 as a homogeneous caste, yet their internal feuds were in the
last analysis less important than their shared feeling of disdain for
the vast majority of Frenchmen who had no claim to nobility. A
policy like Louis XIV's which denied the nobility an effective
political role while allowing them to retain their social identity was
consequently fraught with dangers. On the one hand, the nobility
might tire of their splendid impotence and bid for a political role
that matched their social pre-eminence; if, on the other hand, they
did not win such a role, France, finding that noblemen rendered no
services commensurate with their privileges, might decide that the
nobility were a superfluous burden. Both of these possibilities in
fact did materialize. The entire reign of Louis XIV's successor was

punctuated by the nobles' efforts to enlarge their political role. The second alternative took shape later, during the Revolution. It could be envisioned only when France's social system could be discussed in the light of utilitarian rather than traditionalist criteria.

Though royal absolutism and noble privilege finally perished only in 1789, after a century of conflict, the ideas that justified them had been under attack for much longer. Gradually, in the course of the eighteenth century, the values of the age of Louis XIV were undermined, as the Church of France fell into greater and greater discredit.

The doctrines of the Church had been powerful props for the social and political systems of the seventeenth century. Catholic teaching held that since earthly life was but a transient episode of suffering before the eternity of Hell or Paradise, each individual should strive during it to serve God in the estate of society to which God had called him, rather than envying the privileges that rewarded the calling of others. Abnegation, not emulation, was the social ideal of the Christian. This article of faith helps to explain why so many Frenchmen for so long accepted a social hierarchy that had long since ceased to correspond to social functions.

The relationship between Louis XIV and the Church was one of reciprocal benefit and support. The king offered his strong secular arm for the suppression of religious dissent; the Church preached that submission to authority, whether spiritual or temporal, was the essential principle of a God-fearing polity. During the sixteenth century France had been rent by strife between Protestants and Catholics that occasioned such horrors as the Saint Bartholomew's Day massacre of the Protestants of Paris. Louis XIV's predecessors had alternately negotiated and fought with a virtual Protestant state within the state. Richelieu had already curbed the power of the Huguenots, as French Protestants were called; Louis XIV, who became more bigoted with advancing age, finally decided to root them out completely. In 1685, after years of calculated persecution designed to compel the Huguenots to convert, he revoked the Edict of Nantes, the limited charter of Protestant rights. Henceforth, until the very eve of the Revolution, to preach or to practice the Protestant religion within France was a crime subject to the severest penalties of a legal system that employed torture as a standard method of interrogation.

The Grand Monarch tried to deal no less sternly with dissenters within the Catholic Church. Here his targets were the Jansenists, whose doctrines emphasizing the superiority of religious experience over theological reasoning and repudiating excessive ceremonial ritual have sometimes been characterized as a "Catholic Calvinism." Though the disciples of Bishop Jansen denied that their beliefs posed any threat to the existing religious institutions, they soon found themselves locked in desperate struggle with the Society of Jesus, long the most ardent defenders of strict Catholic obedience against the dissolving influences of religious speculation. This was an unequal contest, since the Jesuits had the ear of the king, and at their urging he asked the Pope to condemn Jansen's teachings. The papal bull of 1713, *Unigenitus,* an anathema upon Jansenism, was declared by Louis XV in 1730 to be part of the very constitution of the realm. Yet despite this papal and royal ban, Jansenism did not completely disappear. There were periodic outbreaks of fervor verging on convulsive hysteria at the news of supposed miracles. And the cult's presence in a less extreme form was detected or suspected in such centers of resistance to royal authority as the sovereign courts, or parlements.

If the high-court judges had reservations about *Unigenitus,* however, perhaps this is to be explained as much by their Gallicanism as by their Jansenism. Louis XIV's appeal to Rome for a judgment against the Jansenists seemed to many an abandonment of the Gallican definition of the Church's organization enunciated in 1682 by the most powerful of Louis's own spokesmen within the Church, Bishop Bossuet. The Declaration of the French Clergy he had then inspired held that the Pope had no temporal authority over the king of France and only limited spiritual authority over the French church.

In fact the relations among the king, the bishops, and the Pope continued to conform to Bossuet's definition, despite Louis's appeal in his last years for papal intervention. The Concordat of 1516 gave the French crown the right to name the archbishops and bishops of the Gallican Church. The fact that he selected its leaders did not mean that the king controlled every act of the Church. It was the largest of those privileged corporations so common under the Old Regime, and paid taxes neither on the ten per cent of the land of the kingdom it owned nor on the tithes it collected from the laity. Its contribution to the state's finances was limited to a so-called free gift voted at the periodic meetings of the assembly of the clergy. It was, again, characteristic of Louis XIV's methods that he did not abolish the principle of voluntary contribution, though in fact he extorted larger "free gifts" than the Church would have preferred to grant.

For the relationship between the king and the high churchmen was not one of master and servants, but the co-operation of men who believed that their functions were inseparable. Since both were God's deputies on earth, religious dissent and civil disobedience really were indistinguishable. It was only natural therefore for the state to persecute heretics just as the Church preached the same submission to royal as to divine authority. Seventeenth-century politics, like seventeenth-century religion, insisted that human affairs must be managed to please an ever-watchful God who intervened constantly in the doings of mortals. The age of the Grand Monarch was the last epoch of Western history that believed this.

For, long before the end of the seventeenth century, an intellectual revolution had begun which by 1789 would undermine not only this view of the nature of the world, but the political and social systems it justified as well. The powerful ideas of three seventeenth-century thinkers, two English and one French, provided the weapons with which the eighteenth-century *philosophes* attacked many of the fundamental assumptions of the age of Louis XIV. From Descartes they learned the method of systematic doubt, the rejection of all beliefs, however widely held, that were not capable of rigorously logical proof. Newtonian physics left them awestruck with its revelation that everything in the universe, from the smallest everyday objects to the solar system itself, acted according to invariable laws that men could comprehend. And the empiricist doctrines of Locke, who insisted that men are born unformed, without innate ideas, and acquire from their experience of the external world all that they know, seemed to represent a breakthrough in psychology as breathtaking as Newton's in physics.

Inspired by the Cartesian, Newtonian, and Lockean examples with the belief that their age represented a turning point in the history of human thought, eighteenth-century thinkers compounded a potent solvent of the *Ancien Régime*'s ideas of the world and of man. Probably the most important change was that belief in God faded. Critical examination of His supposed miraculous interventions in the affairs of man showed them to be spurious. Indeed, such divine meddling was incompatible with the workings of the gigantic mechanism Newton had described. Perhaps a divine being had set the mechanism going, but such a being obviously bore no relation to the God in whose name men had for so long ferociously persecuted one another.

The worldly and intolerant Church was not the only institution that, deprived of the sanction of God's mysterious will, came to seem wholly unjustifiable to many reasonable men of the eighteenth century. Now that Locke had shown that there need be no superstitious awe for things in which men had "always" believed, hardly anything could escape critical scrutiny or even unflattering comparison with the practices of other civilizations like the Chinese, about which Westerners were becoming increasingly curious. Yet the implications of Lockean psychology were constructive as well as destructive. If the newborn child's mind was a "blank tablet," a rational society could take care to inscribe upon it all the lessons necessary for vastly improving—perhaps even perfecting—the condition of the human species. For surely society, when cured by critical enquiry of the blindness of centuries of ignorance, would discover that it was governed by harmonious laws as fathomable as those that regulated the physical world. When men had understood those laws, they might attain on earth the happiness the Church had always preached was only to be found beyond it. It would be possible to change the world, if Locke's chief lesson were learned: "Of all the men we meet with, nine parts of ten are what they are, good or evil, useful or not, by their education."

Such was the message of the eighteenth-century *philosophes,* who were not academic "philosophers" but thoroughly engaged —and often thoroughly intolerant—critics of the society in which they lived. Neither their impact nor their unanimity should be exaggerated. Their polemical speculations hardly touched the vast illiterate masses. Even among the upper classes they were often regarded with the distrust a society usually reserves for its radical thinkers, though few of the *philosophes* went as far as the hedonistic materialism of a Helvétius. Voltaire, less optimistic than some about human nature, regarded its improvement as a long uphill battle and consequently violently rejected Rousseau's contention that men were born good and corrupted only by civilization. Such talk, he exclaimed, made him feel as if he should crawl about on all fours. The two differed as widely in their political ideals as both diverged from Montesquieu.

Despite such differences, however, the *philosophes* imparted to many eighteenth-century Frenchmen a conviction that their society could and must be dramatically improved. While the Sorbonne, the official seat of education, continued through the century to split theological hairs, the salons of Paris and a growing number of provincial intellectual circles bubbled with enthusiasm for every kind of novelty. All sorts of possible improvements were discussed, ranging from the application of scientific methods of agriculture to the Marquis de Beccaria's proposals for a humane justice without capital punishment, torture, or confiscation of the convict's property.

Revolutionary ideas even found scattered support among the very ruling circles they tended to discredit. The efforts of *philosophes* like Diderot and d'Alembert to summarize and diffuse the knowledge of the new scientific age in the *Encyclopédie* were backed by Madame de Pompadour, Louis XV's favorite between 1745 and her death in 1764, against the opposition of the Jesuits. Sympathy for the proponents of the new ideas did not make the royal mistress a reformer. The same cannot be said for Baron Turgot, who as Intendant of Limoges between 1761 and 1774 attempted to put into practice many of the ideas of his *philosophe* friends.

The most convincing proof of the growing influence of the *philosophes* is provided, however, by the remarkable career of an admirer of Turgot's, François-Marie Arouet, known to the century that was uniquely his by his pen-name, Voltaire. Born in 1694 into a well-to-do family on the fringes of the Parisian *noblesse de robe*, Voltaire spurned the respectable legal career his father had marked out for him and earned a precocious literary reputation. (When he was only twenty-four, his tragedy *Oedipe* was a hit in Paris.) He discovered equally early that it was birth, not talent, that the Old Regime really respected. The malicious wit that was never to desert him earned him a thrashing at the hands of the lackeys of a great nobleman, after which Voltaire, rather than his attacker, was imprisoned in the Bastille. He received his release in 1726 on the condition that he quit France for England. The three years he spent there were crucial to his intellectual formation. For the rest of his life he would contrast (not always accurately) English religious toleration with French bigotry, English simplicity with French social pretension, English governmental effectiveness with French incoherence.

By the middle of the eighteenth century Voltaire's feverish outpouring of poetry, drama, history, and satire had made him the chief international celebrity of the age, and his reputation reinforced the impact of his polemics against various abuses of French society. The humble and the great of the whole world vied for his attention. (His collected letters, many of them signed with his motto *Écrasez l'infâme*—"crush the infamous thing," i.e. the Church—fill more than one hundred stout volumes.) King Frederick the Great of Prussia (1740–86) and the Empress Catherine of Russia (1762–96), despotic rulers who attempted or pretended to govern in accordance with the "enlightened" principles of the *philosophes,* sought his advice and approval. At Frederick's invitation in 1751 Voltaire even went to live at the Prussian court. Though a quarrel ended his visit in less than three years, such was the intellectual bond between the two men that they continued an animated correspondence until Voltaire's death in 1778.

That the most famous of sacrilegious wits should become the confidant of one of the most famous of kings suggests the extent to which the *philosophes* had succeeded in demolishing the foundations of divine-right monarchy by the middle of the eighteenth century. More and more, men were learning to ask not what were the traditional origins of human institutions—even monarchies—but what was their present use for the practical improvement of human affairs. It was not the hereditary ruler of Prussia Voltaire praised in Frederick, but the statesman who decreed religious freedom and abolished serfdom and torture.

Few historians would venture to say that a change in intellectual climate has of itself caused any political revolution. But if it is true that the indispensable preliminary step of the process of political "modernization" is a transformation of thought from traditional modes, France may be said to have been about to take that step in the 1760's.

It is essential to note, however, that Voltaire discovered his model sovereigns in Berlin and Saint Petersburg, and not at Versailles. The character and personality of Louis XIV's great-grandson and successor Louis XV (1715–74) were not the only reasons for what some *philosophes* regarded as the failure of the eighteenth-century French monarchy, but, in a system that depended so much on a royal energy matching Louis XIV's, they undoubtedly played their part.

Louis XV was bored by the work of kingship, and often signed without reading them the documents he was handed, including the *lettres de cachet* that consigned men to the royal prisons without trial. Unenthusiastic as he was about his responsibilities, however, he refused to delegate them after the death of Cardinal Fleury, his principal minister between 1726 and 1743. Thus France drifted along in a chaos of conflicting policies inspired by rival ministers and the court factions that backed them. No coherent theory of rule like Louis XIV's was now at work: appointments as intendants, for example, were increasingly given to powerful noblemen with independent positions. Louis XIV had seldom permitted court intrigues to influence his choice of policies; Louis XV had all the weak man's fondness for intrigue as a means of playing off against one another those he lacked the will to control. He even carried on a covert foreign policy at variance with the one his ministers recommended—with sometimes disastrous results. In the three dynastic wars France fought during his reign, she gained no decisive advantage in the continental power struggle; and in the last of them, the Seven Years' War of 1756–63, she lost most of her colonial empire, including much of the North American continent, to England.

The cost of this series of inglorious wars, when superimposed upon the huge deficit left by Louis XIV, grievously aggravated the monarchy's most pressing problem: its finances. John Law, the Scottish banker whose unorthodox fiscal system collapsed in an investors' panic in 1720, was only the first of a series of comptrollers-general (ministers of finance) who struggled unavailingly during short, unhappy terms of office throughout the century to solve the financial problem. Their difficulty was that the tax base was simply too small. The privileged orders—the clergy and nobility—were exempt from older direct taxes like the *taille* and systematically evaded newer ones like the *vingtième* and the *capitation,* which Louis XIV had instituted with the intention that all should pay. Indirect levies like the salt tax or *gabelle,* though they aroused bitter resentment because of the grotesque variation from province to province in the rate at which they were assessed, were equally inadequate.

Rather than modernize the tax base to eliminate these social and geographical anomalies of ancient origin, the government of Louis XV continued to live literally from hand to mouth by a variety of temporary and dubious expedients. The function of tax-gathering was "farmed out," for example, to private individuals in return for ready cash. And the curious practice of selling government offices, from judgeships in the parlements down to subordinate posts in municipal administrations, continued unabated. There was never any lack of buyers, for an office was not merely a safe (though seldom spectacularly profitable) investment, but the means of social promotion. Despite this ever-ready market, however, venality of offices—particularly of high offices—was ultimately a self-destructive practice for the monarchy, since the status of nobility such offices often conferred promptly removed the wealth of the new officeholder and his heirs beyond the reach of the state. Using such methods, the *Ancien Régime* could not indefinitely avoid bankruptcy. When the staggering amount of the deficit finally became known, the extreme remedy of summoning an Estates-General to reconstruct the finances could no longer be avoided. It was summoned for May 1789. A year later revolution had transformed the Estates-General into a National Constituent Assembly which removed two of the obstacles to a complete fiscal reform by seizing for the nation the formerly inviolate property of the Church and abolishing not merely the tax exemptions of the nobility, but the status of nobility itself.

Perhaps only a revolution could have gone this far. Certainly, when faced with the dramatic resurgence of the political activity of nobles after 1715, a less slothful king than Louis XV would have hesitated to take steps much less drastic to re-establish the solvency of his government. Even under Louis XIV, scattered and muted voices had been heard contesting his right to govern absolutely and insisting that kingdoms lived by certain unwritten but fundamental laws that no monarch could breach. In those vague olden times upon which so much of political argument centered, anti-royalist writers recalled, the king of France had been merely the first of noblemen, elected by his peers and governing by compact with them. Thus even when the "royal thesis" of government—the doctrine that the best system was the one that invested the greatest power in the king—was receiving a practical demonstration, the "noble thesis" that the best of governments was rule by aristocracy had not lacked defenders.

After the old king died, however, this undertone of argument against absolutism became much more audible as the nobility emerged from the spell Louis XIV had cast over them. Acting as regent between 1715 and 1723 for the boy Louis XV, the ambitious Duke of Orleans tested the "noble thesis" by entrusting the responsibilities of government to a number of councils composed exclusively of noblemen. The *Polysynodie,* as this experiment was called, quickly proved unworkable. But if the French nobility showed themselves within a few months to be incapable of governing the kingdom, they demonstrated throughout the rest of the century that they were well able to prevent its being governed.

The events of the half-century after 1715 revealed just how the system that Louis XIV had created fell between two stools. His absolutism, eliminating the real function of representative bodies, had given most Frenchmen the feeling that their government was an alien imposition, to be at worst endured and at best defied. Yet at the same time his indirect methods had left in existence the whole medieval maze of privileged institutions and corporations, to be negotiated by a successor who possessed little of the self-confident authority his own presence radiated.

Of all the potentially obstructive bodies Louis XIV had been content to ignore rather than eliminate, the most formidable were the parlements. These citadels of the *noblesse de robe* claimed to trace their institutional ancestry back to the *curia regis,* the medieval royal council whose legal rulings had helped spread the king's authority throughout France. Regarding themselves in consequence as legislative as well as judicial bodies, the parlements after 1715 reasserted their right to "remonstrate," to object to royal legislation they were unwilling to register on their books. Louis XIV had rendered the right of remonstrance meaningless by permitting its exercise only after the law had been duly inscribed; under his successor the whole debate over whether or not the parlements were obliged to defer to the royal will was reopened. As it raged, the remonstrances of the sovereign courts provided a sounding board for an increasingly united nobility, since by 1765 intermarriage and a common feeling of grievance had gone far toward diminishing the hostility between robe and sword.

At its inception, the Brittany Affair was only one of the increasingly frequent conflicts between the proud high judges of France, proprietors of their hereditary offices and defenders, according to their own view, of the ancient liberties of the kingdom, and the royal government. And in their turn, the clashes between the parlements and the crown must be seen as the specifically French manifestation of a phenomenon that could be observed in most of Europe and even in America in the second half of the eighteenth century. Almost everywhere, the most recent broadly interpretive historical account suggests, the expansive tendencies of central authorities were being confronted by the passive resistance or even the active opposition of "constituted bodies" representative of oligarchy rather than democracy. Before the outbreak of the French Revolution, in fact, the "constituted bodies" of Europe had been successful almost everywhere in arresting change, in thwarting the efforts of even such relentless reformers as the Emperor Joseph II of Austria. It was the upheaval of 1789 in one of the world's most powerful and populous countries that reopened the contest between standardizing centralization, on the one hand, and regional diversity and social privilege on the other, a contest that ended when Napoleon constructed an authoritarian state Louis XIV could not have imagined.

Students of the Brittany Affair in particular will be quick to note that it was deputies of the *Breton* Third Estate, grouped in a Breton Club later to become better known as the Jacobin Club, who spearheaded the French commoners' assault upon both royal despotism and aristocratic privilege in the summer of 1789. It might not be too farfetched to suggest that these middle-class Bretons, having witnessed at first hand royal arbitrariness and feebleness and noble intransigence in the course of the Brittany Affair, had determined that the political and social modernization of the *Ancien Régime* could be accomplished only by their own acts, if necessary by revolutionary acts. If this could be proved, La Chalotais's triumphant return to Brittany after the death of Louis XV would appear to have been a Pyrrhic victory for the nobility.

Such a conclusion, of course, would imply that from the long-winded legal blasts and counter-blasts of the Brittany Affair there emerged a pattern of the politics of the *Ancien Régime* that clearly foreshadowed revolution. It would mean that the events of the decade 1765–74 had begun to convince a generation nourished by the ideas of the *philosophes* that both the "royal" and the "noble" theses of government were inadequate, reflecting as they did an outmoded political and social system that would have to be modernized.

This may be too extreme a judgment. Perhaps the 1771 attack by Chancellor Maupeou upon the parlements as a result of their actions in the Brittany Affair was not the "last chance" of the French monarchy some historians have seen in it. Maybe it was only owing to the tragic accident of Louis XVI's personality that under him as under his predecessor the monarchy remained at once too arbitrary and too ineffective to hold the loyalty of Frenchmen who were neither royal menials nor privileged nobles—the middle class that played so decisive a role in 1789. A wiser and stronger king might have continued to back Turgot against the opposition of the nobility in 1776, enabling him to extend throughout the kingdom the modern methods of administration he had developed as Intendant of Limoges, and thereby demonstrating the continuing vitality of the "royal" thesis of government. The later general acquiescence in the rule of Napoleon seems to suggest that many Frenchmen would accept a despotism if it were enlightened and egalitarian. It may have been only an accident that neither Louis XV nor Louis XVI was the man to rule in that manner.

On the other hand, it must be admitted that French public opinion did not turn against the *noblesse de robe* until the very eve of the Revolution, when the Parlement of Paris decreed that the forthcoming Estates-General were to be organized in a fashion that would permit the nobility to control them. Until the end of 1788, the high-court judges enjoyed enthusiastic popular backing in their defiance of Louis XVI's vestigial gestures at absolutism. Conceivably this may mean that if France's "constituted bodies" had been a little more temperate in their triumph over royal authority, Frenchmen would have accepted the kind of oligarchic constitutionalism implied by the "noble thesis" of government. The French nobility, thus vested with political control, would have taken a striking revenge for their eclipse under Louis XIV. (It is difficult, however, to imagine them, eager as they were during those years actually to extend such anachronistic privileges as the collection of feudal dues, in the role of modernizers.)

However improbable the possibilities suggested by these "ifs" of history may appear, to conjure with them is, again, a good reminder that though the Brittany Affair may be useful for diagnosing the ills of the *Ancien Régime,* its future was still clouded in 1774. Neither then nor later was France clearly divided into two camps, the doomed defenders of the old and the prophetic champions of the new, and hardly anyone foresaw a revolution. Both Attorney-General La Chalotais and his antagonist, the royal commander-in-chief the Duke d'Aiguillon, were proponents of change: their differences lay in the kind and extent of change they sought. The escalation of their quarrel into a fundamental constitutional confrontation found some *philosophes* taking each side— with good reason, for there was something to be said on each side. When revolution did come, it was, as Lefebvre has shown, the product of causes more complex than a simple showdown between modernizers and reactionaries.

By 1815, the Revolution had proved little more successful than the Old Regime at achieving its professed goals—a society of both liberty and equality. This is hardly surprising, for equality without tyranny and liberty without privilege have proved equally elusive human goals. Change of the most profound kind, however, the Revolution did unquestionably produce. After 1815 anything like a repetition of the Brittany Affair had become unimaginable. For students attracted to the crisis of the *Ancien Régime* by a presumed analogy with our own times, understanding why this became true may be the chief lesson the Affair affords.

THE POLITICAL INSTITUTIONS OF
THE OLD REGIME IN THEORY
AND PRACTICE

Introduction

Before the student can begin to unravel the Brittany Affair and understand its impact upon the history of the Old Regime, he must have a clear conception of the nature and functioning of the curious institutions within which the Affair was fought out. This drama unfolded at the highest level of the French judicial system, which was surmounted by the parlements, subordinate—if at all —to the King's Council, but which extended downward to include local police courts like the Châtelet of Paris. In this introductory chapter, therefore, the reader will find essential background material, first of all in a description of the French superior or "sovereign" courts by their noted modern American historian. This selection is followed by extracts from the works of two eighteenth-century Frenchmen who knew the parlements at first hand. The first is from the political philosopher Montesquieu's theoretical essay *The Spirit of the Laws,* the second from Voltaire's lively chronicle of the Parlement of Paris, a work that might be called either historical or polemical.

Professor Franklin Ford's intention in his study *Robe and Sword* was to write social, not institutional, history. His aim was to dem-

onstrate that the "noble reaction" of the late eighteenth century
that helped produce the explosion of 1789 had been facilitated by
the fusion, accomplished earliest in Brittany, of two formerly an-
tagonistic castes: the *noblesse d'épée,* or "sword" nobility, and
the *robins,* the nobles who wore judges' robes. In reading this
selection, therefore, the student should not concern himself so
much with mastering descriptive details as with understanding how
the political power and social composition of the parlements might
contribute to the French nobility's reassertion of its privileges.
Thus, though the ritual series of steps in a clash between the
parlement and the government, from the issuing of remonstrances
to the *lit de justice,* should be carefully noted, it is more important
to decide in what ways the right to remonstrate might affect the
executive powers of the king and his ability to legislate in the
interests of French society as a whole, should such be his intention. The American political tradition, owing in part to the influence of Montesquieu, accustoms us to think of the powers of a
government as being clearly divided among executive, legislative,
and judicial branches. It is a question, however, whether the institutions of the Old Regime, and especially the parlements, can
easily be fitted into one of these neat categories.

Having considered the chief political weapon of the parlements,
the reader should reflect on what result might be expected from
entrusting this right to remonstrate to noblemen who owned offices
often made lucrative by the system of *épices*—judicial fees paid
by the litigants—and handed these offices down from one generation to the next. Though the attorney-general of a parlement was
said to be one of the "king's men," did his position make him in
practical terms as much of a king's man as a councilor of state
who sat in the Conseil des Parties—or as an intendant?

Since one can expect to find arguments based upon Montesquieu's
highly influential teachings employed in most political disputes of
the later eighteenth century, the reader should study his definitions
and maxims carefully, and try to predict how they could be em-

ployed in a conflict between the crown and the parlements. What is it that for Montesquieu distinguishes a monarchy from a despotism? What kinds of changes does he emphasize as factors in the corruption of a monarchy—or of an aristocracy? Is the reason that he regards the "judges of the supreme courts of justice" as the only possible "depositary of the laws" that while he believes the nobility to be the "most natural" intermediate power, he also condemns noble "indolence" and "ignorance"? Or could this role implicitly entrusted to the *noblesse de robe* reflect the fact that Montesquieu himself was a *président à mortier*—a judge wearing the honorific mortar-board—in the Parlement of Bordeaux? Would this fact also explain why Montesquieu attaches such importance to the existence of privileged orders in a properly governed state, and why he believes such a state is threatened both by excessive equality and by unlimited royal power? Though there are no direct references to late eighteenth-century France or its parlements in the passages reproduced in this book, the reader should be able to work out the practical implications Frenchmen might draw from the abstract language of *The Spirit of the Laws.*

Voltaire's *History of the Parlement of Paris,* by contrast, is anything but abstract, written as it was in the midst of the struggle that grew out of the Brittany Affair. The selections given here trace the vicissitudes of the parlement through a century, from its participation in the Fronde (1648-53), an actual uprising against royal authority, through its humbling by Louis XIV and its resurgence after his death. The two concluding chapters deal with the role of the parlement in the religious and fiscal controversies of the mid-eighteenth century. Voltaire provides the reader with a concrete demonstration of the power that Ford suggested their composition and function gave to the sovereign courts. Particularly to be noted are the showdown of the 1750's, the new claims made by the parlements as they confronted the king, and the outcome of Louis XV's experiment in doing without the Parlement of Paris. In the light of the distribution of political power that this

narrative reveals, the student might have a try at deciding to which
of Montesquieu's forms of government eighteenth-century France
actually corresponded most closely. And if, as Ford suggests,
France's government was more effective than most of its neighbors, just how effective was it?

Voltaire's tone, though not violent, has little of Ford's detach-
ment, and the reader will have to decide to what extent his narrative is a biased one. But even bias, if it is there, has its uses,
suggestive as it may be of the political outlook of the century's
most influential publicist. To decide what this was, the reader
might begin by asking himself which of the actions of the parlement Voltaire approves, and which he condemns. Within the century he is describing, which period does he find most laudable,
and why? Does the answer suggest that Voltaire was inspired by
quite a different set of political values than was Montesquieu?

Neither of these writers, in any case, was a spokesman for the
vast majority of Frenchmen who were neither noble provincial
judges like Montesquieu nor *philosophes* and intimate correspon-
dents of Europe's "enlightened despots," as Voltaire was. In the
1760's that vast Third Estate was still heard from infrequently in
political discussions. Nevertheless, the reader might consider, finally, which side that mass of Frenchmen could be expected to
support in a conflict between the parlements, whose function of
preserving the fundamental laws Montesquieu thought so vital, and
the kind of ruthlessly logical and efficient royal authority Voltaire
admired in Louis XIV.

A Modern Historian's Description of the Sovereign Courts of Eighteenth-Century France

THE SOVEREIGN COURTS

The structure of French government in the eighteenth century has been variously described by a series of metaphors, all of them designed to convey the impression of a complexity bordering on utter confusion. Behind this situation lay the long process of accretion inherent in the crown's efforts to maintain control of its unavoidable delegations of authority. By the time of Louis XV, that process had produced a bewildering array of governmental organs, many of them fallen into contempt and near uselessness, but each still asserting its claim to control over some portion of the conduct, the personal property, the taxes, the disputes or the physical services of the French population. The social concomitant of such conditions was the existence of numerous groups possessing the titles and trappings of power originally vested in their offices, though the power itself had been wholly or partially transferred to new personnel.

In order to understand the full extent of the confusion, however, it is necessary to bear in mind several other historical circumstances which had left their marks on the institutions existing in 1715. One of these was the practice, characteristic of medieval government, of attaching judicial functions to almost all administrative agencies. A *grenier à sel,* for example, was at once a storage depot for salt under the official monopoly, a collection office for the *gabelle,* and a jurisdictional unit for the trial of accused offenders against that tax. Moreover, the effects of the long reign just ended were apparent in the tremendously overexpanded bureaucracy, swelled by the thousands of sinecures which the government had sold to increase its momentary income. Chancellor Pontchartrain is credited with a remark to Louis XIV which illustrates the spirit of this policy, even as it calls to mind another great entrepreneur of two centuries later: "Sire, every time it pleases Your Majesty to create an office, God creates a fool to buy it."

To these factors there must be added the infinite number of regional variations, deriving from the manner in which the modern French monarchy had been formed. Five hundred years of piecemeal conquest, inheritance, purchase and negotiation, all necessary to bring

Reprinted by permission of the publishers from Franklin L. Ford, *Robe and Sword: The Regrouping of the French Aristocracy after 1715* (Cambridge, Mass.: Harvard University Press, 1953). Copyright 1953 by the President and Fellows of Harvard College. Footnotes omitted for the most part.

the great fiefs of the middle ages under the effective control of the
crown, had everywhere bequeathed local peculiarities. In such great
and once practically independent areas as Brittany, Languedoc, Provence and Burgundy, provincial estates still enjoyed varying degrees
of control over the distribution of the tax load. In Normandy and
Gascony, the vestiges of protracted English rule had never wholly
disappeared from legal customs and legal forms. French Flanders, the
Free County, and Alsace, all incorporated under Louis XIV, retained
institutions largely developed under Hapsburg role—either Spanish or
Austrian—and now simply subordinated to a top layer of French
sovereignty. Little wonder that the total effect should have been one
of seeming chaos.

Nevertheless, French government did function. Inefficient, to be
sure, loaded down with overlapping and conflicting features, it still
managed to provide greater power for the king and greater protection
for the people than did any of its rivals on the continent, with the
possible exception of the new Prussian monarchy. We are thus forced
to conclude that somewhere in all this welter of administrative and
judicial bric-à-brac there must have existed certain institutions which
displayed a substantial degree of uniformity and which represented
effective allocations of power. Aside from the central ministries built
by Louis XIV's great lieutenants, and still powerful under lesser men,
there were, it seems to me, two institutions in the early eighteenth
century standing clearly above and apart from the rest. One was the
network of provincial intendants. The other was the system of sovereign courts. It was the latter which contained the politically significant
portion of the noblesse de robe and which thus constitute the organizational core of the present investigation.

The number of such courts between 1715 and 1748 remained constant at thirty-one: fifteen parlements (including three provincial councils distinguishable only by name), nine *chambres des comptes,* four
cours des aides, two *cours des monnaies* and the *Grand Conseil.* They
were "sovereign" in that each judged by direct delegation from the
king and could be overruled only by his intervention; for the intricate
and often ill-defined hierarchy of appeals normally terminated in this
highest judicial level, allowing always for action by "the king in council." I am concerned with the personnel of these courts primarily as
a social and political force outside the courts themselves; but since the
noblesse de robe drew its power in part from its professional functions, and since those functions provided not only its organizational
form but also the basis for its strong corporate consciousness, it would

be well to have some idea of how these courts were distinguished and how distributed.

Clearly the most important were the parlements, the high courts entrusted with competence over the greatest civil and criminal trials, with extensive administrative powers growing out of their police supervision and with the registration of new acts of royal legislation. The age and jurisdictional area or *ressort* of each of the twelve parlements and three parliamentary-type councils of 1715 may be seen in the following list:

Location	Continuous existence since	Provinces
Paris	1302 (date of separate statute, though *Olim* rolls date from 1254)	Picardy, Champagne, Brie, Île de France, Perche, Beauce, Maine, Touraine, Sologne, Berry, Nivernais, Anjou, Poitou, Aunis, Rochelois, Angoumois, La Marche, Bourbonnais, Maconnais, Auvergne, Forez, Beauiolais, Lyonnais
Toulouse	1443 (after intermittent periods of separate existence in 14th century)	Languedoc
Grenoble	1451	Dauphiné and Orange
Bordeaux	1462	Guienne, Gascony, Limousin, Périgord, Saintonge
Dijon	1476	Burgundy
Rouen	1499	Normandy
Aix	1501	Provence and Barcelonnette
Arras (conseil provincial)	1530	Artois
Rennes	1553	Brittany
Pau	1620	Navarre and Béarn
Metz	1633	The Three Bishoprics (Metz, Toul, Verdun)
Colmar (conseil supérieur)	1657	Alsace
Perpignan (conseil supérieur)	1660	Roussillon
Besançon	1674 (previous existence under the Empire)	Franche-Comté
Douai	1686	French Flanders, Hainaut, Cambrésis

The chambres des comptes, like the parlements, had emerged late in the thirteenth century from a functional specialization within the medieval *curia regis,* that of Paris having been given corporate form under Philip IV, several years earlier than the original parlement. Their principal responsibility was supervision of the king's finances, as well as exploitation of the royal domain. As courts, they exercised sovereign jurisdiction over disputes arising in connection with the domain and had to verify the accounts of all agencies charged with handling the "royal deniers." As recording depots, they registered edicts bearing on these subjects and maintained the official registers of pensions, gratifications and grants of privileges, as well as the declarations of fealty and homage, *aveux,* and *dénombrements* required by feudal law of all who held property of the crown. This broad competence had been seriously diminished on some sides, especially by the encroachments of the *contrôleur-général* and the intendants; but it was still considerable under Louis XV. The Paris Chambre des Comptes enjoyed a discernible but vague superiority, based on its age and the large size of its ressort, over its sister companies in Rouen, Blois, Nantes, Montpellier, Aix, Grenoble, Dole and Dijon.

The cours des aides had a very different background; for their origin lay in the *généraux des finances* set up by Étienne Marcel's rebellious estates general of 1355 in order to supervise the collection and use of moneys voted to the crown by that assembly. They had quickly lost their original appearance of being check mechanisms, however; and before the end of the fourteenth century, Charles V had geared them into the regular machinery of royal government. Over the centuries they had declined steadily in number, as their functions had been transferred to special chambers of one parlement or chambre des comptes after another. In 1715, there remained four which were still independent bodies, at Paris, Clermont-Ferrand, Montauban, Bordeaux. Their jurisdiction covered all matters relating to such taxes as the gabelle, the taille and the various imposts on commercial transactions or goods in passage—*aides, octrois, traites.* Since there existed subordinate courts (*élections, greniers à sel, juges des traites*) to hear such cases in first instance, the cours des aides spent most of their time in considering appeals. Like the chambres des comptes, however, they also had important registration duties, covering especially letters of nobility insofar as the latter involved tax exemptions.

To hear cases based on charges of counterfeiting and to decide the disputes for which the fluctuating royal coinage furnished abundant cause, there were two cours des monnaies, one at Paris, the other at

Lyon, with ressorts covering roughly the northern and southern halves of the kingdom, respectively. Unlike the preceding three types of courts, the *monnoyes* enjoyed a competence sufficiently clear-cut in its special nature to make conflicts with the others extremely rare. On the other hand, they were sovereign only in civil matters, their penal sentences being subject to review by the Parlement of Paris.

A more complicated case is that of the Grand Conseil; for although it was generally termed one of the sovereign companies, it unquestionably displayed some features which might seem to place it in a different category. It was, to begin with, a relatively recent offshoot of the royal council, having received its corporate form only in the last years of the fifteenth century. Furthermore, it did not possess any important sphere of independent jurisdiction, since its principal function was to judge those cases which the king had "evoked" on grounds of the older courts' unsuitability, either because of conflicting rulings or because of some suspicion of bias. It also had a potpourri of detailed assignments, including cases involving consistorial benefices, the oaths of fealty of bishops and archbishops, the litigations of the great religious orders and finally, that peculiar levy on holders of specified privileges, which was instituted in 1723 on the basis of Louis XV's "joyeux avènement," but which, with its re-assessment year after year, tended to make that event seem progressively less joyous.

Part of the difficulty here arises from the fact that not every case evoked by the king was assigned to the Grand Conseil. Some he judged in his Council of State, or more correctly, through a special section of it, the *Conseil des Parties.* There existed no automatic rule of thumb for distinguishing which affairs went to which tribunal. However, an examination of their membership rolls reveals a basic difference between the personnel of the Grand Conseil, on the one hand, and the Conseil des Parties, on the other. The latter was staffed by conseillers d'état, men selected from the royal administration and commissioned to serve as judicial advisers to the king in this privy council. The *conseillers au Grand Conseil,* on the other hand, owned their offices and were chiefly recruited from the lower courts, from the legal profession and from the other sovereign companies. Moreover, they not infrequently left the Grand Conseil again in order to take positions in those courts. They thus formed part of that interwoven complex of personnel in the high judicial service; and, as will emerge later, they displayed considerable solidarity with the Parlement of Paris in its political activities under the Regency, as well as in the religious crisis of the 1730's. . . .

Something of the atmosphere in which the old sovereign companies carried on their functions still lingers in the maze of chambers, corridors and courtyards of the Paris Palais de Justice. Most of the detailed remnants of that earlier period have vanished; but a visitor looking across to the Île de la Cité from the Seine's right bank finds the long wall which faces him broken by the vertical lines of two pointed towers set close together. Between these are the windows of the Grand' Chambre (and later of the Revolutionary Tribunal). Once inside the confines of the Palais itself, he can identify the official residence of the First President of the Parlement, separated from the courtyard of the Sainte-Chapelle by the square mass of the Chambre des Comptes. Also in the Palais before the Revolution were facilities for the Cour des Aides, the Cour des Monnaies and no fewer than eight subordinate tribunals. At the very center of this complex may still be traced the foundations of the original royal dwelling, a reminder that until the time of Philip the Fair the courts, when indeed they were resident in Paris at all, had occupied parts of the king's own palace, and that not until later in the fourteenth century had Charles V moved the royal household completely to the Louvre.

What the modern visitor cannot find reproduced, however, is the shouting, clattering, brawling population of hucksters and small shopkeepers, prostitutes and public scribes who once made the area within the outer walls a town in itself—the "world of the Palais." Only occasionally had this crowd to pause in its affairs when there was a resplendent procession of magistrates to be stared at as it wound through the Cour de Mai en route to a ceremonial mass in Notre Dame, or a condemned prisoner to be jeered at as he began the grim journey to where the wheel awaited him, across the river in the Place de Grève.

The only Paris sovereign court not lodged in the Palais was the Grand Conseil, which had its own quarters in the Hôtel d'Aligre on the Rue Saint-Honoré, just a few steps from the Louvre itself. It was this latter circumstance which in earlier times had aggravated the feeling that the Grand Conseil was not wholly a part of the order of sovereign courts, that it drew its strength too directly from the royal presence; but in the eighteenth century, when the Household remained in the outlying châteaux, save for Louis XV's childhood in the Tuileries, the royal presence was as far from the Hôtel d'Aligre as it was from the Palais de Justice.

In the provinces, court facilities were naturally less extensive. At any rate, those of Dijon failed to impress Baron von Pöllnitz, writing in 1732 from the secure heights of that slightly garrulous condescension with which he described all his travels:

> The palace where the Parlement meets is very old and one of the most miserable in the kingdom. I do not know whether it was here that the old dukes of Burgundy used to reside, but if so, they were not magnificently housed.

Most of the major centers possessed royal buildings large enough for all the local courts; but, except for the fine Palais at Grenoble and Rouen, they were more impressive for age than for charm or comfort. In Toulouse, the parlement sat in the Château Narbonnais, latterly a crown possession but in medieval times the dwelling place of the successive counts Raymond. Even these dark but still awesome piles were not everywhere available. Where there was no suitable building belonging to the king, some former ecclesiastical establishment generally had to serve, as in the case of the Refuge de Marchiennes at Douai or the Maison des Capucines at Pau.

General patterns of interior organization varied from one type of sovereign court to another, though the similarities within each category were more important than the differences. The Grand Conseil and the two cours des monnaies were "semestrial," split into two roughly equal parts with one panel responsible for business arising in the winter semester and the other taking over the court's functions during the summer term. In the chambres des comptes the commonest scheme was that of division into two or more *bureaux,* of which the first normally considered only the weightier and more involved disputes. The same system obtained in the large Paris Cour des Aides, where the first of the three chambers heard the most important cases and was staffed by the senior councilors.

The internal structure of the parlements was much more involved and, from a political point of view, more significant. Only the councils of Artois and Roussillon (at Arras and Perpignan, respectively) were small enough to require no subdivision. Elsewhere each parlement had its *grand' chambre,* heir to the original *Chambre des Plaids* of Paris and focus of the company's judicial and political operations. In the grand' chambre, made up of the first president, the présidents à mortier, and the senior councilors, were heard the oral pleadings of the avocats and the reports on matters referred to it by the lower chambers. Here too, with the junior councilors frequently but not invariably in attendance, were debated the new edicts communicated by the

crown for registration. The Grand' Chambre of the Parlement of Paris
derived additional prestige from the fact that on its high benches might
sit the fifty-odd *ducs et pairs de France* in their capacity as "councilors-
born." But even in the provinces, where this peculiar distinction was
lacking, the grand' chambre everywhere considered the cases most
likely to attract public as well as royal attention.

Over a period of several centuries, the increasing volume of incom-
ing business had resulted in the creation of several other types of
chambers: (1) *chambres des requêtes* to consider cases brought before
a given parlement by holders of the royal letters of *committimus*
which conferred access to the sovereign courts in first instance; (2)
chambres des enquêtes to study prepared briefs and supply examining
magistrates in affairs requiring questionnaires to local officers or interrogation of witnesses; (3) the *tournelle,* usually composed of officers
regularly assigned to requêtes or enquêtes but commissioned in rota-
tion to consider criminal appeals; (4) *chambres des vacations* to carry
on the routine business of the company during the September and
October recess.[1]

The most extreme case of internal complexity was that of the Parlement of Paris, which contained, in addition to its Grand' Chambre, two
chambres des requêtes and five chambres des enquêtes (reduced to
three in 1756), not to mention its tournelle and chambre des vacations, both of which drew on the personnel of the other eight divisions.
The Parlement of Languedoc had one chambre des requêtes and three
chambres des enquêtes. Other companies for the most part varied only
in the number, not in the type, of constituent chambers. The Parlement of Dauphiné alone retained a superficially different organization,
its chambers simply being numbered first through fourth; but in actual
division of functions they correspond closely to their parallels elsewhere.

1. The ability of no more than a dozen presidents and councilors to substitute
for one hundred or more during two full months requires a word of explanation.
Even during the regular sessions, the actual judicial business of the various chambers seems to have been conducted by relatively small working teams of councilors,
while many of the younger, wealthier, or simply less interested members appeared
only for major trials and great ceremonies. In the notes of Bertin du Rocheret,
president of the élection of Épernay, there is a useful list of members whom this
judge considered significant in each of the chambres des enquêtes at Paris: for
two of the chambers, which in theory had about twenty members each, he notes
only six names apiece; for two others, seven apiece; and for the last, eight. B.N.
Ms. fr. nouv. acq. 1313, fol. 55. Given the customary slowness of parliamentary
justice and the possibility of postponing troublesome affairs until after the full
court had reconvened, the members of the "vacations" could manage to collect
their fees without suffering unduly from their sacrifice of a holiday.

Within each sovereign court the individual officer occupied a position carefully defined in terms of its functional title and his seniority at that rank. The names varied somewhat among the different categories of courts, but the same general levels of titular hierarchy were present in each of them. At the very top stood the first president. Just below him, and entitled to act in his absence (in order of seniority), were the other presidents of the court, sometimes as many as twelve, as in the Paris Chambre des Comptes, though more commonly numbering only five or six in the provincial companies. The parlements displayed one peculiarity in this regard: their présidents à mortier were a special group attached in each court to the grand' chambre and sharply distinguished from the presidents of the subordinate subdivisions. Then came the *gens du roi*—the procureur-général and the two to four avocats-généraux [2]—frequently referred to simply as the *parquet* because at ceremonial sessions they addressed the court from the small center space of floor. This was the team of legal officers who represented the king's interests, supervised criminal prosecutions and police functions in the ressort, and were responsible for the registration of all instructions from the crown.

The deliberative mass of a court was composed of the councilors, always led by their dean, who was entitled to extra income and special honors, including that of presiding over the court in the absence of all the presidents. In a parlement the councilors of the grand' chambre (both lay and ecclesiastical) and the presidents of the subordinate chambers, who took rank with them, stood far above the junior councilors of requêtes and enquêtes, who could advance to the grand' chambre only in order of seniority. In the chambres des comptes there were titles of specialization: *maîtres des comptes, correcteurs des comptes, auditeurs des comptes*. These various distinctions, however, should not obscure the fact that in the classification *conseiller* we have a general term covering at least 80 per cent of the high robe officers.

There is no need here to go into great detail concerning the other sovereign court members who were classed as nobles of the high robe: the *greffiers-en-chef* (from one to five per company), who supervised the clerical staff, dispatched correspondence, and saw to the distribution, in some cases the printing, of judgments and resolutions; the *premier huissier,* master of ceremonies in the original sense of the term; and the officers of the chancellery attached to each court— *garde des sceaux, contrôleur, notaires-secrétaires*—who like the gens

2. ["the king's men—the attorney-general and the two to four advocates-general." —Ed.]

du roi were special agents of the crown, in this instance charged with affixing the royal seal to outgoing instructions and rulings.

Finally, if only to emphasize the institutional contact between robe and non-robe noblemen which sovereign court organization permitted, mention must be made of the various honorary officers who were entitled to sit in the various companies: peers of France in the Parlement of Paris, the local governor and lieutenants general in each provincial parlement, the archbishop of Toulouse and the abbot of Saint-Sernin in Languedoc, the bishop of Dijon (from 1731) and the abbot of Cîteaux in Burgundy, the bishops of Rennes and Nantes in Brittany, and so on. By a custom inherited from the medieval Norman *Échiquier,* the lord of Pont-Saint-Pierre was entitled to sit as honorary councilor in the Parlement of Rouen, letters-patent of 1692 having confirmed the holder of this fief in the title of "eldest of the house of Roncherolles" and hence "first baron of Normandy." Finally, there were the two *chevaliers d'honneur* installed in each sovereign court, save the Parlement of Paris, by an edict on July 1702, "in order to tighten the bonds which ought always to exist between the noblesse de robe and the noblesse d'épée." True, Louis XIV's interest had lain primarily in the fiscal returns from this sale of new offices, and in many instances not *nobles de race* but scions of wealthy robe families had purchased places as chevaliers d'honneur; but it was of some importance for the future that certain great feudal houses—Beaufremont and Otselay at Besançon, for example, now had representatives in the strongholds of the robins.

The above discussion represents the bare minimum of institutional detail necessary for an understanding of the various factors involved in individual judicial careers of the early eighteenth century. Against the background of different categories of sovereign courts—parlements, Chambres des comptes, cours des aides, cours des monnaies, Grand Conseil—and titular ranks—first president, president, procureur- or avocat-général, councilor, greffier-en-chef, huissier-en-chef, chancellery officer—we begin to perceive a comprehensible pattern of advancement in otherwise confusing changes of title and transfers from one court to another. The element of geographical movement is particularly striking, for it bespeaks a greater degree of communication and interchange of personnel among the various provincial courts than has generally been assumed to have existed. Thus we find Geoffroi-Macé Camus de Pontcarré leaving his councilorship at the Parlement of Paris in 1730 in order to become first president of the Parlement of Rouen. The previous year Matthieu Montholon, one-time councilor in the

Grand Council, more recently first president of the Parlement of Navarre, had set off from Pau to take up the same office in the distant Parlement of Metz. When Aimard-Jean Nicolai succeeded his grandfather as first president of the Paris Chambre des Comptes in 1734, he vacated a lower position in a more powerful court, to wit, a councilorship in the Parlement of Paris; and First President Claude de Monnier at Dôle had in 1731 received the same relative promotion—in his case, from the Parlement of Franche-Comté. The Paris Cour des Monnaies had been presided over since 1727 by a former councilor of the Grand Conseil, Étienne-Alexandre Chopin de Gouzangré.

Not all the high offices, to be sure, were occupied by newcomers from other courts, this being a circumstance encountered most frequently, though not solely, in the first presidencies, which the king could fill with officers of his own choice. Taken as a whole, presidencies and the high places of the parquet went more often than not to officers already members of the court in question. But the examples given in the preceding paragraph, all selected, incidentally, from just the middle ten years of my prescribed period, will perhaps suffice to show what went to make up the noble de robe's conception of advancement.

*   *   *

In only one French province were the pre-1715 relations between robe and non-robe nobles notably more cordial. . . . This was in Brittany, where the subsequent movement toward amalgamation was to be less striking than elsewhere because the process had been largely completed before the eighteenth century began.

It would not be true to say that noble birth had always been an absolute requirement for admission to the Parlement at Rennes or the Chambre des Comptes at Nantes. Numerous Breton families of Louis XV's era certainly owed their original *noblesse* to high offices in the magistracy; but many more were old aristocratic houses which had simply added high offices to their other attributes. As early as the sixteenth century it had already been relatively difficult for a roturier to enter the sovereign courts of Brittany. The *non-originaires* who had been placed in those companies by a mistrustful monarchy after the union with France in 1532 had quickly sunk their roots and joined their interests to those of the local aristocracy.

By Louis XIV's reign the Parlement and the Chambre des Comptes had in fact become all but inaccessible to common-born aspirants. An *arrêt* of the former court, given at Rennes in 1678, announced that "sous le bon plaisir de Sa Majesté, il ne sera reçu aucuns présidents,

conseillers, ni gens du roy en icelle qui ne soient d'extraction noble ou
de condition avantageuse." [3] Saulnier has found only three cases of
bourgeois recruits to the Parlement after 1671, when the *grande ré-
formation* of the Breton nobility was completed.

This is not to say that there was no separate robe class in Brittany.
On the contrary, there existed a proud confraternity of high magistrates who were exceedingly sensitive on the subject of their official
prerogatives. Perhaps they were all the more formidable because some,
such as Monsieur de Lambilly, former page to the king, joined "à la
fermeté du magistrat l'audace d'un mousquetaire." [4] In any event, the
Breton robe had to overcome no slurs on its gentility. It dominated the
Second Estate in the provincial assemblies. It phrased the demands of
the noblesse to the crown and lashed at the intendant for every trans-
gression against vested privilege. Its officers sat at banquets and café
tables with other noblemen, gambled and hunted with them, discussed
politics and agriculture with them, shared their theatre boxes, and not
infrequently won entry to their wives' boudoirs.

The special case of Brittany is important not only as an exception
to the general situation in 1715, but also as an adumbration of what
to a greater or lesser extent was to be the trend all over France in the
decades which followed. This closing of aristocratic ranks in the face
of royal and popular pressures was exceptional only in the sense of
time, not in that of direction. The integration of the robe into high
society at Rennes and Nantes had come early, but it was not to be
unique.

THE RIGHT TO REMONSTRATE

It is easy to forget, in tracing the political performance and the social
evolution of the high noblesse de robe, that the parlements and their
sister sovereign companies never ceased to be primarily courts of law.
All the political pronouncements of the Parlement of Paris between
1715 and 1753 have been reproduced in a single volume; whereas summaries of the same court's "jugements civils," to mention only one of
the more important technical subdivisions, take up 434 large manuscript volumes for the same period. A collection such as Brillon's
voluminous *Dictionnaire des arrests des Parlemens de France* (three

3. ["At His Majesty's pleasure, no presidents, councilors, or king's men who are
not of noble birth or privileged condition shall be named to this court."—Ed.]
4. ["to the firmness of the magistrate the boldness of a musketeer."—Ed.]

volumes, published at Paris in 1711, greatly augmented—to six volumes—in 1727) provides a good idea of the accretion of case law. In addition, the high courts, particularly the parlements, exercised a wide range of administrative responsibilities based on their loosely defined police powers: forbidding inhabitants of Marseille to leave the stricken city during the plague of 1720, regulating the legal status of actors and actresses in the Toulouse Opera, restricting Paris bakers to no more than two varieties of bread for the duration of the 1740 wheat crisis.

The modern historian, however, must look elsewhere for a full explanation of the high robe's imposing place in the chronicle of the late *ancien régime*. That place depended on the magistracy's judicial and administrative functions, of course; but it depended even more on the ability to interfere with certain actions of the crown and to arouse general support for such interference. The first would have been impossible without the robe's institutionalized role in the legislative process. The second would have been impossible without the robe's great weapon of propaganda: the right to remonstrate.

Although the sovereign courts often expressed themselves publicly on matters not formally submitted to them for consideration, a new act of government came within their official purview only when it was communicated to them for registration. Registration was in itself nothing more complicated than the procedure by which a court entered new ordinances, edicts, declarations, orders in council and letters-patent on its records and ordered their communication to the subordinate jurisdictions of its ressort. It was, in other words, the mechanism by which the will of the sovereign with respect to any concrete issue was incorporated into the "published" body of law. When the king, either alone or in council, ordered some decision to be framed in the form of a written enactment, it was drawn up by the royal chancellery clerks for his signature and that of a secretary of state—in minor matters, this secretarial counter-signature was often the only genuine one. The document was then sealed by the chancellor or by the garde des sceaux and copies dispatched to the procureurs-généraux of all appropriate sovereign courts, with orders to have it registered. Once an individual court had voted the registration, the greffier-en-chef certified this fact by a formal endorsement, entered the substance of the law in the court's registers, and had copies or relevant extracts sent on to the lower tribunals. In theory, discretion was thus reserved to the crown. The courts had only to receive, record, transmit and enforce. For almost as long as any of them had been in existence, however,

the sovereign companies had prided themselves on the right to delay
registration of a questionable law while they presented their objections
to the king and awaited his response. Flammermont has summarized in
convenient form the procedure for drafting remonstrances, and the
boxes of such documents in the Archives Nationales contain numerous
firsthand accounts of the preceding debates themselves. In a parlement
(the other courts had simpler arrangements) much routine registration
was done by the grand' chambre acting alone; but when an act which
threatened to require remonstrances was presented by the procureur-
général, the first president could summon the entire personnel of the
court to meet in an *assemblée des chambres*. Even if the premier did
not think such was called for, it might be demanded by a joint deputation from the enquêtes and requêtes, usually well informed as to
pending business in the grand' chambre. After the law had been read
to the assembled magistrates, any one of several courses might be
adopted: its immediate registration might be voted; it might be entrusted to a *rapporteur* or to a special commission for study pending a
second assembly; or, if the immediate reaction was strongly hostile, a
commission to draft remonstrances might be formed on the spot. These
decisions were all reached by oral vote, each president and councilor
opining in order of seniority, with the youngest and often most rebellious thus accorded the strategic advantage of speaking last.

Draft remonstrances, after a careful editing by the first president,
had still to pass a final reading before the chambers. Once approved,
they were delivered to the king by a delegation of presidents, who
normally carried a written memorandum but who during the early
eighteenth century rendered the message verbally whenever Louis XV
could be induced to listen. Having been apprised of a court's objections, the government might dispatch letters which modified the contested points. It was much more likely to send *lettres de jussion*,
ordering registration in the original form. In the provincial companies
such orders, sometimes repeated several times, never failed between
1715 and 1748 to achieve the desired result. In the case of the Parlement of Paris, however, the crown not infrequently encountered complete refusal to yield until the king appeared in person at a *lit de
justice*. Once the monarch had taken his place on the high, canopy-
covered cushion from which the ceremony took its name, the court's
delegation of sovereignty was suspended—*adveniente principe, cessat
magistratus*. After the chancellor had read the detailed registration
order, the king repeated the standard phrase: "Je vous ordonne de ma

propre bouche d'exécuter tout ce qui vient de vous être dit." [5] Even
this ceremony did not always conclude the matter; for the parlement
might continue to protest in subsequent memoranda, and the crown
might resort to extraordinary measures of coercion. In recognized
institutional terms, however, the *lit de justice* was the final word in
court.

The above summary deals with a subject so familiar to students of
pre-revolutionary French history that it would scarcely deserve discussion here, were it not for the fact that this well-established pattern was
to be revived in 1715 after a long and significant interruption. As has
been pointed out in an earlier connection, Louis XIV had reduced the
whole process of registration to little more than a formality. His
letters-patent of 1673 had in effect stripped the right to remonstrate
of its meaning; for after laying down a time schedule under which all
the stages of registration had to be completed within seven days, the
enactment went on to forbid any officer, on pain of expulsion, either
to raise or to entertain objections. Over the entire period of forty-two
years the courts had never missed an opportunity to protest against the
hated restrictions, but in vain; for the regulations concerning remonstrances seem to have been more sternly enforced than many other
arbitrary enactments of the same era. Not until Louis XIV died did
the magistrates at last see the opportunity to recover their old powers.
Recover them they did, with a sweeping new sanction from the crown
which enthroned remonstrances once more as a key factor in French
politics. . . . The sovereign courts obviously possessed a weapon as
dangerous in its way as was the government's power to imprison or to
exile; and they were prepared to use it. . . .

THE OWNERSHIP OF OFFICE

The change which took place in the status of the high noblesse de robe
after 1715 depended on a combination of family position, wealth, and
the new political opportunities discussed in the preceding chapter, all
inextricably bound into a tight braid of reciprocal reinforcement. The
effort to unravel so complex a phenomenon or at least to identify its
several strands poses a serious problem of causal relationships. How
explain the political influence without first taking into account the

5. ["I personally command you to execute everything that has just been said to
you."—Ed.]

rôle of the sovereign courts' professional solidarity and power, which were in turn dependent on official rank, birth, and personal fortunes? But how understand the protection of this dynastic continuity and wealth, with all the attendant privileges, except by beginning with the political influence? The order in which these separate elements are teased loose and examined involves, no doubt, an unavoidable element of arbitrary choice. But this treatment need not, for that reason, be wholly disparate, if it proceeds from one aspect of the *ancien régime* which was equally crucial for the robe family, robe fortunes, and the robe's political performance. I refer to the fact that almost every sovereign court officer owned his office as a piece of negotiable property.

Few features of the old monarchy are apt to strike the modern reader as so foreign to nineteenth and twentieth century conceptions as does the trade in public functions. In Campan's novel, *Le mot et la chose,* for example, the hero negotiates for a "charge" which his father has offered to buy for him from a widowed friend of the family. (In this case, the young aspirant makes the mistake of discussing the project with an acquaintance, who finds the price so attractive that he quietly buys the office for himself.) A real-life situation, identical save for the outcome with that in Campan's story, is revealed by a sale contract of 1736 in the Gironde archives, involving Montesquieu, who is fulsomely described as "chevalier, baron de la Brède et de Montesquieu, ancien président à mortier au Parlement de Bordeaux, un des quarente de l'Académie française." The philosopher is here seen buying an office of councilor in the Parlement of Guienne for his son, Jean-Baptiste Secondat, and promising to pay to Dame Charlotte Rose de Sacriste de Tombeboeuf, widow of the former holder, the sum of 27,000 livres during the next three years.

Selections from Montesquieu's **The Spirit of the Laws**

BOOK II: OF LAWS DIRECTLY DERIVED FROM THE NATURE OF GOVERNMENT

1. Of the Nature of Three Different Governments
There are three species of government: republican, monarchical, and despotic. In order to discover their nature, it is sufficient to recollect the common notion, which supposes three definitions, or rather three facts: that a republican government is that in which the body, or only

Translated by Thomas Nugent (first published, 1748).

a part of the people, is possessed of the supreme power; monarchy, that in which a single person governs by fixed and established laws; a despotic government, that in which a single person directs everything by his own will and caprice.

2. Of the Republican Government, and the Laws in Relation to Democracy

When the body of the people is possessed of the supreme power, it is called a democracy. When the supreme power is lodged in the hands of a part of the people, it is then an aristocracy. . . .

4. Of the Relation of Laws to the Nature of Monarchical Government

The intermediate, subordinate, and dependent powers constitute the nature of monarchical government; I mean of that in which a single person governs by fundamental laws. I said the intermediate, subordinate, and dependent powers. And, indeed, in monarchies the prince is the source of all power, political and civil. These fundamental laws necessarily suppose the intermediate channels through which the power flows: for if there be only the momentary and capricious will of a single person to govern the state, nothing can be fixed, and, of course, there is no fundamental law.

The most natural, intermediate, and subordinate power is that of the nobility. This in some measure seems to be essential to a monarchy, whose fundamental maxim is, no monarch, no nobility; no nobility, no monarch; but there may be a despotic prince.

There are men who have endeavored in some countries in Europe to suppress the jurisdiction of the nobility, not perceiving that they were driving at the very thing that was done by the Parliament of England. Abolish the privileges of the lords, the clergy and cities in a monarchy, and you will soon have a popular state, or else a despotic government.

The courts of a considerable kingdom in Europe have, for many ages, been striking at the patrimonial jurisdiction of the lords and clergy. We do not pretend to censure these sage magistrates; but we leave it to the public to judge how far this may alter the constitution.

Far am I from being prejudiced in favor of the privileges of the clergy; however, I should be glad if their jurisdiction were once fixed. The question is not, whether their jurisdiction was justly established; but whether it be really established; whether it constitutes a part of the laws of the country, and is in every respect in relation to those laws: whether between two powers acknowledged independent, the

conditions ought not to be reciprocal; and whether it be not equally
the duty of a good subject to defend the prerogative of the prince,
and to maintain the limits which from time immemorial have been
prescribed to his authority.

Though the ecclesiastic power be so dangerous in a republic, yet it
is extremely proper in a monarchy, especially of the absolute kind.
What would become of Spain and Portugal, since the subversion of
their laws, were it not for this only barrier against the incursions of
arbitrary power? a barrier ever useful when there is no other: for since
a despotic government is productive of the most dreadful calamities
to human nature, the very evil that restrains it is beneficial to the
subject.

In the same manner as the ocean, threatening to overflow the whole
earth, is stopped by weeds and pebbles that lie scattered along the
shore,[1] so monarchs, whose power seems unbounded, are restrained
by the smallest obstacles, and suffer their natural pride to be subdued
by supplication and prayer.

The English, to favor their liberty, have abolished all the intermediate powers of which their monarchy was composed.[2] They have
a great deal of reason to be jealous of this liberty; were they ever to
be so unhappy as to lose it, they would be one of the most servile
nations upon earth.

Mr. Law, through ignorance both of a republican and monarchical
constitution, was one of the greatest promoters of absolute power ever
known in Europe. Besides the violent and extraordinary changes owing
to his direction, he would fain suppress all the intermediate ranks, and
abolish the political communities. He was dissolving[3] the monarchy
by his chimerical reimbursements, and seemed as if he even wanted to
redeem the constitution.

It is not enough to have intermediate powers in a monarchy; there
must be also a depositary of the laws. This depositary can only be the
judges of the supreme courts of justice, who promulgate the new laws,
and revive the obsolete. The natural ignorance of the nobility, their
indolence and contempt of civil government, require that there should
be a body invested with the power of reviving and executing the laws,

1. Voltaire is inclined to doubt the justice of this comparison. [Translator's note.]
2. On the contrary, the English have rendered the power of their spiritual and
temporal lords more legal, and have augmented that of the Commons.—Voltaire
[Translator's note.]
3. Ferdinand, King of Aragon, made himself grand-master of the orders, and
that alone changed the constitution.

which would be otherwise buried in oblivion. The prince's council are not a proper depositary. They are naturally the depositary of the momentary will of the prince, and not of the fundamental laws. Besides, the prince's council is continually changing; it is neither permanent nor numerous; neither has it a sufficient share of the confidence of the people; consequently it is incapable of setting them right in difficult conjunctures, or of reducing them to proper obedience. . . .

BOOK VIII: OF THE CORRUPTION OF THE PRINCIPLES OF THE THREE GOVERNMENTS

2. Of the Corruption of the Principles of Democracy

The principle of democracy is corrupted not only when the spirit of equality is extinct, but likewise when they fall into a spirit of extreme equality, and when each citizen would fain be upon a level with those whom he has chosen to command him. Then the people, incapable of bearing the very power they have delegated, want to manage everything themselves, to debate for the senate, to execute for the magistrate, and to decide for the judges.

When this is the case, virtue can no longer subsist in the republic. The people are desirous of exercising the functions of the magistrates, who cease to be revered. The deliberations of the senate are slighted; all respect is then laid aside for the senators, and consequently for old age. If there is no more respect for old age, there will be none presently for parents; deference to husbands will likewise be thrown off, and submission to masters. This license will soon become general, and the trouble of command be as fatiguing as that of obedience. Wives, children, slaves will shake off all subjection. No longer will there be any such thing as manners, order, or virtue. . . .

5. Of the Corruption of the Principle of Aristocracy

Aristocracy is corrupted if the power of the nobles becomes arbitrary: when this is the case, there can no longer be any virtue either in the governors or the governed.

If the reigning families observe the laws, it is a monarchy with several monarchs, and in its own nature one of the most excellent; for almost all these monarchs are tied down by the laws. But when they do not observe them, it is a despotic state swayed by a great many despotic princes.

In the latter case, the republic consists only in the nobles. The body governing is the republic; and the body governed is the despotic state; which forms two of the most heterogeneous bodies in the world.

The extremity of corruption is when the power of the nobles becomes hereditary; [4] for then they can hardly have any moderation. If they are only a few, their power is greater, but their security less: if they are a larger number, their power is less, and their security greater, insomuch that power goes on increasing, and security diminishing, up to the very despotic prince who is encircled with excess of power and danger.

The great number, therefore, of nobles in an hereditary aristocracy renders the government less violent: but as there is less virtue, they fall into a spirit of supineness and negligence, by which the state loses all its strength and activity.

6. Of the Corruption of the Principle of Monarchy

As democracies are subverted when the people despoil the senate, the magistrates, the judges of their functions, so monarchies are corrupted when the prince insensibly deprives societies or cities of their privileges. In the former case the multitude usurp the power, in the latter it is usurped by a single person.

"The destruction of the dynasties of Tsin and Soui," says a Chinese author, "was owing to this: the princes, instead of confining themselves, like their ancestors, to a general inspection, the only one worthy of a sovereign, wanted to govern everything immediately by themselves." [5]

The Chinese author gives us in this instance the cause of the corruption of almost all monarchies.

Monarchy is destroyed when a prince thinks he shows a greater exertion of power in changing than in conforming to the order of things; when he deprives some of his subjects of their hereditary employments to bestow them arbitrarily upon others; and when he is fonder of being guided by fancy than judgment.

Again, it is destroyed when the prince, directing everything entirely to himself, calls the state to his capital, the capital to his court, and the court to his own person.

It is destroyed, in fine, when the prince mistakes his authority, his situation and the love of his people, and when he is not fully pur-

4. The aristocracy is changed into an oligarchy.
5. Compilation of works made under the Mings, related by Father Du Halde.

suaded that a monarch ought to think himself secure, as a despotic prince ought to think himself in danger.

7. *The Same Subject Continued*

The principle of monarchy is corrupted when the first dignitaries are marks of the first servitude, when the great men are deprived of public respect, and rendered the low tools of arbitrary power.

It is still more corrupted when honor is set up in contradiction to honors, and when men are capable of being loaded at the very same time with infamy [6] and with dignities.

It is corrupted when the prince changes his justice into severity; when he puts, like the Roman emperors, a Medusa's head on his breast; and when he assumes that menacing and terrible air which Commodus ordered to be given to his statues.[7]

Again, it is corrupted when mean and abject souls grow vain of the pomp attending their servitude, and imagine that the motive which induces them to be entirely devoted to their prince exempts them from all duty to their country.

But if it be true (and, indeed, the experience of all ages has shown it) that in proportion as the power of the monarch becomes boundless and immense, his security diminishes, is the corrupting of this power, and the altering of its very nature, a less crime than that of high treason against the prince?

6. During the reign of Tiberius statues were erected to, and triumphal ornaments conferred on, informers; which debased these honors to such degree, that those who had really merited them disdained to accept them. Frag. of Dio, book LVIII, . . . by Porphyrogenitus. . . .

7. Herodian.

Selections from Voltaire's **History of the Parlement of Paris**

CHAPTER LVII: END OF THE CIVIL WAR IN PARIS. THE PARLEMENT RETURNS TO ITS DUTIES. IT ADDRESSES CARDINAL MAZARIN

. . . [3 February 1653]. Cardinal Mazarin had returned triumphantly to the capital. Almost all the members of the parlement which had put a price on his head and sold his furniture at public auction to pay assassins, came to compliment him, one after another, and were all the more humiliated that he received them with affability.

The great Condé, prouder and animated by vengeance, did not want to bow down before a foreigner who had taken his liberty. He preferred to continue the civil war that the Parlement of Paris had begun and that the Parlement of Bordeaux was then supporting. This prince was seen at the head of the Spanish troops that he had once fought. Finally, the Parlement of Paris, barely out of the [rebellious] faction, condemned this same Prince de Condé by default, as it had condemned Mazarin, and confiscated all his property in France. This company was an arm that had wounded its master and that the king then used to strike his enemies.

Louis XIV was not yet governing and it was even doubted that he could ever hold the reins of the state himself; but from the year 1655 he made the loftiness of his character felt. The parlement decided to remonstrate on an edict concerning coinage and the minister claimed that since a Court of Coinage had been established it was not for the parlement to interfere in that matter. The king left Vincennes on horseback, and went to the parlement booted, whip in hand. He addressed the first president and told him: "The misfortunes that your assemblies have produced are known. I order that you cease those that have begun on my edicts. Monsieur the First President, I forbid you to allow these meetings. And you (turning to the councilors of inquiry) [*conseillers des enquêtes*] I forbid you to ask for them." They were silent, they obeyed and from that moment the sovereign authority was no longer in question during that reign. . . .

This translation is from the text given in the *Oeuvres complètes de Voltaire* (Paris: Garnier Frères, 1877-85), XV-XVI. The *Histoire du Parlement de Paris* was first published in Amsterdam in 1769. The title page indicated that an "Abbé Big . . ." was its author. A subsequent edition (1770) gave the author's name as "l'Abbé Bigore." Voltaire's disavowals of the work, according to his editor, served only to increase its price. Some copies were sold for six louis, the equivalent of about $140.

CHAPTER LVIII: OF THE PARLEMENT FROM THE TIME THAT
LOUIS XIV REIGNED ALONE

From the time that Louis XIV himself governed the kingdom he was
able to contain all the bodies of the state within the limits of their
duties. He reformed everything—finances, military discipline, the navy,
police, the church, and jurisprudence. There was much that was arbitrary in the forms of justice. At the outset he thought of making procedure uniform throughout the kingdom and of extirpating, if he
could, all abuses. But a part of this great enterprise was not executed
until 1667. It required time and it was necessary to remedy more
pressing evils. . . .

Louis XIV prepared decisions that were more important for the
good of the nation. Early in his reign he had work begun on a uniform system of law which established procedure in all courts of
adjudication for both civil and criminal cases. He set judicial fees
[*épices*] and designated the cases in which judges were permitted to
claim them and the cases in which they were forbidden to take these
emoluments.

There was thus finally a set code—at least for the method of procedure. The manner of judging cases has always remained too arbitrary both in civil and criminal matters.

From the time that he took the reins of government Louis XIV
had to complain about no parlement or any legal body throughout
the course of his long reign.

It is to be noted that in the king's long quarrel with the proud pope
Odescalchi, Innocent XI, . . . the parlements and the clergy vied with
each other in supporting the rights of the crown against the enterprises
of Rome. This was a happily concerted action that had not been seen
since the time of Louis XII. The parlement even appeared quite dis-
posed entirely to deliver the nation from the yoke of the Roman
Church, a yoke that the parlement had always shaken but had never
broken.

The Advocate-General Talon and the Attorney-General Harlay, by
calling one of Innocent XI's bulls an abuse (1678) made it quite well
known how easy it was for France to remain united with the See of
Rome in matters of dogma and to be absolutely separated from it in
everything else.

The bishops did not go that far. Yet it was quite significant that the
clergy, inspired by the great Bossuet, solemnly denied the doctrine of

Cardinal Duperron which had so unhappily prevailed at the Estates-General of 1614.

The clergy, having become more a citizen than a Roman clergy, expressed itself in four memorable propositions:

1. God gave to Peter and his successors no power, either direct or indirect, over temporal things.

2. The Gallican Church approves the Council of Constance which declared that general councils are superior to the pope in spiritual matters.

3. The rules, customs and practices accepted in the kingdom and in the Gallican Church must remain inviolable.

4. The decisions of the pope in matters of faith are not certain until after the Church has accepted them.

These four decisions were, in truth, nothing but four shields against innumerable aggressions; . . . the parlement, which should concern itself only with law and not politics, always preserved them with an unbending vigor.

It was not as inflexible on the subject of the ridiculous and almost fatal affair of the Bull *Unigenitus*. Sent from Rome in 1713 the Bull, which was generally known to have been concocted by three Jesuits in Paris, condemned the most accepted, even the most inviolable maxims. Who could believe that Christians would ever be able to condemn this proposition? "It is good to read books of piety and especially the Holy Scripture on Sunday." Or this one: "The fear of an unjust excommunication should not prevent us from doing our duty."

For the sake of peace, however, the parlement registered the Bull in the year 1714. The parlement did this, it is true, though detesting the Bull and trying to weaken it by every possible modification. This sort of registration was more a stigma than an approbation.

The king wanted his edicts to be registered; if the parlement so desired it could remonstrate in writing afterwards. The parlement did not remonstrate. Louis XIV, satisfied with the parlement's apparent submission, soon made it the trustee of his will which was locked up in a room expressly built for that purpose. He did not foresee that his will would be broken unanimously by the very men to whom he had entrusted it. And yet he should have expected just that, had he only reflected on the clauses his will contained. But he had been so absolute that he believed he was bound to be so even after his death.

CHAPTER LIX: THE REGENCY OF THE DUKE OF ORLÉANS

Louis XIV having died on the first of September, 1715, the parlement met the next day without being convoked. The Duke d'Orléans, presumptive heir of the crown, met there with the princes and peers.

The Guards Regiment surrounded the Palace of Justice and arrangements had been made with the principal members to break the testament of the late king just as the testament of his father had been broken.

Before the will was opened the Duke d'Orléans gave a speech in which he demanded the regency by virtue of his birth rather than by the last wishes of Louis XIV. "But by whatever right I should aspire to the regency," he said, "I make so bold as to assure you, messieurs, that I will merit it by my zeal in the service of the king, by my love for the public good, and above all being aided by your counsel and your wise remonstrances."

To affirm that one would be guided by the same remonstrances that Louis XIV had prohibited . . . was to flatter the parlement. The will was read in a low voice, rapidly and only for form. The will, in fact, deprived the Duke d'Orléans of the regency. Louis XIV had established a Council of Regency in which everything was to be settled by majority vote as though he had formed a council of state while he was alive that was to reign after his death. The Duke d'Orléans, at the head of the council, was to have only a preponderant voice. The Duke de Maine, a son of Louis XIV, acknowledged as such, it is true, but born of a double adultery, was the guardian of the king's person and had supreme command of the troops forming the King's Household, a body of about ten thousand men.

These dispositions would have been wise in the case of a father of a family who was afraid of entrusting the life and property of his grandson to the person who was to inherit it. But these measures were impractical in a monarchy. They divided authority and consequently destroyed it; they seemed to prepare the way for civil war. They were contrary to the accepted customs which took the place of a fundamental law—if there is any such thing on the earth.

The parlement rendered a decision that had already been prepared. It is conceived in singular terms. It is not a judgment made after hearing the parties involved, not a petition, not an ordinary form, not at all a judicial verdict. "The court, with the chambers assembled, the matter having been deliberated, has declared and declares Monsieur the Duke d'Orléans regent in France; . . . orders that the Duke de

Bourbon will from the present be the head of a Council of Regency
under the authority of Monsieur the Duke d'Orléans . . . and, following the declaration made by Monsieur the Duke d'Orléans that he
agrees to conform to the majority decisions of the said Council of
Regency. . . ., [the Court] orders that he may form the Council of
Regency. . . .

These were the expressions of a sovereign. Was this sovereign language legally authorized by the presence of the princes and peers?
Such an assembly, as august as it was, did not at all represent the
Estates-General. It did not speak in the name of the infant king. What
was it doing, then? It was using a right acquired by two precedents:
that of Marie de Médicis, and that of Anne of Austria, the mother of
Louis XIV, who were regents by the same right.

It always remained undecided whether the parlement owed this great
prerogative to the presence of the princes and peers or whether the
peers owed to the parlement the right to name a regent for the kingdom. All of these claims were enveloped in a cloud. Each step we
take in the history of France proves, as we have already seen, that
nearly nothing has been regularized in a uniform and stable manner
and that chance, immediate interests, and short-lived intentions have
often been the legislators. . . .

CHAPTER LXV: OF THE PARLEMENT, THE CONVULSIONS AND THE LUNACIES OF PARIS TO 1752

After the death of Cardinal Fleury and the unsuccessful outcome of
the war of 1741, the parlement's influence began to rise anew. Taxes
aroused public indignation and the faults with which the ministers
were reproached encouraged grumbling. That epidemic disease, religious dispute, found the public in an angry frame of mind and augmented the general ferment. Before his death Cardinal Fleury had
chosen his own successor in ecclesiastical affairs, a Theatine priest
named Boyer whom he had made the dauphin's tutor. This man had
brought to his obscure ministry all the pedantry of his monkish condition. He had filled all the foremost positions in the Church of France
with bishops who regarded the too infamous Bull *Unigenitus* as an
article of faith and a law of the state. Beaumont, who owed him the
archbishopric of Paris, let himself be persuaded that he would extir-
pate Jansenism. He bound the pastors of his diocese to deny the communion called *viaticum* and which means *provision for a voyage* to

the dying who had appealed against the Bull and who had confessed to appellant priests. As a consequence of this denial of communion, known Jansenists had to be refused burial. There have been nations in which this denial of burial was a crime worthy of death; and in the laws of all peoples, refusal of the last duties toward the dead is a punishable act of inhumanity.

The pastor of the parish of Saint-Étienne-du-Mont, a canon of Sainte-Geneviève named Brother *Boitin,* refused to administer communion to a famous professor of the university, the successor of the celebrated Rollin. The Archbishop of Paris did not realize that in forcing the members of his diocese to respect the Bull he was accustoming them to disrespect the sacraments. Professor Coffin died without receiving communion. His burial was obstructed and his nephew, a *conseiller* at the Châtelet, finally forced the pastor to bury him. But this same *conseiller,* being deathly ill six months later at the end of the year 1750, was punished for having buried his uncle. The same Boitin refused to give him the Eucharist, denied him the oils and notified him that he would neither receive communion, nor be anointed, nor be buried if he did not produce a document which certified that he had received absolution from a priest attached to the constitution. These certificates of confession were beginning to be put into use by the archbishop. This tyrannical innovation was regarded by all serious-minded men as an outrage against civil society. Others saw only the ridiculous aspect: scorn for the archbishop unfortunately was visited upon religion. The parlement issued a writ against the seditious pastor, admonished him, ordered him to pay damages and had him put in the Conciergerie for a few hours.

The parlement sent the king several remonstrances, much approved by the nation, to stop the course of the archbishop's innovations. The king, who did not at all want to compromise himself, left the remonstrances without a precise reply for a whole year.

In that interval Archbishop Beaumont succeeded in rendering himself ridiculous and odious in the eyes of all of Paris by dismissing from the General Hospital a superior and a bursar who had long before been placed in those posts by the magistrates of the parlement. . . . All of Paris was indignant. Alms to the hospital ceased, the parlement wanted to open proceedings. The King's Council declared for the archbishop. . . . The parlement had recourse to the usual remonstrances and refused to register the king's declaration (September 1751).

This body had already caused some irritation for it had made a great deal of difficulty about the *vingtième* and the mail contracts. The

king forbade them thenceforth to interfere in the affairs of the hospital
and evoked all matters concerning it to his council. On the next day
First President Maupeou, two other presidents, the advocate-general
and attorney-general were summoned to Versailles. They were ordered
to bring the registers so that all that had been decided on that affair
might be suppressed. The register could not be found. Never had a
littler affair caused greater emotion. The parlement stopped its functions, lawyers closed their offices: the course of justice was interrupted
for two hospital women. But what was horrible was that during these
indecent and absurd quarrels the poor were, for lack of assistance, left
to die. The mercenary administrators of the Hôtel-Dieu [the hospital]
got rich by the death of these poor wretches. There is no charity when
party spirit dominates. The poor were dying in droves and no one
thought about them. The living tore each other apart for foolish
absurdities.

The king had his musketeers bring each member of the parlement
letters of royal command [*lettres de jussion*]. The magistrates in fact
obeyed: they resumed their meetings. But the lawyers, having received
no *lettres de cachet*, did not appear at the bar. Their position is a free
one. They have not bought their offices. They have the right to plead
or not to plead. Not one of them appeared. Their connivance with the
parlement irritated the court more and more. Finally, the lawyers resumed their pleading, cases were judged as usual and everything seemed
to be forgotten. . . .

CHAPTER LXVI: CONTINUATION OF LUNACIES

Denial of the sacraments, quarrels between the civil jurisdiction and
ecclesiastical pretensions multiplied in the dioceses of Paris, Amiens,
Orleans, Chartres, and Tours. The Jesuits secretly fanned this conflagration. The Jansenists cried in fury. Schism seemed about to break
out, the parlement had prepared very ample remonstrances and it felt
bound to send a great deputation to the king. The king was unwilling
to receive them and demanded to see the articles with which these
representations were concerned in advance. They were sent to him
(April 30, 1753): the king replied that, having examined the objects
of these remonstrances, he had no desire at all to hear them.

The chambers met immediately and declared that they would cease
all services except that of preserving public peace from the clergy's
enterprises (May 5, 1753). The king ordered them, by letters of royal

command, to resume their ordinary functions, to dispense justice to his subjects and to stop meddling in matters which did not concern them. The parlement replied to the king that it could not obtemper. This word *obtemper* made a singular impression at court. All the women asked what this word meant. When they found out that it means *to obey* they made more noise than all the ministers and their clerks.

The king assembled a great council. *Lettres de cachet* were dispatched to all members of the parlement, except to those of the *Grand' Chambre*. During the night of May 8-9 the king's musketeers sped through the whole city and sent all the presidents and the *conseillers des requêtes* and *des enquêtes* off to their places of exile. . . .

The *conseillers* of the *Grand' Chambre* met. They were excepted from the general punishment: since several of them held court pensions and since their age was supposed to make them more flexible, it was hoped that they would be more obedient. But when they had met they were seized with the same spirit that moved the *enquêtes*. They said that they wanted to undergo the exile of their colleagues and in that same session they issued warrants for the arrest of several pastors. The king sent the *Grand' Chambre* to Pontoise as the Duke d'Orléans as regent had already banished them. When the chamber was at Pontoise it busied itself only with matters of the schism. No private cases were heard.

Justice, however, had to be dispensed to the citizens. A chamber composed of six *conseillers d'état* and twenty-one *maîtres des requêtes* was created (September 18, 1753). They held their sessions at the hall of the Grands-Augustins as if they did not dare to sit in the Palace of Justice. Custom has such a strong hold over men that the king, in saying that he created this chamber *in his certain knowledge and from the plenitude of his power* dared not make use of his power to register the creation of this chamber in his Conseil d'État although this council had registers just as did the other courts. He turned to the Châtelet, which is only a subordinate court of justice. The Châtelet distinguished itself by not registering. Among the reasons for its refusal it alleged that Clotaire I and Clotaire II had forbidden that the ancient ordinances of the Franks be derogated. The court contented itself with reversing the Châtelet's sentence, and, as a result of its orders, a deputation from the chamber took itself to the Châtelet, had the sentence stricken out of the register and registered the edict itself. After this futile procedure, the Châtelet issued an even more futile protest. The name of this chamber, which up to that time had only been called the *Chambre des vacations,* was changed. It received the

title of *Chambre royale,* sat at the Louvre instead of at the Augustins
and was none the better received by the public for all that. *Lettres de
cachet* were sent to all the members of the Châtelet to register under
the name of *Royale* that which they refused to register under the name
of *Vacations.*

All these little subterfuges compromised the dignity of the crown.
The civil lieutenant registered at the express command of the king.

There were no proceedings. All of Paris persisted in turning the
Chambre royale to ridicule. They accustomed themselves to this so
well that they sometimes met laughing and joked about their decisions.

However a serious matter came up. Some rogue named Sandrin,
having been condemned to be hanged by the Châtelet, appealed the
sentence to the *Chambre royale* which confirmed the sentence. The
Châtelet claimed that the case could only be appealed to the parlement,
and refused to hang the guilty man. The official of the Châtelet who
handled this criminal case, a man named Milon, was put in the Bastille for failing to hang Sandrin. The Châtelet then ceased its functions
as had the parlement (November 27, 1753). There was no longer any
justice in Paris. Immediately there went out *lettres de cachet* to the
Châtelet for dispensing justice; the three most ardent councilors were
seized. Half of Paris laughed, the other half grumbled. The convul-
sionaries insisted that these disputes would end tragically. And what is
called in Paris good society [*bonne compagnie*] asserted that the whole
thing would never be anything but a poor farce.

The other parlements imitated the Parlement of Paris and wherever
there were denials of the sacraments there were decrees and these
decrees were broken. The Châtelet of Paris was filled with confusion,
the *Chambre royale* nearly idle, the parlement exiled and yet all was
calm. The police carried on, the markets were conducted in an orderly
way, commerce flourished, plays delighted the city, the impossibility
of having cases judged obliged the litigants to reach settlements and
people turned to arbiters in the place of judges.

While the magistracy was so disgraced the clergy triumphed. All the
priests banished by the parlement returned. The pastors who had warrants against them exercised their functions. The inclination of the
ministry at that time was to favor the Church against the parlement,
for until then the Archbishop of Paris could not be accused of having
disobeyed the king and the parlement was reproached for its formal
disobediences. However the whole court strove to negotiate because
there was nothing else to do. It was necessary to put an end to this
kind of anarchy. The parlement could not be broken because it would

have been necessary to reimburse the members for their offices and there was very little money. They couldn't be kept in exile forever because men cannot be wise enough to stop litigating.

Finally the king made use of the occasion of the birth of a Duke de Berry [1] to grant mercy. The parlement was recalled. First President Maupeou was received in Paris to the acclamations of the people. The *Chambre royale* was suppressed, but it was very much easier to recall the parlement than to calm men's emotions. That body had hardly reassembled when the denial of the sacraments began anew.

The Archbishop of Paris distinguished himself more than ever in this War of Certificates of Confession. First President Maupeou, who because of his wisdom had acquired a great deal of credit with the king, finally made all the excesses of the archbishop known. The king wished to see if that prelate would disobey his orders as the parlement had disobeyed. He enjoined him to stop troubling the state by his dangerous zeal. Beaumont claimed that God rather than men must be obeyed. The king exiled him (December 2, 1754); but this was to Conflans, to his country house two leagues from Paris. And he did as much evil from Conflans as from his archbishop's palace.

The parlement then had complete freedom to proceed against religious, vicars, pastors, and Eucharist-bearers [*porte-Dieu*] who refused to administer the sacraments to the dying. Beaumont was as inflexible as the parlement had been constant. The king exiled him to Champeau, the most remote town in his diocese. The parlement had been regarded in all of France as a martyr for the laws. The archbishop was regarded by his little party as a martyr for the faith. From Champeau he was sent to Lagny. . . .

The king had ordered silence concerning ecclesiastical affairs and no one kept it. The Sorbonne, at other times Jansenist but then constitutional, supported theses contrary to the maxims of the kingdom. The parlement ordered that the dean, the syndic, six former doctors and professors of theology appear before it with the faculty secretary and the registers. They were reprimanded, their conclusions stricken out and they were ordered to keep quiet in accordance with the king's declaration. . . .

All of the year 1755 passed in these little disputes which began to bore the nation. A greater scene unfolded. France was menaced by that fatal war in which England took from the King of France all that he possessed on the continent of North America, destroyed all his

1. [Who became Louis XVI. He was born on August 23, 1754.—Ed.]

fleets and ruined French commerce in India and Africa. Money was needed to prepare for that war. Finances had been very badly administered. Custom permitted the creation of new taxes only with registration by the parlement. It was time for the parlement to make it known that it remembered its exile. The king, after protecting this body against the constitutional bishops, then protected the bishops against the parlement: thus easily do things change at the king's court! An assembly of the clergy held in 1756 had brought great complaints against the parlements of the kingdom and appeared to have been heard. Moreover, the king then took the side of the Great Council against the Parlement of Paris which was contesting its jurisdiction. The court's difficulty in supporting the coming war made men arrogant and more difficult.

The parlement turned all its batteries, hitherto aimed at the constitutionals, against the Great Council. It convoked the princes and the peers of the kingdom for February 18. The king immediately learned of this and forbade the princes and peers to respond to the invitation. The parlement maintained its right to invite the peers. It maintained it in vain and only displeased the court. No peer took part in its meetings.

What shocked the government most was the association of all the parlements of the kingdom which then took place under the name of *classes*. The Parlement of Paris was the first class and all of them together appeared to form a single body which represented the kingdom of France. This word *class* was severely dealt with by Chancellor de Lamoignon. New taxes had to be registered and nothing was registered. The war could not be waged with remonstrances. This object was more important than the Bull, the convulsions, and the Eucharistbearers.

The king held a *lit de justice* at Versailles in which the princes and peers took part (August 21, 1756). The parlement went to Versailles in fifty-four carriages but beforehand it had decided that it would not give its opinion. In fact it gave no opinion at all and despite it the tax of two *vingtièmes* and several others were registered. As soon as it could assemble in Paris it protested against this *lit de justice* held at Versailles. The court was infuriated. The constitutional clergy, believing the time favorable, redoubled its enterprises with impunity. Nearly all the parlements of the kingdom sent remonstrances to the king. Those of Bordeaux and Rouen had already stopped dispensing justice. The healthiest part of the nation murmured about this and said: "Why punish private citizens for the enterprises of the court?"

Finally, after having held many secret council meetings, the king announced a new *lit de justice* for December 13. He arrived at the parlement with the princes of the blood, the chancellor, and all the peers. He caused to be read an edict whose principal articles are the following:

1. Although the Bull is not a rule of faith, it will be received with submission.

2. Despite the law of silence, the bishops may say whatever they wish, providing that this be done with charity.

3. The denial of the sacraments will be judged by ecclesiastical tribunals and not civil tribunals, except in appeals by writ of error.

4. Everything that has previously transpired on the subject of these quarrels will be buried in oblivion.

Those pertained to ecclesiastical matters. Regarding regulation of the parlement here is what was ordained:

1. Only the *Grand' Chambre* will deal with the general maintenance of order.

2. The chambers cannot be assembled without the permission of the *Grand' Chambre*.

3. No denunciation except by the attorney-general.

4. An order to register all edicts immediately after the king's response to the allowed remonstrances.

5. No deliberative vote in the assemblies of the chambers before the completion of ten years of service.

6. No license before the age of twenty-five.

7. Prohibition against ceasing the dispensation of justice under penalty of disobedience.

These two edicts overwhelmed the company, but it was crushed by a third that suppressed the third and fourth chambers of *enquêtes*. After this meeting the king went out through a vast crowd of people whose faces showed their consternation. He was hardly gone when most of the members of the parlement resigned their offices. The next day and the day after that the *Grand' Chambre* did the same. There were finally only the *presidents à mortier* and ten *conseillers* who did not sign their resignations. If the king's move had astonished the parlement, the parlement's resolution did not astonish the king any less. That body was calm and firm but the talk of all Paris was violent and reckless.

In all there were one hundred and eighty resignations. The king accepted them. There remained but ten presidents and some *conseillers* of the *Grand' Chambre* to compose the parlement. The body was therefore regarded as completely dissolved and it seemed to be quite difficult to find a substitute for it. The party of the archbishop raised its head higher than ever; certificates of confession, denials of the sacraments troubled all of Paris when an unforeseen event astonished France and Europe.[2]

2. [The assassination attempt on Louis XV by Damiens on January 5, 1757. The parlement was recalled, withdrew its resignations and resumed its functions on August 29, 1757.—Ed.]

II

THE ATTORNEY-GENERAL OF THE PARLEMENT OF BRITTANY

Introduction

Louis René de Caradeuc, seigneur de La Chalotais (1701–85), who was raised to the degree of marquis by letters-patent of Louis XVI in 1776, belonged to a family which had long served in the Parlement of Brittany. His great-great-great-grandfather had been named president of the *chambre des requêtes* in 1581, his grand-father became *conseiller des requêtes* in 1672, his father in 1691; his elder brother served as *conseiller* from 1725 to 1754, and his younger brother joined him in 1734.

The family laid claim to very ancient nobility, descending from a fourteenth-century ambassador of the Duchess of Brittany. This claim was accepted by the royal authorities in the "reformation" of the Breton nobility of 1670.

La Chalotais himself entered the parlement as advocate-general in 1730; he became attorney-general [*procureur-général*] by letters-patent issued on May 12, 1752. He became well known beyond the world of Brittany and of the law courts as a result of the central role he played in the judicial condemnation of the Jesuits. He was charged by the Parlement of Brittany in a decree of August 14, 1761, with investigating the Constitution of the Society of Jesus; in his first report (*compte-rendu*) made on December 1 of that year, he concluded that the society's privileges infringed upon French law, the liberties of the Gallican church, and the duties of the universities, and asked the parlement to decree its dissolution. He followed this up with a second *compte-rendu* on May 21, 1762, reaffirming his previous conclusions. A week later the Parlement of Brittany, following the lead of the Parlement of Paris, decreed the dissolution of the Society of Jesus.

In 1763, the year of the publication of his *Essay on National Education,* La Chalotais formally yielded the office of attorney-general to his eldest son, while reserving to himself the right to exercise its functions concurrently. (His younger son was also a *conseiller* of the parlement.)

In this chapter, the reader will become acquainted with this nobleman of the robe at the high point of his career, before his arrest in 1765 launched the Brittany Affair and transformed a provincial quarrel eventually into a national constitutional struggle.

In reading the excerpts from La Chalotais's pleadings in court, his plan for education, and his reverent letters to Voltaire, the student should concentrate on assessing his ideas, to determine whether this man, whose family background and career were so representative of the Breton *noblesse de robe,* was equally conventional in every respect. Though no extract from his reports on the Jesuits is given here, it should not be hard to establish his views on religion in general and the eighteenth-century French Catholic Church in particular. To what extent are they colored by the Gallican or even Jansenist sympathies usually associated by historians with the men of the parlements? In reading his proposals for a new curriculum to replace the one he had helped undermine by his attacks on the Society of Jesus, particular note should be taken of his discussion of such subjects as the course of human development, the necessity for freedom of thought, and France's comparative role in the advancement of science. To what extent does he believe a reformed educational system would be useful to "the nation" and "the State"? By diffusing an easily perceptible truth, could such a system contribute to the ultimate perfection of the human species? The answers to these questions will suggest whether his ideas explain Voltaire's flattering replies in the course of the correspondence he initiated, and whether La Chalotais should be regarded as at least a minor *philosophe*.

Although we have in these extracts little direct evidence of his political and social attitudes, there are perhaps enough clues, particularly in his discussion of who should be educated and for what, to decide whether Montesquieu was right to insist that members of constituted bodies like the parlements represented an essential stabilizing force in a monarchy. La Chalotais is clearly entitled to be called a reformer; the question is, just how far did he desire the reform of the fundamental institutions of French society to go? Finally, the reader should ask himself if it can be foreseen that La Chalotais was the sort of man to be arrested on an unspecified charge amounting to treason. If he were to fall foul of royal or governmental authority, would it be because he had advanced new ideas or because he had defended old ones?

Read between the lines, as Voltaire's writings often must be, his replies to La Chalotais's letters tell us as much about him as they do about the attorney-general of Brittany. In 1762, Voltaire had been living at his Swiss refuge, Les Délices, or at Ferney, conveniently nearby on the French border, for seven years. Enjoying a universal reputation which no twentieth-century author has even approached, he was just beginning his efforts to rehabilitate Jean Calas, the Huguenot of Toulouse who had been tortured and broken on the wheel after a false conviction for murder by the local parlement. This campaign for Calas, which was the first of several in which Voltaire came to the defense of the victims of judicial bigotry or incompetence, only added to the huge correspondence that he superimposed upon his literary work, yet he took time to write more than once at some length to encourage his admirer in Brittany. The reader must therefore ask what it was in La Chalotais's writing and other activities that attracted Voltaire. Did he admire the educational essayist or the prosecuting attorney-general? If Voltaire was really, as he claimed, a "partisan

of the authority of the parlements," what is implied by his sly
reference to "the only philosophical work ever to come from the
bar"? La Chalotais's memoir on the origins of the parlements has
not come down to us, but we can guess at its principal arguments
from Voltaire's objections. What is Voltaire driving at with his
reiterated demonstrations that the parlements are not representative bodies, that their equivalent is not the English Parliament, for
example, but the Court of King's Bench? What can be inferred
about Voltaire's political views from his comments not only on the
ancient origins of the parlements, but on ancient origins in general?
When he has answered such questions as these, the reader will be
less surprised at the attitude Voltaire took when La Chalotais's
misfortunes—and those of the parlements—began in 1765.

Selections from La Chalotais's Speeches in Court on Church and State

[In a case involving the taxing of ecclesiastical fees]
We will begin here by deploring the laxness of ecclesiastical discipline, which has occasioned unprecedented taxes, and which has changed the voluntary fees and offerings of the faithful into forced contributions and exactable rights. During the early centuries of the Church, during those happy times, the memory and the example of which can never be recommended too strongly, the Church's patrimony was derived only from voluntary collections and occasional offerings. But the fervour of these early Christians was great. There was no danger that the revenues based upon such eminent charity and upon the good use which churchmen made of it would ever be anything less than amply sufficient. Let us not be afraid to say it: the fervour of the faithful has declined. Greed and self-interest have sometimes penetrated into the sanctuary itself. Members of mendicant and other religious orders have often dishonored their ministry by an all too sordid self-interest. And the authority of certain laws has been necessary to remedy these ills and the scandals which these ills have caused. The clerics and the faithful ought therefore not to complain too much about these laws. They ought to complain only about the reasons which have made them necessary. . . . One can never go too far in exhorting preachers to prefer the welfare of the people, which God has assigned to their care, to their own interests. And one can never go too far in condemning the ingratitude of people who, contrary to the explicit laws of Scripture as well as to natural and civil laws, refuse the necessary help to the ministers of the altar, and who do not give the necessities of temporal life to those who announce to them the tidings of eternal life.

[In a case involving the legality of Church sanctions against marriages under certain conditions]
The Church, that purely spiritual society, would have the same power over the rulers of nations as those rulers have over the nations they govern! It could impede the effect of civil laws which are contrary neither to good morals nor to religion. It would forbid in the realm of conscience what the civil laws permit in the judicial realm. The priest in his confessional would order those to separate whom the

Translated and reprinted from Gustave Saulnier de la Pinelais, *Les Gens du roi au Parlement de Bretagne, 1553-1790* (Paris, Rennes, A. Picard, 1902), pp. 423-25.

laws regard as united by a true marriage!—And let no one say that
this is to seek a contradiction where there is none, to demand remedies
where there are no ills. What conflicts there have been between kings
and the sentiments of theologians on the subject of secret marriages,
of marriages contracted at the end of life! What conflicts there still
are between canon law and civil law in respect to marriages of minors
contracted against the will of their parents. Canon law permits these
marriages; civil law forbids them. The civil laws assert that there can
be no sacrament of marriage, if there is no civil contract of marriage,
because the contract is the foundation and basis of the sacrament.
Canon law asserts that there can be a sacrament, even if there is no
civil contract. And, through a jumble of powers which degenerates
into anarchy, the ecclesiastical ministry orders couples to live together whom the laws forbid to unite and whose illegitimate offspring
they outlaw. We neglect to mention the other inconveniences which
result from these principles. What occasions of division and discord
between the two powers whom God has established to govern the
world and whose harmony should be eternal!—Let us not seek that
harmony in the intermingling of their powers. That would be to put
an eternal contradiction into our principles. Let us rather seek that
harmony in the exact delineation of the boundaries which God has
established between state and church. Those boundaries are as sacred
as they are inviolable. That which is spiritual must always remain
spiritual and is essentially in the realm of ecclesiastical jurisdiction.
That which is temporal can never become spiritual and is essentially
in the realm of secular jurisdiction. Just as the popes and bishops have
succeeded the apostles in one realm, so the kings and rulers are the
successors of the Caesars in the other, having inherited all the rights
of the temporal power.

[*In a case involving a decree by the Inquisition*]
At the very name of the Inquisition, the most judicious people rebel,
and everyone is overcome with indignation. The sovereign courts [the
parlements] have never deferred to its decrees, or rather they have
always condemned them, whenever anyone has wanted to make use
of them. . . . The maxims about the sovereignty of kings and their
absolute independence of every other power are established within the
universal law of all nations. Just like the other [Gallican] articles which
were renewed in the assembly of the clergy in 1681, they are based
upon the word of God and upon the most respected evidence of tradition. These are the fundamental laws of the realm. Principles which

assert the contrary tend to undermine the foundations of the Church and of monarchies, in making the pope the absolute master of the Church and the dispenser of crowns.

Selections from La Chalotais's **Essay on National Education**

THE HOUSE IN SESSION, 24TH MARCH, 1763

The Attorney-General of the King entered the Chamber and addressed the assembled House: Gentlemen, one of the principal objects of my addresses of 7th December, 1761, and of 24th May, 1762, was to persuade you to represent to His Majesty the great importance of re-forming the schools of the Kingdom, and the education that our young people receive there; to pray him to order the Universities and the Academies to draw up a plan of studies, and to provide the elementary textbooks necessary for putting it into practice. It seems that to-day the nation is fully convinced of the need for thorough reform in the ordinary method of the schools. Some time ago I had the honour of informing you that I intended to put before you a treatise on these matters; they are of such importance that I recommend them to your unceasing care. I now fulfil my promise, and trust that you may find this treatise a not too unworthy response to your patience and expecta-tion. I have not limited myself to indicating the deficiencies in our present system, but have put forward certain reforms that seem to me necessary to remedy them. I have preferred to offer you a useful rather than a pleasing document. My aim is to prove that in place of an education that, at its best, is suitable only for students of scholastic philosophy, we can substitute one which will provide the State with good citizens. You will find herein the opinions of a citizen who pleads for reforms both from yourselves and from the nation at large, for the general good of the State. A Minister is a stranger to nothing that promotes the public good, but he is limited to forming opinions; it is the function of the King to determine what action must be taken. It is for you, Gentlemen, who wield authority in his name, to see that whatever he, in his wisdom, may decree, is duly carried out.

I ask acknowledgement of the delivery I now make of a treatise on

Louis René de Caradeuc de la Chalotais, *Essay on National Education, or Plan of Studies for the Young,* translated by H. R. Clark (London, E. Arnold and Company, 1934).

education, entitled "Essay on National Education, or Plan of Studies for the Young."

Delivered in Court, 24 March, 1763.

Signed, DE CARADEUC DE LA CHALOTAIS.

The Court acknowledged that the Attorney-General of the King had presented and placed upon the table a treatise on education entitled "Essay on National Education, or Plan of Studies for the Young."

Essay on National Education
or
Plan of Studies for the Young
Lodged at the Registry of the Parliament of Brittany by
M. Louis René de Caradeuc de la Chalotais, Attorney-General
of the King

Preliminary Reflections on the Use of Learning, the Unsatisfactory Way in Which It is Taught, and the Quality of the Teachers

For a year, now, the Royal Courts have been deliberating the best means of providing the Colleges with citizens capable of instructing our young people. Destructive criticism without constructive suggestion is of little value. We have had an education that at best was only fitted to produce students of scholastic philosophy. The public good and the honour of the nation require that for this shall be substituted a civil education that will prepare each succeeding generation to fill successfully the various professions of the State.

In this treatise, I propose to show the need for this education, and the means whereby it may be established. To judge well of the matter it is perhaps necessary to give some thought to other matters comparatively remote, to make clear the true use of the sciences and literature, and how a good or a bad education can determine the happiness or misery of a nation; and at the same time to ask what a nation has a right to demand from its educators.

The sciences are necessary to man, and it is important that he should have a knowledge of them if he has incurred duties involving some degree of responsibility. In fact, of all knowledge a real knowledge of science is the most useful, and the man who possesses it is already well on the way to becoming a useful citizen. Ignorance is good for nothing, and harmful in every way. No light can issue from darkness, and the man who walks in darkness cannot fail to lose his pathway.

If the apologists of ignorance only intend to extol that which leads to an intelligent and rational scepticism, which will come to no final decisions because it possesses self-knowledge, they should give it the name of science; for this power of suspending judgment, founded on a realization of one's essential ignorance, is in truth a very real and estimable science. But I speak here of ignorance as commonly understood, which is nearly always presumptuous, and which decides, approves, and condemns with equal temerity; and I submit that if the deplorable effects of this ignorance are observed in relation to the present misuse of the sciences, the case for genuine scientific knowledge becomes overwhelming. There is no one who will not affirm with me that ignorance is harmful in every way, and resolve to establish a sound system of studies in the schools in order to diminish, as far as possible, the evils resulting from lack of knowledge.

The most ignorant and uncultured centuries have always been the most vicious and corrupt. If a man is left without culture, ignorant, and consequently unaware of his real duties, he will become timid, superstitious, and perhaps cruel. If good is not taught him he will of necessity become preoccupied with evil. The mind and heart cannot remain empty. . . .

To deny the power of education is to deny, against all experience, the power of right habituation. What is there that an educational system backed by the laws of the country and administered by enlightened officials could not accomplish? In a few years it would transform the culture of the whole nation. In the case of the Spartans it even changed their natural disposition. There is an art by which the various breeds of animals may be improved; should there not be one for perfecting human beings?

If the human race is capable of reaching a certain degree of perfection, it is by means of education that it is to be attained. The object of the legislator must be to develop in the people, to the highest possible degree, integrity and strength of mind, nobility and enlightenment of character, health and strength of body. This ideal is not to be attained easily; there are too many obstacles to it, particularly in ourselves. But it should be the goal of all our efforts, that we may thus approach the more nearly to it.

The public morality of a great nation is not always sound. The self-indulgence of the young, widespread extravagance, the lack of love of country and the common good, the natural restlessness of our minds, licentiousness, neglect of the duties of our daily work, and a multitude of other well-known failings, are preventing our giving that serious consideration that is always due to true goodness and virtue, and which is its truest reward. Without personal morality any system will be imperfect. *"Quid leges sine moribus vanae proficiunt?"* (Horace, Book III, Ode 23) asked one of the finest and noblest minds of antiquity. But the government can control even morals; the titles, honours, or blame that it distributes have as real a currency as money.

Public education to-day is not directed towards the greatest public usefulness. The truth of this statement requires no demonstration. Happily, the possibility of reform is as fully proved as the need for it. There is an immense number of known truths, scattered throughout a multitude of books, and held in a multitude of minds: these must be collected and methodically summarized for the enlightenment of our school masters and administrators. But since the main principle of our education is wrong, the system must be rebuilt from its foundations. . . .

Our education is throughout founded on the practice of those un-civilized centuries in which only those persons destined for the priest-hood were made to study; the only books then were those copied by the monks; it was necessary to send to Rome for a copy of the works of Cicero. The nobles were hardly able to read and write; war and pillage made books rare and study difficult; the only schools were in the cathedrals and the monasteries. The mother-tongue of the French was then only an unformed and uncertain jargon: barbarous Latin was used in all ordinances, King's charters, and Royal proclamations. Philosophy was reduced to disputation on the books of Aristotle; moral instruction ignored man's duties; Physics was concerned with purely fantastic hypotheses of which the consequences were not even ex-amined. In place of astronomy and natural history fabulous stories held sway that led to the follies of astrology and the employment of superstitious practices in medicine. Theology and jurisprudence were concerned only with scholastic disputation or the opinions of profes-sors, since, in the absence of any science of criticism, texts were abandoned for summaries or commentaries. . . .

With the revival of letters and science the darkness that had covered Europe for so long was at last dispelled. Printing was invented, schools were founded, a spirit of emulation was aroused, and ignorance be-came a matter for shame. Yet education was too exclusively concen-trated in the schools, and it has remained to this day almost wholly scholastic.

The study of letters is only part of the educational system of a nation—such a system has wider aims; it is to a State what learning is to the individual. Its object is to render a nation more enlightened in every way, and consequently more flourishing.

The study of letters provides proper nourishment for the individual mind, and instruction and recreation for mankind as a whole. Plato and Cicero, who taught their contemporaries, are still to-day enlightening the whole of civilization, and remotest posterity will profit by their teaching. The study of letters should be regarded by the State as the source and inspiration of all the human and civil virtues. Unhappy will be that nation in which the love of literature dies.

Our Kings have always given the study of letters their special protection, and the institutions they established to ensure instruction of all kinds might have proved the most solid of foundations for the prosperity of the State had the early education of young people been better carried out. The Universities, the Academies, the Chairs of Languages, and the Schools of Navigation, all seemed in co-operation to produce distinguished citizens. The King who rules us has encouraged science, has aroused emulation by sending explorers to the Arctic regions, the Equator, the Cape of Good Hope; also by founding a Military School. But unfortunately all this help, though of great value, does not go to the root of the problem, if I may dare to say so. The early education of the young of our nation has remained unaltered, and all the rest is determined by it. The education given at the schools restricts that of the remainder of the national system; and it is limited to the study of the Latin language. Only an abstract philosophy is taught there, which can be of no use in daily life, since it propounds none of the moral principles necessary to the individual for his right conduct in society, nor any knowledge really essential to him as a man. Religion itself is taught with as little care; and a youth leaves school having learnt practically nothing that can be of use to him in any of the professions. . . .

Of a thousand students who have completed what is known as the course in the humanities and philosophy, hardly ten would be found able to state clearly and intelligently the elements of our religion, to write a good letter, to tell invariably a good from a bad argument, or a valid from a false proof.

The Greeks and Romans, wiser and more vigilant than ourselves concerning so important a matter, did not leave education in the hands of men whose opinions were not those of a good citizen. It was carried on either by legislators or by philosophers capable of legislating. Solon would never have entrusted the education of Athenians to Spartans, much less to Helots (Spartan slaves); neither would Lycurgus have allowed Athenians to educate Spartans. When Antipater demanded one hundred and fifty children as hostage from the Spartans they answered that they would rather give one hundred and fifty grown men, lest a foreign education might corrupt their children.

The aim of education being to prepare citizens for the State, it obviously must be closely related to the laws and constitution of the State; nothing could be worse than for it to be contrary to them. It is an axiom of all good government that each individual family should be regulated according to the same general principles as govern the State, the great family that includes all others. How is it possible to imagine that men who, caring nothing for the State, put their own priests before the rulers of the country, their religious order before their motherland, and the rules of their religious constitution before the laws of the realm, can be capable of educating the youth of the nation? This blind enthusiasm of religious devotion has betrayed the French people into the hands of such educators, and those educators themselves into the hands of a foreign master. In this way has the foundation of the administration of the entire nation, viz. its educational system, remained under the immediate control of a foreign régime which is of necessity hostile to our laws. It is in the highest degree both irrational and improper that this should be so.

There is no need to follow up all the consequences of this deplorable mistake in order to fully realize that the vice of Monasticism has seized upon the whole of our education. A foreigner to whom our present educational position was shown would imagine that France wanted to people seminaries, cloisters, and Latin colonies. How could the study of a foreign language and monastic procedure possibly be regarded as a suitable method of educating officers, magistrates, and professional men, or, in a word, the whole intelligence of the State?

Without our being aware of the fact, our common life is interpenetrated and to a large extent controlled by monastic conceptions. Our religious masters insist upon the observance of petty details, while the great principles of religion are forgotten. (In daring to say this I am but repeating the words of the wise and virtuous Abbé Fleury.) This practice has led to the rise of all the Orders, Fraternities and Conventicles that lead the would-be Christian from the truly religious path and prevent religious teachers acquiring that intimate knowledge of the essentials of religion which it is necessary to possess in order to be able to instruct others.

The authorities act as if they were compelled to put the full control of all schools and colleges into the hands of the religious communities, or the monks. It is even doubted whether married professors would be able to instruct children. What is one to think of this ecclesiastical prejudice when it is remembered that in the fifteenth century it needed a pronouncement from the Papal legate in France before doctors could marry? [1] Celibacy was enforced in purely civil appointments. It would seem that to have children of his own disqualified a man from bringing them up, and that these precautions were taken with the express purpose of preventing the maintenance of the birth-rate. It is obvious that a civil education is essential to the well-being of society, and as long as our own is not secularized we shall remain in the hands of a pedantic ecclesiasticism.

Why should it be essential for our colleges to be administered either by monks or priests? Under what pretext is instruction in science and the study of letters placed exclusively in their hands? They always put forward the importance of teaching religion to the young, and certainly this is a most vital matter. But is it true that only priests can teach the catechism, French and Latin, and construe Horace and Virgil? We have some excellent printed catechisms; it is not necessary to be a member of a religious order to be able to read to children those of Bossuet or Fleury; and it may be questioned if it is really necessary to be continually making new ones, or even altering the old.

The places where children should learn the elements of Christianity are the bosom of their family and the parish church. The true schools of religion are the churches. The Jesuits, who were real scholars, taught religion, but they were not really ecclesiastics although they dressed as such. Above all, spending forty or fifty half-hours yearly in explaining, well or ill, the catechism of Canisius, is not what educated people would regard as teaching religion. One religious instructor or chaplain in each school would suffice for this purpose; yet under this pretext the ecclesiastics claim exclusive control of the whole administration of our education.

I must not forget an important fact—at the present time practically all our distinguished men in science and literature are laymen. It is continually being stated that there are insufficient priests to carry out the functions of the ministry; why then are they made college professors and school masters? While the towns are filled with a crowd of idle priests, the country districts are without pastors, merely because they do not wish to live there. New appointments are constantly being found for them in the towns, just like transferable livings. One of the present evils of the State is that every priest wants a congregation

1. In 1552 Cardinal d'Estouteville, Papal legate in France, reformed the University, granted doctors liberty to marry, and at the same time, to mark their contamination, prohibited them in future from assembling in the Church of Paris under the towers, as hitherto they had occasionally done.—Pasquier, "Recherches," I, 275.

under his authority, but at the same time does not want to be responsible for it.

To teach children science it is essential to have persons who make a profession of the study of letters. The clergy cannot deny that, generally speaking, they are not in this category. I am not unjust enough to exclude them from it; it is a pleasure to recognize that many of them in the Universities and Academies are well educated, and very capable teachers. I do not forget the priests of the Oratory, who are citizens, and not bound by monastic prejudice; but I protest against the exclusion of laymen. My purpose is to claim for the nation an education which depends only on the State, because it belongs essentially to the State; because every nation has an inalienable and undeniable right to educate its own citizens; because the children of the State should be educated by members of the State.

The exclusive right of instructing the young which is claimed for the secular and regular clergy is not the only disadvantage arising from monastic prejudice; there are others in the procedure of education in the schools that must be considered.

In the schools of the regular orders the object of the work is rather to produce masters than to teach children. In the elementary stages a young instructor is merely an old scholar who finishes his course of study at the expense of the others. He overloads his pupils with long, tiring lessons and essays that give him little trouble to set; meanwhile he uses the time to his own advantage, making summaries and extracts, reading or preparing sermons and lectures. As soon as he is qualified by the knowledge he has thus acquired, he gives up all idea of teaching for the good of others, and passes on to fulfil the vocation prepared for him for the glory and profit of his order.

The manner in which classes are managed is determined by the strict uniformity of the cloisters; the punishments inflicted are inspired by a cloistral conception of discipline, and seem designed to crush rather than elevate the mind. All this coercion produces misery and disappointment, and its most usual result in the pupils is a lifelong hatred of study. Grown men would hardly be able to accustom themselves to the subjection and constraint which is forced upon the children. To keep them seated five or six hours out of twelve is against all nature. The work given them to do is so monotonous that it almost inevitably leads to idleness and boredom. Always Latin and composition! Instead of fostering a taste for any science or art, the monotony and discouragement that attend all their studies lead to a repugnance for the elements of all sciences and arts. Nothing is more usual than to see young people giving up all reading the moment they leave school. The first fruit of what we call the "education" of the young is to leave them with no object of study at an age when there is a growing need of study to combat the increased opportunities afforded by leisure to the dangerous temptations of demoralizing passions. . . .

Masters trained in the subtleties of scholasticism teach these to the young, with the result that they develop a fixed habit of arguing and quarrelling; some of them seem never to escape from the school benches for the rest of their lives.

But the most serious omission in our present system of education (and perhaps the most inevitable so long as it remains in the hands of those who have renounced the world, and who, far from wanting to learn about it, are compelled to shut themselves away from it) is the complete neglect of instruction in personal and social morality. Our education, unlike that of Greece and Rome, takes no account of morals. Having escaped from all the drudgery and boredom of college, our young people find themselves under the necessity of learning the most elementary common social duties. They have learnt no principles by which to judge actions, opinions, morals and customs. They have everything yet to learn about these vital matters, having been taught a devotion that is an imitation of true religion, and rules of conduct that are a substitute for real virtue and but the shadow of it.

The care and preservation of health and physical culture have been lost sight of; the most ordinary matters, which are the bed-rock of communal life, the foundation of civil society, have been neglected. The greater part of our young people are quite ignorant of the world in which they live, of the earth that nourishes them, of the men that supply their needs, of the animals that serve them, of the labourers and artisans that work for them; they have not even the beginnings of knowledge. No advantage is taken of their natural curiosity, to augment it. They do not know how to appreciate the marvels either of nature or of art. Both the matter and manner of what they are taught and what they are not taught bear the hall-mark of the monastic mind.

The sole aim of this mind is to subdue all spiritual forces to the service of a religious order, and in its dealing with the sciences its only concern is to limit them, isolating them, so to speak, one from the other. The point of view that recognizes that all truths are inter-related, that they are easier to comprehend when this interrelation is demonstrated, and that for the purpose of understanding them it is essential to juxtapose them, since it is a characteristic of error to remain unique and in isolation—all this can have no place where the study of sciences useful to mankind is a completely subordinate one.

In an educational system based on the method of a religious order that treats all its members exactly alike, one cannot hope to find diversity of instruction, or any variation of it to suit the varying needs of individuals. A man who is one day to command armies, or to fill one of the higher judicial positions, is brought up like the son of a major in the bourgeois militia, or the son of a village patriarch. I am not complaining that we are giving as good an education to the poor as to the rich; I am complaining that we are giving an equally bad education to both.

It is, then, only by delivering ourselves from this spirit of monasticism that, by hindrances of all kinds, has embarrassed the educational policy of our state for more than two centuries, that we can establish a basis of general education upon which all particular education must rest. As the author of "Considérations sur les mœurs" wisely said fifteen years ago, this basis can be founded only on an organized system of human knowledge, since it is indispensable that every section of education should have the same general aim and tendency.

CONCERNING THE NUMBER OF SCHOOLS AND SCHOLARS

Everything without exception is held within the moral order, as it is within the physical; the education of individuals and of schools is relative to the educational system of the nation and to the constitution of the State.

Be the nation military or commercial; a monarchy, a republic, or an aristocracy; densely or thinly populated; it is evident that all general policy and every political enterprise must depend on an exact assessment of the numbers in the different professions, such as the clergy, the nobility, the military, the legal, the commercial, the labourers, the artisans, etc. For example, it is asked if there are too many or too few schools in France. To answer this question it is necessary to know if there are sufficient labourers, sufficient soldiers, if there are not too many lawyers, too many or too few priests, or men of letters. In short, the answer depends upon the proportion that holds, or should hold, between the different professions, according to their usefulness and necessity to society. Without entering here into unnecessary detail, and accepting the proportion of the military class as fixed by the experience of ages and nations at a hundredth, I affirm that there are not enough agricultural labourers in this country. We have large stretches of land lying fallow, and though our State is rich enough to produce sufficient foodstuff to have a surplus for export, we often import food from the very countries to which we should be supplying it.

Numerical predominance is not to be feared in a profession that produces wealth for the rest, and continually adds to the real prosperity of the State; but it is dangerous in a class that, while producing no new wealth itself, lives on that of the State which has created it.

Is it essential to the proper education of the people and the good of religion that there should be at least 250,000 priests, men and women, in the Kingdom? At the time of Pope Cornelius there were only forty-six priests in Rome and only 154 clerics altogether, although the city was very populous; now there are many thousands. Either there were too few then or there are too many now. The number of ecclesiastics has very greatly increased in all Catholic countries. What functions have they to-day that they did not have in those early days when religion was most flourishing?

Does instruction in matters of law require the incredible number of legal agents and officers that despoil the inhabitants of our towns and countryside? Seyssel, under Louis XII, decided that there were more officers of justice in France than in all the rest of Europe. This was undoubtedly an exaggeration, but to what extent has their number increased since then?

Are there not too many writers, too many academy scholars, too many schools? It was difficult to study at one time owing to the lack of books; the difficulty now is that there are too many books. We can say, with Tacitus: *"Ut multarum rerum, sic litterarum intemperantia laboramus."* Never before have there been so many students in a country where everyone is complaining of depopulation; even the working people want to study. Labourers and artisans send their children to school in the small towns, where it costs little to live; and after a poor education that teaches them only to despise their fathers' professions, they turn to the cloisters and join the clerics; they take posts as officers of the law; they often become persons harmful to society. *"Multorum manibus res humanae, paucorum capita sufficiunt."*

The Brothers of Christian Doctrine, called the "Ignorantins," are pursuing a fatal policy; they are teaching people to read and write who should have learnt only to draw and to handle planes and files, but who now no longer wish to do so. These clerics are the rivals or the successors of the Jesuits.[2] The good of society demands that the knowledge of the people should not exceed what is necessary in their occupations. Every man who sees further than his dull daily round will never follow it out bravely and patiently. Among the common people it is really only necessary for those to learn reading and writing who live by means of these accomplishments, or who need them in their daily tasks.

It is recognized that under a good administration the classes of men that live on the labour of others must not be too numerous; they must be limited to the essential minimum. In practice we seem to have adopted exactly the opposite policy. The common people will soon consist exclusively of discontented artisans, militiamen and students.

It is, then, more helpful to the State to have few schools, provided that they are good and offer a complete course of study, than to have many poor ones. It is better to have few students provided they are better taught; and they can be taught more easily when there are fewer of them. . . .

It is very surprising that the cultured classes and the intelligentsia of last century were able to tolerate an education as crude as ours, even while continually criticizing it. The bodily routine and habit by which men are controlled allied to a sixteenth-century educational system which had never been, and, I repeat, never could be, purged of monastic ideas, had combined to perpetuate their errors and abuses. The slight reforms that were begun improved education a little; but it is just this that led to the consolidation of the faults and imperfections. The Jesuits were convinced that the plan of studies (*ratio studiorum*) drawn up under Aquaviva in the sixteenth century, and Jouvenci's feeble pamphlet, were masterpieces of literature. Wedded to old prejudices, they were the last to relinquish them, and they opposed all reforms; they recognized no books but their own, and they began to adopt Cartesianism only when everyone else was preparing to renounce it.

It is easier to banish the darkness of ignorance than a presumption of false knowledge. During ten years Russia has advanced further in Physics and Natural Science than other nations would have done in a hundred: the reports of the St. Petersburg Academy are sufficient to

2. Since they have been established at Brest and St.-Malo there are hardly any ship's-boys to be found there—that is, lads who work in the vessels and eventually become sailors. Thirty years from now it will be asked why there is a shortage of sailors at these ports.

make this clear. Perhaps Portugal, who is drastically reforming her system of studies, will progress further in proportion than we shall, unless we seriously consider the reform of our own.

During the last few centuries all instruction has been in the sphere of language study: in the present century the craze for culture has seized the nation and disorganized the professions. The life of society has perhaps become more congenial for a few individuals; but in the matter of the nation at large the State is the loser. Its interests demand that the professions should be filled by capable men. Sick people are not perturbed if their doctors' orders are not written in epigrams. A counsel is required to know the law, not to be a wit. In a word, the good of the State demands that each man should occupy himself primarily with his profession, and unless our outlook changes, the only professions in which this really occurs will be those of the skilled artisans. The taste for wit has become a craze, and has banished science and that true learning to which we have owed so much in the past; on this foundation our great men based their wisdom, yet to-day it is largely if not entirely neglected.

It can happen that while there are highly cultured individuals in a nation the people as a whole may be ignorant. It is the schools that are the measure of the culture of the ordinary citizen; but the reports of the academies and published books are the evidence by which we may point to our men of genius.

When our schools, with their bad methods, are compared with those of Oxford, Cambridge, Leyden and Göttingen, which have elementary books better written than ours, it is clear that the Germans and the English are better educated than the French. In the same way it is impossible that a well-bred Roman, cultivated by the conversation and society of educated men, who pleaded cases at law, became ædile, prætor, augur, consul, presided at the Senate, and commanded armies, was not as a man superior to contemporary Englishmen and Frenchmen, since it is only experience that can really fashion men.

But when the reports of our academies of science and those of London, Leipzig, etc., are compared, and our books with those of foreigners, it is clear that a Frenchman, if only he is put on the right road early enough, is as clever as, and perhaps better educated than others; he has more sense of order and method, and better taste. We must do justice to the French nation; she will become, eventually, all that she herself and others wish her to be. In all departments of human activity she can rival antiquity. She has had her Themistocles, Miltiades, Pericles, Demosthenes, Sophocles and Aristophanes; and,

when she seriously wants them, will have them again. It is the State
as a whole, the greater part of the nation, that must be chiefly kept in
sight in the matter of education; twenty million men are more to be
considered than one million, and the peasants, not yet an Order in
France as they are in Sweden, must not be neglected in any educational system. Its aim must be the cultivation of letters, but no less is
it the cultivation of the soil. All the useful arts and sciences must be
developed, the administration of justice assured, religion taught; gen-
erals, magistrates, well-educated and efficient ecclesiastics, artists and
skilled artisans must all be produced in proportion to the needs of the
State. The government's business is to make each citizen content with
his walk in life, so that he will not feel impelled to abandon it.

In carrying out these different aims there is no need for the State
to constrain individuals or the liberty of the citizens. It must govern,
inspire, remove obstacles and give facilities and encouragement to the
functioning of an industrious nation; and I personally think a nation
like ours (I speak of the common people) only needs to be well taught.
We have a large number of excellent books, but few classical and
elementary books. Let books suitable for children and the ignorant be
written, let genius be left free to act and freedom of thought be respected; let love of country and the public good be inspired; and let
talents, provided they are not improperly used, be no longer a draw-
back to their possessors.

There will be learned men in France when science is honoured, and
not considered only from the point of view of party, vested interests
or diplomacy, as we have seen ecclesiastical learning reduced during
the last century to what was called the fashion of the period, or,
better, of the moment. There will be real professions when apprenticeship is a reality, and when application and talent lead to advancement. . . .

A man of great intelligence has said that the greatest service literary
societies can render to the study of letters, the sciences and the arts is
to devise methods and courses by which labour and error are reduced
to a minimum, and truth is reached by the surest and shortest route.
By such means a young man will know more at twenty-five than another, badly taught, would know at thirty-five.

Courses of study at present are too long and difficult because they
are encumbered with too much useless material; this is evident in the
schools, and is the reason why, after so much labour, so little is known.
When you are on the wrong road the more you advance the farther
does the journey's end recede; a good guide would spare you much

useless toil. It is the inutilities and falsities that are long and prolix; the truth still retains the merit of being more easily understood—it is the false that is unintelligible. . . .

Selections from the Voltaire–La Chalotais Correspondence

To M. de La Chalotais
Attorney General of the Parlement of Brittany

"Délices," 17 May [1762]

I was at the point of death, Monsieur, when I received the letter [1] with which you have honored me. I hope that I live to see the effects of your excellent *compte-rendu*. I did not know that you were to do me the honor of sending it to me and I must send my thanks for two things: for having enlightened France and for remembering me.

Your indictment has been published in Geneva and has spread throughout all of Europe with the success that is due the only philosophical work ever to come from the bar. Hopefully, once France is purged of the Jesuits, it will be obvious how shameful it is to be yet under the ridiculous power that has established them.

I assure you, Monsieur, that it is a great consolation for me to see my sentiments justified by a magistrate like you. I can boast that I first attacked the Jesuits in France. . . .

To M. de La Chalotais

"Délices," 11 July [1762]

Monsieur, I am almost blind and yet I am writing. But that is because passion gives strength and the sentiment which your kindnesses inspire in me is a passion. You confound the Jesuits and you instruct historians. The memoir that you have deigned to send me is very plausible: if you were the attorney-general of some parlement in my neighborhood I would fly to you to thank you although I no longer stir from my cottage. I would come to ask you to cure me of the

1. [On May 4, 1762, La Chalotais wrote to Voltaire from Rennes telling him that he was sending him a copy of his book against the Jesuits and the backwardness of French education. Cf. Besterman, ed., *Voltaire's Correspondence*, XLVIII, 233. —Ed.]

Voltaire's letters have been translated from the texts in the *Œuvres complètes de Voltaire* (Paris: Garnier Frères, 1877-85), LXII-LXIII. The letters of La Chalotais have been translated and reprinted with the permission of the editor and publisher from Theodore Besterman, ed., *Voltaire's Correspondence*, 107 vols. (Geneva, Institut et Musée Voltaire, 1953-65), LI, 239-40; LII, 2-3.

scruples that remain with me. If things had been as you say they were, the Parlement of Paris (the capital of ancient France) would have been the assembly of the Estates-General. Why, during the estates of the fourteenth century, did the parlements not meet? Why is the King's Bench in England different from the estates named Parliament? Why does the English government—having in everything imitated, and preserved, our usages—still have its Estates-General while those of France have been abolished? Why does the attorney-general of the King of England argue at this royal bench and not at the nation's parliament? That which is called the Great Bench in France is still the Great Bench in London. The old formulas of your sessions are preserved there and the attorney-general acts only at that bench. That which is called parlement in France is therefore the King's Bench, just as that which is named Parliament in England represents our estates-general.

If the Gothic-Vandal-Teutonic government was everywhere the same, why would we be the only nation in which a supreme court of justice was substituted for the representatives of the heads of the nation? The Spanish Audiences are not *las cortes* and they are in no way related to them. The Imperial Chamber of Vetzlar,[2] although a prince always presides over it, is not at all analogous to the Diet of the Empire.

In no European country does any superior court represent the nation. How could France alone have established this public law? If she had established it, why would it not be in due legal form? If each parlement took the place of the Estates-General during the recesses of these estates, it is clear that it would be there [merely] in its place; what would the King's Council then become?

You are well aware, of course, that this is embarrassing. Make an effort to be sincere. Anyway, I am not selfishly interested in this because, as far as I know, I'm not the descendant of any Frank who ravaged the Gauls with Ildovic named Clovis, nor of any Lord who betrayed Louis V and Charles of Lorraine, belonging to no constituted body [*corps*], being neither tonsured nor a Master of Arts; having one foot in France, the other in Switzerland and both of them on the edge of the grave. I pretty much agree with the Englishman who said that all origins, all rights, all establishments are like plum-pudding; the first cook puts in only flour, a second adds eggs, a third sugar, a fourth raisins and in this way the plum-pudding takes shape.

2. [Wetzlar was a free imperial city of the Holy Roman Empire, seat of its supreme court.—Ed.]

Consider what Lin and Clet [3] were—supposing that there were Lins and Clets: would they recognize their successors today? Would Mary's son recognize his religion? Everything in the universe is made of bits and pieces. It seems to me that society resembles a great shipwreck: Every man for himself! is the motto of poor wretches like me. For you, Monsieur, who have a nice seat on the ship, it is a completely different matter. You've dumped Loyola into the sea and your ship sails all the better for it. There is something that they must realize in Paris, providing they reflect on it: true eloquence now exists only in the provinces. The *comptes-rendus* in Brittany and Provence are masterpieces. Paris has nothing to oppose to them—far from it.

Nevertheless there are still a dozen Jesuits at the court. They triumph at Strasbourg, at Nancy. In Brittany, your country, yes your country, the pope distributes benefices four months during the year. Your bishops, *proh pudor!* entitle themselves bishops by the *grace of the Holy See* etc., etc.

Monsieur, you fill me with respect and hope.

To M. de La Chalotais

"Délices," 21 July [1762]

I believe, Monsieur, that I owe to your kindness the gift of your new masterpiece. The two of them are all the more powerful because they are, or appear to be, rather moderate. The Jesuits will say *Haec est aerugo mera.* All good Frenchmen owe you thanks for those words "in a word, ultramontane maxims."

These two works are the voice of the fatherland, expressing itself with eloquence and erudition. You have sown seeds which one day will produce more than people think. And when France no longer has an Italian master who must be paid, she will say: it is to M. de La Chalotais that we are obligated.

You have given me such enthusiasm, Monsieur, that I will go so far as to take the liberty of recommending to your justice the case of M. Cathala, a businessman of Geneva. He is imploring the parlement in order to be paid a debt. He is a very honest man, very precise, incapable of asking for something he is not owed. I know very well that being a Huguenot, he is condemned to eternal damnation; but, in the meantime, he must have his money in this world.

Pardon me, Monsieur, for making this request of you. I know that it is quite useless to solicit you, but I could not refrain from telling you how much I value the honesty of my Huguenot. I can hardly be

3. [Lin and Clet are Voltaire's nicknames for Saints Linus and Cletus, the traditional successors of Saint Peter. He doubted their existence.—Ed.]

suspected of favoring evildoers, because I have just had a church built.

I cannot express to you with what respect I have the honor to be, etc.

To M. de La Chalotais

November 6 [1762]

You will undoubtedly present, Monsieur, a plan for education worthy of your excellent memoirs which have served to destroy those who give our youth a pretty terrible education. May it please God that you will want to add some lessons for those who believe themselves to be grown men! They are terrible children, these men with bearded chins who pay an Italian priest the first year's revenue from land in France that the king has given them. And they go on to complain that they are wronged because they aren't allowed to be the absolute masters of everything. You are the attorney-general of a province in which an Italian still bestows benefices. The English, it is true, were for a long time more imbecilic than we. But look at how they have improved themselves. They no longer have monks or convents, but they have victorious fleets. Their clergy writes good books and educates good children. Their farmers have made fertile land that once was not. Their commerce embraces the world and their *philosophes* have taught us truths that we had no notion of. I admit that I am jealous when I cast my eyes upon England.

You have rendered the nation an essential service, Monsieur, by enlightening her on the Jesuits. You have demonstrated that the emissaries of the pope, foreigners in their own country, are not made for the education of our youth. You believe that it is better that a man learn the four fundamental maxims of the year 1682 early, rather than know by heart the verse of Jean Despautère. In a word, I am persuaded that you are able—with your usual skill—to add to your plan for education quite a few things that will serve the education of mature men. The century of the acorn [*gland*] is over. You give men bread. Some superstitious people will still regret the acorns which suited them so well. The rest of the nation will be nourished by you.

It is a splendid age that abolishes the Jesuits. I would dare to say with Horace:

> *Quid te exempta juvat spinis e pluribus una?* [What good does it do you to pluck out a single one of many thorns?]

I will be told that, of all the thorns, this was the most pointed and the most troublesome and that it is necessary to begin by tearing it out. I would reply:

> *Perge quo coepisti pede.*

Reason has made great progress among us. But beware that one day Jansenism doesn't create as much evil as the Jesuits have! What use is it to me to be freed of foxes if I'm handed over to wolves? May God give us many attorneys-general who have, if it is possible, your eloquence and your philosophy! I've noticed that philosophy has almost always come to Paris from northern countries. In return Paris has always sent them fashions.

I am forgetting, Monsieur, to talk to you about the case of my Huguenots. Were they Mohammedans you would award them the decision if they were right.

Allow me, Monsieur, to renew the sincere protestations of my esteem and my respect.

To M. de La Chalotais

Ferney, 28 February [1763]

I would have much preferred, Monsieur, that you had done me the honor of sending me your work in print rather than in manuscript— the public would already be enjoying it. I believe quite sincerely that it is one of the best presents that one could make it.

I was obliged to have almost all of your *Memoir* read to me because I am becoming a bit blind as a result of a great inflammation that affected my eyes.

I cannot thank you too much, Monsieur, for giving me a foretaste of what you've destined for France. To mould children you begin by moulding men. You've entitled your work *Essay for a Plan of Study for Secondary Schools;* I myself would entitle it *The Teachings of a Man of State to Enlighten All Stations in Life.* I find all your views useful. How I am grateful to you, Monsieur, for wanting those who teach children to have children themselves! They certainly sense better than those bachelors how children and youths should be educated. I thank you for proscribing study for plowmen. I who cultivate the earth present you with a petition for having laborers and not tonsured clerics. Above all send me some Ignorantine [4] Brothers to guide my plows or pull them. I am trying to make amends at the end of my life for the useless thing that I've been in the world. I'm expiating my

---

4. [Not a Voltairean pun but rather one of the names given the Brethren of the Christian Schools (Frères des Écoles Chrétiennes), a teaching order organized in 1683 and dedicated to providing the poor with free, especially religious, education. So called because the Order's rules did not admit priests who had a theological education.—Ed.]

pointless occupations by clearing land that has borne nothing for
centuries. In Paris there are three or four hundred paper-scribblers, as
useless as I, who should do the same penance.

You do Jean-Jacques quite an honor to refute his ridiculous paradox
which excludes history from the education of children. But you do
M. Clairaut justice in recommending his *Elements of Geometry* which
is overly neglected by instructors and which leads children along the
route that nature herself has indicated. There will be no father of a
family who won't regard your book as the most necessary furnishing
in his house and it will serve as the rule for all those who engage in
teaching. . . .

As for religion, I hold with what you say with the Abbé Gedoin
and even with what you do not say. The religion that is simplest and
most visibly founded on natural law is doubtless the best.

I am rendering you an account, Monsieur, with as much good faith
as gratitude, of the impression that your *Memoir* has made on me.
For the present, what would you have me do? Do you want me to
send the manuscript back to you? Do you allow me to have it printed
abroad? I will obey your orders exactly. Your confidence honors me
as much as it is dear to me. . . .

I am quite weak, quite old, quite sick. But I defy anyone to be
more alive to your merit than I. I cannot express to you with what
respect and esteem I have the honor to be, etc.

To M. de Voltaire

Rennes, March 11, 1763

The letter which you have done me the honor to write me, Monsieur,
gave me one of the greatest pleasures I have had in my life. Imagine
someone who is far from all human help, who has been writing a
work on literature at intervals amid the tumult of affairs, who receives
the approval of that man who is, as the Latin puts it forcefully,
Litteratorum facile princeps.

You have given me courage, Monsieur, and I shall bring out my
Memoir. To see a work of literature written by a man of the king
deposited in the register of a parlement is a landmark of the fortunate
progress we have made. I confess, Monsieur, that I would certainly
have been glad had you condescended to make some corrections of it
and to give it a few of those flashes of Enlightenment which you
diffuse everywhere.

The society is falling to its doom; it is the fate of fanaticism to collapse completely as soon as it has been exposed. I am pleased to have struck it several blows. . . .

Being a farmer, do you have, Monsieur, our two volumes of the observations of the Society of Brittany for Agriculture, Commerce, and the Arts? If you do not have them I shall send them to you. We are beginning to be born. I should like very much to be able to send you at Ferney all our Ignorantins whom you could harness to your plows. Because you work the land, Monsieur, one can say of Ferney as of the countryside of Rome, *Gaudet tellus vomere Laureato*.

I do not wish my *Memoir* to be printed, I am reworking it every day. I shall send it to you when I have it ready and if later I am done the honor of having it printed at Geneva I shall be delighted. . . . I saw with pleasure from your letter to Mr. Dalembert that you are expecting to publish a new edition of your universal history. If it is not yet printed I shall take the liberty, with your permission, of sending you some notes on the origins of the parlements of France.

Your good health, Monsieur! live for the honor of literature and philosophy, for the honor of the century, the nation, and humanity. No one desires it more than I, and none, Monsieur, is with more respect and sincerity,

Your very humble and obedient servant,
LA CHALOTAIS

To M. de La Chalotais

"Délices," 21 March [1763]

I have the honor, Monsieur, to send you by M. d'Argental the manuscript that you were good enough to entrust me with and I assure you that it is with a good deal of pain that I part with it. . . .

Don't doubt that your work will be printed in more than one city after it appears in Rennes. It will be quite a bit easier to counterfeit it than to imitate it. You do me a very great favor, Monsieur, in deigning to forward the memoir on the origin of the parlement to me. If the package is large, I would beg you to address it to me care of M. Damilaville, first clerk of the *vingtième,* quai Saint-Bernard in Paris. If the volume is not considerable, as I fear it is, have the kindness to send it directly to me.

I'm afraid that I don't have very accurate notions about this origin, for, beginning with the origin of the world, I see nothing about them that is clear. Origins resemble the genealogies of great houses: they all begin with fables. Although the new tableau of the stupidities of the human race has already been printed under the title of *Essai sur l'histoire générale,* I would not profit any less from the knowledge that you would have the goodness to communicate. Everything can be made up by means of a few boxes.

Truly, Monsieur, *The Judgment of Reason* is a nice subject. But the *Appeals of Reason* are already forgotten. Witticisms are good only when they are served piping hot. Moreover, it seems to me quite difficult for reason to pronounce on the children of Loyola without speaking its mind on those of that extravagant Francis of Assisi, of that fanatical Dominic and of that insolent Norbert and of all those schoolmasters of the papal militia who are always an expense for citizens and always a danger for governments.

I would, however, quite willingly undertake to be the registrar of reason in a court in which you were the first president. But I have for a long while been occupied with a matter that is neither less reasonable nor less pressing. Unfortunately it is against the Parlement of Toulouse. Destiny had decided that I be sought out in the caves of the Alps to help an unfortunate family sacrificed to the most absurd fanaticism, and whose father was condemned to the wheel by the most misleading evidence. You have doubtless heard about this adventure: it interests all Europe for it is religious zeal that has produced the disaster. It seems to me that, thanks to you, Monsieur, people are more reasonable in Armorica than in Septimania. Breton heads take after Locke and Newton and Toulousian heads take somewhat after Dominic and Torquemada.

I admit that I was greatly satisfied when I learned that the whole council, to the number of a hundred judges, had unanimously condemned the zeal with which eight Toulousian Catholics had condemned a father of a family to the wheel because he was a Huguenot; for that is what the whole trial amounts to.

I've read the two volumes of your *Agricultural Society* and I've profited from it. I've had oat-grass sown; I've cleared land. I've turned a piece of property that wasn't worth three thousand livres into one that produces seven to eight thousand livres of income. This occupation of old-age is better than making an *Agesilas* and a *Surena.* Yet, I am still making them—to my misery. But I won't be making them for very long: *vox quoque Moerim deficit.*[5] What doesn't *deficit* me at all is the very respectful esteem and the sincere attachment with which I have the honor to be, etc.

5. [Cf. Virgil's *Eclogues* ix, V. 53, *vox quoque Moerim/ Jam fugit ipsa.*—Ed.]

To M. de Voltaire

Rennes, April 2, 1763

Here, Monsieur, is the memorandum which I had the honor to tell you I was sending. A long time ago I had written several observations on this subject, I have lost them in a pile of papers. I have dictated this very hastily as you will see, and the desire to please you has caused me to hasten to send it to you. I do not know why it is, Monsieur, that I fear less to send you a crude and unformed piece of work than I do to anyone else. If you condescend to make the slightest use of this one, you will understand as you read it that there is not the slightest reason to give me any credit because of the few principles which it contains. Moreover, these are only undigested observations which would gain much from your attention. I believe them to be basically very true. . . .

The Estates of Brittany would owe you their thanks, Monsieur, for the complimentary remarks you were kind enough to make about Breton Heads, certainly the Calas affair would not have happened in the Parlement of Brittany. Who is there who has not heard of that affair and of the noble and generous way in which you took up the cause of the oppressed? I read all about it and I trembled at it. Let them say after that there must be no more denunciations of fanaticism, I would wish that that case be sent on appeal to some parlement, it would be an honor.

[La Chalotais quotes six lines of the *Aeneid*, not quite correctly.] I only wished, Monsieur, to give you one quotation, I could not stop myself from copying all these verses and I have not been able to alter any, I could not add anything to them and I conclude by begging you to accept my homage, my respects, and my profound veneration.

To M. de La Chalotais

At the Château of Ferney, June 9, 1763

I haven't received, Monsieur, the book which you deigned to honor me with and which pleased me so much in manuscript. It could quite easily happen that I will not receive it no matter how many times it might be countersigned—at least unless it be addressed to M. Janel, postal intendant and the absolute master of all printed matter that is mailed, or unless the package be dispatched to me on the Lyon coach to the address of M. Camp, a banker in Lyon. For a short time there has been a little inquisition against books. They are cutting off the nourishment for our poor souls as much as they can. I think that we are indebted to M. Jean-Jacques Rousseau for this, because of the letter that he took it into his head to send to Christophe de Beaumont.

I am not at all astonished, Monsieur, that the *pedant, heavy, filthy,* and *vain,* is angry that a man who doesn't have the honor to be a university pedant is teaching him his job. You have chased the Jesuits out and you've done well, sir. I praise you for it, I thank you for it. But one day you will have to repress the *bacheliers en fourrure* as well as the people in three-cornered hats. La Fontaine was right to say:

> *Je ne connois de bête pire au monde*
> *Que l'écolier, si ce n'est le pédant.*
> [I know no worse animal in the world
> Than the schoolboy, unless it's the pedant.]

As soon as I have your excellent work I'll recommend it to a book-seller and I'll have the honor to advise you of it.

Let me say, Monsieur, that the Senate in Sweden is a perpetual council of regency. You know better than I that each government has a different form and that nothing resembles anything else in this world. I am a partisan of the authority of the parlements and I would passionately love the one in Paris if you were its attorney-general. I would especially like it to be a bit more enlightened. It is not that at all and that makes me angry. But you console me as much as you instruct me. May God give us many magistrates like you so that we can pride ourselves in equaling the English in something!

Accept, Monsieur, the very sincere respect of a poor man who is close to losing his eyes and who wants to keep them to read you.

To M. de La Chalotais

Ferney, June 22 [1763]

I have finally received, and hastened to read, your excellent *Treatise on Education.* The miserable job of instructing youth used to be scorned by capable people, and was abandoned to pedants or, what is even worse, to monks. You instill a desire to be master of physics and rhetoric; you make the upbringing of children a great object of government. Why should not the best individuals who would be willing to devote themselves to a job which you have made so honorable be drawn from within our academies? But that would require Michel de L'Hospital, or M. de la Chalotais for chancellor.

A supply of your book has just arrived at Geneva; it is being read and admired. Geneva will believe I amount to something, seeing the way in which you have been kind enough to speak of me. In fact that is the only thing which can be criticized in your book. It seems to me, from the eagerness with which all the fathers of families are reading you, that a new edition must soon be printed here, although a great number of copies has been sent from France; if so, I shall ask you for the additions with which you will wish to embellish your work.

Did you not mean, in saying that it would take a cannon-ball twenty-five years to cover the distance between our globe and the sun, that you were supposing that the speed is constant? It's a small matter. I shall carry out your instructions precisely.

You give some good examples of more than one kind to the prosecutors of Paris. It could be claimed that the learned Omer de Fleury did not follow them when he made his denunciation of vaccination.

I am afraid that the government may be so embarrassed by the difficulty that so many grown men will have in paying their taxes that it will not be able to give to the education of children the attention that it deserves.

Curtae nescio quid semper abest rei

Certainly that will not be said of your book, although people think that it is too short.

Accept, Monsieur, the respect, the devotion, and the gratitude of your most humble etc.

To Louis René de Caradeuc de La Chalotais
                                        Ferney, September 26, 1764

Permit, Monsieur, M. de La Vabre, who last year presented to you a letter of introduction from me, and whom you received with so much kindness, to have the honor of presenting you another one. He will tell you of his case; as for me I can only speak to you of yourself, of your eloquence, of the excellent methods that you have condescended to offer for bringing up young people as citizens and cultivating their reason which has for so long been perverted in the schools. You seem to me to be the attorney-general of all of France.

I have several times reread everything that you have been willing to make public, always with new pleasure. You are not content to enlighten men, you come to their aid. I have seen from agricultural proceedings how much you encourage agriculture in your native land. I have taken my place among the ranks of your disciples; following your example I have sown some rye-grass, and I have compelled the poorest land to yield something. I think that Virgil had as much reason to say *o fortunatos nimium sua si bona norint* as he was wrong to abandon the kind of life he praised. He gave up the plow for the court; I have had the good fortune to abandon kings for the plow. Would to

God that my small properties adjoined yours! Thinking men are too widely scattered; and the number of *philosophes* is still very small, although much larger than it was in our youth. I have seen the domain of reason expand, or rather reason's chains have become lighter. A few more men like you, Monsieur, and the human species will be of greater value.

I beg you to be well convinced of the infinite respect with which I shall forever be etc.

ROYAL SOVEREIGNTY AND PROVINCIAL LIBERTIES IN BRITTANY

Introduction

This chapter concludes with a chilling account by a nineteenth-century historian of Attorney-General de la Chalotais's midnight arrest by royal troops on November 10, 1765. Public interest in the fate of this well-known and highly respectable nobleman, so harshly punished for what he was to insist was no reason at all, and in the fate of those he declared responsible for his sufferings, would soon make the "Brittany Affair" a byword in French political argument. Ultimately the consequences of the Affair were to produce what Voltaire called a "revolution" in the institutions of the Old Regime. In this chapter, however, the reader will be concerned only with understanding the origins and development of the Affair itself.

He is faced with a double task. First, he must reconstruct from the documents the sequence of events that culminated in La Chalotais's arrest. Having compiled as fully as possible a blow-by-blow account of *what* happened, he must then turn to the historian's even more difficult responsibility of explaining the *why* of November 10, 1765. There are two levels on which this explanation can be attempted. First, the reader might try to see whether this punishment fitted a crime. Was La Chalotais the writer of illiterate anonymous letters to the king's minister, and, even if he was not, had he been plotting against the royal authority? Or was the attorney-general perhaps the innocent victim of a powerful enemy or "society" of enemies, i.e. the Jesuits in whose condemnation he had played such a part? Even helped by his previous acquaintance with La Chalotais, the reader may find that the conclusions he can form through this kind of detective work are not very satisfying. This result may prompt an effort to provide another kind of explanation, suggesting as it does that the important question to ask in order to explain the Brittany Affair is not what La Chalotais had done or not done, but what he represented. In other words, even if he was, as he was to claim, an innocent bystander, his tragedy may have been an incident of the confrontation of two historical forces, of a showdown somewhat reminiscent of American conflicts over states' rights, between the representatives of royal centralizing authority and the defenders of Breton provincial liberties.

The reader may find it just as difficult to allocate "guilt" as an explanatory factor on this level as it was to choose between La Chalotais and his accusers. He may find that there is something to be said on both sides when he considers the fundamental question: was provincial resistance justified because monarchical authority had become exploitative despotism in Brittany in the 1760's, or was the defense of Breton liberties in reality the defense, at the cost of general progress, by one social class of its own vested interests? To answer that question, and thus to understand the struggle in which La Chalotais was caught up, the reader must acquaint himself with the history, economy, social structure, and institutions of that remote peninsula swept by Atlantic storms.

In the first of the selections in this chapter, Armand Rébillon, a modern historian of Brittany, suggests that the Breton conflicts of the eighteenth century were constitutional questions paralleled throughout France and did not arise from a nationalistic spirit peculiar to the province. Certainly if Brittany were completely untypical, studying the Brittany Affair would afford far fewer insights into the general problems of the Old Regime. Yet the reader should be alert for expressions revealing that some Bretons did not yet feel themselves entirely French. Even today, in the second half of the twentieth century, a Breton autonomist movement, emphasizing the region's linguistic and cultural differences, is still in existence. Of course, no Breton now would conceive of declaring war on France in alliance with a foreign power as a conspiracy headed by a "gentleman"—i.e. nobleman—named Pontcallec did in 1719, but many Bretons still complain of what they feel to be Paris's simultaneous interference and neglect.

In reading Rébillon, as well as the selection from the handwritten notes for a "Dictionary" of Breton government by an anonymous royal official of the 1760's, in order to discover the pattern of the developing conflict that led to La Chalotais's arrest, the reader should bear in mind this modern Breton feeling of incomplete integration into the national community. Last of the great provinces to be joined to the French crown, Brittany enjoyed what exceptional privileges, legal and fiscal, denied to other parts of France? Was it possible for eighteenth-century Bretons to believe themselves sincerely "devoted" to the king, and yet to insist upon the maintenance of those privileges, ambiguous as they sometimes were?

What specific evidence is there that by the middle of the eighteenth century, the crown was beginning to interfere more in Brittany, and perhaps also to neglect the province less? Does the explanation for this increased interest lie at least partly in the state of the royal treasury, and in the fact that such taxes as the *taille* had not been introduced in Brittany, while traditional taxes remained at their sixteenth-century levels?

If the action of royal authority was being increasingly felt in Brittany, the reader should take careful note of where the corresponding *re*action in defense of provincial liberties appeared. Why, when Brittany was one of the "provinces of estates" (*pays d'états*) having a legislature in which all citizens were at least theoretically represented, was opposition to the crown's encroachments first voiced by the "bastion" of "guardians," by a cabal within the second—or noble—estate? Is the reason that the numbers and way of life of the Breton noblemen, as well as their position in the estates, made them particularly vulnerable to change? Or were the first and third estates comparatively quiescent because the crown had succeeded in controlling them through what Rébillon calls "docile elements"?

A careful study of the fees listed in the "Dictionary" as being paid to various individuals by the estates or by the crown, and of their fluctuations, may suggest answers to these questions. But these lists of payments are not the only material of interest in the "Dictionary." For example, ceremonial often is the reflection of basic social and political attitudes. The reader should try to imagine what was symbolized in a Breton nobleman's mind by the ritual in which the representatives of royal authority, the king's commissioners, met the Estates of Brittany, as well as by the differing seating and processional arrangements for the three orders. In the light of such symbolic ceremonial, what would be the reaction of noblemen to any threatened infringement of Brittany's privilege of contracting biennially to make its contribution to the French treasury by a "free gift" or by "subscriptions" managed by the estates themselves through elected commissioners? If customary law was unclear, as on so many matters, as to when unanimity was required among the three orders of the estates to enact legislation, how would the nobility react to a royal declaration that two orders could outvote a third?

According to Rébillon, the Parlement of Rennes had not always co-operated with the estates in disputes with the crown. Yet, as the reader might expect after reading Ford, there is evidence that by the 1750's the Breton *noblesse de robe* was in close touch not only with the judges of the other sovereign courts of France but also with the leaders of the nobility in the provincial estates. Certainly the behavior of both the Parlement and the Estates of Brittany was enough to dissuade the Duke de Croÿ, the nobleman of the court whose diary will frequently be quoted from now on, from purchasing the command of the province. Do the conversations Croÿ had at Versailles suggest that the royal government was united in a determination to override Breton resistance to its authority? How, in fact, had the government responded to Breton opposition thus far? Was this response a factor in Croÿ's reluctance to take the Breton post?

There was no change in command in 1762. The Duke d'Aiguillon, commander-in-chief since 1753, returned to Brittany to lead the king's commissioners before the estates. D'Aiguillon's is the other famous name besides that of La Chalotais at the very center of the Brittany Affair. It was in fact his efforts to cleanse his name of the stain the Affair had left upon it that precipitated, as the reader will discover in later chapters, a major crisis of the Old Regime. From the brief written to exculpate him by his lawyer, Linguet, the reader can begin to construct a chronology of the events that were the immediate cause of La Chalotais's arrest. Linguet's credibility can be checked in two ways: by comparing his introductory account of the problems of Brittany with the picture the reader has already drawn for himself of the nature of the conflict there, and by examining Linguet's references to remonstrances and letters in the light of the texts of these documents, which complete the chapter. In testing for bias, one might ask to what extent he recognizes the legitimacy of Breton grievances. Should his contention that the Bretons ought to have blamed ministers in the capital, and not d'Aiguillon, for any infringement upon their liberties be believed, or is this merely the argument a clever lawyer would naturally adopt?

The reader might divide his chronology into two periods: September 1762 to June 1764, and June 1764 to November 1765. In the first period, it is important not only to look for incidents that might have generated a feud between the commander-in-chief and the attorney-general, but also for evidence that both at Versailles and in Brittany, attitudes were hardening. If the estates balked at a 5 per cent (sou per livre) tax increase, is there anything to suggest that the government was prepared to send in "foreign clerks"

to collect it? Note should also be taken of M. Coëtauscours's defense, in the estates, of the Jesuits whom the parlement of Brittany
had just dissolved. Does the aftermath of this incident suggest that
the Breton nobility of the robe and of the sword were united by
common vital interests that overrode the religious quarrels about
which contemporaries talked so much?

The answer is suggested by the complaints of the parlement in
its registration of the royal fiscal edict of November 21, 1763, on
June 5, 1764. Why should the judges go out of their way to declare that the "immemorial essence of the estates" had been destroyed by the order on voting procedure of October 1762? And
why the objections to d'Aiguillon's roadbuilding program, since
only peasants were liable for the compulsory labor service of the
corvée? Was the parlement complaining on this count in its role
as "guardian" of Brittany's privileges from genuine concern over
peasant hardships, or in a demagogic effort to gain popular support? Or has the fact that the peasants subject to the *corvée* were
the tenant-farmers of these landed judges something to do with it?
Indeed, the underlying problems raised by the parlement's opposition to d'Aiguillon's efforts to develop Brittany by improving its
municipal facilities and its communications are well worth ponder-
ing. What was the parlement doing: defending liberty, or obstruct-
ing progress? Was it, perhaps, doing both?

It is essential to note that after reading these complaints from
Rennes, Louis XV summoned four delegates of the parlement to
Versailles, scolded them, and gave La Chalotais his personal warning to "conduct himself with more moderation." Is there anything
in the remonstrances of August 11, 1764, to suggest that the parlement had heeded these royal admonitions? Both the language and
the argument of this document should be carefully studied. How,
in its general conception and even in its specific phraseology, is it
reminiscent of Montesquieu? Was it true that royal authority was
seeking to "change the principles of government" in Brittany, and
to "crush the magistracy"? Had Brittany been "enslaved," its constitution "overturned"? If there was room for honest differences

of opinion on such questions, does this suggest why Voltaire complained in his *History of the Parlement of Paris* that in France "nothing has been regularized in a uniform and stable manner"? What could be done about such a state of affairs?

Certainly the reader may find it difficult to decide which party had "the law" on its side in the long process of litigation that began when the Vacation Chamber of the parlement decided in favor of the estates in their suit against the collection of 10 per cent (two sous per livre) in additional taxes. Contrasting this year-long exchange of legal blows and counter-blows with the outcome of the stormy Breton Estates of 1764-65, he should perceive why a judicial body was a more effective center of opposition to the assertion of royal authority than a legislative one could be. In this struggle between the parlement of Rennes and the government, which side can be said to have been on the offensive, and which on the defensive? Which was the more patient, and the more anxious to end the confrontation? If both the representatives of the royal authority and the defenders of provincial liberties finally resorted to their ultimate weapons, who would the victor be? Had this been decided in November of 1765? Public opinion would play its part in a victory; is there any evidence to suggest that whether or not its actions were primarily dictated by concern for the interests of the nobility, the propaganda of the parlement had won it widespread support?

In this connection, the reader should evaluate the effectiveness of the propaganda on the other side. Some historians have suggested that the monarchy of the Old Regime became so unpopular that it finally gave way in 1789 to revolution less because it was ineffective than because it had no gift for clever public relations work. Thus even when its actions were in the general interest, popular opinion backed its opponents, even though they were representatives of a privileged class. Does Comptroller-General L'Averdy's pamphlet bear out these historians? Were citations from Gregory of Tours the best way to make the crown's case? Why could L'Averdy not simply demonstrate that a selfish mi-

nority were denying the government the funds it required for
essential measures in the public interest? How much royal authority
in Brittany did even the Comptroller-general think it wise to claim?

Whatever the efforts of L'Averdy to prove that the king exercised "full sovereignty" there, Brittany in the summer of 1765 was
in turmoil after the resignation of the parlement. Lower courts
kept the battle going. After Audouart, one of the royal intendant's
sub-delegates, had ordered to jail some pro-parlement rioters, he
himself was sentenced by the police tribunal of Rennes, composed
of friends of La Chalotais. The royal council at Versailles had to
intervene to quash this verdict.

Audouart's case was just one more episode of the conflict between Versailles and Brittany, yet it may throw some light on the
question with which the reader begins this chapter: of what, if
anything, was La Chalotais guilty? Though a question subordinate
to the great issues at stake in the Brittany Affair, it is certainly not
without interest. Can at least a circumstantial case of subversive
activities be made out against him? Though there was no trial by
jury under the Old Regime, the reader, as La Chalotais's retro-
spective juror, should weigh carefully the amount of credence that
should be given to the reports of police informers and handwriting
experts of the eighteenth century, or of any other. Is the worst that
can confidently be said of La Chalotais that he kept dangerous
company and thought dangerous thoughts? In the light of the circumstances of November 1765 was his arrest then surprising, or
predictable? Was it in any way *justifiable*?

A Modern Historian's Description of Breton Institutions and Society before 1789

CHAPTER VI: BRITANNY AND THE ROYAL POWER

I. *The Privileges and Organization of the Province*

The last obstacle to the complete incorporation of Brittany into a united France disappeared with the end of the ducal dynasty (1515). The royal authority, in truth, seemed always to fear that the memory of its ancient independence would preserve in the province the spirit of resistance. Such a fear is evident in the continuing concern to secure the development of docile elements and in the uneasiness about the particularistic tendencies of the historians and the Breton jurists. . . .

However, events would prove that in all the realm no province was more devoted to the monarchy than Brittany, nor more resolute in opposition to the enemy in time of war. In Brittany there were uprisings against the Huguenot danger or taxes; but nowhere was the population more attached to the king, and to the security and the integrity of the realm. The conflicts with the government became at times indeed lively, but they were always constitutional rather than national. Too often the character and scope of these conflicts have been poorly understood because of the desire to view them only as a manifestation of a particular Breton political situation. They offer us no more than a local instance of affairs common to the whole kingdom, and their interest lies really in the manner in which they illustrate some general problems of French politics.

The privileges of Brittany—These conflicts ordinarily originated in the exercise or the defence of those privileges recognized in the province at the time of the union; these privileges, analogous to those of the several *pays d'États*, were not unique. Completely negative, they were not intended to return to the Bretons the administration of their province, but rather, above all, to preserve in their arrangement with the king those guarantees which they had enjoyed with respect to their dukes. . . .

Except for the case of the dealers in contraband salt who had been dragged before the chamber of the salt-tax of Saumur, there could be no complaint that the privilege of the Bretons to be judged by the tribunals of their own province in accordance with their own customary

Excerpts translated and reprinted with the permission of the publisher from Armand Rébillon, *Histoire de Bretagne* (Paris: Librairie Armand Colin, 1957), pp. 103-71. Copyright 1957.

law had been deliberately infringed upon. When that law was first officially codified in 1539, the estates, called together for this purpose in an extraordinary session, were, true enough, compelled to assert firmly their right to discuss the text decided upon by the royal commissioners. But the new draft of 1580 was their own work. It had been undertaken at their request; the commissioners of the king, who were all Breton magistrates, had been designated upon their nomination, and the chief role in the deliberations fell to the *sénéchal* of Rennes, Bertrand d'Argentré, the most knowledgeable and the most resolute defender of the provincial traditions. It was, moreover, an accepted rule that the king's function was not to proclaim private law on his own authority but only to promulgate the customary law "of which the first birth and life," said Guy Coquille in 1665, was "by the will of the Estates of the province." In other regards neither the estates nor the parlements ever offered objections to the principle of the exercise by the king of his right of legislative sovereignty in Brittany. . . . By the creation of the parlement, which took place in 1554 . . . Brittany was endowed with a real sovereign law court, independent of appeals to the parlement of Paris and armed with the rights of registry and remonstrance. Because of its concern for its own prerogatives, it would prove even more jealously vigilant in the defence of the province against the establishment of new jurisdictions and the encroachment of external jurisdictions. . . . The financial privileges of the provinces are ultimately the only ones that can be said to have been the basis of important quarrels with the royal power. They are summed up in the right of the estates to give final consent to all levies of money in the province; on this right was grounded the very existence of the estates. . . .

The financial organization of Brittany—Nothing that concerned the province was foreign to the estates. Their deliberations at all times ranged over the most diverse questions. However, they had hardly any effective powers except in the matter of finances; this was the case in the other provincial estates as well. But the predominance in the Breton assembly of an independently minded and combative aristocracy, and the maintenance in the province of a unique financial organization which was particularly fitting for the expansion of a self-governing administration—these taken together facilitated a resistance to unreasonable demands of royal power, a resistance more efficacious than in any other *pays d'État;* they facilitated also the winning of new authority. In Brittany neither the *taille* nor the *aides* nor the *gabelle* were introduced. The king collected, of course, by right the revenues of the old ducal domain along with the various charges connected to them. He continued to ask from the estates an annual vote of the traditional ducal taxes: the *fouage,* a tax on commoners analogous to the land *taille* but lower, and the *impôt et billot,* a retail tax on the sale of beverages. The revenue from this was directly collected by special and general receivers, officers of the king, or by the tax farmers. Toward the middle of the sixteenth century the rate of these two taxes became fixed and their vote was henceforth no more than a formality. The disputes between the estates and the royal power dealt then with the amounts in extraordinary subsidies which were often asked of them to make up for the insufficiency of the old ducal taxes, whose revenues had become ridiculously small as a result of the depreciation of money. At the beginning of the seventeenth century these subsidies took the form of an outright gift (*don gratuit*) bargained over and voted on regularly during each session under conditions stipulated in a contract in which the king solemnly renewed his promise to respect the privileges of the province. An examination of the breaches of contract resulting from failure to live up to the terms of the previous contract preceded the vote of this gift until the time of Louis XIV. . . .

The parlement—The parlement, created in Brittany by an edict of March 1554, was organized along the lines of the other parlements of the kingdom. . . . An understanding between the province's two political bodies, the estates and parlement, was normally not so simple as the common interest in privileges which dominated in both bodies would appear to dictate. The parlement should have insisted upon the previous assent of the estates as a condition for the registering of all fiscal edicts; then, if the king proceeded further (beyond the bounds of the law) they had formidable means of resistance at their disposal: to welcome the opposition of the estates to the levy of taxes not. previously agreed to, to threaten to prosecute—not an idle threat—anyone involved in the collection of the taxes, and, on the other hand, to prevent all coercion of recalcitrant rate-payers. The parlement, however, often registered taxes which had not been agreed to. They never admitted that their decision should depend upon a vote of the estates. The parlement considered itself absolutely independent of the estates and never tied its policies to theirs except when it judged such an action useful. The parlement viewed the estates, not so much as their natural allies, but rather as an institution with regard to which it was essential to maintain their superiority and to defend their prerogatives. The creation by the estates of permanent organic bodies invested with an administrative jurisdiction, such as the *Commission intermédiaire* and the *Commission des Domaines et Contrôles,* always aroused their suspicion; they did not stop to consider the obvious advantages of these institutions for the province.

Although the political powers of the estates were, historically, more solidly based than those of parlement, the opposition of the latter was at all times more feared by the royal power, which was always most concerned with mastering it. The parlement possessed the advantage over the estates of being a homogeneous and permanent body, invested with a portion of royal authority and thus armed with means of action which the estates lacked. The government encountered in the parlement of Rennes the same adversary it faced in the other parlements of the realm; it sought more than once to conciliate the estates so as to isolate the parlement.

Governors, commanders-in-chief and intendants— . . . Brittany's governor from 1695 to 1737 was the Count of Toulouse, the son of Louis XIV and Madame de Montespan, who never came there, and his son in turn, the Duke of Penthièvre, who only appeared twice, to convoke the estates of 1746 and 1774. Consequently it was on a permanent basis that one of the two lieutenant-generals, holding a commission as commander-in-chief, acted as governor. Ordinarily he came to Brittany only for the sessions of the estates or when his presence was required, as in time of war.

Since 1689, an intendant had been in residence in the province, where there had been none until this date; he directed the administration. . . .

II. *Brittany and the Absolutism of Louis XIV (1661-1715)*

*An absolutist policy—*Under Louis XIV Brittany underwent the universal fate: reduction to obedience and endless financial exploitation to serve the ends of an expensive policy. . . . All political opposition was overcome early. The parlement, which until 1672 had stood up on several occasions in opposition to the edicts of reform, was then forbidden to communicate to the estates the royal decrees submitted for their registration; and next, in 1673, to accept from the estates any opposition. At the same time they were deprived, along with the other sovereign courts of the kingdom, of the practical right of remonstrance. As for the estates, Colbert barely tolerated the bargaining over their free gift and he did not consider that their assent was needed for the new universal taxes imposed throughout the whole of the kingdom, although he admitted that formality for the special traditional taxes of the province.

CHAPTER VII: THE BRETON OPPOSITION IN THE EIGHTEENTH CENTURY

In the history of the aristocratic reaction which, from the death of Louis XIV to the Revolution, would hold in check royal absolutism and its attempts at reform, Brittany played a part, in which the incidents most often included in its own history of the period—the conspiracy of Pontcallec, the affair of La Chalotais and the troubles of June 1788—cannot sufficiently be explained . . . as the manifestation of a kind of Breton nationalism. The opposition of the parlement of Rennes was in reality not unique either in its motives or in its means, but that opposition was able to join forces with the opposition of an assembly of estates more favorably constituted than anywhere else to sustain the general claims of the nobility of France. . . .

The interim commission— . . . [After 1720] the opposition completed its organization. From 1732 people began to speak of a *bastion,* a group of opponents from among the more stubborn of the nobility united behind *les tuteurs* (guardians). . . . The royal power was also disturbed by the relations of the opposition with the parlement when the latter, around 1730, played a part in the awakening of the religious agitation. Though the Rennes parlement did not include many declared Jansenists among its ranks, it pronounced an opinion against the papal bull *Unigenitus* in 1716; it refused to register the declaration of 24 March 1730, which prescribed acceptance of the bull by all the clerics, and its remonstrances cost the attorney-general, La Bédoyère, whose son was a *convulsionnaire,* four years in exile in Paris. It should be noted that among the members of the opposition in the estates who were then prominent were such Jansenist militants as the abbot of Trémigon and the lawyer Lolivier, deputy public prosecutor. The Estates of 1734 were managed quite harshly, without any partiality toward the *bastion.* If some advantages accrued to the estates and thereby opened a new era in the history of provincial self-government, this happened because the comptroller-general, Orry, obliged to re-establish the *dixième* by the War of the Polish Succession, found it convenient to permit it to be subscribed to by the *pays d'États* and offered at the same time to the Estates of Brittany to resume the subscription for the *capitation,* increased on this occasion from 1,400,000 francs to 1,800,000.

. . . The interim commission, charged with raising all taxes which affected the privileged orders and with the use—or at least the control—of the funds for which the royal power required their vote, gave the estates a powerful administrative agent whose functions they were always eager to extend. The commission, composed of nine members and then eighteen from 1737, sat at Rennes with the bishop serving as chairman. . . .

The vingtième tax—Until 1749 the estates, thanks to subscriptions, accepted without resistance the fiscal burdens stemming from the War of the Austrian Succession. But the policy inaugurated in 1749—when the comptroller-general Machault, by substituting the *vingtième* for the *dixième,* claimed thereby to abolish the subscription—to require of all property-owners tax declarations which would be verified and to bring into Brittany for this purpose a staff of tax-collectors working under the direct authority of the intendant, revived the opposition in all its force. In 1750 and 1752 the nobility began a campaign of obstruction which was destined to prolong indefinitely many of the sessions. The royal power, however, held firm. The first *vingtième* was levied in Brittany for seven years, as in other provinces under the authority of the intendant; it finally produced about as much as the former subscribed *dixième.* But when the recurrence of war in 1756 forced the government to impose a second *vingtième,* the government spontaneously offered the subscription to the estates, and that of the first *vingtième* at the same time. This was done under the pressure of events but also at the request of the Duke d'Aiguillon, commander-in-chief in Brittany since 1753.

The Duke d'Aiguillon—The resounding impact of the "Brittany Affair" has given to the Duke d'Aiguillon a reputation as a violent enemy of the liberties of the province. The truth is that he came with the hope of succeeding and therefore of living on good terms with the estates, whom he hoped to associate with the important work which he was seeking to accomplish. Young, active, authoritarian, he personally took in hand the general administration of the province, as well as the defence of the coast and the preparation of a landing in England. Often he spent more than six months of the year there; the intendant Le Bret, who had proved from 1753 to 1764 to be a dedicated colleague and a good adviser, was relegated to a secondary status. Thus d'Aiguillon had to shoulder the responsibility for the unavoidable conflict.

. . . Unfortunately he had the misfortune of governing in Brittany during and after a war which opened for the monarchy the period of maximum financial difficulties and led it to attempts at reform most likely to disturb the privileged orders. No commander-in-chief applied himself, however, more actively and with more success to reducing government demands to a minimum. The Estates of Brittany received the subscription or the redemption of new taxes under particularly advantageous conditions.

. . . Although the *bastion,* now under the leadership of MM. de Coëtauscours and Kerguézec, had resumed its influence over the assembly since the affair of the first *vingtième,* it is not easy to see how a quarrel of importance could arise directly between that body and d'Aiguillon. But the parlement had also to be reckoned with. Since 1756 this body had joined in the great movement of the parliamentary opposition, adhering to the *union des classes* in opposition to . . . Silhouette's schemes of general subsidy and Bertin's *cadastre* [a register of property to serve as a basis of taxation] which before too long were bound to make the privileged orders aware of all the dangers. . . .

CHAPTER VIII: SOCIETY AND CIVILIZATION IN BRITTANY UNDER
THE OLD REGIME

Agriculture—When the Englishman Arthur Young took a three-week tour of Brittany in 1788, he was struck most by the extent of uncultivated land, the backward state of the methods of cultivation and the miserable appearance of the rural dwellings. This state of affairs was, however, no worse than in certain other parts of the realm.

. . . Steady progress and the comparative wealth of some cantons lessened only slightly the unfavorable general impression. If one can cite great landlords, from the seventeenth century on, who were interested in the improvement of agricultural techniques, they were but rare exceptions. The Society of Agriculture established in 1757, on the initiative of the Rennes lawyer Abeille and the economist Vincent de Gournay, originally a native of Saint-Malo, brought together some, among them La Chalotais. Thanks to subsidies from the estates, the society was able to introduce the use of better flax seeds and better breeds of cattle in the province. However, the society disappeared after 1768 without having attained noticeable results. The written proceedings which they had assembled and their *Corps d'observations* bear witness to a state of affairs more often than not deplorable. The lack of fertilizer accounts for the general practice of leaving land fallow. We find only timid attempts at the creation of artificial grasslands, and the natural grasslands remained in most cases poorly drained. Cattle, the breeding of which often required the use of the moors, were numerous enough but hardly valuable. . . .

The nobility— . . . The Breton nobility remained until the revolution a numerous class (from 1500 to 4000 families, depending upon the method of counting them); the great majority were of modest circumstances and simple, even occasionally rustic, manners. The "reformation" effected under Louis XIV made them, as elsewhere in France, a caste better protected against usurpation, and also a more exclusive one. That reformation cut off the lesser nobility from the lower positions in the judiciary and closed to them the possibility of participating in commerce by "forgetting" their gentle birth. It was at that time that the army and the navy, like the Church, became for them the eagerly sought professions. A current of emigration toward "the islands" . . . appeared in the seventeenth century. Often the younger sons of a noble family, unable to find a means of living without losing caste, dropped down to a commoner's position. In the eighteenth century, many sought employment in the tax-farms of the king or of the provinces. The problem of the impoverished nobility preoccupied everyone at that time. The estates took into their charge, in 1750, the establishment founded in Rennes by the Abbot Kergu for the free education of some forty needy young gentlemen for service under the king or in the Church; under Louis XVI they undertook the support of some young women of the same impoverished condition at the Home of the Infant Jesus in the same town. In 1745 a gentleman, Pinczon du Sel, had established a cotton mill at Rennes with the financial support of the estates, and had published a short treatise in which he argued against the prejudices which kept the nobility away from industrial enterprises. These prejudices were not, however, overcome. Maritime trade, once carried on by the nobility in the region of Morlaix, was only practiced in the eighteenth century by a few noble families, in the majority of cases only recently ennobled, in Saint-Malo.

. . . At the end of the Old Regime the Breton nobility was thus more exclusively than ever a rural nobility, living from their lands and their dues, and abstaining, in most cases, from the economic activities of the province. We need not judge their morals on the basis of the deplorable examples which Charles Colbert reported in his investigations of 1665. Nonetheless, it is certain that the idle existence which many impecunious and uneducated squires led on their lands produced among them, all too often, violent and dissolute customs which their vassals had to endure. These customs were better regulated in the eighteenth century, but the participation of well-born gentlemen in coastal smuggling continued to impede the repression of this activity.

Selections from a "Manuscript of a Dictionary of the Administration of the Province of Brittany" Written in the 1760s.

I. OPENING OF THE ESTATES . . .

The convocation [of the estates] is made by *lettres de cachet* from the king, addressed to the bishops, abbots, and chapters of the province, to the barons, and to a certain number of gentlemen to whom the king deigns to accord that honor, and to the municipal governments of the forty-one towns of the province who have the right to send deputies to the estates, and thus are composed the three bodies or orders of the estates: the clergy, the nobility, the third estate. . . .

On the eve of the day chosen for the meeting, the commander-in-chief commands its proclamation, which is made at all the street-corners by the herald of the estates, clad in his tabard, and riding a horse caparisoned in cloth of silver, dotted with *fleurs de lys* and bordered with ermine; he is preceded by his trumpeter.

As a consequence of the proclamation of the opening of the estates, the three orders, with their presidents at their heads, proceed separately and successively, the next day, at the appointed time, into the hall designated for the assembly, starting from the *hôtel* of their president; first the order of the third estate, then the nobility, and the order of the clergy last. This procedure is followed each day for the entry into the estates.

The orders of the clergy and the nobility are led in their march by the mounted constabulary, with their officers and trumpeters, and the herald of the estates; the order of the third estate by the herald alone.

Before the king's declaration of June 26, 1736, the members of the order of the nobility had the right to enter and be inscribed on the

Translated and reprinted from the text reproduced in N. L. Caron, *L'Administration des États de Bretagne de 1493 à 1789* (Paris, Bordeaux, and Nantes, 1872).

rolls even as children, but, by the first article of this declaration, no member of any order might have the right to enter and sit in the assembly unless he was at least twenty-five.

The hall of the assembly is usually the chapel or the refectory of one of the convents of the city, where the herald of the estates has supervised the construction of a sort of theater, rising by seven or eight steps, which occupies half or two-thirds of the room; at the top, against the wall, is a dais of velvet covered with *fleurs de lys* and embroidered ermine, under which are placed two identical chairs, joined to one another and with their backs to the wall: the president of the order of the clergy sits in the right-hand one, and the president of the order of nobility in the left-hand one; beside each, on upholstered benches, the bishops take their places on the right, and the barons on the left, and, since generally there are few or no barons present, their places are filled by the most important gentlemen and generally the most aged, who choose to sit there; the abbots do the same on the bishops' bench, when there are empty places.

The remainder of the theater is divided into three sections; the one, in the middle, opposite the dais and the chairs of the presidents, which remains empty; the other two, on the right and left, corresponding to the benches of the bishops and barons, are made up of two sorts of grandstands of three or four wooden steps. The grandstand at the right is divided in two by a simple wooden balustrade at arm-level, the abbots and the deputies of the chapters occupying the upper part, next to the bishops' bench, and the order of the third estate the lower part at the bottom of the grandstand; the president of the order of the third estate has his place here, at the head of his order on the lowest step, but with a raised seat upholstered in green. . . . The grandstand on the left is entirely occupied by the order of the nobility. These two grandstands are separated by the empty space in the middle, and were also separated, until quite recently, by a wooden balustrade on each side; but now that balustrade is to be seen only at the place occupied by the president of the order of the third estate.

At the two extremities of the theater, and at the left of the steps located in the middle by which it is climbed, are, on the right, a bench for spectators, which is guarded by a sentry of the mounted constabulary, and which cannot be approached by the steps of the grandstand, but is reached by other steps and an exit door, and on the left, the desk of the clerks of the estates, behind which is the desk for the recorder.

The three orders having taken their places, the *procureur général syndic,* speaking from his seat, asks the assembly to send deputies to the king's commissioners, who are, for this purpose, assembled at the house of the commander-in-chief, in order to ask them to come open the estates. . . .

The deputation having returned to its seats, the commissioners of the king make their entrance, preceded first by the mounted constabulary, the grand provost, the officers and the trumpeter at their head, then by the liveried servants, the pages and the gentlemen of the commander-in-chief, then by his guards, captain, officers, and trumpeters at the front, marching in two files.

When sometimes the weather is so bad that it is impossible to go on foot, everyone is carried in his sedan chair to the hall of the estates.

The comptrollers-general of the domains and of the finances come first, then the receivers-general of the domains and those of the finances, all in cloak and hood; the grand master of woods and water, wearing his sword; the general agents of the finances in cloak and hood, the procurator-general of the chamber of accounts and the second commissioner of the council in their robes, then the commander-in-chief walking alone, then the first president [of the parlement] with the attorney-general and the two advocates-general walking slightly behind him on each side; and when, either in entering the hall or otherwise, the two files are obliged to form one, then the intendant walks directly before the commander-in-chief, and the first president immediately behind him.

The commissioners of the king are received within the door of the hall of the estates by the same deputies who have asked them to come open the proceedings, and having mounted the theater they take their places, while the guards of the commander-in-chief occupy all but the last step of the staircase.

Whenever the commissioners of the king enter the estates (and they may enter whenever they send word that they desire to) it is always with the same ceremonial, the herald having arranged the empty space in the middle of the theater in the following manner:

Under the dais, which is in the middle of the theater, a throne or platform raised by three or four carpeted steps is erected, on which, in an armchair, his back turned to the two presidents of the clergy and the nobility, the commander-in-chief takes his place, with his pages seated on the steps, his captain of the guard, his secretary, his gentlemen standing around and behind his chair.

On the right and left of the throne . . . two chairs are placed, for the first president on the right and for the intendant on the left.

With the assembly thus formed, the commander-in-chief, who, after greeting upon his entry the presidents of the three orders, has seated himself in his chair and put on his hat, takes the general commission from the hands of his secretary and has it handed to the recorder of the estates, and the first clerk of the records reads it aloud; the same is done for the other individual commissions, which are successively read, except for those of the intendant and of the second commissioner of the council, which are not presented or read until the next day. These commissions remain in the hands of the clerk, to be registered.

After the reading of the commissions, the commander-in-chief and the first president of the parlement each make a little speech, with their hats on, to which one of the two *procureurs syndics* of the estates responds, and it is noteworthy that whether or not the commander-in-chief is a marshal of France, the *procureurs généraux syndics* of the estates, when they address him in the assembly, refer to him as Monseigneur, for so it was decided at the behest of M. the Marquis de Brancas at the Estates of 1738, before he became marshal of France.

This first sitting is closed by the choice of the bishop and his assistants who are to celebrate on the morrow the Mass of the Holy Ghost. . . .

After the pontifical Mass of the Holy Ghost, the three orders having returned to their seats in the hall, and the commissioners of the king having sent word to the estates that they were coming and having entered, been received, and taken their places in the same order and ceremonial as on the previous day, the commander-in-chief begins by having the commissions of the intendant and of the second commissioner of the council read. After which, the intendant makes a speech, at the conclusion of which, in the name of the king, he requests the free gift. The *procureur général syndic* replies, pointing out the position of the economy in the province and its need for relief, he refers to the intendant as Monsieur. . . .

For each assembly there is a budget of honoraria, for attendance by commissioners of the king at the estates, to a total of 33,000 livres, paid for by the king, and this budget has been drawn up by the Duc de Penthièvre; there figure on it:

The first president of the parlement, for	3,000	livres
The intendant, for	6,000	"
The second commissioner of the council	3,000	"
The three lieutenants of the king, 3,000 livres apiece	9,000	"
The nine bishops, each 1,000 livres apiece	9,000	"
The three senior *présidents à mortier* of the parlement	3,000	"
	33,000	"

The estates, to compensate the attorney-general and the two advocates-general of the parlement, along with the first president of the chamber of accounts, who are also named commissioners of the king, for not being on this budget, give each a gratuity of 1,000 livres for each session.

In 1762, the estates earmarked funds of 5,000 livres to be distributed to one Becdelièvre, first president of the chamber of accounts of Nantes, to de la Chalotais, attorney-general of the parlement, to Parc-Porée and le Prestre, advocates-general of the parlement, and to de la Tulaye, attorney-general of the chamber of accounts—1,000 livres to each, as commissioners of His Majesty.

The estates elect, for each session, the commissioners to manage the taxes for which the estates are responsible; there has never been a clear rule on this question. The only practice common to the three orders of the estates, for the choice of these commissioners, is that in general the orders each elect the commissioners residing in the bishopric of Rennes, and that those residing in each of the other bishoprics are elected, within each order, only by the members of the diocese whom they will principally represent.

The costs of traveling and lodging for the estates, for the deputies of the towns and communities, were fixed by decrees of June 28 and July 18, 1681, and October 11, 1684, at 300 livres for each of the two deputies of Rennes and of Nantes, and at 350 livres for the deputy of Brest; Vannes, Saint-Malo, and Morlaix each send two deputies, who get 200 livres apiece; the other towns have only one deputy, who gets only 200 livres. There are thirty-five of these towns. . . .

In all, forty-one towns, sending forty-six deputies. By a decree of August 30, 1754, double the fees mentioned in the above decrees were granted to every deputy who had attended the assembly of 1752.

When the assembly lasts longer than forty days, it is usually customary for the intendant to authorize the treasurers of the communities to pay the deputies an increase proportional to the length of the assembly, and there are several cases of increases having been accorded by decree. . . .

In 1758 M. Le Bret [the intendant] asked for authorization to pay the deputies of the order of the third estate exactly twice what was due them for their attendance at the estates. He said, "They merit this new mark of the bounty of the king, because of their good conduct during the session, because of the proofs they have given of their zeal, and because they must be compensated for the expenses occasioned for them by the length of the session and by the high cost of living at Saint Brieuc." This was granted to them.

. . . It has been claimed that the estates can commit the province to something only until their next session, and that therefore, while the rest of the kingdom pays annual and perpetual taxes by virtue of one single edict, the king would in some manner be obliged to ask the Estates of Brittany, at each session, for their consent and establishment of these same taxes in the province; but this contention is equally contrary to the constitutions of the Estates-General and individual estates as it is to the authority of the king and the maintenance of good order. If the Estates of Brittany meet biennially, it is because His Majesty has condescended to allow it, in order that their management of their affairs may be simpler and more convenient; but, however, since the estates, at each session, represent equally fully the whole of the province, it follows clearly that they can commit the province for the same purposes and for the same length of time for which all the other subjects of the king are bound by his laws. Since the meeting of the estates which consented to the *dixième,* there has been no debate on whether or not this tax would be submitted to; the later sessions have only deliberated upon the continuation of the subscription and on the sum to be collected to pay for it, and it is particularly to be noted that by the second article of their remonstrances of 1748, they asked that the king be pleased to exempt the Province of Brittany from the *dixième,* as soon as peace had been made. In so doing they admitted that the province was subject to it and had to pay it, not only through the year 1750, but for as long as the king desired and until he judged it proper to relieve all his peoples of its collection. . . .

It is the lot of all overly numerous assemblies to be managed by a small number of people. The meeting of the Estates of Brittany gives the right of entry to seven or eight hundred gentlemen, the majority of whom understand nothing of its business. Each president has influence only on the deliberations of his own order; as a result it is important for those in the service of the king to see that the orders of the clergy and the third estate do not have presidents who, by their incompetence, stubbornness, or other improper views, might make the conduct of business difficult and the sessions stormy; consequently, it is essential that the assembly be presided over by men whose fidelity and good intentions are known.

M. Baillon, master of requests and seneschal of Rennes, president of the order of the third estate in the assembly of the Estates of Brittany, is asking for a gratification to compensate for the unusual expenses he had to meet at the last session of the estates (1760).

According to an old rule, the presidents of the orders of the clergy

and the nobility each have a fixed sum of 15,000 livres for the cost of
their table during the meeting, paid out of the budget of the province.
The president of the third estate only gets 10,000 livres, which barely
covers half of his expenses. His Majesty has paid the costs of M. the
Duke de Rohan, who presided over the nobility; Baillon hopes that
His Majesty will be kind enough to treat him with the same liberality.

In 1742, His Majesty granted M. Baillon an extraordinary gratuity
of 8,000 livres, in addition to the 10,000 paid by the estates.

In 1746, the estates paid him 10,000 livres, and he asked nothing
of the king.

In 1748, His Majesty granted him 8,000 livres, although the meeting only lasted thirty-two days.

In 1750, he similarly obtained a sum of 8,000 livres, the meeting
having lasted forty-six days.

In 1752, he received an increase of 4,000 livres.

Baillon begged His Majesty to grant him a gratuity to help him
meet, during the next session, the expenses which the good of the
service requires him to undertake in his position during their meetings.
He was given an extraordinary gratuity of 8,000 livres.

M. Baillon thus depicted his life during the session of the estates:
at eight o'clock in the morning, he says, I must be at breakfast, to
which I invite those going to the estates at ten o'clock; when business
is concluded at two o'clock, I go to dinner, inviting anyone from the
three orders who chooses to come; generally there are forty to sixty
people at my table. After which I urge anyone who wants to, to stay,
and join in parlor games; at seven o'clock, I take leave of the crowd to
go confer with the other presidents and at eight o'clock we all three
confer with [the commander-in-chief], the first president and the intendant on the next day's order of business, and I do not finish with
this until ten o'clock, etc.

M. Baillon asked a decree granting him 1,000 livres a year from
the local tariffs of Rennes, like the one granted in 1729 to one Rallier,
who served as mayor of Rennes; this is, he says, to pay those who do
his work as mayor during his absence.

The king, by a decree of May 8, 1757, gave an extraordinary gratuity of 10,000 livres to Baillon, intendant of La Rochelle, to compensate him for the losses he suffered as a result of the delay of more
than two years in the sale of his office as seneschal of Rennes, and for
other reasons listed in his petition. . . .

III. THE CABALS

Several letters of the king's commissioners report the existence of cabals in the estates, formed with regard to the *vingtième;* when the minister expressed his intention to take steps against the most troublesome spirits, the intendant, M. Pont-Carré de Viarme, in his letter of November 22, 1750, observed that there must be a proper punishment and not half-measures; that is why he refused to name, for the present, seven or eight gentlemen who were the driving force of the troubles, observing that the punishment which would be inflicted on them during the session of the estates would only ignite in the assembly a blaze which perhaps could not be extinguished, which might bring about the most harmful consequences which it would be prudent to avoid. He thought that a simple letter of the king, ordering them to leave the town of Rennes and return to their lands, would only serve to make them bolder and create respect for them in their neighborhoods as martyrs of the fatherland and to sow a spirit of rebellion, so contrary to the good of the service. His opinion was that the estates must be allowed to conclude, and if the king then was still inclined to punish the troublemakers, it would be proper in every respect to confine for a while in fortresses two or three of the guiltiest, or at least to exile them far from the province.

The Duke de Chaulnes, writing on the same subject, observes: (1) that the cabals are never more discredited than when no attention is paid to them, and this method, he says, has worked for him; (2) he thinks that in an affair which may influence others of the same type, punishment, even after the conclusion, would serve to persuade people that there had been difficulties of execution, which might encourage them to create even greater ones; (3) there is no doubt that there are people unreasoning enough to regard punishment as a sort of title of honor, which proves their zeal for their fatherland; often they only make up their minds to behave badly from an aspiration to distinguish themselves; the best way to punish and discourage those who might think of emulating them is to allow them to be forgotten.

Steps were taken, after the session, against several persons who had caused trouble.

MM. Langourla, Beschard, le Mintier, Troussier de Sceaux, and Vavincourt were condemned to prison.

M. and Mme Piré, M. de Begasson de la Lardais, former councilor of the parlement, the elder M. de Begasson, uncle of the former, the Count de Kersauson, MM. du Lattay, de Kerguézec, de la Bennerays,

La Bédoyère, the Chevalier de Kératry and the Deputy de Quintin were exiled.

The following were noted for exclusion from the assembly [of the estates]: MM. Camarec, Begasson, son of the older of the uncles, de la Villethéart, the Chevalier de Nétumières, La Bédoyère, son of the former attorney-general, Gazou, Pontphily, the Chevalier de Kervasy, Keruzan, Perrirn, Poillève, Kératry L'Argentais, du Grosquer, Villeneuve de Rocher, Hercules de Lescoët, Mongermont, Quebriac, the Chevalier de Champsavey, Talhouet (the uncle), de Boishorant, Bire, the Tourbillons, Charlette Colinière, du Dresnay, Kermadec.

On September 1, 1754, the king decided to remove the orders given against the person named above.

Exile of two councilors of the Parlement of Rennes, de la Gascherie and Dupargo, who were forming cabals in the parlement and in the estates, and who were carrying on a correspondence with the parlements of Paris, Rouen, and Bordeaux.

The cabal of the nobility screamed its head off at the time of the vote of approval, in spite of the nobility, of the subscription for the tax of two sous per livre, in addition to the *capitation;* one de Vay, a gentleman of Nantes, carried his extravagance and frenzy so far as to throw himself upon the Bishop of Saint Brieuc, at the moment he was signing it, and to snatch the pen and the register from his hands; several others, like Rauléon, des Aulx, etc. shook their fists under the nose of the Duke de Rohan, to prevent him from signing; nevertheless, the presidents signed the transcript of the vote, despite the clamors of the cabal.

M. de Vay, by order and under the threat of the Duke d'Aiguillon, made an apology to the Bishop of Saint Brieuc; the prelate had asked pardon for him.

The spirit of sedition and independence made itself felt principally in the session of 1760. Yet the period of this way of acting and speaking irresponsibly can be traced back to the session of 1752, which was very long, very difficult, and very stormy; it ended in several punishments, inflicted for the most part on people of little importance, of whom some were sent to fortresses, the others exiled; but all were recalled before the session of 1754, from which none was excluded. They treated their punishments as a sign of merit in the estates, by whom they were received in an indecent manner, but the authorities closed their eyes to this, so that these examples had no effect in the sessions of 1754, 1756, and 1758, and the audacity, the spirit of independence, the rashness and indecency went on increasing, encouraged as they were by the impunity they enjoyed; in the session of 1760 they were carried to an extreme point.

We shall record here the principal features of the cabal, drawn from the letters of the Duke d'Aiguillon to the Assembly of 1760.

"MM. de Coëtauscours and de Begasson wanted to attach conditions to the free gift, and demanded that a gift from the towns not be discussed at all; they were not heeded. MM. de Coëtauscours, Begasson and Kerguézec, who take advantage of every opportunity to get the assembly excited, stirred up a little trouble about the sergeant named by the Duke de Penthièvre. The cabal of MM. de Kerguézec and de Coëtauscours carried on its usual clamor, and although it was composed of only twelve or fifteen people, for more than two hours it prevented the nobility from agreeing to the proposal made by the other two orders to suppress the debate on the list of the order of the nobility. Three persons ruled the assembly despotically: MM. de Coëtauscours, de Kerguézec and de Begasson la Lardais; only they had the right to speak and be heard. M. de Nétumières read, with great emphasis, a speech which put the finishing touches on the rage of the assembly; there are many hotheads because of the indecent utterances of MM. de Coëtauscours, de Kerguézec, de Nétumières, Begasson, etc.

"A gentleman said yesterday, in my house, in my presence, and before a numerous assemblage, that it was very strange that the estates did not cause a monument to be erected to the four gentlemen who were beheaded in 1722, and bury them in the church; that no one was more worthy than they of this distinction. I asked him to say no more, and he fell silent, but I dared say nothing more to him.

"The leaders of the cabal are called the 'guardians'. When the *procureur général syndic* read the request for the [tax] rolls, M. du Lattay and two or three madmen or imbeciles like him shouted that they should be handed over, but that it would not be quite so easy to put them into effect, when the nobility had refused to pay the tax; but the rest of the assembly, not excepting the chiefs of the cabal, kept silence and appeared embarrassed.

"M. Coëtauscours said, about the subscription, that the nobility asked nothing better than to come to agreement with the other two orders, but that it could not abandon the common people, who would be crushed if the subscription proposed were enacted. There was much murmuring at this, and M. de Berthou had the courage to say to him openly: 'It is your bad faith, Sir, your stubbornness and that of your adherents, which will bring about the ruin of the people; we are not duped by the patriotic sentiments which you display with so much emphasis, and we can easily read what is deep within your heart.' The chief of the cabal was the more disconcerted by this challenge because it was followed by much applause, which let him know that his party was not the stronger at that point.

"The Duke de Rohan, having remained with his order, wanted to begin the vote, but the cabal made such a frightful uproar that it was totally impossible to hear the names which the clerk called, there were even some blows struck against the first people on the list who wanted to hand in their ballots, etc.

"I shall not report to you the indecent, I may even say insolent, words spoken about M. de Rohan and me by the cabal. According to them I am a true commissioner of the king, that is to say a rogue and a man of very bad faith, and the Duke de Rohan is a traitor.

"M. de Noyan, one of the principal aides-de-camp of the leaders of the cabal, said that all the stipends of which the estates customarily dispose must be abolished. The third estate said that it would gladly consent to this abolition, but that it asked at the same time the abolition of all the pensions paid to the nobility. M. de Coëtauscours replied that he would be glad to agree, since almost all of them were paid to military men who had sold out to the king and were traitors to their fatherland.

"M. de Begasson de la Lardais replied that if the king acted in agreement with the estates when he sent troops into Brittany, the province would not be so badly vexed as it is, and I asked him to employ more respectful expressions when he spoke of the king, etc. MM. du Lattay, de Kervyon and de Rauléon distinguished themselves throughout the session by their zeal in supporting violent and indecent expressions. The presidents adjourned the session, in spite of the cries of the cabal.

"M. de Noyan stopped the Duke de Rohan in the middle of the room to prevent him from leaving, and the latter had a good deal of trouble getting rid of him.

"M. de Coëtauscours, who, on all occasions, shows the greatest respect for the parlement and his desire to unite it indissolubly with the estates, proposed to communicate to it the decisions taken with regard to the third *vingtième*.

"M. de Coëtauscours spoke just as lengthily and strongly against the so-called tyranny of the Duke de Penthièvre with regard to the naming of deputies.

"I think that it is equally necessary to punish the seditious of the

orders of the clergy and the third estate severely. The principal ones
in the order of the clergy are the abbés des Fontaines, de Villeneuve
and du Lorent. In the order of the third estate, Géry and Terrien.

"The Abbé de Villeneuve, who had been elected a deputy, made a
long speech thanking the assembly for its good will toward him, and
assuring them that he would render himself ever more worthy of it by
his zeal in supporting the liberties of the fatherland.

"He did not bother to inquire if the king would approve his elec-
tion, and if the Duke de Penthièvre might not oppose it; I have not
even seen him. Such insane and insolent conduct must not be tolerated. . . ."

Selections from the Diary of the Duke de Croÿ

[Emmanuel, Duke de Croÿ and Prince de Meurs et de Solre (1718-
84) was a professional soldier, though the diversity of his interests
is reflected not only in the keeping of his diary, but also in his
ventures into theoretical physics and his encouragement of oceanic
exploration. He served first in the Musketeers, then in the cavalry,
and his brigade played a decisive part in the French victory at
Fontenoy (1745). In 1757 he was given command of the troops
in Artois, Picardy, and the neighborhood of Calais and Boulogne.
He was promoted to lieutenant-general in 1759, and supervised
the restoration of the defenses of the port of Dunkirk in 1763.
A year before his death, he received the supreme military rank:
Marshal of France.—Ed.]

. . . On February 24 [1762], Ash Wednesday, Mme de Leyde informed me that Portugal had joined the war on the side of England,
that the English were sending 15,000 men there, and that to do so they
were evacuating Belle-Isle, which was useless to them. . . .

The rumor was spreading, at that time, through all Paris, that M.
the Duke d'Aiguillon would receive the command in Alsace, which
Marshal d'Estrées had just nobly refused. . . . And the public thought
that I would have the command of Brittany: I had almost refused it.

Translated and reprinted with the permission of the publishers from the *Journal
inédit du Duc de Croÿ*, 3 vols., edited by the Vicomte de Grouchy and Paul
Cottin (Paris: E. Flammarion, 1906-7), II, 34-35, 45-51.

... The reasons that I did not care for it, although I recognized all its good features, were that at the court I could hope neither for any money nor for support against the Estates of Brittany, which were rather difficult, or against the parlements, whose heads had been turned, especially in the affair of the Jesuits, and that I would have had to pay 500,000 francs for the lieutenant-generalcy, and to be inconvenienced by the necessity of going there; moreover, it would have meant expatriating myself—giving up my plans for Flanders and the pleasures of my home, for which I still wanted to have time. However, I would have been rather flattered by the command of Brest, provided that there were no more wild schemes about England, but, in any case, I was very glad that this rumor was spreading, since it would accustom the public to regarding me as capable of playing such a role. . . .

March 18, [1762] was a very important day. M. the Comptroller-General informed me that he wished to speak with me. . . .

The Comptroller-General appeared, took me immediately into his office, and said, "I have asked you to come here to tell me why you will not accept Brittany. I can sense your objections and I am going to overcome them." I told him that I had only too many to make, that in the end I would be a failure there, that the job seemed beyond my abilities and my physical strength, that I had an income of only 40,000 livres, that going there would be my financial ruin, and that there was no way of dealing with estates of such a kind, with a rebellious parlement, no way to set the navy to rights without money, to reconquer Belle-Isle without the necessary means . . . and that I only desired, for a year, to calm my mind and restore my health.

He tried to overcome my resistance on all these points; he told me a great deal about the difficulties with the estates and I saw thereby that they were even worse than I had thought, the worst thing being that he wanted to get a great deal out of them, at a time when they were almost in revolt. He admitted to me that they were unbelievably tumultuous, that they might go on for three months, with a bunch of little so-and-so's of gentlemen who ought never to have been allowed to enter them; that they would have to be reduced and reformed eventually, but that this was a job for peacetime. He betrayed a great dislike of M. the Duke d'Aiguillon, with whom he was on the worst of terms, neither seeing him nor answering his letters. He astonished me by saying that M. the Duke d'Aiguillon really wanted to go back there, that he only complained so much in order to be better rewarded for it, that he would certainly ask for his 600,000 livres, but that he, the Comptroller-General, would help me and do everything possible for me; that, for private expenses he would willingly help me from his own pocket, and would even give me the 300,000 livres the farmers-general gave him in cash for the renewal of their contract; that there was nothing he would not do to have me there . . . that he could not envision anyone else in the post, that it was an opportunity for me to get everything I wanted from the court, that in four conversations he would tell me everything I needed to know for the estates; that, if I could deal with them, the parlement would not amount to much. . . .

He added that M. the Duke d'Aiguillon put everything, even his carriage, on his expense account, and that he doubted that he had ruined himself financially there; that it was M. de Saint-Florentin who made nominations for that job, the uncle of the Duke d'Aiguillon, who privately wanted to return there. To say this was against his own line of reasoning, for it meant that I would have to worry about having the two of them against me [if I took the command] and, since the Duke de Choiseul would give me little support, I would have only the Comptroller-General behind me, and he could not be counted on. . . .

Ultimately there was nothing he did not try in order to persuade me. I remained cool to the idea, asking him for time, but saying that I was not inclined to take it. . . .

On the twenty-second, things became more complicated. . . . I went to take coffee with M. the Duke de Choiseul, to whom I confided the story. . . . Whereupon M. de Choiseul, frowning, told me, "M. d'Aiguillon is the only commander I can see for Brittany, unless the king names another. If he orders a change, fine! You could certainly command the troops, but for dealing with the estates, I can think only of M. d'Aiguillon!"

I saw that the Comptroller-General, on the worst of terms with M. d'Aiguillon, wanted desperately to get rid of him, and that this would cause all sorts of trouble. I said to M. de Choiseul that I knew only what he told me, that I was interested only in doing his bidding, and wanted no trouble with anyone else. He said, "Then go tell the Comptroller-General that you don't want the job; you would not be a success in that province. . . ."

Selections from Linguet's Brief for the Duke d'Aiguillon

[Emmanuel-Armand, Duke d'Aiguillon (1720-88) was a grand-nephew of Cardinal Richelieu. After distinguishing himself in military service, in 1753 he bought the office of the Duke de Chaulnes as commander-in-chief in Brittany. In 1761 he was accorded the high honor of right of entry to the king's bedchamber. After quitting the command of Brittany in 1768, he was brought to trial in the Court of Peers of the Parlement of Paris on April 4, 1770, for abuses of his authority as commander-in-chief. The selections that follow are taken from the brief drawn up in his defense and published by his lawyer. The trial was brought to a close on June 27 of the same year, and in 1771 the Duke entered the government as minister of foreign affairs. He is best remembered by historians for his role as minister during this period, called that of the "Triumvirate" (of Maupeou, Terray, and d'Aiguillon). With the advent of a new king in 1774, he lost influence, and soon thereafter left office.—Ed.]

It is true, then, that one must defend oneself, even against slander; the generous bravery of a soul which scorns it often serves only to give it credit; it is sometimes more dangerous for innocence to be silent than for crime to flaunt itself; the situation in which M. the Duke d'Aiguillon finds himself only proves too conclusively this sad truth.

His silence has emboldened his enemies; long bound by orders which his first duty was to respect, by superior considerations which it was not his responsibility either to condemn or to combat, he resisted only with patience the intrigues, the audacity of his enemies; they have taken advantage of this involuntary inaction; libels, produced by fanaticism and hatred, have been broadcast; they have given rise successively to enthusiasm and imposture; they have seduced, misled the public, which will believe anything without examining it, for whom audacity takes the place of truth, and who always confuse impudent falsehood with truth.

The Duke d'Aiguillon, finally obliged to put an end to this inconceivable hysteria, has asked and obtained permission to take as judge between his accusers and himself the most august of tribunals. While

Mémoire pour M. le Duc d'Aiguillon, par Me Linguet, avocat (Paris, 1770).

a judicial investigation was going to bring to the light the secrets of his private life, while slander animated by a fear of being unmasked was on the point of probing into the most hidden mysteries of his private conduct, and of seeking in the shadows, as is its custom, those false nuances, those deceptive impressions which it needs, he thought that he should place before the eyes of the king and of the Court of Peers an accurate record of his public life, and of his administration in a province where he commanded for more than fifteen years.

Responsible to the nation, to Europe, and to posterity for the usage he has made of the confidence of his master, he wishes to publish the most accurate report possible; to prove that very far from having provoked the troubles of Brittany, he had a hand in them only to appease them; that very far from having been the oppressor, the tyrant of the province, he was its guardian, its most zealous defender; that he has never done anything for that society of which he is accused of being the protector; that instead of asking for rigorous orders against subjects whom a pardonable anger perhaps carried to excesses, he made it his duty to warn them and to lighten the consequences when he was compelled by an unhappy necessity to carry them out; that if there has ever been a commander-in-chief to whom Brittany should have shown some gratitude, it is perhaps he whom Brittany allows to be reproached in its name with having worked to ruin it; that finally if it is true that he had to fear real enemies, they were only the enemies of the public good.

These assertions will no doubt appear novel and most audacious, but when this *mémoire* has been read, they will be found perhaps too modest; it will be difficult to conceive how so much moderation could produce so much bitterness, that so many services were rewarded by such outrageous protestations, so much concern by such furious resentment, so much zeal and affection by such an obstinate hatred. What a lesson it is for men in office!

I

Duties of the Commanders-in-Chief of the King in the Regions of Estates. Idea of the Constitution of Brittany

There is perhaps nothing more delicate and thorny than the functions of a first commissioner of the king in the provinces which have preserved, under a monarchy, the right to govern themselves.

If this sort of administration bears some resemblances, insofar as its advantages are concerned, with democracy, it also has its inconveniences. It is natural that parties are formed; that clever minds try to make themselves a name by gaining the confidence of others, either to acquire celebrity and prestige in their country, or to make themselves necessary to the administration which may need their credit and influence.

The safest method for them to succeed is to display an ardent zeal for the defense of the rights of the country. Since these rights can only be attacked in the name of royal authority, since they are usually attacked only in a matter already somewhat unpleasant in itself, that of finances, it follows that those who adopt this course are inevitably hailed by the mob who regard them as its defenders, and that they also inevitably find themselves in opposition to the will of the king, though they are nonetheless his faithful subjects: it is obvious how many embarrassments and difficulties this singular mixture of resistance and submission creates for all the activities of a commissioner of the king. . . .

If the country has a parlement, the embarrassments are even greater, and the difficulties more thorny still; it is one more body which has to be conciliated, and with great delicacy; a body perpetually on its guard against foreign enterprises. If these two authorities are not in agreement on the manner in which the will of the king should be obeyed, this is a very serious subject of concern for the commander-in-chief who must pass on to them the orders; if they come to agreement on the means of resisting such orders, the difficulties and dangers are doubled.

Brittany is one of the largest and richest provinces of the kingdom. Fertile lands, a temperate climate, excellent ports, rivers useful for commerce, great forests, numerous iron-works, and several very rich mines of lead and silver are a profusion of gifts which nature has given her, and sources of an opulence which is constantly renewed. To these advantages she joins the advantage of being populated by an industrious, brave, submissive, and faithful people, well-made to adore their king and to be cherished by him.

A numerous and ancient nobility, praiseworthy by reason of its services either in the army or in the parlement, which it glories in making up, and to which it brings its virtues, sets the nation the example of the sentiments for its country and for its prince by which it is animated. The Duke d'Aiguillon has studied the Bretons and knows more of them than anybody; he finds it a duty and pleasure to give them their due, and even to his enemies; this is the only vengeance he will ever take upon them.

The estates in Brittany are composed of three orders; of the clergy, the nobility, and the third estate. The order of the clergy is composed of nine bishops, of the deputies of the nine cathedrals, and of all the abbots of the country, numbering thirty-seven. But since some are always absent, this order is never composed of more than forty persons; the third does not provide many more voting subjects; it is composed of the mayors of towns or of deputies elected by them, which produces only forty-eight people, since there are only forty-three towns which have the right to choose deputies, and Rennes, Nantes, S. Malo, Vannes, and Morlaix are the only ones with a right to two deputies. Thus, these two orders together never make up more than eighty or ninety people, if the substitutes, who have the right to attend but not to vote, are not counted.

It is not the same with the nobility. Attendance at the estates being a sort of sign of patriotism, all the gentlemen take great care to be inscribed on the rolls; thus their list is often composed of six or seven hundred names, and sometimes even more.

Two consequences result from this: the first is that the debates in the orders of the clergy and of the third estate are generally more thoughtful, better arranged, and more peaceful than those of the nobility; the second is that the equal power of the three orders, despite the prodigious inequality of numbers, inevitably causes a secret jealousy on the part of the nobility of the other two orders on which it is dependent, and who can defeat the nobility, in almost every case, when the orders are brought together.

In the first place a small number of opinions are easier to examine and reconcile than that incredible number of votes, which it is hard even to count; the more numerous an assemblage is, the more prone it is to becoming heated, to being carried away, to that sort of enthusiasm which confuses minds and renders good intentions vain. The clergy and the third estate are more moderate in their activities, the one out of respect for its own character, the other by reason of the quality of its deputies, accustomed to work and to juridical discussion. The nobility brings to the assemblies the impetuous zeal, the haughty frankness which characterizes it, and these traits, so useful when it is a matter of supporting the honor of the throne by force of arms, sometimes become dangerous when it is only a matter of proceeding calmly to pacific negotiations between the prince and his subjects.

Moreover, it is only natural that six hundred gentlemen are jealous of not having more influence in the affairs of their country, which are their own affairs, than forty ecclesiastics some of whom are foreigners, and whom the gentlemen suspect of lacking their own interest in the public good, and an equal number of individuals, for whom prejudices permit the gentlemen to have in some ways little regard, if their personal qualities, their patriotic spirit and their talents do not suffice to diminish the distance which separates the latter from the nobility.

This simple summary demonstrates how many quarrels, arguments, and troubles can at any moment arise in the assemblies, and what dangerous consequences this collision of opinions may produce, if the commissioners of the king do not take care, by extreme prudence and wise firmness, to avert them and to stamp out every spark which might produce a conflagration.

The estates thus composed have charge of the finances of the province. One of the articles of their franchise is *that no tax or raising of funds will be made without their consent.* A custom founded on their part on a wise policy has authorized them in recent years, when they have granted the king a new tax, or any kind of subvention, to ask for its *subscription.* That is, in some fashion to make the [tax] farmers responsible for payment, in return for a sum agreed on and fixed which they [the estates] themselves later collect from the province. This method of distribution is more equitable, and the collection goes more easily. This method guarantees the people against the incursions of clerks foreign to the province; it is thus unquestionably advantageous; but since the ministers have felt that a tax was almost always susceptible to increase, a subscription fixing it has often not been allowed.

If one is obliged to divide the burden of taxation among all the subjects of the same realm, it is only natural that there be a desire to know exactly what they produce, and even what could be produced in every part of the monarchy; but subscription is a sure method of concealing this interesting statistic.

In the assemblies, the clergy has precedence, and the third estate the rear rank. But this inequality of honor has no influence on the votes; in this respect they are absolutely equal. Each of the three orders has the same weight as the other two in the deliberations; two prevail over one in most cases, though there are some in which unanimity is required. It would seem that these exceptions must be indicated by a fixed and recognized law; but by a fatality which seems inseparable from all public establishments, a very dangerous uncertainty has been allowed to subsist in this regard in Brittany.

The text of the law certainly limits the occasions on which unanimity is required; it says that it only is required in the case of *gifts and contributions;* but since the estates claim that all the payments which they

make to the king are *gifts,* because they can only be made with their
consent, there are thus obviously no cases in which the rule of unanimity cannot be required, and this pretext has more than once served
troublesome individuals for the purpose of raising difficulties and has
given a tempting air of justice to their opposition to the will of the
king. . . .

VI

*Administration of the Duke d'Aiguillon from the Estates of 1762 to
the Estates of 1764*

Of all the sessions of estates attended by the Duke d'Aiguillon, none
began in a more brilliant and flattering manner than the session of
1762. To the usual wartime grant of a free gift of three millions, this
assembly added, in perfect unanimity, a present of a ship of a hundred
guns. A great province could not make a more noble gift to its king.
The remarkable thing is that it was offered by acclamation on the
first day of the meeting, a day on which it was customary to take no
action. But the Duke d'Aiguillon did not long enjoy the satisfaction
which he experienced at this proof of the zeal of the estates.

His orders required him to propose the same requests as those to
which the estates had consented two years previously: the only difference was the addition of the sou per livre, which the minister was
firmly determined to demand. There were several reasons for this;
the principal ones were that this tax being general throughout the whole
kingdom, Brittany could not escape it, and that since this tax weighed
upon many objects consumed outside the province, it was no great
burden upon its inhabitants. The orders were explicit on this point, and
the Duke d'Aiguillon was not permitted to disregard them.

As soon as he had informed the assembly of this, it fell into a state
of consternation which was expressed at first only in an obstinate
silence. An entire fortnight passed without its being possible either to
persuade the estates to debate or to obtain their answer; and when
finally they recovered their voices, it was only to express a bitter
anguish, to reveal a stern determination to resist. In the midst of a
period of uncertainty which rightly alarmed the Duke d'Aiguillon, an
unforeseen incident occurred which increased his apprehensions and
the anger—already too strong—of the assembly.

On September 15, in the hall under the benches were found a great
number of printed *mémoires,* lacking the name of an author or printer,
in which the estates were reproached with the greatest boldness for
their deference to the commissioners of the king and their submis-

siveness to the demands which the latter were responsible for making; the estates were accused of allowing themselves to be deceived and managed by their presidents. They were exhorted to act in a fashion completely opposed to that of previous assemblies, if they wished to prevent the entire ruin of the province and of their privileges. This was the first case of the distribution of these clandestine writings which have since become so common and so audacious.

Such a piece of writing certainly had all the earmarks of a libel: the Duke d'Aiguillon, a scrupulous observer of the forms of judicial procedure, asked M. de la Chalotais, the attorney-general, to carry out the prosecution of this crime.

An indictment was brought on the eighteenth in the Vacation Chamber [of the parlement] which replied on the twentieth by a formal verdict of nil.

Impunity emboldened the author and his adherents; the party of opposition declared itself violently. There was then talk of peace [with England], the preliminaries were thought to have been signed, or to be on the point of being signed; this expectation encouraged the opposition to protest against the request for a new tax made at the very moment in which circumstances should have brought about its withdrawal and even the reduction of older taxes. Moreover, they said that the sou per livre had never been known in Brittany; that the [tax] farms, since they belonged to the estates, could never be subject to a tax of this kind, and that if it were accepted, their property would thus be compromised.

In vain the Duke d'Aiguillon pointed out to them that peace was not yet certain and that, moreover, since the war had absorbed during so many years the resources of the state, it had produced requirements which would not permit the king to follow as soon as he would have liked the dictates of his heart. As for the sou per livre, he tried to make them understand that the farms of Brittany had no more right to be exempt from it than those of the rest of the kingdom; that the king did not intend to take them over any more than he did any other property on which he was obliged to assess taxes; that submission on this point was becoming indispensable, and that a refusal could bring the greatest misfortunes upon the province, because the result would be that taxes would be raised there in the same manner as they were elsewhere, and that Brittany would thus lose control of a useful and honorable part of its own administration. Moreover, he offered the same modifications of which he had demonstrated the advantages at the last session, that is, permission to pay certain subscriptions by means of loans, which would make their weight in some ways imperceptible.

The clergy, convinced by his reasoning, gave way; the third estate was not far from obeying; even among the nobility, many of the more mature and thoughtful people, considering how far things might go if there were a simple refusal, were inclined to submit; but a party had formed in that order which had been emboldened to the point of fanaticism by the indulgence of the Vacation Chamber on the charge of libel. One of the men who dominated this party one day proposed to his followers *that they should pledge themselves by a formal oath never to give way to the acceptance of the sou per livre*. This sort of league was rejected; but they acted nonetheless as if they had sworn the oath.

The Duke d'Aiguillon, seeing how serious the battle was going to be, torn between his affection for the province and his zeal in the service of the king; convinced that too much firmness would be just as dangerous as too much weakness, appealed to the minister. He asked *precise orders to determine his conduct in all possible cases, no longer daring to act on his own responsibility*. The orders came; they enjoined the commissioners of the king to hold firm and to make an effort to overcome the opposition.

One scandalous scene followed another: several bishops were insulted in the hall, the third estate was roughly handled. The prudent understanding of these two orders at a time when such understanding had become indispensable was regarded as cowardly treason; it looked as if soon there would be no way out but a noisy breaking up of the estates, which might have done irreparable harm. . . .

The affair of the sou per livre was not the only one which caused the Duke d'Aiguillon the liveliest apprehension during this session. It was not the only affair which became for him the source of the cruelest suffering, for his enemies the basis of the foulest slanders, and for the public the occasion of the most inconceivable misconceptions.

The Society of the Jesuits was at that time collapsing throughout the kingdom; the feelings of the Duke d'Aiguillon toward them were known in Brittany and elsewhere. M. de La Chalotais, who had become such a celebrity on account of his successes in this sort of war, was better informed of these sentiments than anyone else; nothing was farther from his mind in those days than regarding the commander-in-chief of the province as an hysterical partisan of the Jesuits. The Duke d'Aiguillon was among the first he allowed to read his *comptes-rendus*. In sending them, he wrote from Rennes on July 4 of the same year

[1762], "You do not pay particular attention, M. the Duke, to the constitutions of the Jesuits, NO MORE THAN DO I; however, you should know what has been said about them for better or for worse in Brittany." These few words might provoke many reflections. This confidence of a magistrate *philosophe* to a commander-in-chief, by the man of the robe to the man of the sword, clearly proves the similarity of their ideas, that is, at least an equal indifference on the part of both toward anything relating to that society.

The Duke d'Aiguillon was far from believing that the estates should in any way concern themselves with the Jesuits, and even less with their re-establishment; the society had just been dissolved in the whole kingdom, but it still had supporters in Brittany. A great number of gentlemen, accustomed to the education which they had received in the Jesuits' secondary schools [*collèges*], wanted nothing else for their children.

By a rather singular coincidence, quite contrary certainly to the accusations which have since been advanced against the Duke d'Aiguillon, those who were of this opinion were precisely the same stubborn individuals with whom at the time he was locked in such violent struggles on behalf of the interests of the king. MM. de Coëtauscours, de Pontual, and other gentlemen very well regarded in the party of the opposition, and its real leaders, were publicly regarded as the people who had the most sympathy for the Jesuits.

It was difficult to imagine that they could create an opportunity, in an assembly solely concerned with the regulation of finances, to speak in favor of the proscribed religious; however, one did occur. The estates had made their [tax] farms responsible for a due of 10,000 livres payable to the Jesuits who were established at Rennes and La Flèche. At every session it is customary to review all disbursements made by the province; this item came up in its turn like all the others. M. de Coëtauscours interrupted the Bishop of Nantes who was reading it.

Instead of turning to the question of what use could be made of this bounty which now had no purpose, he spoke at length in praise of the Jesuits, on the scandals afforded to the public by the secular instructors who had been called in to replace them; he claimed that the parlement was incompetent, without the approval of the estates, to bring about such an important and essential change in the constitution of the province; he concluded by proposing to inquire, through an express deputation to the commissioners of the king, if His Majesty would be willing to receive very humble remonstrances on the harm caused to the province by the expulsion of the Jesuits, begging him to restore them to the schools which they formerly had there.

No one had foreseen this or at least very few people had; this speech aroused both approval and condemnation; the clergy and the third estate took no stand, but the nobility was divided; tempers were the more aroused because it was so delicate a matter, and because the proposal had been made by a man who was accustomed to instruct the desires of his order; it was impossible to decide anything, but the presidents, seeing how excitement was growing, took the wise decision to close the proceedings for the day.

This happened on October 26 [1762]. . . .

The year 1763 had been a fateful, one might even say, a critical year for the commanders-in-chief, almost everywhere in France. The king, saddened as he was by the misfortunes of the peoples and the calamities of the war, was unable, to his very great regret, to grant, when peace had been signed, all the relief which his heart felt to be necessary, but which the position of the finances rendered impossible; several taxes had to be maintained; the commanders-in-chief of the provinces had been made responsible for notifying everyone in their departments of the intentions of His Majesty. At Rouen, at Grenoble, at Toulouse, the most violent disputes had arisen in this regard, but there were none in Brittany.

The Duke d'Aiguillon had obtained a decision that the edict of 1763 would not be presented to the sovereign courts before the session of the estates, which would convene only at the end of 1764. So far he had had no sort of difficulty with the parlement. The little misunderstanding of 1757 had blown over almost as quickly as it had arisen; since that time, the Duke d'Aiguillon had shown only the most courteous regard for that body; he had received from all of its members only proofs of friendship and esteem. One can imagine his surprise, when on his arrival in Rennes, he was informed that the company had just drawn up and sent to the king remonstrances against abuses of authority attributed to the commander-in-chief of the provinces, and against him in particular.

It is true that he was not personally named, but in this document the administration of the highways was attacked, and there was no doubt that he was in charge of that. The order of 1762, registered in the estates of that year, on the preponderance of two votes [i.e. the votes of two orders] over one was harshly criticized. It was pointed to as the natural product of the commander-in-chief's despotic mentality, to which, indeed, it was solely attributed. The Duke d'Aiguillon was bitterly hurt by an attack of this kind, at a time when he had no reason to expect it.

Nothing was more natural or more legitimate than that the parlement of Rennes should join its remonstrances and pleas to those of the other parlements to defend the conduct of those among these bodies with which the king seemed dissatisfied.

But what deeply hurt him was that it should take advantage of this occasion to blame a commander-in-chief about whom it had no reason to complain, that it should impute to him as a crime a step in which he had only carried out his duty and obeyed the orders of higher authority, which neither he nor the estates could escape, that an effort should be made to dishonor an administration in which he had tried to act with all the equity and mildness possible, by violent accusations and charges of injustice and harshness. . . .

Toward the end of 1763 the king, desirous of proving to his peoples his affectation and good will, had chosen from within the membership of the parlements the minister of his finances [de L'Averdy].

The first act of this magistrate was the famous edict of November 21, 1763. This announced the most sincere desire to re-establish the economy and to complete the freeing of the state [from debt]. It announced, it is true, an increase of one sou per livre on all existing taxes; but this increase was intended to facilitate the elimination of all charges; it established a fund reserved for the amortization of the public debt; it invited all the superior courts to share, so to speak, the patriotic views which animated His Majesty, and authorized them to communicate to him any plans for reform which might appear to them easy to execute and advantageous. This declaration was registered throughout the kingdom. M. de L'Averdy desired that it also be registered by the parlement of Brittany.

Since it involved the establishment of a tax, and the consent of the estates was necessary for this, it seemed that its verification should have been postponed until after their meeting; but the comptroller-general desired that registry precede the approval of the estates; he pressed the Duke d'Aiguillon to act as mediator with the company [the parlement] in this affair, which did not seem to the minister to present any difficulty; however, there were obstacles.

The parlement seemed to pride itself on its deference toward the estates; it displayed at first a great deal of reluctance to verify a tax to which the province had not consented. The Duke d'Aiguillon himself certainly thought this method of procedure irregular; his principle had

always been that the estates should be consulted first of all; that registration [by the parlement] in Brittany was only what might be called the
legal endorsement of their will, and could not take its place. However,
out of deference to the minister he tried to combat the resistance of
the parlement of Rennes.

The negotiations were long-drawn-out. . . .

In the meantime, M. d'Amilly had busied himself with the edict
[of 1763]; some changes and modifications had been asked for Brittany, and the king had granted them. On June 5 [1764] it was registered, and a copy sent to the comptroller-general. That minister was
extremely surprised to find that in the act of registration all the themes
of the preceding remonstrances which had so pained the Duke d'Aiguillon, and which the parlement had seemed to abandon, were recalled.

The order of October 12, 1762 [on voting in the estates] was mentioned; it was said to have been *enacted in disregard of the king's good
conscience, and inscribed on the registers of the province for no reason
at all; corvées* were described as *having become unbearable in Brittany
because of the great number of roads opened at the same time, because
of the violent orders tearing the peasant away from cultivation and
harvest;* it was claimed that *the costs of the coast-guard were collected
without the consent of the estates;* so-called *compulsory improvements,*
which, said the act of registration, *were ruining the bankrupt communities,* were also brought up, and in conclusion reference was made
to *disorder, acts of despotism* which would be repressed by the *parlement, armed with the sword of justice to strike down the guilty party,
whoever he may be.*

Such an unforeseen declaration of war rightly grieved deeply the
Duke d'Aiguillon. If one considered the facts, such an attack could
not be directed at him; but if only the language of this act of registration were examined, it was all too clear that it was directed solely
against him. In the case of remonstrances, at least the attack would
remain unknown; these documents not being designed to be made
public were not so heavy a blow; but now, in an authentic document,
in the sanction given a law which would be recorded in the archives
of the province, in a decree to be printed, publicly posted to serve as
a rule for the conduct of the citizens, widely publicized, thus to utter
reproaches of this kind was obviously an attempt to dishonor him, to
place arms in the hands of the discontented who are always to be found
wherever even the most temperate authority is exercised, to suggest
to all turbulent and disorderly spirits that impunity was assured them,

as well as a reliable means of carrying out without risk either their private vengeance or their general aim of upheaval and confusion. The Duke d'Aiguillon, however, contained his chagrin. Confident in his own innocence, he contented himself with placing proofs of it in the hands of the king and the members of the council. . . .

Registration, June 5, 1764, by the Parlement of Brittany of the Edict of November 21, 1763

The attorney-general having entered the court, all chambers assembled, placed before it an edict of the king given at Versailles, November 21, 1763, signed Louis . . . by which His Majesty was pleased to desire what follows: . . .

[Two-and-a-half pages detailing the specific demands of the king and the modifications to be requested by the parlement are omitted.]

The said lord king will be implored to consider that the excessive *capitation* paid by the province is in no way proportionate to the number and to the households of the taxpayers, that nevertheless this tax is made even heavier by others for the collection of which it serves as a guide, that the *corvées* are ruining and crushing the farmworkers, that this sort of work, always onerous, has become unbearable in Brittany by reason of the multitude of roads opened all at once, by the haste sought for their completion, by the violent orders which drag the farmworker away from tilling and harvesting the fields; that the province pays, in peacetime, the costs of the ordinary militia and the coastguard; that the levy for the special coastguard militia is being collected without the consent of the estates and without the registration of the parlement; that the expenses imposed on the towns on the pretext of improving them are hopelessly ruining the citizenry although the owners of property taken by eminent domain are almost always insufficiently compensated and the financial position of the province is far from being favorably altered thereby; that its commerce will long feel the effects of the misfortunes of war, that the tax on hides destroys one of the principal branches of that commerce; that the others have been dried up by a host of surprise decisions of the tax-farmer which are extended as his greed may dictate; that the new efforts made today by a faithful and submissive people as testimony

This and the following selection are translated and reprinted from the texts reproduced in A. Le Moy, *Remonstrances du Parlement de Bretagne au dix-huitième siècle* (Paris: Champion, 1909), 81-85, 86-95.

to their love and enthusiasm for the best of kings would be infinitely
beyond their capacity if they were not reassured by their confidence
in the promises of His Majesty; that the assurances which the said
lord king condescends to give that he will reign in his kingdom fill
his parlement with the greatest gratitude and guarantee that everything
will be restored properly, that acts of arbitrary authority will be forever banished, that the acts of despotism of which the said lord king
declares he is the enemy will be punished everywhere by the parlement,
armed with the sword of justice to smite the guilty party, whoever he
may be . . . Brittany will return to its own. His Majesty only awaits
the assembly of the three estates to revoke the order of October 12,
1762, promulgated while he was being misled and inscribed for no
reason whatever on the registers of a provincial assembly which had
just given the king new proofs of its zeal by the grant of extraordinary
assistance in the amount of 460,000 livres. The said lord king will be
very humbly begged to consider that this order destroys the immemorial essence of the estates, that as long as it remains in force no grant
can be legitimate, since only the nation composed of all its three orders
has the power to make grants, and that it is one of the chief duties
of his parlement to claim with the most urgent and respectful insistence
privileges of which it is the guardian and over the preservation of
which it will never cease keeping watch. The said court commands
that copies of the said edict shall, on the motion of the attorney-general
of the king, be sent to the presidial and royal courts of this district,
there on the motion of his subordinates to be read, published, and
registered, that no person may be ignorant of it, and this court shall
be informed within the month that they have carried out this duty.

Remonstrances of August 11, 1764, of the Parlement of Brittany on the Necessity for Its Decree of June 5, 1764

Sire,

The magistracy of your kingdom has been exposed at all times to the
resentment of those who have undertaken to change the principles of
government. At this moment, your parlement is undergoing a cruel
proof of this truth. Brittany has immunities and franchises which have
never suffered harm; they are consecrated in the most authentic titles.
They form a law similar to the common law of the kingdom, whose
force was until recently tranquilly assured.

The establishment of Saint Louis, the decisions of the Estates-General at the beginning of the thirteenth century, the ordinances of 1355, 1560, and 1576 permit little doubt that under the common law of France, the consent of the three orders, in the assembly of the Estates-General, is necessary for the establishment or the prorogation of taxes. The particular law of the province conforms to the common law as attested by Lobineau in his history, volume one, on pages 295, 673, 685, 707, by the declarations of 1459, 1463, 1468, by the edicts of 1532 and 1579, and by the letters-patent of Louis XIII in 1611; finally, the evidence of possession conforms to the common law and to particular law resulting from the verbal proceedings of the assemblies of the estates of the province, notably 1573, 1574, 1602, 1603, 1604, 1605, 1638, 1718, 1750, and 1752.

Your parlement, Sire, trustee of the laws of the kingdom and guardian of the franchise and liberties of the province, has not been able to see them attacked without claiming the justice of Your Majesty against this abuse of his authority.

Bound by oath to this precious duty, it cannot keep a culpable silence when the laws are violated; it is their preservation which, in a monarchical state, guarantees the security of the monarch and the subjects. This government, which is more perfect than all others, assures a prince who, like Your Majesty, wishes to reign in accordance with the laws, the obedience and love of his subjects; quite unlike those despots, who recognize no other law than their will, the monarch has nothing to fear from that resolution which tyranny excites: always in agreement with the law which his people have voluntarily received, his will cannot fail to become theirs.

Your parlement, Sire, has also very humbly beseeched you to take cognizance of the excessive taxes of all kinds which crush the province; here is its crime and the pretext for the dishonoring orders Your Majesty has falsely been advised to issue.

The zeal of your courts has often subjected them to punishments, but never as crushing as those which your parlement experiences at present. The fidelity which it has sworn to you and from which it has never deviated is attacked. It is accused before Your Majesty of "having wanted to besmirch an administration with which you are as satisfied as the province, or even of having wanted to create difficulties which could excite dissension among your subjects, if they were less attached to you."

What audacity, Sire, in such an indictment by those who have deceived you! Magistrates whose loyalty is suspect, whom one can reproach with having wished to instigate dissension among the people, although they have not met with success, because these peoples are more attached to the sovereign than they are! Such magistrates, if one may find their like, are liars who merit the laws' strictures; the people shall close their ears to such voices; such magistrates should abdicate their offices, which the confidence of the sovereign and the most correct conduct can alone make respected by, and useful to, the nation.

Your parlement, sire, in receiving the afflicting orders Your Majesty was falsely induced to issue, would have abandoned the sanctuary of justice had it not been persuaded that the truth could penetrate to the throne, and that you would announce to your people that the innocent can be accused, but that your justice protects and will avenge them.

If it had been permitted to the deputies of your parlement to be heard in the presence of their accusers, what a triumph for it, and what confusion for those who had dared to slander them! But in order to strike with more certainty and with more force, the voice of the deputies has been stifled, they have been ordered a hundred leagues from their seat of residence that the accusations might be heard by the entire nation (not on your orders, Sire, your parlement will never think that; it is neither in the goodness of your heart, nor in your justice, to deal such crushing blows) but on the orders of those who have deceived you, dictated by the hatred and interest of your enemies and the enemies of your parlement.

Silence would become, in this circumstance, a criminal acquiescence which would tend to the subversion of public order in the province; it is the sacred bond which unites prince and subjects which they wish to break asunder, it is the magistracy they want to crush under the weight of arbitrary authority, and however humiliating it may be to fulfill our office after the mortal blow which we have just been delivered, your parlement, counting on the justice of Your Majesty, awaits with the respectful confidence with which it is penetrated and with the inner calm born of irreproachable conduct, the restoration of the honor which is its due.

Sire, we owe you the truth, we present it to you openly and without fear. We know that you cherish it and that it has always triumphed when it has been able to reach you. It is in this confidence that we present the particulars of the grounds for the decrees of last June 5th, and to prove to Your Majesty the necessity and the accuracy, the conformity to usual rules, and the connection of our decrees with the decree of registration of your declaration.

It has been the duty of your parlement, Sire, to place before the eyes of a king, father of his subjects, the misfortunes of a people crushed under the weight of excessive and multiple *corvées*. For so long as the agreements concerning the roads made by the estates of the province and your commissioners were carried out, your parlement has kept silence. These agreements contained several rules, and notably these which fixed for each *corvée*-worker the distance he can be required to travel to work, and the length of road for which he is responsible. He may be sent two leagues at most from his parish, and may only be required to build one running *toise* [one *toise* equals 1.949 meters] for each twenty *sous* paid in *capitation,* and having accomplished this task, he is responsible only for maintaining it and must forever be discharged from all other *corvées* for the highways.

These rules, though onerous, caused the *corvée*-worker to work actively in the hope of finishing his labors, but he is far from seeing the promises made to him come to pass; everything has become arbitrary; he is transported from one road to another, he always wonders, when he has finished his task, if another is not being prepared for him; no attention is paid to the distance he is required to go to reach his work. . . . From this results the discouragement which arbitrary action always produces, and consequently the frequent need for garrisons, about which your parlement, Sire, has complained justly and necessarily; all the trouble results from the great number of roads opened so to speak all at once and from the haste sought for their completion, even during the war and at a time when your peoples are overloaded with taxes.

But if the completion of the roads now open or projected has become at this moment impossible, their later maintenance, if ever they could be completed, would be infinitely beyond the capacities of those who are held responsible.

An unfortunate *corvée*-worker who pays 40 sous of *capitation* and who lives only on what he can earn by his day's labor will be held responsible for maintaining about six running *toises* of road. The cost of that maintenance cannot be reckoned at less than nine livres per year, i.e. more than four times the total of his *capitation*. How could the poorest and most necessary class of the population support such a crushing surtax on a tax which is already so excessive?

It is thus, Sire, that the *corvée,* onerous in itself, has become tyrannical for the farmer and destructive to agriculture. It is thus that any agreement which does not receive in your courts the authentication it needs to assure its execution is left open to the excesses of an arbitrary and despotic management. It was also, Sire, the duty of your parlement to make known to you that it was not at a time when the state had need of the strongest aid that superfluous expenditures should have been made for the embellishment of the cities of the province. Never have these cities had more need for economy, to repair the losses inflicted by war, to make up for the decreases they were obliged to endure in tax-revenue, and for all the different kinds of expenditures with which, until the present, they have not been afflicted; they are obliged to have recourse to forced loans to satisfy their ordinary bills and the arrears of the new debts they have had to contract. And, Sire, it is at this unhappy time that it was decided to deliver the final blow in the form of public works projects which could only have been undertaken with difficulty had the cities been at their most opulent.

Your Majesty, Sire, has given yourself the example of economy by the reductions which you have announced your intention to make in all expenses; should not this example, so worthy of your paternal kindness, have served as a model and guide for anyone who thought only of the real needs of your peoples? But, Sire, you are assured that no one complains. Would it not be truer to say that no one dares complain? All individuals are in a condition of dependence; their voices are muffled by fear. Only a body still free and subsistent, like your parlement, can make itself heard and carry to the feet of the throne the cry of despair which the nation itself would carry there, if your parlement made a judicial case of the facts about which it is complaining to Your Majesty.

We cannot, Sire, conceal it from you. The work of enslaving a province hitherto free under your fortunate government has long been going on. The constitution is shaken and overturned; everywhere limitations are being placed on the franchises and liberties which you yourself engage us to preserve; the mayors, the deputies of the towns to the estates, elected from time immemorial by the free vote of the communities, now cannot be elected without the approval of your commissioners. It is now also required that the commissioners approve the choice which the province once made freely of the men to whom it entrusts the division and collection of subscribed taxes. Finally, the good faith of your council has been abused to the point that by its order of October 12, 1762, it has destroyed the estates, by destroying their essential and immemorial constitution.

A decision which, though couched in no legal form, dismisses as meaningless titles and customs, ordinances and constitutions, common law and national law, a decision which without any excepting clause contradicts and abrogates the oldest and wisest law, cannot but be regarded as having been falsely defended to Your Majesty. Such, Sire, is, in general, the character of the administration which people have had the temerity to assure you satisfies the province.

Would those who have exaggerated to Your Majesty the advantages of the present administration dare to contend that their audacious assertion would be confirmed by the free vote of the estates, whose most important privileges have been destroyed, by the vote of the towns whose revenues are being wasted, and funds used up; by the vote of the inhabitants of the countryside who are groaning under the weight and abuse of the *corvées?*

Mendacious letters and attestations, praise and petitions, dictated by flattery, by fear, or by vested interest, will never prove that the province is satisfied, when it is unfortunately only too true that it is suffering in every respect and needs the most urgent rescue.

It only remained, Sire, to attack the most redoubtable adversary of despotism. Your parlement enjoyed the advantage of having completed negotiations with your comptroller-general on the subject of your edict of November 21 last; it had just sealed its co-operation by registration and by offering to Your Majesty the last efforts of an exhausted people. It thought that there could be no more favorable moment to beg you to cast a paternal regard upon the burden of the *corvées,* with which the province is crushed, upon the extraordinary and superfluous expenditures in the towns, upon the destruction of the immemorial constitutions of the province, and finally upon the other taxes which were neither registered nor included in the contract between the estates and the twenty commissioners at the last session, and which are nonetheless being collected.

It was the representations on these subjects which have been reported to you as being criminal, with the suggestion that your parlement had interfered with concerns not involved in the registration of your edict, concerns which might provoke the kind of controversy which it is the parlement's duty to avoid or punish.

Such an accusation, Sire, can only be made by those who have reason to fear that your parlement might reveal to you the different kinds of over-taxation which would make it impossible for your province to raise the new taxes contained in your edict; and it was to assure the execution of that edict in accordance with the terms of its registration that your parlement begged Your Majesty to put an end to these abuses which are destructive of all production and hence of all taxation. To assure the collection of legitimate taxes, those which are not legitimate must be abolished.

Was it not proper, we dare ask Your Majesty, to mention these things while registering an edict in which you announced in the most solemn way, in a way consoling for your peoples, that you wished to rule only with the laws and by the forms established in your kingdom, was it not proper to consecrate that pronouncement from your own lips by announcing it to the people as a sure pledge of its happiness and as a happy forerunner of the restoration of their franchises and liberties? Was it improper to call for the immemorial constitutions of the province, of which your parlement is the guardian and depository, and would the parlement not have failed in its duty to Your Majesty if it had not asked for their re-establishment with the liveliest and most respectful insistence?

Is your parlement reproached, Sire, for the form of its decrees, because they were inserted after the registration and were sent to all the local courts of the province? Is it really necessary to reply to such an allegation, and does it not betray the most determined effort to treat customary usages, which Your Majesty has so often witnessed without disapproving them, as crimes? What would be wrong, Sire, indeed, in your peoples knowing that your parlement, as mediator between sovereign and subjects, is soliciting in their favor some relief from the ills that are crushing them and a return to the franchises and liberties which are so dear to them? The hope of relief encourages them, and the hope of recovering their ancient rights makes them capable of even more love, zeal, and gratitude to their well-beloved king. Such, Sire, is the peculiarity of the Bretons. The more you spare their liberty, the more you will extend your power over them.

What a difference between the motives which animated your parlement, and the views which have been imputed to it in order to accuse it of the most serious crimes! Is then one of your subjects permitted to trouble the relations established between Your Majesty and his parlement, and to cast suspicion on the purest intentions by accusations dictated by ambition and vested interest?

Far from you, Sire, and far from the throne, these men who employ such means to impair the confidence you have shown in your parlement, interrupt the natural communication between the sovereign and the essential officers of the laws of the kingdom, who seek to have you regard the legitimate liberty of your subjects as incompatible with your sovereign power, who intrigue to inspire you with suspicion of the purest zeal and the most inalterable fidelity. It is these men, Sire, whom Your Majesty will blame for provoking difficulties which might create divisions among your subjects, if they were less attached to you.

What a striking contrast there is between their conduct and the conduct your parlement has always maintained!

We appeal, Sire, to your justice, we ask it of you insistently: punish your parlement if it is guilty; but if it has been slandered, the laws demand vengeance of you and expect from your royal justice a proportionate and complete reparation, without which your parlement would become unworthy of rendering justice in your name. Announce, Sire, its justification to France, and show how truth rules the heart of the best of kings, when it can reach him.

These are, Sire, the most humble and respectful remonstrances, etc.

Further Selections from Linguet's Brief for the Duke d'Aiguillon

VII

Administration of the Duc d'Aiguillon from the Estates of 1764 until the Estates of 1766

While the king and his council were treating as an error the extraneous additions to the registration of the edict of November 21, 1763, and the parlement was making an attempt to justify them, the time came to hold the estates. They were convened at Nantes. The Duke d'Aiguillon went there as usual.

As a result of the registration of June 5, 1764, collection had begun in Brittany, as everywhere else, of the two sous per livre established by the edict of November 21, 1763, on the taxes which were not managed by the estates. The nobility broached the idea of bringing suit in the parlement against this collection carried out without the consent of the estates. The third estate, after long debate, accepted this point of view, though with some modifications; but when it had agreed, the modifications were ignored and only its agreement with the views of the nobility was taken into account; the clergy was opposed, but the measure passed with the affirmative vote of the two orders. . . .

The Vacation Chamber of the parlement was then sitting. The ordinance of 1669 forbids this court *to judge any case provisionally which it could not judge definitively;* there can be no doubt that a case of this importance, a suit brought against the execution of an edict registered by the whole parlement in a regular session, was not a case which the Vacation Chamber could have judged definitively.

Mémoire pour M. le Duc d'Aiguillon, par Me Linguet, avocat (Paris, 1770).

Moreover, the ordinance of 1673 *prohibits the courts, in general, from accepting any suit by public bodies, communities or individuals, whoever they may be . . . against the registration of ordinances, edicts, declarations and letters-patent, concerning public affairs and emanating from the authority and action of the king himself.* According to this text, the entire parlement itself would not have been competent to judge the case.

Indeed, of the eight judges, three took the side of law and reason. They wanted at least to put off the case until the full parlement was again sitting, but the other five accepted the suit brought by the estates. They handed down a decree [October 16, 1764] prohibiting, on pain of indictment for fraud, the collection of the two sous per livre; and the next day they adjourned.

This was a new affront to the minister, whose work the edict and its registration were; it was perhaps lacking in respect to the king, who had disapproved the parlement's modifications and who would not be pleased to see a very small section of the parlement annulling at one blow the registration and even the edict itself. Moreover, it was a sort of indication given to the estates to encourage them to refuse to co-operate with His Majesty, and a hint of the encouragement they would receive from the parlement. This at least was the way the council evaluated this verdict; it was promptly revoked; the suit was called to the Council of the King, which ordered that the estates should register both this revocation and the intervention of the royal council; which was done October 22. This act of authority done on the orders of the comptroller-general and on the king's own authority has been publicly blamed on the Duke d'Aiguillon. He, however, was not even consulted on this subject, and clearly there was no reason why he should have been.

The idea of an agreement, of a secret union between the members of the nobility who were opposing the collection of the taxes and the members of the parlement who had prohibited such collection, was not destitute of truth. The latter company now came to suspend its activities; it had decided to uphold the decree of the Vacation Court of October 16, 1764. . . . The king had sent the parlement letters-patent imposing silence upon it; his letters-patent had been sent back to the king through the mail, and the activities of the parlement had not resumed.

The lower jurisdictions, the subordinate officers, prosecutors and others, already were refusing to appear for trials; the execution of justice was soon to be abandoned. They flattered themselves that they could thus force the king to give in to the protests of the parlement, from fear of the evils and even disorders which could result from the inactivity of that great instrument of government, the most visible embodiment of the principle of public order.

To apply still more pressure, they had the idea of preventing the estates from deliberating, uniting them with the cause of the parlement, raising obstacles to the collection of funds, and thus forcing the [royal] council to give up on this measure as a sign of its indulgence for the company, against which it seemed to be prejudiced. It was this idea which caused such scandalous scenes, such picayune and childish deliberations, such improper proposals; it was this stubbornness which prolonged the duration of that session [of the estates] for more than six whole months, to the great detriment of the interests of the province and to the members of the estates themselves.

This, then, is the explanation of everything that happened during that unfortunate session, in which the Duke d'Aiguillon, though not yet the target of personal abuse, and though his affection for the province and his attention to the interests of Brittany were not yet called into doubt, nevertheless now began to be underhandedly portrayed to the people as a secret enemy to be feared, and as an imperious man who always insisted on the adoption of his own ideas, and who worked by devious means to wreak his private vengeance. . . .

After six whole months of altercations, trickery and dishonesty of all sorts, it finally came time to think of closing this fatal session. The efforts which the leaders of the opposition had made to prolong it indefinitely were now exhausted. The majority of the members were horrified by such a long period of disorder, and were suffering from the expense and inconvenience which an absence of six months had caused in their affairs. The bishops had to look to the cares of their dioceses. The third estate, almost completely made up of lawyers and businessmen, longed for the quiet of their offices and were being urgently recalled to their occupations; even the nobility, most of whom are not rich, regretted thus having been snatched from its farms, its property, its peaceful dwellings, to come to witness involuntarily these interminable debates; thus there were serious thoughts of an adjournment; everything for which the Duke d'Aiguillon had asked in the name of the king was granted.

Even the extraordinary [financial] assistance was finally consented to by the nobility, not, in truth, by simply agreeing to the resolution of the other two orders, but by granting permission to the treasurer to brorow 700,000 *l* in the name of the estates and pay them into the coffers of the king; thus they avoided in theory what they did in fact. . . .

Finally, the estates were adjourned April 1, 1765. But those who had caused so much trouble had taken the precaution of keeping the seeds of discord alive. They had had drawn up in the name of the nobility, a long self-justifying memoir addressed to the king; the purpose of this memoir was, by appearing to exonerate the nobility from responsibility for the improper activities of the session and for its length, to throw the blame on the other two orders, and make them responsible for everything reprehensible which had occurred during the session. . . .

After the adjournment of the assembly, and the departure of the Duke d'Aiguillon, the troubles increased at Rennes; the king, during the session of the estates, having seen so many of the orders he had given eluded, had finally summoned the entire parlement in order to communicate to it his will; that company had had an audience on March 15 [1765].

One of its great complaints, on which it had based most of its remonstrances, was the supposed lack of information available to the king on the orders which were being given in his name; His Majesty addressed himself specifically to this point.

"I have read your remonstrances; they are written in a tone of which I do not approve; I forbid you to have any of them printed up. In them you say that I am not informed; nothing could be more false. I have read everything you have written and nothing has been addressed to you which I have not myself commanded. Get you back without delay to Rennes; reopen your proceedings on the first day of your return; thus expressly I command you; I shall not answer you further until you have obeyed me. Only in this way will you make yourselves again worthy of my benevolence."

The parlement returned to Rennes; it met at the Palace [of Justice] but only to declare, on April 6, 1765, its determination *to resign from all its functions and to continue them only until it pleased His Majesty to send out other judges.*

On April 24, a letter was received from the minister which left the way open to conciliation: the king, to calm the situation, asked only obedience; their decision of April 6 could still be forgotten, annulled; but it was not. On April 26 the magistrates, who were only continuing to exercise their functions in a spirit of duty, handed down a decree forbidding the collection of the two sous per livre on all taxes included in the general [tax] farms, and ordering the restitution of all money thus collected so far. On April 27, there was another decree, which required the attorney-general to investigate and prosecute anyone collecting in the province taxes which had not been registered.

On May 3, the [royal] council handed down a decree contrary to the parlement's decree of April 26. On May 20, the resignations were completed; on the 22nd, they were signed; on the 23rd, the document bearing the signatures was mailed to the king; on the 24th, the province learned with certainty that it no longer had any judges, and thus that crime had no restraint, innocence no more support, the laws no more instruments; hitherto this cruel situation had existed in fact, but there was still some hope of seeing it change; by the act of May 20, even this faint hope was eliminated.

Things then took the course they usually do in such great events; surprise was followed by chagrin, and excitement by fanaticism; this final period of hysteria leads to all sorts of evils, and creates fears of even those evils which do not come to pass. Twelve members of the parlement had refused to join their colleagues in resigning; they became the targets of the most bitter mockery and the most outrageous slander; during the night gallows were drawn in chalk on their front doors; a cartoon was passed around in which their names were depicted inscribed on an escutcheon formed of yew-boughs, and surrounded by the letters I. F. intertwined.[1]

This obscene buffoonery enjoyed a great success; these faithful subjects were no longer called anything but "the IFs."

Songs were composed, the dispatches of ministers were parodied; the king had ordered one of his secretaries of state to write to the first president, and to authorize him to express to the twelve magistrates who had not resigned his satisfaction at their steadfastness; this letter was travestied in ironic couplets, in which even the king was attacked. Other anonymous letters, even more obscene and licentious, and addressed directly to ministers, followed one after the other. Two notes in particular, which have since become famous because of the handwriting which was thought to be recognized in them, provoked the strongest indignation and could even justify alarm; the government thought the time had come to prepare to take steps.

---

1. [*If* is the French word for the yew-tree. But in the eighteenth century, I and J were the same printed character, so that *If* might also be *Jf*, the initials for Jean-Foutre. As the word might suggest, Jean-Foutre ("Jean-F - - -") is an obscene generic term for idiots or cowards. —Ed.]

There was no longer in the province any authority capable of avenging the outraged dignity of the king and restoring good order, violated in so many ways; the lower courts had also withdrawn, and were refusing to sit. It was necessary to make up for the absence of regular justice, which no longer existed, by orders emanating directly from the throne. The authors of these libels, and those suspected of being their accomplices, were put in prison; several were transported to Paris, there to undergo judicial interrogation.

On November 11 [1765] by order of the king, three councilors of the parlement were arrested, as well as the attorney-general and his son; then it was that the misfortunes of M. de la Chalotais began, and he himself began to arouse real interest.

He has written publicly since, that his celebrity had brought his misfortunes upon him, but he must have felt at the time how helpful it is for a man in trouble to have become a celebrity. His *comptes-rendus* had given him readers, his detention assured him supporters, and when they were clever enough to make his detention look like persecution, when the idea had become widespread enough that the disaster of M. de la Chalotais was the consequence of the resentment of a society overthrown by his eloquence, he got on his side all the enemies of that society, which gave him a numerous party of men of wit, and through them, won the public to his side.

However, the king was greatly troubled by so violent and open a conflict: he could not at all get accustomed to the idea of having to punish the entire personnel of one of his courts; he had not completely given up his desire of a reconciliation for which he still had ardent hopes, though he was on the verge of ordering the prosecution of several members of a company which had incurred his disgrace, while respecting the privilege claimed by everyone of that order of themselves trying the cases of the magistrates who compose it. He decided to make one more attempt to persuade the resigned parlement to resume its activities.

His Majesty wrote to all the councilors; he commanded them to return to their functions, and as their first act in so doing, he demanded only that they consent to the tax of one sou per livre. This simple step would return them to their sanctuary; those of their colleagues who were prisoners would be handed over to them; the task of investigating the charges pending would be entrusted to them; the proof of innocence or the conviction of crime would be decided by them alone.

But they persisted in their fatal abnegation; they appeared only to refuse their services once again; they referred to themselves in their reply to the king as *people who formerly composed his Parlement of Brittany*. This was to announce only too clearly that they no longer considered themselves to be that parlement.

Then His Majesty no longer hesitated; he formally abolished the titles of that court which had already dissolved itself voluntarily; he announced that it was his intention to form another to take its place, to be composed of a smaller number of judges than the previous one. Until he was able to take steps to carry out this plan, he sent to Rennes twelve magistrates of his council to deal with the most urgent requirements of the people and to set about re-establishing the normal course of affairs. These twelve departed, and installed themselves at Rennes; they took over the [hall of] parlement now vacant, and assumed the functions attached to it; the accused were brought before them, and trials were begun. . . .

Nothing was more alarming for the party which had given rise to the confusion, and which was eager to keep it going, than the prospect of the restoration of the parlement. Therefore, they hastened from the first to oppose themselves to the good results which might be expected from these preliminaries. The new company had to be rendered untrustworthy or contemptible. Wherefore that name of the *"Baillage d'Aiguillon"* ["d'Aiguillon's private court"] which was bestowed on it; thus those criminal lists, with their slanderous notations, in which respectable magistrates were attacked and dishonored with an impudence which reason and political sanity should not have tolerated even if the charges made against the men were true, but which was an atrocious crime in circumstances where it was merely a signal for revolt, and an instrument of the most unjust defamation. . . .

Extracts from Letters Written by La Chalotais to His Son During January 1765; Later Seized and Produced at His Trial

Your little despot is, then, very angry at the remonstrances of the parlement. . . . M. d'Aiguillon wants to ruin the parlement and some

This and the following three selections are translated and reprinted with the publisher's permission from the texts given in Barthélémy Pocquet, *Le Pouvoir absolu et l'esprit provincial: Le Duc d'Aiguillon et La Chalotais,* 3 vols. (Paris: Perrin, 1900-1901), II, 19, 52, 63, 218-19.

individuals in the eyes of the king, he is a lunatic who was discrediting himself in the minds of the public and the nation. . . .

You know the funeral preparations for the parlement and the estates which the ministers would like to make; but the king, who is a better man than they are, desires no harm, he wants peace and he deserves that peace be made for him at any price. As for the ministers, M. d'Aiguillon, his uncle, etc., they merit hatred both public and private. . . . Everything for the king and nothing for M. d'Aiguillon who is, I hope, discredited here. . . .

The ministers have gotten themselves into a bad pass which they will have trouble getting out of without using a violence which is very far from the gentle and human character of the king. . . . The king is the best man in his kingdom, they are trying to push him to acts of violence. . . . In a word, everything for the king, who, basically, is very good, and nothing for M. d'Aiguillon, who is bad. . . . If M. d'Aiguillon is a madman, that is not a reason for the Bretons to go insane, and the cause of the king must always be kept separate from his. . . . As for M. de Saint-Florentin, *nepotism* has turned his head, he wants at any price to avenge M. d'Aiguillon. . . .

Letter from the Count de Saint-Florentin to the First President of the Parlement of Rennes

The king, sir, is beginning to interest himself in the affairs of the Parlement of Brittany. His Majesty has noted with satisfaction that in the midst of an almost general desertion, twelve magistrates remain who refuse to resign and to abdicate responsibilities to which they are bound by their oath to His Majesty and his peoples.

His Majesty has expressly charged me to write you so that you might express to them in his stead that he is the more pleased with their zeal and their attachment to his service and to the general welfare since he is well aware of all the methods being employed to detach them from the most legitimate of duties.

It is the wish of His Majesty that you assure them that he is firmly determined under all circumstances to afford them the most courteous gages of his protection and benevolence.

Versailles, June 7, 1765

Signed: SAINT-FLORENTIN

Texts of Two Anonymous Letters, Posted from Rennes, Received by the Minister, the Count de Saint-Florentin, in June 1765 and Attributed to La Chalotais by the Crown's Handwriting Experts

(1) To Monsieur
     Monsieur de sain Florantin [sic]
     Minister segretary [sic] of state
     At the Court

     tell your Master that in Spite of him we'll chase out the 12 j
     and you to [sic]
(2) you're j f just as much as the 12 j f
     Magistrats [sic] who stayyed [sic] out of
     the general runawway [sic] raport [sic] this
     to Louis so that they'll be awarre [sic] of our
     affair and then write in his name butt [sic]
     without him knowing it pretty letters to the 12 j f
     Magistrats [sic]

Letter of Du Poulpry to La Chalotais of October 27, 1765, Referring to **Proofs of the King's Full Sovereignty over the Province of Brittany**

. . . These three letters are deadly boring, and certainly kept us yawning. M. de L'Averdy makes a great display of erudition in them, of the history of Brittany and of the subtleties and fine points you would expect of a prosecutor, but the whole thing is designed to dazzle the ignorant and does not deal with the facts. . . . It would have been a good idea not to reply to the first two letters, for these replies are weak and have the appearance of having been agreed on in advance. Nevertheless, they are attributed to du Parc-Poullain, they certainly reflect no honor upon him. He is said to have been paid to leave the last word to the author of the letters, and thus the victory as well. What is the point of all this, if not to make the public laugh? . . .

Selections from the Pamphlet Proofs of the King's Full Sovereignty over the Province of Brittany

PUBLISHER'S NOTICE

The three letters and the two memoirs, which are here presented to the public, are already known in Brittany. . . . The troubles instigated in this province have given an all-too-free field to controversy; and if, in these important matters, it is no longer possible to impose silence on the people, it is all the more necessary to enlighten them.

One does not hold at fault a minister whose correspondence is published. One would never blame men of state for wishing to promote authority with the weapons of reason.

PROOFS OF THE FULL SOVEREIGNTY OF THE KING OVER THE PROVINCE OF BRITTANY. FIRST LETTER OF MONSIEUR THE COMPTROLLER-GENERAL, TO MONSIEUR D'AMILLY, FIRST PRESIDENT OF THE PARLEMENT OF RENNES, 12 JULY 1765

You will recall, Monsieur, that the parlement in its remonstrances of the month of August last advanced, as an indisputable principle, that Brittany had submitted itself to the power of the king, and consequently set out the privileges of this province as so many conditions of a free compact, the covenants of which created the title of HIS MAJESTY. THE KING, in his response, suffered to observe to his parlement that this company ought never to allow Brittany to forget its ancient and primary dependence upon his crown.

Surprised to see a fact, so contrary to the conceptions which I had formed of the sovereignty of the king, advanced by a company which ought to regard itself as a repository of the laws and maxims which form our public law, I resolved to examine myself the historical monuments which could instruct me in the rights of H. M. I knew that if our sovereigns had little by little recovered the exercise of the power united to their crown, the title to which might have been disregarded but never alienated, it was principally the zeal of their parlements which they had employed in achieving this end. I was not unaware that even in the period of feudal anarchy, when the great vassals saw in the king only a superior within the order of seigneuries [lords], the parlement, constantly bound by the ancient constitution, had never lost from view the title and rights of the royal sovereign. I was indeed astonished that a parlement which has for its jurisdiction one of the

Preuves de la Pleine Souveraineté du Roi sur la Province de Bretagne (Paris, 1765).

156

most ancient fiefs of the crown could have considered this fief as having been in olden times entirely and irrevocably withdrawn from the sovereignty of our kings, and the peoples of this province as having been free to choose masters for themselves.

I believe it my duty today, Monsieur, to confide to you the result of my researches, and I do this after having begged the permission of the king. With the rest of his subjects, it is only necessary to make mention of his authority; to his parlements, whose obedience ought always to be enlightened, he makes it a rule to utter reason, truth, and justice; he is persuaded that it suffices to expose these to them in order to lead them back to sound maxims. I shall rapidly survey the history of the province. I shall indicate to you the monuments, I shall draw from them the most simple inductions; but should my letter be regarded as a dissertation, I shall never regret having descanted upon the laws and the maxims of the monarchy with magistrates whose first duty is to maintain them in all their purity! I pass to the subject.

All authors acknowledge, Monsieur, that Clovis [King of the Franks, 481-511] made himself master of the provinces known today under the name of Brittany, and dispute only the manner in which he made this acquisition. It would appear that the peoples of this territory contributed to the Armoric line, of which they formed a principal part. [Armorica: Latin name of territories in northwestern France.] Did Clovis make conquest of the territory of the Armoricans, or was it by a treaty that he subjugated this province? We shall not examine this here. The fact of the sovereignty of Clovis suffices for us, and it is supported by a passage of Gregory of Tours,[1] who says: *The Bretons have always been under the dominion of the Franks after the death of Clovis, and their chiefs have been designated counts and not kings.* . . . [Gregory's Latin is reproduced in the margin: *Semper Brittani sub Francorum potestate post obitum Regis Clodovici fuerunt & Comites non Reges appellati sunt.*]

Under the last descendants of Clovis, the counts of Brittany saw the mayors of the palace [principal royal lieutenants, founders of the Carolingian line] in possession of the supreme power, regarded themselves as absolutely independent, and little by little freed themselves from the sovereignty of our kings. Charlemagne was obliged to subjugate this province anew in 786 [and] he established there counts whose power was no broader than that enjoyed under this monarch by any of the officers who governed the provinces in his name, under this title

1. [Gregory of Tours (*ca.* 538—*ca.* 594), Saint, Bishop of Tours, author of *Historia Francorum,* an essential source for the history of Merovingian Gaul.—Ed.]

or under that of duke. In 818, the Breton princes revolted, and Emperor Louis the Pious [814-40] subjugated them again.

This same prince gave the government of all Brittany and the title of duke to Nomenoë, whom he had already made count of Vannes, striking proof that even if the power of the king was not absolute in this province, at least his right was recognized there. . . . [Seven further pages of medieval evidence are omitted.]

François II [last duke of Brittany, d. 1488] left only one daughter, who was Anne of Brittany.

All the evidences anterior to this princess, under whose posterity we shall see Brittany reunited to the crown of which it was a fief, prove indeed, Monsieur, that although the dukes of Brittany enjoyed most of the regalian rights which the lords had usurped, they nonetheless regarded the king as their sovereign lord, and were regarded by him as his subjects. In all the documents in which the dukes of Brittany had occasion to name the king, they designate him only *my most dread Lord, Monseigneur the King.*

[Two pages of styles and titles are omitted.]

. . . [I] think that those [titles] which I have just cited demonstrate sufficiently that the Duke of Brittany, although enjoying most of the rights of sovereignty in the province, was nonetheless vassal of the king, bound to answer to his justice and subject to confiscation in the case of forfeiture or rebellion; from which it follows that the sovereignty of the king over the province of Brittany had never been alienated, and that this duchy had never ceased to form a part of the direct domain of the crown. . . .

In 1491, Charles VIII [King of France, 1483-98] repaired to Brittany in order to maintain the rights which he claimed over this province. We see that he began by speaking and acting as sovereign.

On October 27, he named commissioners to convene the Estates at Vannes. The letters which ordained the convening of these estates fixed the relief or hearth-money which the king wished to have solicited in the province, and which amounted to a sum of six livres, six sols per hearth, in coinage of Targe [ancient Breton coin].

In the month of November 1491, the king was so far the master of the entire province, that Anne was obliged to conclude a treaty by which it was covenanted that the king and she would each name a dozen commissioners who would assemble to discuss the rights and claims of the parties, that this examination might last one year and even more, and that, while waiting, the king would remain master of

Brittany and would pay forty thousand écus per year to the princess, who would be free to retire to Germany.

This treaty preceded by only one month the contract of marriage between the king and the princess [Anne of Brittany], which was concluded December 6, 1491.

By this important document, you know, Monsieur, that they made mutual gifts to one another, and to the survivor of the two in the case that they might die without issue, of all their rights over Brittany, but on the condition, however, that if it were the queen who survived, she might espouse only the succeeding king, or upon his refusal a prince heir-presumptive of the crown, *who in this case would be bound*

> *to make and exhibit* to the King the acknowledgements and feudal dues, both honorary and profitable, due from the former by reason of the said Duchy, County, and their said appurtenances, & could not alienate the said Duchy, County & appurtenances into any other hands than [those of] the said Lord & his successors Kings of France.

One sees from these terms that the principal aim proposed to one another by King Charles VIII and Queen Anne was to reunite at last to the crown this great fief, whose lords had sometimes had difficulty in complying with the duties and obligations of a vassal. . . .

The reunion of Brittany to the crown occurred in 1532, [and] you are going to see whether it is true, as I recall having read in the remonstrances which the parlement presented to the king in 1760, that the legitimacy of this union depends absolutely on the consent of the estates of the province; whether it is to the people that the king owed this increase in his dominion, and whether it is they who have voluntarily submitted to the French government, as the Parlement of Brittany has again said in its most recent remonstrances, which gave rise to my researches. . . .

Francis I wanted to execute this reunion during his lifetime. He repaired in 1532 to Vannes, where the estates were meeting, and these presented to him a request by which they begged: first, that it might please him to accord and grant them that Monseigneur the Dauphin make his entry into the city of Rennes as duke and prince proprietor of the said Territory of Brittany, reserving at all times to the king the use and entire administration of the province. Second, that it might please him to unite and join perpetually the said Territory and Duchy of Brittany with the Kingdom of France, that there might never arise war, dissension and enmity between the said countries, reserving at all times and holding good the rights, liberties and privileges of the said country. . . .

The king upon this request executed letters-patent . . . by which he granted to the estates their demands, and among other things united and joined the Territory and Duchy of Brittany with the Kingdom and Crown of France perpetually, in such manner that they might never be separated nor fall into discord for any reason whatever. These letters-patent were registered at the Parlement of Paris on September 21, 1532, and in the Council of Brittany on December 8 of the same year. . . .

It is from these evidences that we must judge whether the king enjoyed the sovereignty over this province only with the consent of its peoples. If this were true, it would necessarily be equally true that the estates possessed the liberty to prevent our kings from becoming their sovereigns.

But tell us, Monsieur, to what prince were the estates of Brittany free to give themselves? I willingly implore the composer of your recent remonstrances to answer this question.

Was not Anne of Brittany duchess of Brittany? Was she not in this quality vassal of the king? The fief which she held of her fathers, under protection of the King of France, did she not hold it with the acknowledgement and due consent of the Bretons: could they alienate it? Could Anne herself have alienated it without the consent of her lord? Have not the parlements of the kingdom always upheld the principles which serve to solve all these questions?

How, indeed, was your company able to think that Brittany had submitted itself? . . .

After that, Monsieur, let us review the titles which have at all times assured to our kings the sovereignty over Brittany, independently of the acknowledgement and due consent of the estates.

[Here are omitted ten pages of examples from the Merovingians to Francis I.]

It follows [from examination of the letters-patent of 1532, described above] that the Bretons did not voluntarily yield, [and] could not impose any conditions on the king, but that the fact is that they could not exact any. They begged a grace from their sovereign; what is it? The confirmation of their privileges; it was granted to them. That is all that is contained in the letters. . . .

Let us conclude that Brittany has never given itself at all to the king, [and] that it is his by right of succession, like the majority of other fiefs which have been reunited to the crown at various times.

That the king has always upheld and confirmed the privileges of the province is a result of his justice and of his benevolence toward his peoples, but not the consequence of the execution of any treaty nor of any convention with the estates.

The king unites over Brittany all the rights of sovereignty which belonged to the issue of Clovis, to Charlemagne and to his descendants, and all those which belonged to the dukes proprietors of the domain and vassals of the crown; thus he is in Brittany sole and supreme legislator, and the estates have only the right of representation and remonstrances.

Do not fear, Monsieur, from all that I have said that the king ever draws the barbarous conclusion that he can at his pleasure abolish the privileges of Brittany; he knows his rights and the plenitude of his power; but he has never supposed that the attribute of royalty is to have neither a rule to follow nor duties to fulfill. He knows that his law is the constitution of his state, but this constitution itself assumes full and complete authority which it [derives] only from God.

I believe that I have proved to you that the title to this authority is in Brittany anterior to the reunion, which was itself only the result of the general Laws of the monarchy.

I remain, etc.

OBSERVATIONS ON THE LETTER OF M. THE COMPTROLLER-GENERAL OF JULY 12, 1765, RENDERED TO THAT MINISTER BY M. D'AMILLY . . .

One cannot take it ill that the parlement has recalled to mind an event so glorious at once to the French government and to the Breton nation.

The more free the union on the part of the Bretons, the more it proves that the French government was dear to all those who recognized its excellence, and the more it makes felt the attachment of the Bretons to the crown; since they freely renounced the advantage of being governed by particular sovereigns [who were] interested in conserving their laws, their customs, and their privileges.

Moreover, when the parlement recalled this truth in its remonstrances, what was its motive? It was solely to engage the king to maintain the rights, the liberties, and the franchises which H. M. himself declares that he wants always to preserve; it was to make still better known the devotion of a province [which is] always submissive to the king and distinguished by its inviolable attachment to his sacred person: has the parlement said, and has it even thought, that the dukes of Brittany were not vassals of the crown? Has it recalled the least traces of what some authors have said to prove the former independence of Brittany? Has it sought to assert the nature of simple, [that is,] not liege homage, which some dukes have rendered? Far from wishing to renew these ancient historical discussions, pointless ever since that so solemn union, the parlement has only recalled to mind the fact of an unlimited submission, founded upon the love of the Breton people for the French government. . . .

Extracts from Police Reports from Rennes in September 1765, Now Preserved in the French National Archives

September 15—Next Tuesday, M. de la Gacherie is expected at Vern, the country estate of M. de la Chalotais, two leagues from Rennes, where the latter has been since the marriage of one of his daughters, and where it is reported that he is working on a pamphlet destined to be published, though the subject of this pamphlet is unknown.

September 20—M. de la Chalotais did not come to Rennes last Sunday for no reason; people are meeting at his house, they are working on, or rather they are finishing there, so it is reported, answers to be made to the letters of the comptroller-general and to the *Historical Memoir*. M. de Kerguézec is at all these meetings, and is probably the most informed and most influential person there. Last night there was a great supper at the home of Mme de la Courpéan, the sister of M. de Begasson, one of the leaders of the leaguers of the estates, and wife of another. The leaders of the league of the parlement and the estates were present at this supper, notably MM. de la Chalotais, de la Gacherie, de Kerguézec; it is reported that they put the finishing touches on the answers which they are proposing to make public.

September 22—The last pages of the *mémoire* written at the home of M. de la Chalotais in reply to the letters and *mémoires* of the comptroller-general must have been sent to the printer's in Paris. They are

This and the following selection are translated and reprinted with the publisher's permission from Pocquet, *Le Pouvoir absolu et l'esprit provincial: Le Duc d'Aiguillon et La Chalotais,* II, 68-69, 95-98.

written in the hand of M. de la Chalotais's secretary and corrected by one Jousselin, his assistant. We are assured that it was M. de Kerguézec who must have given each person his share in the work. He kept a part of it for himself.

September 25—The first part of the famous pamphlet which is being fabricated here using a secret press has appeared. We know, however, that out of vanity M. de la Chalotais had this anonymous letter dated from the "castle of V***" in order that people would know it came from the castle of Vern, which is the name of his estate.

The Arrests on the Night of November 10, 1765

At one o'clock in the morning, the mansions of the two attorneys-general and those of the three councilors were surrounded by soldiers; the officers knocked at the door, were admitted, and placed sentries, with fixed bayonets, at the doors of every room.

Soldiers entered the bedroom of M. de la Chalotais; they brusquely awakened him and ordered him to get dressed and follow them.

He asked for his valet, but was forbidden to call him. He asked to write . . . to the intendant, but was not allowed to do so. He asked to see the orders and to be informed of the reasons for his arrest. This was harshly refused.

He was forbidden to communicate with anyone and even to see his children.

M. de Caradeuc his son came out to discover the cause of the noise he had heard. He was arrested and prevented from returning to his room.

Mme de Caradeuc was seven months pregnant, confined to her bed and very ill; she was not permitted to see her husband again. A dragoon was posted with fixed bayonet at the door of her room, and ordered not to allow anyone to enter. . . .

With the prisoners thus in hand, two notaries, accompanied by locksmiths, arrived, examined the papers and put seals on the desks and doors. . . .

M. de la Chalotais and his son were thus guarded throughout the night. Mlle de la Chalotais succeeded in getting a letter to the intendant. The latter authorized father and son to receive the farewells of their family "in the presence of the sub-delegate. . . ."

At five o'clock in the morning, November 11, in darkness, they were ordered into a carriage. Two officers rode by each door, and an escort of dragoons surrounded the vehicle. Where were they taking these magistrates who had become state prisoners, and were being treated like dangerous criminals? To the farthest reaches of Brittany, forty-five leagues from their home, to a fortress isolated by the ocean's waves, to the castle of the Bull [*château du Taureau*]. . . .

IV

THE BRITTANY AFFAIR IN RENNES AND PARIS, 1766-1770

Introduction

This chapter opens at the castle of Saint-Malo in February 1766, with Attorney-General La Chalotais under interrogation by a special commission of royal officials sent out to Brittany from Versailles. It was from Saint-Malo, the second of his prisons, that he published two self-justificatory *Memoirs,* selections from one of which, a letter to the Count de Saint-Florentin, are reproduced here. (The popular story was that he had written them with a toothpick, using ink compounded from sweat and soot, and had had them smuggled out of the castle.) Saint-Malo was not to be the last of the attorney-general's prisons; he was taken from there to Rennes, where he was held until the government found that it could not recruit sufficient judges to its new court to try him. From Rennes he was moved to the Bastille in Paris; finally he was exiled to the town of Saintes in southwestern France, where he remained under surveillance, together with his son and four other councilors of the Breton Parlement, until 1774. In considering his answers to his interrogators and the arguments of the pamphlet that bore his name, the reader will have yet another opportunity to judge why La Chalotais endured so long a punishment. Is his story of a feud between himself and the Duke d'Aiguillon plausible?

Can his description of his own role in the troubles of Brittany be trusted? Does it seem clear that he was in fact being "framed" by the commissioner Calonne, whose future career is worth noting? Does the reader perhaps find himself in agreement with Voltaire on the question of the attorney-general's guilt?

The selections from Voltaire's correspondence given here reveal the tremendous interest of public opinion in La Chalotais's case. But the reader should be careful to determine in what ways Voltaire's reaction differed from that of such friends as the tax-collector Damilaville and the *philosophe* Jean Le Rond d'Alembert (1717-83), author of the Introduction to the *Encyclopédie*. How much sympathy does Voltaire's letter to his niece, Madame de Florian (whose son d'Hornoy was a young councilor of the Parlement of Paris), suggest he now had for the attorney-general of Brittany?

The Calas affair had already revealed just how aroused Voltaire could become over a miscarriage of justice; indeed, in 1766 he was engaged in a new crusade on behalf of the Chevalier de la Barre, a young nobleman of Abbeville who had been tortured and executed on July 1 after his sentence for blasphemy had been confirmed by the Parlement of Paris. Does Voltaire's reaction to the words of Louis XV, "protector" of the French Academy, in his address to the Parlement of Paris at the "Session of the Scourging," suggest why he did not mount a similar campaign in favor of La Chalotais?

The "Session of the Scourging" underscored dramatically the fact that the Brittany Affair had become in 1766 a national constitutional controversy involving far greater issues than the fate of the attorney-general. The reader's principal concern in this chapter must therefore be, after again establishing a careful chronology of events, to determine how and why the struggle between royal authority and the defenders of the liberties of Brittany (or of the privileges of its nobility) should now be carried on not only in Rennes but in Versailles and Paris.

Perhaps the best way to answer this question is to compare the constitutional theory and the definition of the role of the *noblesse*

de robe expressed in the remonstrances of the Parlement of Paris
of February 2, 1766, with those articulated by Louis XV in his
speech to the Parlement a month later. Why did the Paris Parlement feel compelled to remonstrate on the case of "the members
of the Parlement sitting at Rennes," and what is implied by its
choice of this phrase to describe La Chalotais and his colleagues?
What great principles or interests did it feel to be at stake in their
cases? Was it the principle of judicial integrity or the principle of
noble privileges that the parlement was seeking to defend? To what
lengths did the nobles of the robe hint that they were prepared to
go to defend it?

The reader should also ask himself why Louis XV chose to
come to Paris to reply in person to these remonstrances. In his
reply, how many of the constitutional doctrines that the parlement
had advanced did the king reject? What point was he making by
ordering certain passages stricken from the parlement's records?
Did he concede that his royal authority was in any way limited?
Do the preparations made for this confrontation in the Palace of
Justice of Paris suggest that popular opinion sympathized with this
royal constitutional doctrine, and, in this connection, why was it important for Louis XV to kneel in the street before the passing Host?
In confronting the men of the parlement, how far did Louis XV
hint that he was prepared to go if he continued to encounter interference? In the long run, how effective was this "scourging" of the
parlement?

These last two questions prompt the thought that the outcome
of a constitutional conflict may be determined less by the theoretical merits of the positions taken by the two sides than by their
different degrees of perseverance in upholding those positions.
Taking into account not only the Duke de Croÿ's account of the
later developments of 1766, but also the Paris Parlement's remonstrances of March 1768, the reader should try to decide whether
the crown or the parlement got the upper hand in the Brittany
Affair and the constitutional conflict it dramatized. Or, three years
after La Chalotais's arrest, was it a stalemate?

In order to make this judgment, the significance of the king's

decision in November 1766, after having partially restored the
former Parlement of Brittany in July, to have La Chalotais tried
by the Conseil des Parties, should be considered. Why did Louis
XV then decide to close the case in December, though without
freeing La Chalotais? Did he take this way out because of the
opposition of the Parlement of Paris to the attorney-general's being
judged by such a court, or was it perhaps because there seemed
no chance of convicting him, at least without embarrassment to
the government? Was this a solution that reflected royal strength
or royal weakness? In answering all these questions, particular
attention should be paid to the Duke de Croÿ's appraisal. On
which side of the conflict did his sympathies lie, and just how
optimistic was he that his side would finally prevail?

In reading the remonstrances of 1768, three points in particular
strike the student. The first is the justification the parlement advanced for remonstrating. Does it suggest that the "Session of the
Scourging" had made a lasting impression upon the *noblesse de
robe* of Paris? Then there is the attribution by the parlement of
blame for the Brittany Affair to the machinations of the Jesuits.
The reader will have noted that their sinister role is alluded to at
every turn of this tortuous Affair; he may well at this point want
to ask himself once and for all if the events described in this book
can be explained without postulating that they played some significant part.

The victims of their plotting, according to the Parlement of
Paris, were not only the Breton magistrates, but the Estates of
Brittany as well. The "entire province," in fact, had been falsely
depicted as rebels. In order to decide, finally, how many Bretons
of what sorts were resisting the royal authority, the reader should
turn back from Paris to Brittany and reconstruct the continuing
struggle there by comparing the petitions of the various Breton
corporations with the concluding chapters of Linguet's brief for
the Duke d'Aiguillon. How much support do the petitions suggest
the nobility of Brittany were getting from the first and third estates

in their demands for an end to interference with Breton liberties and for the return of the entire former parlement of the province, including La Chalotais? When the other estates did not join the nobility, was it because of Jesuit influence and royal bribes, as the nobility suggested, or were they perhaps swayed by other considerations? How much do we know about what the mass of Bretons who were not nobles thought? Was this essentially a conflict between the crown and the Breton noblemen of both robe and sword, backed by the *noblesse de robe* of Paris? How far was the second estate of Brittany prepared to go in resisting royal authority? And, on the other side, should the policies of those responsible for asserting that authority be characterized as firm, or vacillating?

Linguet's arguments for his client should be helpful in resolving these questions. Is there any hint in them that d'Aiguillon's retirement in 1768 was really a dismissal? Was it perhaps significant that the former commander-in-chief permitted his lawyer to quote in his defense from letters from Comptroller-General L'Averdy? Voluntary or not, was d'Aiguillon's retirement after fifteen years in Brittany a sign of governmental determination or weakness?

The answer to this question really requires from the reader a judgment on whether or not d'Aiguillon had been a good administrator. Did his road-building program, for example, reflect despotic caprice, as the Parlement of Brittany had charged in 1764, or was it a well-conceived plan whose implementation was essential for the future well-being even of the Bretons who opposed it? Had difficulties with the parlement arisen because d'Aiguillon was seeking to avenge the Jesuits, or because the parlement had been led by narrow political motives to undertake a suicidal course of action?

In any case, the fact that d'Aiguillon was obliged to have this brief written for the trial he demanded in 1770 to clear his name —a trial that was to have the most dramatic consequences—suggests how public opinion judged him, and thus which side may be said to have won the first round of the Brittany Affair.

Excerpt from the Transcript of the Interrogation of La Chalotais by the Royal Commissioners at the Castle of Saint-Malo, February 6, 1766

QUESTION—After the resignation of the parlement, did you not become enraged at M. de Saint-Florentin, whom you thought to be your enemy, and was it not at this time that, giving way to the most hysterical animosity toward that minister, you wrote and sent to him anonymous notes?

ANSWER—I entirely contest the question.

Q.—Here are two letters signed de la Chalotais; are they in your handwriting?

A.—Yes, I recognize these.

Q.—Well! the writer of those two letters is incontestably the writer of the anonymous letters?

A.—I can say nothing as long as I have not seen those letters, but I deny here and now that they are in my handwriting.

Q.—The sight of those notes is not necessary to convince you to admit a personal and positive action. I call on you to admit that you are the writer of the anonymous notes addressed to M. de Saint-Florentin.

A.—I formally deny it; I deny having written them, or having had them written, or having had any part in sending them; I ask that they be shown to me and I shall deny them.

Q.—Do you consent to accept the testimony of the handwriting-experts?

A.—I completely deny having written these anonymous notes. When they are shown to me, I shall ask for recognition and verification of the writing by all possible means.

Q.—That verification has already been made and the identity of the writing in the notes and the writing in the two letters signed La Chalotais has been demonstrated.

A.—I persist in my answer; I ask to be shown the anonymous notes · and the report, if there is one.

Q.—Was it not when you saw that you had been discovered as the writer of the anonymous notes that you conceived this plan of defense which consists of asking for the production of the originals which you think *perhaps* are not in our hands?

A.—I have never been discovered as the writer of the anonymous let-

Translated and reprinted with the permission of the publisher from the text given in Barthelémy Pocquet, *Le Pouvoir absolu et l'esprit provincial: Le Duc d'Aiguillon et La Chalotais*, 3 vols. (Paris: Perrin, 1900-1901), II, 225-29.

ters, and I have never intended to say to anyone that I was, because
the truth is that I am not; I had no part in the writing or the sending
of them, and the plan of defense which I offer today is so simple and
so natural it requires no meditation; I persist in asking for the production of the documents.

Q.—How does it happen that among the persons prosecuted, you have
considered yourself the only one affected by this accusation?

A.—I contest it formally, because I know very well in my conscience
that I did nothing of the kind, and I would never have believed that
such a violent procedure would have been undertaken against me on
such false grounds.

Q.—You suggested to your son his answers on the various counts of
the indictment, and you said nothing to him about the anonymous
notes, and that means, then, that you thought that you alone could be
accused on this count.

A.—I have had no reason to suggest anything to my son, not having
seen him since I learned of the letters-patent. I deny a charge obviously false with regard to me as to my son; moreover any doubt
will be removed by the presentation of these anonymous notes for
which I am asking.

Q.—Among the papers seized in your chamber in this castle, one was
found in which you referred to the anonymous letters.

A.—I admit that, I knew of the accusation from the letters-patent
which were shown to me. I deny having sent any such letters, having
written any note. Moreover, all this rather metaphysical emphasis on
looking for contradictions where there are none falls, in the face of the
formal declaration I now make: namely, that if it is proved that I am
the writer of the anonymous notes, I consent here and now to my full
and entire condemnation on all charges, and even to losing my head,
and I offer to sign my declaration.

And immediately the attorney-general seized a pen, wrote his declaration and signed it.

He was shown a copy of the anonymous notes.

A.—I reply, he said, by the offering of my head, as I have already
done. I shall not cease so long as I live to ask for the production of
notes so crude and insulting so audaciously imputed to me. This cannot be denied me without obvious injustice.

Q.—The sending of the notes is explained by the animosity you have
displayed toward M. de Saint-Florentin; you have been heard expressing yourself against him in insulting terms.

A.—I had reason to complain of M. de Saint-Florentin, and I have complained of him, because I claim to have received many injuries at his hands; but this (the notes), this would not be animosity, it would be hysteria, frenzy, extravagance, an outrage against the king, an act of insolence for which I can find no name. . . .

Repeated Remonstrances, Decrees, and Representations on the State of the Parlement of Brittany and the Commission of Saint-Malo by the Parlement of Paris

February 2, 1766

Sire,

The good of the service of Y. M., the interests of your justice and your authority, the security of the state all make it imperative for your parlement to convey to Y. M. the just protest of the magistracy crushed by continuous irregular acts, the last of which clearly reveals the use of absolute power, subversion of the authority of the laws and open infraction of the most sacred rights of the state; while your parlement, Sire, was awaiting with respect and confidence the reply of Y. M. to the representations which it had the honor to make on the illegal establishment of a commission at Rennes to replace, if that were possible, and to prosecute criminally several of its members; while public opinion was augmenting its confidence in the success of its representations on the subject of that commission and was preparing the expressions of its respectful gratitude, suddenly your parlement was plunged again into new consternation on learning that new orders had formed a body of commissioners at Saint-Malo responsible for continuing the prosecution of the members of the parlement sitting at Rennes.

If the criminal impulses of the enemies of the magistracy, the secret enemies of the state and of Y. M. can prevail to such a point that magistrates could be tried before commissioners, then all rights of station and dignity are henceforth trampled underfoot, and henceforth extinguished in the kingdom.

According to the precise wording of a law of the state, "none of the peers, chancellors, presidents, masters of requests, councilors and others of the body of the court of parlement can be taken away or summoned

Translated and reprinted from the text reproduced in Jules Flammermont, ed., *Remontrances du Parlement de Paris au XVIIIe siècle,* 3 vols. (Paris, 1888-98), II, 534-37.

elsewhere nor before other judges or commissioners in cases involving their honor, their persons, or their dignity."

If this law, Sire, can be infringed, all orders of birth and distinction, all bodies, all ranks, all dignities must henceforth fear the imperious force of absolute power and watch with terrified eyes all the movements of a small number of persons transported at a word to the farthest extremities of the kingdom, transformed at a word into a tribunal, put into action at a word, suspended and removed at a word, but placed immediately, under a new disguise, by a word in possession of sole power, to which all the legitimately established powers in the state would be subordinated.

Your parlement, Sire, has already represented to Y. M. the contradiction in the establishment of these commissions with the laws of the state, the injuries they cause to the security of the citizens, the impressions of fear and terror which they arouse in the citizens' minds, and the slow but inevitable deterioration they would cause even in the authority of the sovereign whose principal strength is closely bound to the love of his subjects and their confidence in his justice. . . .

There are no circumstances, Sire, in which these invariable statutes and these maxims of public law can be avoided; it is part of the essential order of a well-regulated monarchy that the law does not lack legitimate officers any time, anywhere; as the communication of the law's authority is irrevocable, so it is indivisible and hence unified; in the constitution of the state there is an order and hierarchy of jurisdictions fitted for all possible cases, and always capable of safeguarding in a regular manner the prerogatives and inviolable rights of each class of citizen accused of crime. . . .

The Duke de Croÿ Describes the "Session of the Scourging" (Séance de la Flagellation), March 3, 1766

On March 3, as I was going on an errand to M. Bomare's, while passing along the Quai des Quatre-Nations, at ten o'clock in the morning, I was very surprised to see the other side of the *quai* lined with troops, and to hear the cannon of the Bastille firing. The people in the street told me that the king was passing by. I could not believe it, but

Translated and reprinted with the publisher's permission from the *Journal inédit du Duc de Croÿ*, 3 vols., edited by the Vicomte de Grouchy and Paul Cottin (Paris: E. Flammarion, 1906-7), II, 220-28.

I found the Pont-Neuf covered with French Guards, in a line which extended up to the Palace [of Justice, where the parlement sat], and the king came by a moment later. That day was one of the most important and glorious of his life, and one which did him the most honor.

The Parlement of Paris, on account of the king's affliction [the death of the dauphin], had taken no action on the Breton Affair, in which the court, for the first time, had taken the upper hand by breaking the Parlement of Brittany, whose members had compelled the court to take this step by refusing to withdraw their resignations; the king had formed a new one, less numerous and more submissive to the court.

At the end of February, the Parlement of Paris had come to life again, and, making common cause (in accordance with its idea of the interrelationship of all the parlements), forcefully urged the king to re-establish the former Parlement of Brittany, and to hand over to its judgment the case of M. de la Chalotais. If the court gave in, the remains of its authority would be lost. Thus the council was most embarrassed.

It convinced the king that an act of force was necessary. The king undertook it personally and carried it off in the best fashion. Never did he display more firmness, presence of mind, and grandeur. M. de Gilbert prepared the king's speech, but he himself put the finishing touches on it, and displayed the greatest dignity and majesty in delivering it.

With the decision taken, the previous evening, orders were sent during the night to the two regiments of guards to line the streets in the usual way, and to the first president to warn the parlement that the king was going to come, not to hold a *lit de justice,* but to conduct his parlement in person. No one, in Paris, knew anything about it. At quarter past ten, the king arrived; a circumstance which had a very good effect was that the king encountered, on the Pont-neuf, the Host which was being carried to a sick man. He promptly stopped the procession, dismounted alone, and knelt, among the people, in the mud. When the Host had passed, the crowd, charmed by this gesture, cried over and over "Long live the king!"—something which has not happened for a long time.

Having arrived in the Great Hall, and having taken his seat with the princes and peers who had been collected, the king ordered that the various chambers [of the parlement] be summoned. They assembled, much astonished at the suddenness of this step. The king overpowered them with that air of majesty which he possesses beyond all description. He said, "I have come to give you my answer in person and to explain to you my will. Here it is, written by my own hand!"

And he ordered that it be read. Scarcely had this been completed when, rising with the greatest majesty, he said, "Yes, that is exactly my will, which I shall know how to ensure is carried out. Dufranc (this was the clerk of the court), bring me the register containing such and such a decree!" It was the most recent. Having looked at it, he said, "I order you to strike that out!" When Dufranc appeared to hesitate, he said, in the tone of a real master, "Dufranc, strike it out at once!" He struck it out; "Bring it here, so that I can see if it is really stricken out!" Then, having spoken a little more, firmly, but not rudely, he rose and returned to Versailles.

Everyone who saw him that day, in the parlement, agreed that no one could have displayed more grandeur and majesty. And the whole display being one of the few well conceived, well managed, and well supported, overwhelmed the whole parlement, which stood confounded.

It wanted to resist, but was held back by the wiser heads and by the personal firmness which the king had shown: some remonstrances were decreed. When a deputation carried them to the king, he displayed the same firmness and the parlement contented itself, according to its custom, with drawing up a decree, but in more humble terms (it meant a lot to have gained that!) in which it recalled what had been stricken out, and reinscribed it in part on the register, to maintain, according to it, the rights of the nation. The court prohibited what had been done, and both sides, as usually happens, thought that they had caused their opinion to prevail. But, in general, the king supported the [new] parlement he had created in Brittany, and regained part of his authority. It was one of the principal landmarks of the reign.

Excerpts from the Official Transcript of the "Session of the Scourging," March 3, 1766

This day, after the report on several cases, the king's guards having seized control of the doors, the court, informed that the king was coming to parlement, deputized messieurs . . . to go and receive him, who . . . met the said lord king at the foot of the steps, opposite the Sainte-Chapelle, and accompanied him. . . .

When the king had been elevated to his high place, had seated

Flammermont, ed., *Remontrances*, II, 555-59.

himself and put on his hat, he said "I wish the present session to be
an exceptional one. Monsieur the President, have the chambers assemble." The President, having put on his hat, said, "Go to the Tournelle, to the Chambers, and send for the Courts of Requests of the
Palace." When all these gentlemen had entered, taken their ordained
places, and sat down, the king removed his hat, and, having put it on
again, said:

"Gentlemen, I have come in person to reply to your remonstrances.
Monsieur de Saint-Florentin, have this answer read by one of you."

Whereupon the Count de Saint-Florentin, having approached the
king and knelt, took from the hands of H. M. the reply, and, having
resumed his place, had it handed to Joly de Fleury, named above, who
read it as follows:

"What has happened in my parlements of Pau and Rennes is no
concern of my other parlements; I have acted with regard to these two
courts as my authority required, and I owe an explanation to nobody.

"I would have no other answer to give to the numerous remonstrances made to me on this subject, if their combination, the impro-
priety of their style, the rashness of the most erroneous principles, and
the pretension of the new expressions which characterize them had not
revealed the pernicious consequences of that idea of unity which I
have already prohibited, and which people wish to establish as a principle at the same moment in which they dare to put it into practice.

"I shall not tolerate in my kingdom the formation of an association
which would cause the natural bond of similar duties and common
responsibilities to degenerate into a confederation for resistance, nor
the introduction into the monarchy of an imaginary body which could
only upset its harmony; the magistracy does not form a body, nor a
separate order in the three orders of the kingdom; the magistrates are
my officers, responsible for carrying out my truly royal duty of rendering justice to my subjects, a function which attaches them to my
person and which will always render them praiseworthy in my eyes.
I recognize the importance of their services; it is an illusion, which
can only tend to shake confidence by a series of false alarms, to imagine
that a plan has been drawn up to annihilate the magistracy, or to claim
that it has enemies close to the throne; its real, its only enemies are
those within it who persuade it to speak a language opposed to its
principles; who lead it to claim that all the parlements together are
but one and the same body, distributed in several classes; that this
body, necessarily indivisible, is the essence and basis of the monarchy;
that it is the seat, the tribunal, the spokesman of the nation; that it is

the protector and the essential depositary of the nation's liberties, interests, and rights; that it is responsible to the nation for this trust and
that it would be criminal to abandon it; that it is responsible, in all
concerns of the public welfare, not only to the king, but also to the
nation; that it is a judge between the king and his people; that as a
reciprocal guardian, it maintains the balance of government, repress-
ing equally the excesses of liberty and the abuses of authority; that the
parlements co-operate with the sovereign power in the establishment
of laws; that they can sometimes on their own authority free themselves from a registered law and legally regard it as nonexistent; that
they must oppose an insurmountable barrier to decisions which they
attribute to arbitrary authority, and which they call illegal acts, as well
as to orders which they claim to be surprises, and that, if a conflict of
authority arises, it is their duty to abandon their functions and to
resign from their offices, even if their resignations are not accepted.
To try to make principles of such pernicious novelties is to injure the
magistracy, to deny its institutional position, to betray its interests and
to disregard the fundamental laws of the state; as if anyone could
forget that the sovereign power resides in my person only, that sovereign power of which the natural characteristics are the spirit of
consultation, justice, and reason; that my courts derive their existence
and their authority from me alone; that the plenitude of that authority,
which they only exercise in my name, always remains with me, and
that it can never be employed against me; that to me alone belongs
legislative power without subordination and undivided; that it is by
my authority alone that the officers of my courts proceed, not to the
formation, but to the registration, the publication, the execution of
the law, and that it is permitted for them to remonstrate only within the
limits of the duty of good and useful councilors; that public order in
its entirety emanates from me, and that the rights and interests of the
nation, which some dare to regard as a separate body from the monarch, are necessarily united with my rights and interests, and repose
only in my hands.

"I am convinced that the officers of my courts will never lose sight
of these sacred and immutable maxims, which are engraved on the
hearts of all faithful subjects, and that they will disavow these extraneous ideas, that spirit of independence and these errors, the consequences of which they could not envisage without terror.

"Remonstrances will always be received favorably when they reflect
only the moderation proper to the magistrate and to truth, when their
secrecy keeps them decent and useful, and when this method [of re-

monstrance] so wisely established is not made a travesty of libelous utterances, in which submission to my will is presented as a crime and the accomplishment of the duties I have ordered as a subject for condemnation; in which it is supposed that the whole nation is groaning at seeing its rights, its liberty, its security on the point of perishing under a terrible power, and in which it is announced that the bonds of obedience may soon be broken; but if, after I have examined these remonstrances, and, knowing the case, I have maintained my will, my courts should persevere in their refusal to submit, and, instead of, registering at the very express command of the king (an expression chosen to reflect the duty of obedience) if they undertook to annul on their own authority laws solemnly registered, and if, finally, when my authority has been compelled to be employed to its full extent, they dared still in some fashion to battle against it, by decrees of prohibition, by suspensive opposition or by irregular methods such as ceasing their service or resigning, then confusion and anarchy would take the place of legitimate order, and the scandalous spectacle of an open contradiction to my sovereign power would reduce me to the unhappy necessity of using all the power which I have received from God in order to preserve my peoples from the terrible consequences of such enterprises.

"Let the officers of my courts, then, weigh carefully what my good will deigns once again to recall to their attention; let them, in obedience only to their own sentiments, dismiss all prospects of association, all new ideas and all these expressions invented to give credit to the most false and dangerous conceptions; let them, in their decrees and remonstrances, keep within the limits of reason and of the respect which is due me; let them keep their deliberations secret and let them consider how indecent it is and how unworthy of their character to broadcast invective against the members of my council to whom I have given my orders and who have shown themselves so worthy of my confidence; I shall not permit the slightest infraction of the principles set forth in this response. I would expect to find these principles obeyed in my Parlement of Paris, even if they should be disregarded in the others; let it never forget what it has so often done to maintain these principles in all their purity, and that the court of Paris should be an example to the other courts of the kingdom. . . ."

Letter of Voltaire

To M. d'Alembert

March 12 [1766]

My very dear *philosophe*, had you gotten married you would have done very well; and, by not getting married, you do no harm; but, in one fashion or another, give us some more d'Alemberts. It is a terrible thing that the Frérons multiply, and the eagles have no young. I would certainly imagine that your dioptric does not resemble that of the Abbé Molière's; you were not made to see things as he does.

If you resemble a Molière in any way, it is Jean-Baptiste Poquelin; you have his good wit, and I expect it will appear in the little supplement you are preparing for those foxes of Jesuits and for those wolves of Jansenists.

It is certainly a great misunderstanding that a minister who has a great deal of intelligence should not have given recognition to your merit, and should have left that honor to foreigners. I think that he had a great desire to be once more on good terms with you; but you are not a man to make advances. I am presently serving as the Tiresias of my neighborhood. The inflammation of my eyes prevents me from writing, and I could certainly be blind for a few more weeks. M. de Chabanon is visiting us here; he is a musician, a poet, a *philosophe*, and a man of wit; he speaks of you in the way that he should. We were all very satisfied by the reply of our protector to the gentlemen of the parlement; that script seemed to us to have been nobly conceived and nobly written; and if its author were not our protector, I would wish him to be my colleague.

I flatter myself that your friend M. de la Chalotais will emerge as brilliant as a swan from the mire into which he has been pushed; he is too intelligent to be guilty.

You know that the parliament of England has revoked its stamp-tax; I do not think that it is amending that of Jean-Jacques.

Farewell, my very dear *philosophe:* I imagine that the person with whom you are living is also a *philosophe,* and I trust that the number will increase. Do not forget to remember me to M. Turgot, if he is in Paris. I have a great feeling of tenderness for thinkers.

Voltaire, *Oeuvres complètes* (Paris, 1877-85), XLIV, 241-42.

Excerpts from a Pamphlet Entitled **Letter from M. de La Chalotais,** Attorney-General of the Parlement of Brittany, to M. the Count de Saint-Florentin, Minister and Secretary of State, Written in the Castle of Saint-Malo, June 18, 1766

Monseigneur,

I take the liberty to complain to you about yourself. Why did you have to start out with me by being inhuman; and, because you were inhuman one time, was that any reason to persevere?

I had been known to you for a long time as a good magistrate, and I am sure that you will always grant that I carried out my duties with honor.

You always had the goodness to make those feelings known to me, until the moment that M. the Duke d'Aiguillon—for reasons of which you are well aware—became my enemy.

You know that at the Estates of Rennes in 1762, there arose a conflict which might have become dangerous, over the affair of the Jesuits. A cabal formed whose purpose was nothing less than to stir up a civil war between the members of the estates and between the estates and the parlement. I have only to remind you that two gentlemen of quality drew swords against one another in the theater of the estates.

I was afraid—I admit it—that the fatal consequences of this conflict might have repercussions all over the kingdom; and because it had become very obvious that M. d'Aiguillon was supporting the party which intended to stir up the question, I talked to him three or four times about the matter and finally I described the state of affairs to the Duke de Choiseul. But I ended by telling him (and he will testify to this because he is an honest man) that so far as this concerned M. d'Aiguillon, one might possibly say that perhaps he wasn't worried enough, but that perhaps I was a little too worried.

Could you possibly question, Monseigneur, whether I had done anything in this matter counter to my duty and to the service of the king? Perhaps I prevented a civil war in the kingdom.

Nevertheless, this action earned me the implacable enmity of M. d'Aiguillon. I continued in all of my obligations toward him—visiting him at Rennes and at Paris, writing him on the first of the year and on special occasions: he did not do me the honor of answering me.

Lettre de Monsieur de La Chalotais, Procureur-général du Parlement de Bretagne, à M. le Comte de Saint-Florentin, Ministre et Secrétaire d'État. . . .

He said openly that he would ruin me and he said it to so many people that I was persuaded he meant it.

In 1763, I asked His Majesty's assent that my son assist me and succeed me in the office of attorney-general. You did me the honor to say to me at Versailles, in the presence of the Prince de Soubise, the Duke de Duras and the Duke de Gontaut, that this was proper and usual enough.

The Duke d'Aiguillon set himself against this with all his power; and he declared publicly at Nantes, at Redon, at Vannes and elsewhere that I would not obtain any of these favors and that he didn't care who knew he opposed me. Then you turned against me too, Monseigneur—for rather evident motives. You know from whom I learned these facts, and how that powerful person explained them: I will not repeat all she said on the subject; you are well enough aware of it.

When I was granted this favor, M. d'Aiguillon became more vitriolic than ever against me. You are well enough acquainted with him yourself to know what that meant. He swore to avenge the injury which he alleged I had done him by obtaining these favors against his counsel and despite his efforts.

These are, in truth, the sole and unique causes of our disgrace—to speak in legal terms: the whole *corpus delicti*.

The remonstrances of the Parlement of Brittany in January and February 1764, and the registration of the edict of the preceding November furnished him with pretexts against me. He said that I was behind these remonstrances which injured him—even though I hadn't even seen them and was in Paris at the time—and he had them sent to the Count de Maurepas.

In June when it registered the edict of November, the parlement renewed the complaints it had made in its first remonstrances about the administration of the highways. I was attacked for the clauses added to the edict in this registration although I had had no part in them because they were decreed in the assembled chambers. My only role had been to look after the interests of the king as best I could, i.e. to get the edict registered. I was also specifically accused for my alleged opposition to the administration of the highways. At Compiègne you criticized me very bitterly and harshly; and people abused the king's good faith to accuse me.

I cleared myself fully of both accusations. The comptroller-general said to the deputation of the parlement, that there could be no complaint about the way I had handled the registration of the edict (he will remember this well); but that one could complain about the opposition which I had demonstrated towards the highway administration. But you accused me of having written to all the tribunals against this administration, of having sent my deputies to them along with protocols of questions regarding it.

I had no trouble clearing myself of these suppositions. I had the honor of sending you a memorandum stating: that if my deputies had really been everywhere they ought to have been seen somewhere; that if I had written to all of the tribunals and sent lists of questions, some copy or some trace of them ought to have been found; and that there wasn't anybody who claimed to have seen them or even heard of them; that I defied anyone to produce any proof or any witness in the whole province; that even on this point I would be happy to abide by the testimony of M. d'Aiguillon who had all the means to be informed in this respect and who (in my case) would certainly ignore nothing.

I pleaded with you to present this memorandum to His Majesty to correct the false impressions which he had been given; and I sent copies of it to the ministers. M. de Calonne [1] kept this memorandum from the commissioners, even though I had asked in my statements to the court that it be included in my testimony.

This accusation failed: the ministers agreed that it was without foundation. New ones, thus, had to be found, and they thought they had found them in the action I had taken on the decree of the council, forbidding the secret printing of new remonstrances of parlement against M. d'Aiguillon. His Majesty was given to understand that I had had the notices of the decree seized. I was summoned to Versailles: you, Monseigneur, and the vice chancellor, reproached me on the dubious grounds that the decree bore the inscription (which was usual, regardless of what action was taken): "taking absolute precedence."

It was easy for me to prove to both of you that I was being charged on the basis of suppositions, it was sufficient for me to hand over to you my formal conclusions, which only required that the irregular notice be stricken from the records. I gave you a memorandum on this subject to be presented to His Majesty; I gave a similar one to the

1. [Charles-Alexandre Calonne (1734-1802) was the son of the first president of the Parlement of Flanders, and in 1758 himself became the attorney-general of that body. In 1766 he was named intendant of Metz, and in 1778 intendant of Flanders. His role in the commission made responsible for investigating the case of La Chalotais and his fellow magistrates at Saint-Malo earned him the lifelong hatred of the parlements. He is best known to historians for his tenure as comptroller-general (1783-87). His radical plans for financial reforms were thwarted by the resistance of the privileged orders, and Louis XVI dismissed him.—Ed.]

ministers which M. de Calonne again did not allow to be presented. The parlement, in a letter to the king, fully exonerated my conduct, and all were forced to admit that they had been duped. I say this to you, Monseigneur; I call to witness the Duke de Choiseul, M. the Vice-Chancellor, M. the Comptroller-General.

Thus this second accusation was as unsuccessful as the first; still I stayed five months at Versailles with three other magistrates of parlement who, it was said, had been summoned for remonstrances against M. d'Aiguillon: these are three of those who are involved in the same trial as I, and who are presently being held at the château of Saint-Malo.

During this time I had to *convince* the parlement not to suspend its functions. The comptroller-general knows the fidelity with which I carried out this task and how much I compromised myself on this occasion. Even M. de Calonne, who was involved in one part of the negotiations, cannot deny this.

On our return to Brittany at the end of March 1765, my son and I did all we possibly could to persuade the parlement to resume its functions according to the will of the king and not to resign the following May! I could cite M. the F. P. himself to attest to these facts, but I take the liberty to cite more particularly the comptroller-general whom I kept informed of all the difficulties we went through daily in this business, until we had compromised ourselves more than once with several members of the parlement. He knows that perfectly well, and I am convinced that he would be glad to attest to it.

After the resignations, I began to keep continually to my office; and for seven months before and after them, I didn't leave more than seven times, seeing very few people, and not having seen even three times those persons with whom I have been accused of being in league.

Around St. Martin's Day arose the possibility of reconvening the parlement; I drew up a rather long discourse outlining the most compelling reasons for it to resume its functions. I was arrested on St. Martin's eve with my son; and my discourse, which M. the intendant had seized in my office, was confiscated by M. de Calonne, although I asked several times in my statements that it be returned as exonerating evidence which belonged to me.

These have been, Monseigneur, all of my crimes; this is why my son and I are being held in a castle, treated by the military as inhumanly as in the prisons of the Inquisition.

I ask what we could be accused of; and I ask that M. de Calonne—who came not to find the truth but to condemn us, who would consider himself lacking if he did not find us guilty (as he has imprudently admitted to gain favor at the court)—draw up a list of accusations against us, and offer to undergo our punishment if they are not true; this is the least of the penalties which foolhardy and calumnious accusations deserve.

You do not believe, Monseigneur, that I wrote or that I sent to you those anonymous letters, put together by a hired forger; no, you can't believe it. I hope you still have a better opinion of me than that. Come now! could I have written these vile letters, as silly as they are insolent, supporting the resignations to which I had always firmly declared myself opposed? Would I have sent them to you, written with my own hand but disguising my handwriting, to your office where there are two hundred original letters from me? You couldn't think me crazy or stupid enough—because I would have to have been both at the same time—for that. But I have offered my head if anyone can prove it, and I still make the offer.

M. de Calonne—having obtained several notes which I wrote at the castle of the Bull dealing with an incomplete excerpt of the indictment made against us at Rennes, notes which had been seized from my pockets along with several other papers and receipts (of which, incidentally, an inventory has never been made)—concluded directly that I must have admitted to the part which I had had in the letters because I didn't mention them in these notes. I demonstrated exactly the opposite in my replies: I said that the real reason was that I didn't imagine at the time that I was suspected of having written the letters, and that in truth I had only learned of it in interrogation. Another reason was that the open and secret letters-patent which M. de Calonne specializes in are constructed with so much verbiage that it is impossible to find anything personal in them.

There is yet another thing of which I am accused, and which, as I learned in interrogation, has furnished grounds for the accusation of a supposed conspiracy. M. d'Aiguillon worked three years secretly, through devious methods, to trump up these charges and this project was brought to perfection by M. de Calonne. This, as I also learned, is supposed to have been the starting point of all our imagined criminal intrigues: the knot which held them together.

This was a trip which we are supposed to have made, the count of Kerguézec and I, to visit the Marquess de la Roche, at the Castle of Boschet, a week before the convocation of the Estates of Nantes— and a plan between this gentleman and me to unite our opposition in order to ensure the failure of the demands which M. d'Aiguillion was to make in the name of the king at the estates (demands of which it was impossible that I had the least knowledge). I know that the king had already been told this lie in the month of December 1764, and the comptroller-general did me the honor of speaking to me about it then at Versailles. I easily destroyed this charge by maintaining (which was the truth) that I had never set foot in the castle of Boschet with M. de Kerguézec, at that time or any other. I maintained this equally in my statements; I demanded that they question people who had been with me at the time and the people who had been with me for the three preceding months. I demanded this of M. de Calonne, but he didn't ask anyone; I don't even believe that M. de Kerguézec was interrogated.

Now they want to bring up this unbelievable story against me again and give it the appearance of truth by corrupting one single witness, the wife of a certain trooper of the constabulary. She was made to testify that she had heard one of the chambermaids of one of my daughters say that she had heard her mistress (whom I had summoned from Versailles) say that the Count of Saint-Florentin had discussed with me all the arrangements which M. de Kerguézec and I had made at Boschet. You know, Monseigneur, that you never said anything to me at Versailles or anywhere else about this mythical journey, and that consequently I have never been able to cite your testimony in this matter. Finally in my statements, I maintained the same thing and I have consented to be considered convicted on all counts if this particular one can ever be proved against me.

How could you fail, Monseigneur, to find all this clear, and to find my answers to the indiscriminate allegations of M. de Calonne sufficient?

.   .   .   .

I admit, Monseigneur, that I have complained of certain persons and even ministers who have tried to deprive me of the good graces of the king. But I would not be worthy of his graces if I did not fear to lose them or did not regret their loss. And to whom did I make these complaints? To my son, in private letters which I did not write to be seen or to be divulged, and which wouldn't have been if they hadn't been seized in his office where they were gathering dust. Furthermore, M. de Calonne has made a misleading exhibit by selecting only some letters and avoiding those written at Nantes in which I instructed my son to do everything he could for the success of the demands of the king at the estates, to spare no pains, no cares, no

efforts in this and to do it for the love of the king. I have demanded
several times in my statements that these letters be exhibited along
with the others, and I believe that my son has demanded the same
thing; but M. de Calonne is still keeping them hidden. I don't know
what he has done with them, but he ought to know that it is the duty
of a public minister to present evidence favorable as well as unfavorable to the accused.

Should anyone be condemned for his own secret thoughts? And does
not what is written without being divulged come under this heading?
In society every man's own home ought to be his refuge, as M. de
Montesquieu says; and when I complain about something in a private
conversation, are these complaints, within my own family, a crime
against the state?

Furthermore—when was it that I complained about certain of the
ministers who were trying to deprive me of the good graces of the
king and about you, Monseigneur (for I admit that it was you almost
solely that these complaints concerned)?

It was during the time that I was at Versailles, working with all my
might, as the comptroller-general knows, to obtain peace, when you
were doing your best to deprive us of fire and water if that were possible, when I told you (and you may remember this) that I would
have liked nothing better than to withdraw to my office and wash my
hands of the whole affair. (M. de Calonne ought to remember too, for
I had written just this in one of the letters which he has confiscated.)
This was a time when, having been well treated one year before, as
you know, and having received flattering evidences of the favor of the
king, I was suddenly ill-received by persons whose favor I might possibly have had the right to anticipate, but from whom I could at least
have expected justice.

. . . .

These have been, Monseigneur, all of the counts of the accusation
which has been brought against us. After these trivial explanations
which I have gone into in great detail, I would like to ask you if there
has been the slightest shadow of crime or of harassment in all my
conduct and in that of my son. For a few imprisonments of common
lawbreakers and of prostitutes, made on the recommendation of the
police commissioners, can hardly be considered harassment.

Nevertheless, although the two slanderous accusations which were
brought to the very foot of the throne were unsuccessful, we are still
treated like criminals. First, without any right or any reason, we were

deprived of our liberty: we have been held captive for eight months. The arrest of men of position, gentlemen, office-holders, was made without any crime having been proved; for whatever M. de Calonne says, an expert's report does not constitute proof of a crime: when it is alone it means very little; when it is extrajudiciary it means nothing; when it agrees with an arbitrary authority it is suspect. They have been trying to drive us insane by this long and harsh imprisonment, by inhuman and cruel treatment; they have been trying to deprive us of our honor, our property and our lives.

Knowing that I have had weak lungs for thirty years, they have put scaffolding outside of my window to cut off the air. The vapours of tallow, of pepper, of sulphur, and of tar from the port of St. Malo caused me to collapse twice this spring. I have contracted in these accursed castles an ailment caused by retaining my urine after emitting a bloody secretion. For three months you have seen the certificates of doctors attesting to this and you haven't paid the slightest attention. A man of my age—after thirty-six years of service—Ah! Monseigneur, this is unbelievable! I would never believe this of you if I were not going through it.

I protest against the illegal harshness with which my son and I are daily treated by your order or by the order of M. d'Aiguillon, our opponent and our denouncer.

The notaries I asked for to draw up legal documents were denied to me by your order. We are being kept under closer security— counter to the implication of the laws which say that after interrogation the accused are to be allowed to confer with anyone they please. All of the commissioners were of this opinion including M. de Calonne. M. le Noir, the court secretary told me this at the time. The military, by whose order I do not know, opposed it although they had no right to. You know that by both divine and human laws, to augment a sentence is a crime worthy of punishment.

We are deprived of every means of defence; I can defend myself only by making accusations and that would evidently be, according to M. de Calonne, a crime against the state. You will probably make the contents of my letter known to him; this I consent to. His accusations are too obviously unjust for me to fear his answers: those are arrows which could only wound in the dark. He has been the mere mechanical instrument of an arbitrary power; but by his blundering he has compromised the king's authority and yours also. I do not know whether he has since surrendered those pieces of evidence which he had kept from the trial. If so he should have notified me of this, for I have asked for copies from the intendant who has promised them but has not had them made. I do not know, but perhaps they have been suppressed entirely.

As for the present, unfortunately, I can come to nobody but you: I would gladly have had you for a judge, Monseigneur, if you had not yourself had an interest in the matter; and I would have wished that you had not been my accuser and prosecutor in that you furnished evidence against me.

Our accusation was trumpeted all over France with publicity and uproar. It is to my interest that our vindication be made public: also I owe it to myself, and to my family; I owe it to the entire magistracy of the kingdom. I am asking permission of His Majesty to have one given to him; it ought also to be presented to the ministers, to my judges, to the public, to the whole nation which has known of my distress.

I entreat you not to take offence if I am forced to complain about you. I will try to forget neither the respect which I owe you nor several of your past favors for which I am grateful. I will never forget them and I would have liked to be able to preserve the friendship I have long felt for you: it is painful for me to forget it.

I have had the honor to give you my thanks at Versailles in the presence of M. de Livry, and I must say that one of the things which has been the most painful for me has been the harsh way in which you received them, especially at Compiègne.

You have made my case, Monseigneur, your very own affair, because it concerned M. d'Aiguillon, your nephew; and that ought to have been a reason for you to keep out of it.

But, Monseigneur, if you continue with M. d'Aiguillon to give orders and to solicit in the name of the king against us, then there is no use in deceiving His Majesty, in compromising his royal dignity, in contradicting his humane and gracious nature, in order to persuade him to abandon his role as sovereign judge of the nation and assume the role of prosecutor in a capital case (this I don't believe, it would simply be too inconceivable) against his own subjects, against his magistrates, against the attorneys-general.

There was no use in going through so much work dissolving and reconvening the parlement, and in choosing, dismissing, intimidating, and seducing judges all under the cover of the august name of His Majesty.

There was especially no use in instituting, as M. d'Aiguillon did long ago, the vile network of spies with which he has filled the cities and towns, which he has spread throughout almost all the orders and organizations of the province.

For we will bring our heads to the feet of His Majesty; he will do whatever he deems just with us and with our lives. Our honor only he cannot touch.

I am, Monseigneur, your etc.

Signed, DE CARADEUC DE LA CHALOTAIS
from the Castle of Saint-Malo, June 18, 1766

Selections from the Correspondence of Voltaire
From Etienne Noël Damilaville

July 31, 1766

Here, my most illustrious master, are some new *mémoires* for the history of the splendors of this century. In truth horror redoubles from one moment to the next. Yesterday it was children twenty years old sacrificed to fanaticism, greed, envy; today it is an old man of sixty-five whom slander hurls, loaded with chains, into the dungeons. His age, his talents, his virtues, his merit, his services, his public reputation avail him nothing. On the contrary all this only arouses the rage of the wicked and the good man is called a criminal. It is said that the king has read these *mémoires* which made me shed tears of blood. I don't believe it because M. de la Chalotais has been arrested on the denunciation of his accusers and [if the king had read them] no doubt they would now be defending themselves against his accusation if justice were done to the guilty. This reciprocity is, it seems to me, part of natural and civil equity. In any case, tell me, after you have read these writings, if any action in life, even the most innocent and virtuous, can safely be done. Who is there who, alone in his chamber, will not tremble at a knock? Who will dare write to his son, his father, his friend? O unhappy humankind, to what fate are you condemned? It is unbelievable good fortune that the *mémoire* of M. de la Chalotais could pierce the walls of his prison and reach the public. It has created a terrible sensation; there is no one who does not bewail his fate, and I dare to hope that this effect can change his fate. O Calonne, where will you hide the infamy with which your treason must cover you?

Damilaville's letter is translated and reprinted with the permission of the editor and publisher from Theodore Besterman, ed., *Voltaire's Correspondence*, 107 vols. (Geneva: Institut et Musée Voltaire, 1953-65), LXII, 82-84. The source for the remaining three letters in this section is Voltaire's *Oeuvres complètes*, XLIV, 377-78, 383-84, 510.

Who can ever repair the injuries and misfortunes which the good man has undergone? What monsters men are! how I counsel them still to boast of their superiority over the other animals! . . .

I embrace you, my most illustrious friend, with as much grief as respect and tenderness. All our brothers do the same.

To d'Alembert

[*Ca.* August 10, 1766]

You can well imagine, my true philosopher, how my blood boiled when I read that *mémoire* written with a toothpick, that toothpick is cutting its way to immortality. Woe to him to whom reading that pamphlet does not give a fever. It must at least make the . . . and the . . . and the . . . die of apoplexy. Don't you admire the nicknames which the stupid populace gives to certain people! What it means is that on all sides is a contest to see who will cover himself with more horror and infamy. I pity you for being where you are. You can say to me, *ubicumque calculam ponas ibi naufragium invenies.*

You have ties, pensions, you are enchained. As for me I shall die soon, and I shall die detesting the country of apes and tigers where the folly of my mother caused me to be born almost seventy-three years ago. I ask you as a favor to write yourself to the King of Prussia and to paint everything for him with your brush. I have strong reasons for wanting him to know to what an extent we deserve to be scorned. One of the great misfortunes of honest people is that they are cowards. They bewail themselves and fall silent, they go to dinner and forget. I thank you in advance for the thunderbolts with which you will crush the Jansenists. It is good to tread upon the basilisk after having crushed the serpent underfoot. Have the pleasure of pulverizing the monsters without risking yourself. Geneva is a ridiculous bedlam but at least such horrors don't happen here. They wouldn't burn a young man here over two songs composed eighty years ago. Rousseau is nothing but a madman and an empty windbag. Farewell, I honor you with justice and love you with tenderness.

Let us keep our pain and indignation to ourselves; let us preserve the secrecy of our hearts.

From d'Alembert

Paris, August 11 [1766]

As far as I know there is nothing new, my dear and illustrious master, on the atrocious and absurd affair of Abbeville. It is only reported— but this is nothing but a rumor—that young Moinel, who had re-

mained in prison, and who is sixteen years old, has been condemned
by the Torquemadas of Abbeville to be *censured,* with regard to which
I beg you first of all to note the cruelty of this sentence, which declares
infamous a poor child who deserved at the most to be whipped at
school, and second to contemplate the singular variation in the sentences which these Busirises in robes, as you so properly call them,
have pronounced against young men who were all equally guilty: the
first burned at the stake, the second beheaded, the third censured. I
hope that the fourth will be commended. I wish to say no more of
this abomination, which makes odious for me the country where it
was committed.

You know that there are at present eighty-three Jesuits at Rennes,
no more, and that these scoundrels, as you can imagine, are not going
to sleep in the affair of M. de la Chalotais. He has been transferred to
Rennes, and apparently will soon be tried. His *mémoire* has won over
public opinion entirely, and makes his persecutors look despicable;
Laubardemont de Calonne[1] especially (for so he has been called)
will not recover from the infamous reputation he has gotten; this is
what I have heard the wisest and most respectable people say.

Another idiocy (for we are rich in that sort of thing) which is attracting much public attention is the argument between Jean-Jacques
and Mr. Hume. . . . Farewell, my dear master, how many fools and
villains there are in this best of all possible worlds! I embrace you
ex animo.

To Madame de Florian

November 24 [1766]

My dear niece and dear nephews, does Mme de Florian still have gout
in her three writing fingers, and can she never show the slightest sign
of life to an uncle who loves her tenderly? As for you, Monsieur her
husband, you are another matter; you answer regularly, you give news
to those far away, your letters are instructive.

And you, my dear big nephew, who are now buried up to your neck
in land charters, lend me your help and your knowledge to resist some
ifs of monks who are trying to oppress Mama Denis and me. When
you have a deliberative vote in the first class of the parlement of
France, put together for me a first-rate cabal against all these *ifs* of
monks; relieve us of this vermin which is gnawing at the kingdom;

1. [Laubardemont was a notorious seventeenth-century hanging judge, the creature
of Cardinal Richelieu. It was said of him that three handwritten lines were enough
to convince him of the guilt of the defendant before him.—Ed.]

stick a big needle [*donnez des grands coups d'aiguillon*] in the skinny
backside of the Abbé de Chauvelin. It's not much to ask; it was not
enough to drive out the Jesuits, who at least educated young people,
if we still have bloodsuckers who are good for nothing except getting
fat on our blood. . . .

I embrace you all three with all the force of my heart, and with
my long and feeble arms.

Selection from the Diary of the Duke de Croÿ

On the twenty-fourth of November [1766] I went to spend two days
at Grosbois, at the home of M. de Moras, and had a wonderful time
with the good hunting of all sorts of game and the good company of
my fellow sportsmen.

M. de Quincy arrived there, having come the day before from the
famous extraordinary council at which the king ordered that the case
of M. de la Chalotais (the only one, at that time, of which people
were talking) would be judged by the Conseil des Parties by all the
maîtres des requêtes, even the honorary and retired ones.

This was an assertion of authority of the strongest kind.

If the court had its way, this would become a new tribunal which
could gain ascendancy and deprive the parlements, and especially the
Paris one, of their authority. Thus, this in a sense changed the nature
of the case, making it the affair of all the parlements, which all seemed
to be up in arms.

If the court gave in, it would lose more and more of its authority,
being continually defeated by reason of the kind of steps it was compelled to take. Thus this affair—the only one attracting attention at
this time—came to be one of the utmost gravity.

The parlement, regarding the case as fundamental for the laws of
the kingdom, claimed that the king could not have a member [of a
parlement] tried by anyone but his colleagues, who were his proper
judges. The court took the opposite view and claimed in particular that
the servants of the king [including La Chalotais] depended only upon
His Majesty.

The king, weary, hoping to avoid a *lit de justice,* and wanting to

Translated and reprinted with the permission of the publisher from the *Journal
inédit du Duc de Croÿ,* 3 vols., edited by the Vicomte de Grouchy and Paul Cottin
(Paris: E. Flammarion, 1906-7), II, 235-39.

make an attempt to get out of the whole business, summoned his whole Parlement [of Paris] to Versailles. It was, I think, on December 16 that they came. The king forbade them to interfere further in the case. Upon which, the parlement drew up some verbal objections. A postponement was sought. The king granted it, repeating what he had said, whereupon the parlement drew up even more strongly worded remonstrances.

On December 21, I saw the first president arrive to ask another postponement. The king replied that he would again summon his whole parlement for the next day. All this was decided only after very long committees and councils. . . .

December 22, 1766, was a very remarkable day (I was at that time staying at Versailles to keep an eye on my prospects for a regiment.) At ten o'clock in the morning, without anyone's expecting it, the king came down to the meeting of the royal Privy Council or Conseil des Parties at which a place is always provided for him, since theoretically he is always regarded as being present. It was a Monday, the ordinary day for the meeting of this council, and, during the night, all the *conseillers d'État* and *maîtres des requêtes* had been summoned. The king ordered M. Le Noir to report on the affair of M. de la Chalotais, as if to judge it on the spot; after which he said: "I am very satisfied with the report you have made on this case! It confirms my decision to bring it to an end. I do not want any verdict rendered; my intention is that all the indictments and procedures be quashed and suppressed. Therefore I order that letters-patent to that effect be drawn up, and I charge my vice-chancellor to have them published in the Great Council. . . ."

Returning upstairs, he held a Great Council, while in the meantime the parlement arrived. I had never seen this ceremony. I now saw it with my own eyes and found it very instructive. The parlement, which had been convened early in the morning, and had received the summons, came in about fifty carriages, all traveling together in line, at a slow pace. There were no honors or ceremony at their arrival. They got out, like everyone else, in the Courtyard of the Princes, and went to wait below, where the Grand-master of Ceremonies received them in the Halls of the Council, while all their carriages were drawn up at the side of the Courtyard of the Ministers, behind the guard (who had come in because the king was going to go hunting) and the horses were not unhitched.

After the council had gone on for two hours, about one o'clock in the afternoon the king called for the parlement. It came in, led by M. de Saint-Florentin, secretary of state for Paris, and the grand-master of ceremonies, preceded by six of their ushers. . . .

I counted one hundred and thirty-six people in judicial robes, in all, and wanting to see what would happen, I pushed so far forward, though no one was supposed to follow them in, that I was close enough for the usher to allow me passage; but the door remained open, as is the custom in a public session.

The king was as usual in his armchair near the fireplace at the rear of his bedchamber. He took off his hat as they entered, then put it on again and gave them his orders or his answer, which he read as if speaking it from memory. He spoke with as much nobility as firmness, and always with an air of politeness. Behind his chair, and on both sides, were his great officers and his council, while the parlement stood in a circle in front of him, the first president in front.

I admit that this spectacle deeply moved me; this sort of ceremony is always very imposing.

The king said to them: "I wished to learn, by the investigation which I ordered, the source and the development of the troubles which have arisen in my province of Brittany. The account which has just been given me has led me to decide not to allow the whole procedure to go any further. I do not wish to find a guilty party. I am going to have letters-patent sent on my own authority to annul, with the plenitude of my power, all indictments and accusations in this regard. Above all I impose the most absolute silence, and, moreover, I shall restore neither my confidence nor my good graces to my two attorneys-general [La Chalotais and his son] of my Parlement of Brittany, whom I think it wise to keep at a distance from that province. This is my answer to your representations. My parlement should not have lacked confidence in my good will. It should never forget that the spirit of good sense will always regulate my usage of my authority."

After which, the king removed his hat, and each member of the parlement bowed and withdrew.

This is what happened on that remarkable day, about which everyone will have his own opinion.

However, as soon as that affair had been virtually terminated by the full authority of the king, he had M. de La Chalotais and the others removed from the Bastille, and sent him, with his son, also an attorney-general, into exile at Saintes, an act which provoked their family to make a great outcry, demanding a verdict and complaining that to refuse the justice which the king owes to his subjects was to continue to dishonor them; everyone had an opinion on the question depending on which side he was on. But if the affair could end there, the king could not have taken a firmer decision to maintain his authority.

The day after this decision, the Duke de la Trémoille left with his wife to preside over the estates, as president of the nobility . . . and the Duke d'Aiguillon went again to convene the estates as commander-in-chief of the province. The Duke de la Trémoille succeeded beautifully at first, . . . but, later there was plenty of trouble: the Bretons gladly granted the money asked, but made many efforts to restore M. de la Chalotais and the former parlement.

MM. de la Chalotais meanwhile were more at ease than people thought, and so was the Parlement [of Paris] which contented itself with drawing up some remonstrances, and then turned its fire on the ecclesiastics. Thus, this long and singular affair was at a standstill for the time being, and the court seemed to have come out of it less badly than usual. In general, since the step the king had taken in going suddenly to the parlement to speak firmly to it, and since he had been making his own decisions, he seemed to possess more firmness, and his authority was a little bit strengthened.

Supplication of the Corporation of Merchants of the City of Rennes

Presented to Their Worships of the Estates-General of Brittany on February 1, 1767

Their Worships, the Estates of Brittany,

The community of the merchants of Rennes humbly entreats you, SAYING that the state of collapse and of exhaustion to which the commerce of this city has found itself reduced during the last two years authorizes it to seek recourse in your authority, Your Worships, to be relieved of all or of a part of its contributions to the taxes. Up until the present moment it has completely satisfied its obligations and would continue to do so if the present misfortunes had not placed it in the most deplorable of situations and in an almost complete inability

The two "Supplications," Maupeou's "Answer," the "Petitions of the Order of Nobility" and the "Testimony of the Diverse Orders of the Province of Brittany" on this and the following pages have all been translated and reprinted from contemporary pamphlets.

to bear its share of the public burden. The community does not exaggerate in saying this, kind sirs; to convince you of the truth of its claims, it has need of nothing but a simple observation.

The chief commerce of Rennes, which has provided the subsistence of the members of the community of merchants, and has enabled them to pay their share of public expenses, has always been in retail sales of diverse merchandise to their fellow citizens and to the strangers who are daily drawn by their affairs to the parlement. But this commerce has been considerably diminished since the unhappy days of the resignation of Their Worships of the parlement. The citizens of all the orders, especially those whom this event first affected, have ever since then been more occupied with their misery than with providing for themselves. The absence of the greater portion of the magistrates who resigned has reduced the number of consumers; the flow of strangers into the city has stopped completely and has never resumed; and thus the chief trade of the community is languid and sickly.

On the other hand, each member of the community has been obliged to contribute to payment of the common debt, to pay the *capitation,* to pay for raw materials and to pay personal debts previously contracted by the purchase of stock now uselessly lying in stores and warehouses.

In these circumstances the community hopes, Your Worships, that you will heed the petitions of citizens bowed beneath the weight of public misfortune; and that you will consequently excuse it from the totality or from the greater part of the taxes to which it is subjected, until a happier day will return the city of Rennes to the affluence it enjoyed during the existence of the whole parlement. The restoration of this august body would restore the country to its ancient splendor, and would renew the sources of commerce and of public felicity. The community can do nothing but wish for so happy an event. It is up to you, Your Worships, to the fathers of our country to solicit this favor of the monarch who governs us. You can obtain it out of the goodness of his heart through the sentiments of love and fidelity which you bear for his sacred person. (Signed etc.)

Supplications of the Lawyers of the Parlement of Rennes to the King

Sire,

The lawyers of the Parlement of Brittany would be betraying the confidence of their fellow citizens if they were to hesitate any longer in bringing to the attention of Your Majesty the misfortunes which afflict their country. The cries of need, kept at first within the family, are breaking out everywhere; they can no longer be hidden. Our concern carries them to the feet of the throne in these humble supplications which we dare to address to Your Majesty for the restoration of the entirety of the members of your parlement.

After a cruel war which has ruined the ports of Brittany and destroyed all the branches of her commerce, we saw new subjects of dissension arise whose fatal consequences are still making themselves felt. We have seen our magistrates scattered, exiled, some of them even subjected to all the rigors of a criminal prosecution.

It is not our business, Sire, to divine the original causes of these events; but we perceive their end in the declaration which His Majesty has just made, that, "the honor of our magistrates has not been at all compromised." [answer of the king to the Parlement of Paris, January 21, 1767]. If, then, those who were thought to have been suspect are not guilty, how can any of the others be reproached?

They only resigned from their posts because they feared they could not reconcile what they owed to the interests of the province with the sentiments of respect, submission, and love for the sacred person of Your Majesty with which they were filled.

This act has not changed their zeal and loyalty; and we assume that Your Majesty has found nothing which ought to deprive them of your confidence, because you have since decided to restore to your parlement a portion of these same magistrates who abdicated along with them. All the resignations were handed in in the same spirit, for the same and unique reason; how can Your Majesty justly make a distinction among those who resigned which seems to incriminate some and vindicate others?

It is only too obvious that the very small number of magistrates who have been recalled and even the sixty established by your edict of November 1765 cannot suffice for the needs of the nation.

If your Parlement of Brittany at its creation was composed of only 36 magistrates, 4 presidents and 32 councilors, the insufficiency of this number was soon recognized: in the space of about 40 years, the volume of affairs demanded new creations.

In 1581 the number of magistrates had risen to 84
                                    in 1598 to   86
                                    in 1637 to   96
                                    in 1689 to   107
                                    in 1704 to   126

Unfortunately all of these additions provided only tardily and by degree a court adequate to the needs which had made them necessary. What sufficed at the end of the sixteenth century no longer sufficed in the middle of the following century; and the growth in the volume of affairs since that time demands an even greater number of judges.

This truth cannot be denied even if no comparisons are made. The prosperity of these last reigns, in augmenting the wealth of the state, has necessarily augmented the objects of legal contention.

Even the most hardworking and zealous magistrate has to look after his own affairs. Whatever his devotion to the public welfare, his private interests interrupt his official function in spite of himself. He does not cease to be the father of a family and to be responsible for the conservation of his fortune. Thus the personal affairs of some, the age and infirmities of others, and any number of other necessary or accidental causes is diminishing their number and slowing down service.

Brittany, Sire, is one of the greatest provinces of your kingdom: four presidencies, twenty-five royal jurisdictions, seven seats of admiralty, five consulates, five masters of waters and forests, fourteen customs jurisdictions, and over four thousand seigneurial jurisdictions —such is the dominion of the parlement of a maritime, agricultural, and commercial province; and besides these conventional areas it has many special duties.

.   .   .   .

Sixty magistrates cannot suffice to fulfill Your Majesty's responsibility to render justice to all your subjects; it is evident that the very few whom Your Majesty has recalled are absolutely powerless to satisfy these wide responsibilities.

The restoration of one portion seemed to herald some sort of negotiations for the return of the entire group. More than a year has gone by, and far from seeing the number of magistrates grow, we see it shrinking every day: death has carried off some of them; others are absent due to sickness, personal affairs, and other reasons; there remains only a very small number to perform the numerous and laborious functions of the magistracy.

This eminent station (the magistracy) is a sort of militia or a priesthood which exacts great tribulations and requires great virtues. The magistracy does not come into being all at once; it can only acquire the knowledge and qualifications which it needs through long study and experience, through long meditation upon the laws, through the examples of the wisdom of the ancients which teach principles and maxims. We will not see an adequate professional body until the very far distant future, unless the totality of the magistrates who compose it is recalled. And cases are piling up all the time: the inventory of trials which were waiting almost a year ago stood at over ten thousand, and since that time the number has grown considerably. Whatever the small number of recalled magistrates may undertake, their zeal cannot exceed the limits of the possible. This obstacle to the entire administration of justice has brought the ruin of the capital of the province, reduced now to a very limited retail trade; Rennes, scarcely reborn from the ashes of war, has no other means of subsistence than to serve the people who come here in search of justice. For two years we have seen the city practically deserted. Victim of a series of disasters, the city has seen its losses multiply practically every day. At the same time the burden of taxes has not diminished; indeed it has grown because of the necessity of replacing losses, and the burden is becoming more and more onerous as the number of those able to contribute shrinks. The surcharge will soon rise to the point where it will be impossible to meet it.

All of the corporations are suffering, advocates, bailiffs, notaries, merchants and others, each in proportion to its station. The decline of each one necessarily affects the others; all lament that they cannot make their cries heard at the feet of the throne of Your Majesty.

. . . .

The most essential duty of the lawyers has always been to make heard the voice of truth; this duty becomes all the more sacred when they have just reason to fear the slightest decline in the administration of justice. Their silence could only be a species of prevarication, and the same oath which destines them to the defence of the poor and the oppressed, obliges them even more to do their utmost to prevent public and general distress.

Faithful to these principles and full of confidence in the royal promise which guarantees to all your subjects the right so natural and so consoling of recourse to their sovereign, we dare, Sire, to hope that the paternal bounty of Your Majesty will not reject the humble and respectful supplications which we have believed it our duty to address to Your Majesty, we your humble, obedient, loyal, loving and submissive subjects and servants,

THE LAWYERS OF YOUR COURT OF PARLEMENT
Rennes, Saturday, the 7th of February, 1767

Answer of M. de Maupeou, Keeper of the Seals, Vice-Chancellor, Addressed to M. Eveu, President of the Order of Lawyers at Rennes

Versailles, February 14, 1767

I have received, Monsieur, with your letter of the eighth of this month the deliberations of your order of last January 31, and the petition which it has believed it its duty to make to the king as a consequence of these deliberations. His Majesty will not waver in the execution of his edict of November 1765; and he can but disapprove of the action taken by your order in asking its revocation. I am, Monsieur,

Yours truly,

signed
DE MAUPEOU

[This answer of M. de Maupeou was read at the assembly of February 21, and it was decreed that a new petition would be addressed to the king on the part of the order. This new petition was approved by the assembly on March 7.]

Petitions of the Order of Nobility to the King, in the Hall of the Estates of Brittany at Rennes, Enacted April 21, 1767

Following the decision taken by the order of nobility on April 3, by which it proposed a respectful petition concerning His Majesty's order of March 30, delivered on the first of this month, the said order of nobility has decreed that it most humbly petitions His Majesty:

1. That the accusation of resistance to the will of the king which has been brought against this order fills it with the greatest grief; that it can regard this new charge only as the result of the scheme, originated in the estates of 1764 and perseveringly pursued ever since, to

disgrace the order in the eyes of His Majesty. That, believing itself obliged to give an example of obedience and loyalty to the other orders of the state, this order is far from desirous of resisting the will of the king; that it is more important to this order than to either of the others to defend and maintain the royal authority, because the higher positions of state have been conferred upon it since the establishment of the monarchy, and thus any resistance or threat to the power of His Majesty lessens the dignity and prerogatives of the nobility. That, although this order seems to be retarding the execution of the momentary wishes of His Majesty, this can only be intended to make known to him the harm which these wishes would bring to his true grandeur, which is necessarily united with the tranquility of his provinces, with the happiness of his peoples, with the preservation of the laws. That resistance such as the present resistance ought doubtless to be very rare even for the most compelling reasons; but that the plight of this province shows its necessity. . . .

3. That the order of nobility, in seeking to bring to His Majesty, in a solemn deputation, its humble petition concerning the state, the present administration of justice in Brittany, is only following the usual practice of the estates when the commissioners of His Majesty have not been given sufficient authority to receive the petitions of these estates. That their registers testify to several deputations formed for infinitely less important reasons. That, because the present state of the province requires the most rapid aid possible, the order of nobility feels it necessary to solicit this aid by all of the means allowed to good and loyal subjects. The order of nobility, far from having ignored the usages and customs of the estates, has stayed within the limits of the deepest respect and more entire confidence in the bounty and justice of His Majesty, in requesting a grace which the estates have always enjoyed when the commissioners of the king have not been authorized to handle their petitions. That there is no lack of examples for His Majesty to consider of diverse deputations sent by the estates after deliberation, always received graciously and terminating in the happiest success; and that His Majesty is very humbly begged to take this into account. That the aforesaid order has been forced to combine its petition of recourse to the sovereign with its opinions concerning the requests of His Majesty. That in any other matter the weight of the two other orders would have prevailed over this petition; that it is thus necessary to explain to His Majesty the reasons for the perseverance of the nobility in its opinion. That all the tribunals of the kingdom have felt the repercussions of the accusations, the intrigues,

the plots and the leagues (supposedly) formed in Brittany against the
interests of His Majesty; that, among the things which have come to
the attention of the judges who have looked into this great affair, one
of the most important has been an agreement between distinguished
members of the nobility and of the parlement to oppose the demands
made by His Majesty to the last Estates of Nantes; and that the opposition to the tax of two sous on the livre and all that arose out of it
has been attributed to this supposed intrigue. That the order of nobility
is well aware of the necessity to wipe out all the traces of so public and
so injurious a slur upon its love for His Majesty. That, since the efforts
of the nobility at the estates of 1765 to destroy these imputations have
had thus far no success, the nobility owes it today to all of France and
especially to itself to bring to the feet of the throne decisive proof of
its love, its respect, and its loyalty. That the affairs of the province are
important enough to require recourse to the sovereign, since the happiness and the peace of mind of the populace depend upon this, and
this so natural and so consoling right of petition thus became an indispensable necessity when the commissioners of His Majesty were not
authorized to accept the memorandum which the order of nobility
brought them on February 13.

4. That His Majesty is humbly begged to recognize that by the terms
of article 4 of the order of March 30, delivered on the first of April,
the nobility has found itself faced with the absolute impossibility of
deciding definitively for either an acceptance or a refusal of extraordinary [financial] aid.

5. That every time that the momentary and individual wishes of the
king come into conflict with and destroy his edicts, ordinances, declarations, contracts, in a word with his legal wishes, the duty of those of
his subjects who have the honor to represent a part of the nation is to
invoke the laws and to demand respectfully their maintenance and conservation; because it is under the safeguard and the rule of the laws
that the people have always faithfully served their sovereign. That the
deliberations of the 1st, 2nd and 3rd of April undertaken by the order
of nobility concerning the order delivered on the first of the month
were founded on this inalterable and certain principle; that all the
contracts entered into since the union of the duchy and the crown,
indeed that all of the terms of this union, have stipulated and insured
that there is to be no levy of taxes in Brittany without the consent of
the estates; that these solemn promises—preserved in the most authentic of documents and drawn up in accordance with all of the forms
prescribed by the laws of the kingdom—have been rendered powerless

by the order delivered on April 1, which admits the exercise of this national right by the nobility only to destroy it simultaneously by declaring that in case of a refusal His Majesty will simply decree the levy. That under these circumstances the nobility had no other choice but to resort to the goodness and the justice of His Majesty by respectful petition, to take refuge in the law and to invoke, according to time-honored custom, the basic, constitutional foundations of the estates in opposition to a summary order of His Majesty. That the order of nobility cannot imagine that it could be the intention of the best of kings to destroy in a single order a national right, solemnly recognized by His Majesty and by his commissioners in his name. That, obliged by its duty to watch over the conservation of the rights, franchises, and liberties of the province, the order of nobility begs His Majesty please to preserve them in their full extent. . . .

10. For these reasons the order of nobility hopes that His Majesty will be more and more convinced of the subservience of the order to his will, of its devotion to his service, of its zeal for the glory of his reign, and of its respect and of its love for his sacred person. That, taking into consideration the devotion and the loyalty of one of his greatest provinces, he will deign to cast a paternal eye upon the deplorable situation to which it is reduced, to stop the calamities of every kind from which it suffers, to abolish all the causes of the hate, the discord and the disagreement which plague it, to restore peace and quiet there, and to bring back, in accordance with the general wish of a submissive and faithful province, the worthy magistrates who, through their wisdom, their impartiality, their integrity, their devotion to the laws and especially through their loyalty and their zeal in serving His Majesty, have been able to gain the esteem, the confidence, and the devotion of the whole nation.

11. The order of nobility goes so far as to hope that His Majesty would be willing to retract all the orders entered in the registers of the estates, and notably that of March 30, as being absolutely destructive of that liberty which the nobility will never cease to claim as the most precious of its privileges, because it alone can bring to the foot of the throne homage and tribute truly worthy of the best and most cherished of masters.

Testimony of the Diverse Orders of the Province of Brittany, Concerning the Necessity of Restoring the Parlement of Rennes in Its Entirety, as It Was before the Edict of November 1765

Testimony delivered by the nobility as a body in the estates begun December 29, 1766, and still in session May 1767

[The order of the clergy [1] and the third estate having refused to agree to the plan proposed by the nobility to send a deputation to the king to ask him to restore the parlement; on January 15, 1767, the order of the nobility requested the Duke de la Trémoille, its president, to communicate to the Duke d'Aiguillon, as commissioner of the king, the following statement.]

"The order of nobility is fully convinced of its inescapable duty, as a portion of the nation, to bring to the foot of the throne the truth as it sees it and the wishes of the nation concerning the restoration of the entirety of the parlement; a truth which the nobility wishes to get off its conscience, and whose veracity the king must judge sovereignly, according to justice. The order of nobility has all the more right to be heard as can be seen from the letter of the king dated the sixth of this month, addressed to the Duke d'Aiguillon, which he had read to the assembly on the ninth, and which showed that His Majesty has been given an entirely misleading idea of what course of action the nobility desires. The nobility, in demanding the restoration of the entirety of the parlement, is far from demanding the dismissal of subjects recognized as faithful [the twelve magistrates who did not resign]. The

1. No one will be surprised to see that the clergy had not agreed with the other orders in demanding the restoration of the parlement. Since the bishops claim to be independent of any sovereign authority, they would just as soon see all the superior tribunals abolished. The dissolution of the former Society of Jesuits has furnished the prelates of Brittany with new grounds for opposition to the parlement. These prelates are so attached to the Jesuit fathers that, without taking any of the necessary precautions to guarantee the doctrine and the loyalty of these so-justly suspect men, they confide in them all the functions of the holy offices, preferring them to all other priests. As for the deputies of the third estate—since the Duke d'Aiguillon dispenses at will municipal offices and all of the rewards which can fall to this order, it is well known that the deputies have sold themselves to him and that they are willing to sacrifice to him the interests of their country. This is why the Duke d'Aiguillon, who wanted to be the despotic master of the Estates of Brittany, assured of the blind submission of the clergy and of the third estate to his will, had the council issue a decree which ordered, contrary to the most formal rights of the province, that if two orders agreed and the third did not yield within twenty-four hours, the deliberation would be considered closed. The unanimous outcry of the province obliged the annulment of this decree, but this had not stopped the machinations of the despot. [Footnote in the text.]

nobility therefore believes that duty imposes the necessity to let no opportunity whatsoever go by to reach so desirable a goal. And since the orders of the third estate and of the church are opposed to sending a deputation to the commissioners of the king and refuse to recognize the opinion of the nobility and even refuse to put this opinion on the record; the order of the nobility instructs me to protest in the presence of the commissioners of the king against the persistent refusals of the other orders. The nobility instructs me to tell you, Monsieur the Duke, that it is resorting to your good offices as the only means left to get the commission to recognize the requests it is making of the king, to bring its respects and its petitions to the foot of the throne; convinced as always that recourse to the sovereign is the incontestable right of a loyal nation, and that to demand to be heard by the king is not to disobey him."

(The Duke d'Aiguillon answered, first, that the king had forbidden him to receive any requests of the estates concerning the restoration of the parlement; then that one order alone did not have the right to ask a deputation to the king and if the three orders would unite behind this request, then perhaps he could bring it to the attention of the king; finally he maintained that the estates had neither the right, the interest nor the power to ask that the parlement be restored. . . .)

Remonstrances of the Parlement of Paris on the State of the Province of Brittany and on the Situation of MM. de La Chalotais and Consorts

March 18-20, 1768

Sire,

Nothing which concerns the glory of Y. M. and the happiness of your peoples can be regarded as lying outside the concerns of your parlement. The daily exercise of the administration of justice may be confined within the limits of a certain territory, but the responsibility for bringing the truth to the throne knows no limits, it is founded on a devotion which knows none. Remonstrances are neither a verdict nor an assertion of jurisdiction, they are but the expression of fidelity. When the parlement presents supplications to Y. M., it is not a tribunal which is deciding, but a body of the magistracy which implores your good graces, or the depositary of the law which points out to the

Flammermont, ed., *Remontrances,* II, 839-51.

legislator the violations committed against the laws he has himself made. . . .

Public order, Sire, is as indivisible and as universal as the monarchy of which it is the basis and the support; if it is violated in one province it is damaged throughout the kingdom, and the magistrate who implores the justice of the sovereign to persuade him to protect and maintain the liberty of the subjects and the laws of the state, in whatever part of the monarchy they may be violated, never transgresses the limits of his authority; thus he watches over the preservation of the general constitution and acts only for the common good. . . .

Your parlement, Sire, thus would betray your interests if, while order is impaired in the province of Brittany, the liberty of the subjects injured, the rights of the province violated, it should, on the pretext of a distinction of jurisdiction, cease to call for the re-establishment of public order in the monarchy and to support the confidence of a faithful province by continual efforts to enlighten the sovereign's justice.

That a simple citizen without support, without any other resource than his innocence, be accused by a powerful and accredited enemy, is too frequent an event for the honor of humanity; but judges exist for an affair of this kind. The accused finds means of defense in the scrupulous observation of the forms of criminal procedure, and the protection of the law alone, when its exercise remains free in the hands of its depositaries, suffices to make him triumphant over calumny; but, when an entire province is depicted to its sovereign as rebellious, when an entire parlement is accused of having been disloyal, who will speak out in favor of innocence and bring truth to the sovereign? The wisdom of the sovereign would inspire the greatest hope in the accused if they could be sure that his conscience was correctly informed; but if intrigue is so well plotted by the enemies of the public good that the prince cannot discover all their maneuvers, if the parlement is dispersed, if the estates are oppressed, if that part of the nation is refused the consolation of prostrating itself at the feet of the sovereign to bring him both the tribute of its affection and the list of its needs, what resource will remain to faithful subjects unjustly slandered? Under any other prince, despair would become the lot of the oppressed; under Y. M., there remains to them an assured resource, the kindness of your heart; but they cannot hope to feel its effects before your conscience is enlightened by that portion of the magistracy which has access to the throne. Such, Sire, is a faithful depiction both

of the events which have taken place in Brittany and of the present
state of the province.

The assembly of the three estates, as well as the magistracy of
Brittany, that is to say the entire province, have been represented to
you as lacking in the respect and submission which nature has engraved on the heart of every Frenchman for his sovereign; a protest
judicially and legally lodged by the assembly of the three estates in
the records of your parlement of Brittany has been depicted as an
act of revolt against Y. M.; provisional prohibitions dictated by the
fear of seeing violated in your name privileges which Y. M. is certainly eager to preserve have been represented as a struggle for authority. Your parlement, Sire, will not undertake to discuss the limits of
the privileges which Brittany enjoys; it will content itself with pointing
out to you that there can be no crime on the part of the Estates of
Brittany in claiming that privileges exist, and that, if they extend them
further than they should be extended, only enemies of the nation
would attribute to a spirit of revolt, in that case, what could only be
an involuntary error. . . .

Your parlement, which owes you the whole truth and which would
regard itself as culpable if it left you in ignorance of anything which
might affect your justice and the glory of your reign, cannot help
representing to you, finally, that this conduct, whether by the estates
of the province, or by your Parlement of Brittany, is not the real cause
of the disgrace which they are undergoing. The enemies of the magistracy have seized this opportunity to destroy it, and to render suspect
to Y. M., if possible, all the parlements of your kingdom; they [the
parlements] have all equally incurred the hatred of the enemies of
the good, by prohibiting that proud and intriguing society which has
been judged in the greater part of Europe to be both the enemy of all
legitimate powers and incompatible with the tranquillity of all states.
Among the proofs of fidelity which the magistrates charged with public
office in the different parlements had all equally given Y. M. in the examination of the rules, mentality, and acts of that society, the magistrates of
Brittany and Provence had attracted the attention of the public in the
most precise fashion; thus the maneuvers of the hidden friends of that
prohibited society were directed with the greatest care against them;
both would have been attacked at the same time; the circumstances
were not equally favorable in Provence, where none of these delicate
questions regarding the independent power of the sovereign and the
legitimate liberty of the people were pending; but in Brittany it was

easy to profit from the opportunities to which the nature of affairs gave rise; everything has been misrepresented in accordance with interests and emotions; the recourse of the people to royal authority has been represented as an act of disobedience, and the reception which the magistrates could not refuse to the pleas of the people has been described as the signal for a struggle for authority.

What parlement here reports to Y. M. as being the real cause of the misfortunes of Brittany is not based on simple conjecture; the prohibited society has made and is still making too visible efforts to profit from the circumstances, and there can be no doubt that it has at least employed all the means of politics to block any attempts which might have been made to bring about a return to peace. Indeed, from the moment when the parlement of Brittany ceased to hold its regular sessions, clandestine meetings composed of both the public and the secret members of that society were seen to increase in the capital of the province. Such a gathering of discontented and suspect subjects, at the moment when the tribunal which had scattered them was destroyed, carries in itself the imprint of an intrigue; the rank and personal influence of several of those who joined with the ex-Jesuits gave these meetings the means to take decisions as contrary as possible to public tranquillity and the power to execute those decisions.

Despite the precautions, Sire, which the organizers of these troubles took to eliminate at least the proofs of their illicit meetings, the public outcry, the evident notoriety forced the judges who still existed in that province to carry out an investigation of the existence of these meetings; the forms of judicial procedure were employed and, although this investigation was not carried out with all the energy and vigilance which the glory of Y. M. and the peace of the province demanded of those who were responsible for the exercise of justice there, the mere announcement that they were prepared to employ the regular judicial means sufficed at first to bring about the cessation of these meetings. Thus they must have been dangerous, because they stopped when they were denounced, and those who took part in them must thus have felt that there were no judges before whom they could justify the meetings. . . .

Your parlement, Sire, cannot pass over in silence . . . what is well known to all the orders of the estates, that it was the bad relations which developed between the parlement and the commander-in-chief of the province which brought about the unfortunate circumstances so desired by the partisans of the destroyed society. These people, who know how to foment and excite so cleverly selfish interests and emotions, were able to profit from the division which developed between this commander and the parlement in order to continue and increase the troubles. The parlement felt itself obliged to protest against various acts of the administration, to bear the plaints of the province to the foot of the throne and there to call for the legitimate liberties of the subject. . . .

Private quarrels broke out, personal interests took a hand, and, uniting everyone for personal reasons against the Parlement of Brittany, finally that parlement was dispersed. However, Sire, one considers this unfortunate affair, the Parlement of Brittany can only be regarded as being the victim of its most disinterested, purest zeal for the true interests of Y. M., while everything reveals, on the part of the enemies of the magistracy, the blackest, most involved and continuous intrigue to poison the most innocent actions, to provoke and maintain personal animosities, to depict to Y. M. as a crime the complaints against the administration of the commander-in-chief in that province, and to depict as resistance to royal authority recourse to that very same authority.

It is in the intrigues and maneuvers of the destroyed society, it is in the usage it has made of the powerful interest of an administration angry with the parlement, guilty in its eyes of having represented at the foot of the throne the cries of the nation, that the real source of these troubles, which Y. M. called on his parlement to investigate by letters-patent of July 18, 1765, must be sought; it is the maneuvers of that same society which made it impossible for your parlement entirely to carry out those letters-patent, and, if it pleased Y. M. to restore to your parlement all its authority in that regard, it dares to assure you that criminal investigation would promptly add the certitude of evidence to the light of notoriety; but if Y. M. persists in wishing, as you made known by your answer of December 22, 1766, that the whole case be annulled, if you think it better for the public good that the guilty parties not be known, your parlement presumes to point out to you that the views of the administration should never be contrary to the desire for justice; that, if reasons of prudence may require leaving the guilty to be sheltered by a veil of darkness, justice will forever oppose allowing the same fate to befall magistrates whose honor Y. M. yourself has admitted was not compromised. Yet this would be the consequence of the most recent decisions of Y. M., if you continued to allow the six magistrates of Brittany to remain groaning under the burden of your disgrace, and to refuse them any judicial means of justifying themselves.

The reply which it pleased you to make to your parlement on December 22, 1766, left these magistrates exposed to all the suspicions to which a criminal trial might give rise; in this situation, your parlement believed that for the sake of the honor of the magistracy, which cannot tolerate within it any member tainted with the slightest suspicion, it was essential to beg Y. M. to hand over to its attorney-general the documents which might serve as a basis for an indictment of these magistrates, in order that they might be tried by the court according to the rigor of the laws and in conformity with the letters-patent of July 18, 1765. Y. M. having declared, in replying to these remonstrances, that the honor of these magistrates was not in question, your parlement, Sire, with the most respectful confidence in the spirit of justice and mercy of Y. M., has hoped and waited for the moment when it would please you to restore these magistrates to their functions and give them the opportunity to offer new proofs of their zeal and fidelity. Not only does this happy moment become daily more remote; but also these magistrates continue, because of their exile and their loss of the confidence and bounty of Y. M., to suffer a real disgrace and actual punishment, which may, in the circumstances of the case, give some reason for suspecting their innocence.

However consoling, Sire, the testimony which you have been pleased to render to them may be for these magistrates, it nevertheless cannot be regarded as sufficient; it is only private testimony against a public indictment, verbal testimony against a great number of documents still existing from an immense criminal investigation, it is testimony, finally, which can be regarded as dictated by kindness rather than a verdict marked with the most rigorous exactitude. Magistrates who have been accused before the eyes of the whole of Europe by letters-patent broadcast everywhere and stamped with the name of Y. M., who have been denounced to the nation as guilty of cabals, intrigues, disobedience, criminal conspiracies, have been unable to regard as a verdict of innocence the decision taken by Y. M. not to allow the trial to continue; they feared, and could not but fear that their exile, which followed the pronouncement of the annulment of all indictments and accusations, would seem to mark them as being those "guilty parties" whom Y. M. did not wish to find. . . .

Your parlement, Sire, presumes to suggest to Y. M. that it is part of natural law that any criminal investigation be followed by a verdict; that the horrors which accompany a criminal investigation are neither legitimate nor compatible with humanity except if the innocent person who is exposed to them can be quite confident that, when with the aid of the rigorous forms of judicial inquiry the light of truth has pierced the veil of calumny, justice, having attained its sole objective, will hasten to make known his innocence and to compensate him for the risks he has run by the vigor with which his innocence is proclaimed and the seal of authenticity attached to that proclamation. If Y. M. regards the six magistrates of Rennes as innocent, justice and the rights of the innocent cannot permit the rejection of their lamentations when they renew their pleas that all the doubts which have been cast on their honor be removed by the destruction of whatever caused them, or dissipated by the authenticity of a regular verdict. . . .

Your parlement, Sire, in calling the attention of your justice and mercy to the situation of these six magistrates, cannot omit to appeal equally in favor of the other magistrates of the Parlement of Brittany who also, though to a different degree, have been the victims of maneuvers executed in order to excite trouble in that province . . . For more than two years now, the administration of your sovereign justice in Brittany has been reduced to a vain apparatus of pure theatrics, arranged and supported with great difficulty solely to convince, by exaggerated accounts, those who cannot see it in person, and the daily spectacle which is provided by those who are undertaking to substitute for the absence of most of the officers of the law would become an occasion for the citizens to scorn the sanctuary of justice, if it were not for them a cause of bitterness and prostration.

It is evident, Sire, from the most recent letters-patent for the regulation of the service and for the administration of justice in Brittany, that Y. M. feels sure that the number of members of the court is presently considerable; but these letters are but one more instance in which your good faith has been abused, and even if this number were what it is claimed to be, it would hardly suffice for the handling of judicial affairs in a district which encompasses a province with so much commerce; but your parlement can assure Y. M., because it is a fact of public notoriety, that most of those whose names appear on the table drawn up in consequence of those letters-patent do no kind of service. Whatever the number of judges attained by different means on the present tribunal in Brittany, this incomplete assembly, because of its form and of the persons who compose it, is incapable of taking the place of all the officers of the parlement of that province; a great number of those whose names are inscribed on the list with which attempts are made to deceive the public are, by reason of their age, the state of their health or other personal reasons, quite incapable of assuming the functions of magistrate with the necessary energy. Some, obliged by orders personally addressed to them, have not been able to refuse the appearance of their names on the table which has recently been composed; but, united in sentiment with those of their colleagues who felt obliged to give way before violence and gave up their useless offices, they continue to abstain from carrying out any duties. . . .

Further Selections from Linguet's Brief for the Duke d'Aiguillon

VIII

Administration of the Duc d'Aiguillon, from the Estates of 1766 until His Retirement. . . .

In 1766 he proceeded to Rennes to open the estates. They had been summoned for December 29, 1766. The Duke d'Aiguillon certainly expected that the meeting would be tumultuous, and from the very first day he could see that he had not been mistaken. It is the custom that on that day no business be taken up, the first commissioner of the king and the first president each making a ceremonial speech, after which the proceedings are adjourned. The orders of the clergy and the third estate, and even a part of the nobility, conformed to this custom; but the remainder of the nobility remained in the hall and proposed the sending to the king's commissioners of a deputation to ask above all: (1) a reply to their memoir presented toward the end of the estates of 1764; (2) the revocation of orders issued against two gentlemen exiled since the resignations, and lastly, (3) the recall of the *entirety* of the parlement. This word *entirety* has become famous; it served throughout the session as a rallying cry for the party which had invented it. . . .

Unexpected resources were set to work to move minds and agitate the assembly; there suddenly appeared in the hall a grandson of M. de la Chalotais, only five years old. A gentleman related to him acted as his spokesman and guide. This tutor, in the name of his pupil, implored the help of the assembly for his grandfather. In support of this theatrical surprise, a great number of copies of the letter from the attorney-general to the Count de Saint-Florentin were distributed.

While this scene was being acted out at the estates, others, less

Mémoire pour M. le Duc d'Aiguillon, par Me Linguet, avocat (Paris, 1770).

touching but equally peculiar, were being played at the Palace [of Justice]. The prosecutors decided in a body to represent to the first president *the extreme hardship into* which they had been plunged, *and to beg him to use his good offices to come to the aid of their guild.* However, it was this same guild which had first stopped coming to trials, long before the resignations. If their affairs were not going well, it was because they had refused to undertake them, and the *good offices* they were asking were requests for the return of the entirety [of the former parlement]. The ushers fell in with the prosecutors. The law students, the guild of merchants, the guild of artisans all presented their petitions complaining of the harm being done by the absence of the *entirety,* and asking the estates to solicit its return.

These signs of popular feeling are not cited in order to ridicule the idea that the misfortune of the magistrates could inspire concern. In any other circumstances, these activities might have been regarded as pardonable if imprudent reactions, but at the time they occurred, their possible consequences were feared and it was decided to halt their development. The police imposed silence on this popular outbreak, and this wise precaution was looked on as yet another act of despotism. . . .

For a long time there had been ideas of collecting into a single compilation the different rules in force to establish the form of the estates; those which were in force during the meetings had been established one by one, as circumstances dictated. A set of general rules had been promulgated in 1687 which seemed to include all parts of the administration; but it had become insufficient owing to the changes which had occurred since it had been drawn up. From the time of the ministry of Cardinal Fleury [1726-43], the necessity had been felt of issuing another; that minister had had work started on one, under the supervision of the Keeper of the Seals Chauvelin and of M. Orry the comptroller-general; the notes drawn up as an outline for this work still existed in the bureaus.

The disorder of the meeting of the estates, in 1764, had brought forward again the idea of finally putting these to use; the minister had spent a great deal of time on it for a year; he had taken the advice and collected information from the people who knew most about the administration of Brittany. After these preliminaries, a draft code of rules which appeared to reconcile all interests and remedy all the abuses was drawn up; the comptroller-general had sent it in the month of March 1766 to the Duke d'Aiguillon, informing him that what had been going on in the assembly for the past three months made the publication of this code of rules indispensable, and that it was the intention of H. M. that it be inscribed on the registers before the closing of the session; the Duke d'Aiguillon communicated it at once to the commissioners of the king, to the presidents, and to several of the most enlightened and best-intentioned members of the three orders.

These people gave him their comments, which he passed on to the comptroller-general, along with the draft code of rules; he added that however convinced he was that these rules might be useful, he did not think it a favorable moment to present them to the estates, and that a calmer session should be awaited in which to have them adopted. He received no answer to this advice; he imagined that the minister had taken it into account; but six days before the date which H. M. had irrevocably fixed as the date for the adjournment of the estates, a courier brought back the rules, with a precise order to the Duke d'Aiguillon to have them registered before that date. The commissioners of the king and the distinguished persons to whom he reported this news all thought that he had no choice but to obey; however, in the chapter [of the rules] concerning the nobility there was an article which granted entry into that order of the estates only *to gentlemen of noble extraction possessing in Brittany lands containing at least one parish, and possessing the right to dispense justice*. The Duke d'Aiguillon felt that this reduction would be infinitely displeasing to nobility. The greater part of the order would thus be deprived of an honorific right it had hitherto enjoyed; he took it upon himself to make repeated pleas to obtain some reduction in the rigor of this rule. The king deigned to take notice of his pleas; the article was changed, and the code of rules sent out once more. The Duke d'Aiguillon then had it read and registered in the last sitting, conformably to the will of H. M. The estates applauded the speech which he made at that time, and most of those present seemed to approve of it. . . .

With the estates at an end, the Duke d'Aiguillon came to Paris; upon his arrival at the court, he was most astonished to learn that this code of rules, which the minister had seemed convinced was so useful that he had had it drawn up under his own supervision after the longest and most careful examination, and registered both by the estates and by the parlement on his repeated and positive orders, was now causing considerable uneasiness, and fears that it might provoke trouble in the next session; he learned also that it had been decided to convene an extraordinary session of the estates to have the code of rules adopted again, without change, in order that the despatch of business would not be retarded in the ordinary session. The Duke d'Aiguillon offered no opposition to this indulgence of the minister for the estates. He limited himself to pointing out that the custom was that the commander-in-chief did not attend extraordinary sessions, that the king had never sent to them as his commissioners anyone but the intendant and the first president; and that consequently he begged H. M. to spare him this new ordeal, and that he had all the more reason to expect it because the king had finally allowed him to hope for permission to give up the command in Brittany; the king condescended to consent, but added one condition as flattering as it was difficult. He insisted that the Duke d'Aiguillon, before leaving Brittany, must work at completing the parlement. This operation was regarded as indispensable, but this only made it all the more difficult.

In the absence of the Duke d'Aiguillon, his deputy had been pressed by the minister to complete this task. Four members of the former parlement, who appeared inclined to take back their jobs, were mentioned to him; he had not been suspicious of their intentions, and had addressed to them the orders of the king necessary to allow them to display the good will which they were supposed to possess; but he had been deceived; these four magistrates did indeed return to the palace, but only one remained there; the other three only appeared in order to be able to say publicly that they would not come back, until their entire company was recalled.

This demonstration had produced a most lively sensation entirely opposed to the views of the government, which the Duke d'Aiguillon noted on his return to Brittany in December 1767. His invitations remained useless; no one wanted to run the risk, by taking the opposite course, of heaping more praises on the three Magistrates who had just so noisily refused; the Duke d'Aiguillon reported to Paris on the state of things and the views people held; the minister replied that since there was no further hope of being able to win over any of the former magistrates, the places must be filled by subjects foreign to Brittany, but capable of occupying them with honor; this being a positive order, the Duke d'Aiguillon did not feel that he could avoid carrying it out. Therefore he informed some gentlemen of the best nobility of the intentions of the king; some of these were somewhat advanced in age, but had had a taste for the magistracy in their youth, had studied for it, and had not entered it only because they could find no office to buy; others were of families already illustrious of the robe; they were only awaiting a moment when favorable circumstances would permit them to assume the dignity to which their birth destined them; all were approved by the king and the parlement, and installed some time afterwards. With this important task fulfilled, the Duke d'Aiguillon left Brittany never to return. . . .

After the adjournment of the extraordinary Estates of Saint-Brieuc, the Duke d'Aiguillon felt that it was no longer possible for him to battle against the resentment, ill founded though it was, of an order which seemed to have conceived such unjust prejudices against him; there had been no session of the estates since 1760 after which he had not begged the king to approve his retirement; His Majesty had always imposed silence upon him by assuring him of his good will and satisfaction; in 1768 he insisted more strongly than ever, and finally obtained the consent for which he had been longing. He left Brittany not happy to see that beautiful province a prey to the activities of an aroused party, which did not shrink from the cruelest slanders, and which was already then displaying that spirit of fanaticism, of rancor, the proof of which has been demonstrated over and over since by so many libelous pamphlets. His only consolation was that some there missed him; he was pained at leaving all the faithful servitors of the king exposed to the most painful incidents and affronts. The numerous letters he received served to prove that injustice toward him was not general, and that some well-balanced people had remained immune from the enthusiasm which had been stirred up by so many means.

The bare account, the details stripped of elaboration which the reader has just gone through, no doubt have already justified him on the counts to which the greatest importance has been attached; it might have been presented more excitingly and with more flourishes of style, but the most beautiful ornament of truth is truth itself. The Duke d'Aiguillon has desired to be himself, and this memoir has presented him as he is. It has served to destroy beyond redemption that shadow of an accusation to which malignity has given rise, these absurd charges which hidden interests have spread about, these fairy tales of all sorts which an abandoned frenzy has consigned to so many printed works.

BASICALLY, what does this monstrous accusation, which for three whole years has scandalized Europe and rightly saddened honest people to whom the frenzy of the spirit of party is unknown, consist of? What are the elements of this inconceivable hysteria, which accepts so many impostures at the expense of truth? If we go through these anonymous pamphlets, we find that they blame the Duke d'Aiguillon:

(1) For having made Brittany suffer under a cruel despotism, for

having overwhelmed her with abusive and repeated, or rather continual, acts of authority.

(2) For having protected the Jesuits, and for having followed the advice of several turbulent and vindictive monks.

(3) For having set to work to humiliate and ruin the magistracy and the magistrates.

(4) For having favored criminal conspiracies of all kinds, formed to ruin honest men, for having either ordered, or at least tolerated, that the lives of these honest men be attacked by poison, in order to please him, and their honor by mendacious and falsified testimony.

So that everything at once is imputed to the Duke d'Aiguillon, poisoning which is the way of cowards, subornation which is the crime of knaves, indulgence for monks which is the weakness of superstitious souls, but at the same time an imperious haughtiness which at least is the vice only of a lofty personality, and an open and inflexible hatred such as a frank and vigorous person would display in his very misconduct.

The incompatibility of these charges already suggests their injustice. The account the reader has just read demonstrates this; but in order to carry the testimony as far as possible, the Duke d'Aiguillon will add to the preceding details some reflections on each of these charges.

IX

First Charge against the Duke d'Aiguillon. Despotism and abuse of authority . . .

Here, no doubt, there will be protests against our truthful enumeration of the *lettres de cachet* executed in Brittany under the Duke d'Aiguillon; that famous list, that printed chronological table, will be cited, in which were reported "The *Lettres de Cachet* and other violent acts of absolute power carried out in Brittany from the time of the signature of the resignations of May 22, 1765, to September 1766." In this pamphlet one may count 158 of these letters or absolute acts. This chronological table, like all the libels which have followed it, is merely a compilation of untruths. It impresses only people who examine nothing closely, and who, in calculations especially, look only at the totals.

First of all, there are included 78 letters addressed to the members of the parlement six months after the resignations, although the Duke d'Aiguillon was taking the waters at Bagnères, on the Spanish frontier, when the king, judging it proper to send magistrates of his council to conduct the Parlement of Rennes, did not think it suitable to leave within the same town the officers who had themselves given up their right to sit in it.

Second, there are included fifteen other letters, by which fifteen of these same magistrates received the order to change the place of their exile.

Third are included the six detentions of the magistrates arrested in the name of the king, at a time when the Duke d'Aiguillon was two hundred leagues from Brittany, when regular justice having abandoned its responsibilities, there was no other means available than a direct order of getting hold of a person under indictment.

Fourth are included the removals of six persons suspected of composing insulting cartoons, libelous pamphlets, etc., and among others the removal of Bouquerel, the young fanatic who wrote to a minister that if the king did not change his policy "someone would pay for it." This precaution of protection against the enterprises of such a dangerously aroused mind is what is called a violent act of absolute power.

Fifth are included three letters by which these same individuals suspected of having had a hand in the composition of libelous pamphlets were ordered to be removed from the Bastille; so that the undoing of the so-called act of violence serves in this table to increase the number of incidents listed to prove the use of violence.

Sixth are included the punishment of a vagabond beggar and of three sedan-chair porters imprisoned for some time by the police.

Seventh is included the dismissal of the relatives of M. de la Chalotais, who had gone to Paris to broadcast the *Mémoires* attributed to that magistrate.

Eighth and finally, these orders are imputed, whatever they were, to the Duke d'Aiguillon, who had no hand in them, who did not even know of most of them, who allowed the rest to be executed because he had neither the right nor the power to oppose them, as even the authors of the attacks on him would have done, had they been in his place. . . .

There remains the accusation about the *corvées*. If the Duke d'Aiguillon violated neither the rights of the province, nor those of natural liberty with regard to the inhabitants of the towns, was he equally respectful of the rights of those unfortunates who spend their lives in rustic labors, of those worthy men whose sweat makes possible the luxurious lives of the towndwellers who disdain them? Never has a charge been more positive than the one made against him in this regard; has it any foundation? This is what must be examined.

There must be roads; and in almost all of the kingdom we have hardly any other means of building them than the strong arms of the peasants. No doubt of all the men in office who have employed this destructive method, the least guilty, or rather those most worthy of praise, are those who have modified it in such a way as to diminish its devastating effects. No one has turned his attention to this with greater humanity, or greater success than the Duke d'Aiguillon.

. . . The dispositions of his celebrated regulation of 1757 . . . tended to preserve the countryside from the vexations so common elsewhere; they certainly in every way merited the praise made of them by a minister, who said in a letter . . . *that it would be desirable to see them adopted throughout the kingdom.* And yet these measures were not sufficient in the mind of the Duke d'Aiguillon, he felt that in many cases, it was not enough to have limited the tasks of the peasants to a fixed and determined level, to have guaranteed them against arbitrary surcharges, to have proportioned their labor exactly to their strength. . . . The differences of terrain and the differences in the location of the roads still created inequalities within the equality of his general regulation; therefore the Duke d'Aiguillon was always careful, at each session of the estates, to ask for funds destined for the lightening of the *corvée,* and for paying for work at least on the most unusual or painful parts of the construction, to which the unfortunate condition of the villagers condemned them.

Not only to the estates did he set forth the necessity for relieving the people of the countryside; he asked it also of the court, with the same insistence. Here is what he wrote on the subject to the minister in 1757.

"The first report which I had the honor to send you will have informed you of some of the difficulties of the *corvée,* which is much more onerous in this province than in the others, not only because of the depopulation, the dispersion of the houses of the inhabitants, the distances separating them from the highroads, and the quality of their diet, but also because of the bad quality of the soil and of materials, the scarcity of the latter and the distance separating the places where they are to be found from the places where they are needed, the intemperance of the climate, and especially because of the prodigious number of enormous wagons which pass continually over the roads to Brest, Lorient, Nantes, and Saint-Malo in the armament service; all these difficulties taken together make it impossible to hope that the roads of Brittany can ever be kept practicable by the sole means of the *corvée,* however much is demanded of the *corvée*-workers. I am convinced that after this report, and with your knowledge of our roads, you would under no circumstances hesitate to grant the permission which the estates are asking to take 400,000 livres from their special fund to aid the *corvée*-workers to fulfill their task; it appears to me all the more essential not to refuse this that it will result in the greatest advantages for the public service and the relief of the inhabitants of the countryside, who are crushed in every way. . . ."

Such is the language of this inflexible individual, who has been portrayed as the oppressor of the countryside and a tyrant over agriculture.

Not only was he wise enough to respect these useful men, and to demand of them only what the ancient customs compelled them to give; but he also reformed these ancient customs in their favor; not only did he not force them to interrupt their necessary labors on their lands, to drag themselves to the roads and exhaust in excruciating labors arms needed for the cultivation and harvest, but he also put an end to an abuse introduced and sanctified before he came to Brittany. The rules previous to the year 1754 left only the months of August and September free to the peasants; they were absolved from the *corvée* only during this short interval, and among the days lost for their own fruitful labor were those which in a rural economy are the most important of all; the Duke d'Aiguillon would not tolerate such harsh and pernicious laws. By the regulation of 1754 he limited the period of time during which the peasants could be called on to work on the highroads to the months of October, November, half of December, March, April, May, June, and half of July. . . .

It has been charged that he crushed the whole province at once by his ambition to open simultaneously all possible routes of communication; it has been said that he had staked his reputation on this ruinous complication of a multitude of roadworks which could only have been possible and really useful if they had been separated and executed one by one. Calculations have even been made of the number of leagues of road thus constructed with an ambitious and ferocious haste.

One can never cease to admire the audacity of the accusers who have added these charges one to another, and who even succeeded in persuading the parlement to support them, because it included them in its fatal decree which has been regarded as the starting point of all the trouble which has occurred in Brittany.

First of all, all these roads were not constructed at once, because new ones are still being built every day; because at the very time that there was the greatest outcry against the old plans, several cantons were insistently requesting that they receive the same benefit; at the very time that the magistrates were misled to the point that they were persuaded to denounce to the king a tyrannical multitude of road-works destined to re-establish all the communications of the province, a number of parishes complained of not being given any, and presented petitions in this regard.

But even supposing that all at once all the roads needed by a maritime province, surrounded almost completely by the sea and deprived by the inadequacy of its communications of the advantages of its numerous ports, had been undertaken, what evil would have resulted from this? We must not lose sight of the regulation of 1757, a celebrated law, always scrupulously executed, a law which the most violent enemies of the administration have never dared to say has been infringed in any way.

This law limits the amount of work for which each peasant is held responsible, and it is neither permissible nor possible to ask more of him in any case. With this limit thus set, what would it matter to the inhabitants of one canton what happened in another? . . .

X

Protection Given to the Jesuits.

To ally himself with powerful monks would be a humiliating thing to do even for a private individual; but to attach himself to condemned monks would be an act of irresponsibility quite inconceivable for a man holding office. And yet this is what the Duke d'Aiguillon is accused of. . . .

At the end of 1765 there commenced to appear those tables which have become so well known on which were inscribed the names of so-called affiliates of the Jesuits, souls who were said to be sighing for their re-establishment, and who while imploring it from Heaven, were working to facilitate it on earth by their intrigues; in this public denunciation no holds were barred, men and women of every estate were listed, and even the names of people who never existed, so honest were these authors and so well informed; however, the name of the Duke d'Aiguillon was not yet included in these fatal tables designed to produce about the same effect as tables of proscription, to designate for universal hatred and scorn all those unfortunate enough to be inscribed on them.

It was only in 1766, when M. de la Chalotais was implicated in a capital trial; when there seemed to be a need to create partisans for him; when it was necessary to claim that the reasons for his detention were odious pretexts, and to give his defense an honorable passport; it was only then that we were informed that Rennes had become the retreat of the Jesuits driven from France; that the blood of the attorney-general of the parlement was intended to be spilled in expiation to the idol that he had overthrown; and that the Duke d'Aiguillon, honored with the leading role in this tragedy, had taken it upon himself to lead the victim to the sacrificial altar in person.

We do not wish in these pages to lift a veil which the king himself has lowered; we do not wish either to rekindle an affair now died out, or to give grounds for new suspicions; but is it not sad that the partisans of a man like M. de la Chalotais have felt that they needed to use slander to defend him, and that to justify him they have called falsehood to his aid?

The first libel in which this appeared, was the letter published in his name in 1766; the obscure writer who in it dared hide himself behind a celebrated name has long enjoyed great success with his lies. The Duke d'Aiguillon has so far not replied other than with a righteous scorn; but now that it is a question today of setting all of Europe straight on a fact of this importance, he calls upon the author of this libel, and his adherents, to produce proofs of the atrocious imputation with which they have blackened his name.

"His hatred of me" (M. de la Chalotais is made to say) "went back farther than his affair with the parlement. In the month of February 1762, when my first *compte-rendu* on the constitutions of the Jesuits appeared, I learned that the Duke d'Aiguillon, to whom I had sent a copy, said nothing more to those who spoke to him about it than that I was a HOTHEAD."

This word, if indeed it was spoken, would have hardly reflected a mortal enmity; but if M. de la Chalotais had been informed of it, would he, on July 14, 1762, have complimented the Duke d'Aiguillon on his coolheadedness? Would he have bantered with him on the unimportance of these monastic illusions and on the credulity of the public, if he had thought him so seriously concerned about them? This first reflection on a fact which has served as a basis for all of the recriminations of this kind is very essential.

This libel adds "I do not know the motives of M. d'Aiguillon in this regard, but I know that at the following estates, at Rennes in 1762, when a movement arose among some ecclesiastics and some gentlemen

to persuade the estates to declare themselves against the decrees of
parlement which had dissolved the Society of the Jesuits, M. d'Aiguillon favored, first covertly and then quite openly, this faction of the
president of the clergy." It is not enough to talk of facts, they must be
proved, and the Duke d'Aiguillon challenges the writer who advances
them to do so. His actions have not been concealed, because the libel
declares itself that his favor was expressed "quite openly." It should
therefore be very easy to name witnesses of these so-called intrigues,
which, it is said, had such a distant, but nevertheless such a powerful
connection with the disaster of M. de la Chalotais. However, witnesses
have never been produced. The Duke d'Aiguillon repeats that he confined himself to the most scrupulous impartiality; he calls to witness
the two parties whose efforts he suspended; if he seemed at that time
to be inclined to one side, it was that in which the opposition prevailed,
and one can see that it was not the side of the protectors of the society.

"I was afraid, I admit," continues this anonymous author, "of a
surprise, and of the civil war which such a step could bring about in
the kingdom. I was quite aware that the estates would be pushed into
opposition to the parlement, the nation to the nation, and knew very
well the arguments which such a subject could provide to fanatical
people and even to people who would not be fanatical. From time to
time I had made a few representations to M. d'Aiguillon, who, as is
usually his method of judging what is contrary to his opinion, found
them absurd."

Nothing proves better than this passage that indeed M. de la Chalotais is not the author of this memoir; he knows very well that he
never spoke to the Duke d'Aiguillon of this so-called fear of his, of
seeing civil war begun in the hall of the estates, and the kingdom ablaze
over a few innocuous words spoken in Brittany. But if M. de la Chalotais had had such fears, and if he had spoken of them, the Duke
d'Aiguillon admits that he would have treated them in the fashion the
libel supposes, though not thereby being animated by any spirit of partisanship, without being either a Jesuit, or a partisan of the Jesuits. . . .

"The affair of the Jesuits was defeated three times in the estates.
M. d'Aiguillon knew of my letters; he said that I had wished to ruin
him, and that I could count it certain that sooner or later he would
ruin me. . . . This is the origin of the charge of *Lèse-Majesté:* the
hatred which the Duke d'Aiguillon conceived against me."

And indeed that is what the whole accusation, by which they have
tried to condemn the Duke d'Aiguillon, refers to. A word, a phrase,
with neither time, nor place, nor witnesses cited; a threat to which an

unknown is the only witness; this is the only proof of the abominable conspiracy attributed to a man in office; this is why the public believes him to be guilty of having sought to ruin a magistrate, of having sought to ruin him by the use of judicial machinery, uniting hatred to condemnation, infamy to torture, of having tried to make accomplices in such a black strategem a king known for his extreme beneficence, his ministers, and his whole council.

This is what the Duke d'Aiguillon affirms, and he challenges anyone to prove the contrary. Since he left school he has had no connection direct or indirect with the Jesuits; he is perhaps the man in France who had the fewest relations with them, even before their fall. . . .

What becomes, then, of this artificial indictment, to which, however, M. de la Chalotais owes almost all of the partisans who have served him, and the Duke d'Aiguillon almost all the enemies who are attacking him? There has been an outcry against the violation of rules in the person of the attorney-general, against the infringements made upon the freedoms of his office, against the inhumanity of his detention, against the forms of the indictment brought against him, etc. The Duke d'Aiguillon has neither the competence nor the right to approve or reject these complaints; but is a citizen's honor less precious than his liberty? To break the chains of M. de la Chalotais, is it necessary thus to cover the name of the Duke d'Aiguillon with opprobrium?

His friendship for the Jesuits, the libels have said, is the only cause for his hatred of M. de la Chalotais; but if he was not the friend or the protector of the Jesuits; if M. de la Chalotais himself admitted this at a time when he could not imagine that anyone someday would claim the opposite; if the Duke d'Aiguillon never quarreled with him for their sake or for any other reason, he is then innocent of the misfortunes of M. de la Chalotais. The memoirs resting on this inconsistent base are thus pointless recriminations, and the libelous pamphlets which have copied them are criminal satires, to which justice owes only an inflexible severity.

XI

Hatred for the Magistracy, Conspiracy for the
Destruction of the Magistrates.

The magistracy, so it is said, is the stumbling-block for despotism; the accused magistrates had been the opponents of the society; that is why the Duke d'Aiguillon is alleged to have wanted to annihilate the one and ruin the others. This charge has already been refuted by what has been said. If the Duke d'Aiguillon never had any idea of establishing despotism in Brittany, and even less of supporting the society there, no more did he think of sacrificing the magistracy or its members to these two idols; it has just been proved that he was neither a despot nor a protector of the Jesuits; this charge thus fails of its own weight.

But it was under the command of the Duke d'Aiguillon that the parlement was dissolved and reduced by half. That company had had quarrels with him which were not yet resolved. After the reduction in numbers, he worked in person to complete the number of members destined to compose the new body, and this, no doubt, in order to spare the king the need for re-establishing the old one; therefore he was responsible for the dissolution and the reduction.

It was under his command that six distinguished magistrates were put in irons, their trial elaborately prepared, and that they ran the risks of criminal procedures. These magistrates were suspected of having been the principal instigators of the quarrel which arose between their company and the Duke d'Aiguillon; therefore their destruction was his work, and he plotted their ruin.

Thus reason Hatred and Suspicion; in these pages we beg Hatred to hearken, if it can, and Suspicion to listen, if that is possible.

During the first eleven years of his administration, from 1753 to 1764, the Duke d'Aiguillon had no quarrel with the parlement; from that company he received only testimonials of esteem and had no reason to feel for it anything but the same sentiments . . . until 1764, no seed of discord, no source of division; each did his duty, and the people were happy.

At that fatal moment, the parlement felt obliged to embrace the cause of the parlements of Toulouse, of Grenoble, of Rouen. It was no doubt unfortunate that to justify its participation in a quarrel foreign to it that company felt obliged, at the end of its remonstrances, to insert a few words insinuating that it had a personal interest in the matter; it was another misfortune that these words, designed to serve as a pretext rather than a serious denunciation, happened to refer directly to the commander-in-chief, who did not deserve them; it was yet another misfortune that in their haste to articulate some sort of criticism to conclude these remonstrances, they chose the most unjust; it was a far greater misfortune that the company, having let itself be deceived by false reports, preferred rather to uphold them than to disavow them, as it had had the honesty to do in 1757, and that it believed that its honor was engaged to prove facts which did not exist; finally it would have been one more misfortune if the Duke d'Aiguillon had felt a profound resentment at all this, and had nourished a deep desire for revenge.

Suppose for a moment that this last article were true, what would have been the result? What could a commander-in-chief of a province do against a judicial tribunal supported by its own weight, by respect for ancient customs, by its guardianship of the laws, by the confidence and love of the peoples? At the very most cause it some annoyances which would have been amply paid back. In this sort of attack, an individual has never won out over a body. Certainly the hatred of the Duke d'Aiguillon would have been powerless, however strong it might be, if the parlement had not allowed itself to be dragged into the actions with which we are familiar.

If it had purely and simply registered the edict of 1763, as had been promised, it would not have given cause for the displeasure of the minister . . . if the Vacation Chamber had not thought itself competent on the eve of the day when it would cease to sit, to overthrow by a plurality of five votes to three the work of the entire parlement; if the entire parlement had not preferred to support the decision of the Vacation Chamber rather than its own; if it had not refused to give in to the reiterated injunctions of the king; if these refusals had not been accompanied by aggravating circumstances, like the return by mail of letters-patent, like its pretension to decree that decrees of the council be torn down from the walls; if the company had not decreed its resignations, and thus decided, unintentionally, either to punish the people for the apparent wrong done to them by royal authority, or to force royal authority to give in, out of consideration for the resulting misfortunes of the people; if its only usage of its power, after the decree of resignations, had not been a new infringement on the will of the king, by a prohibition of the raising of the two sous per livre on the general farms, a levy specially ordered and reserved by His Majesty; if, finally, when the resignations had been consummated, it had not stubbornly rejected the series of invitations by the king to resume service, which hinted that this single proof of obedience would be rewarded with all the marks of favor which might be hoped for, it would never have been dissolved.

Among these events, was there a single one which the Duke d'Aiguillon could have—we will not say overcome—could have foreseen and prevented? These are the real causes of the dissolution of the Parlement of Rennes; he knew nothing about it; he was in correspondence neither with the court nor with the province.

If he had been, if he wanted to seize a favorable opportunity for his vengeance, he could have done it without risk; he would only have had to abandon that company, which a terrible rashness was carrying to its ruin, to itself; he would have profited from the situation without exposing himself to the slightest reproach, or even to the slightest suspicion; but that idea would never have entered his mind; had he been present, he would have forgotten everything and concerned himself only with pacifying the quarrel. He presumes to believe that his advice, his pleas, his prayers would have opened the eyes of the magistrates, and that the disorders over which Brittany had shed so many tears would never have taken place.

But in any case, he was not present; after more than six months of absence he arrived at Fontainebleau; he learned all that had happened; he found the resignations accepted, the edict of suppression issued, the commission departed for Brittany; he himself was ordered to proceed to Rennes, and to work there on rebuilding a parlement according to the new rules laid down; in such circumstances, what ought, what might the Duke d'Aiguillon have done?

He knows very well that his real crime, his only one in the eyes of the magistrates in this cruel affair, is to have accepted a task which seemed designed to avoid the recall of the entirety, and to prolong indefinitely the punishment to which the king had limited himself with regard to the officers who had resigned, namely to allow them to be forgotten; but could he refuse that task? Should he have? . . .

He does not conceal the fact that from the end of 1764, at the opening of the estates, he could not free himself of a sad presentiment of the evils with which Brittany was threatened; the bitterness with which the parlement took its steps; its links with the members of the estates most known for their opposition to the will of the king; the nervous avidity to play a role displayed by some individuals and the extreme desire they betrayed of engaging some dispute between the king and their company, in order to win the glory and merit of being the mediators, these things afflicted and terrified the Duke d'Aiguillon.

Moreover, the letters of ministers made it clear to him that these doings were not unknown to the court, and that steps were being taken to deal with their consequences. M. de L'Averdy, then comptroller-general, had spoken frankly to him about this internal agitation and its causes; it was clear that this minister, a former magistrate, had understood the situation and was already thinking of preventing its further development, or of applying punishment.

On July 1, 1764, M. de L'Averdy wrote to the Duke d'Aiguillon; speaking of the imminent return [to Rennes] of the deputation from the Parlement of Rennes, that is, of MM. de la Chalotais, de Montreuil, de la Gascherie, etc., the same who were later arrested on orders of the king, he said, "I am convinced that on their return they will make every possible effort to stir up the greatest scenes."

Writing on September 10, 1764, he reported the details of a conversation he had had with a Breton gentleman who had a great reputation in his region. He wrote, "I told him that I myself had been a councilor of a parlement, that I was convinced that it was essential to preserve that body in France, that I was well aware of their rights and would never infringe them, but that I could not defend them to the king when they exceeded their limits, that indeed I thought it would be dangerous to allow them to exceed those limits, because their own destruction would follow, and royal authority would get the upper hand sooner or later." He wrote to the Duke d'Aiguillon in a letter of October 24, 1764, "If the clergy and the third estate do not hold firm, all is lost. . . . I do not know what decisions will be taken on all this, but I can clearly foresee a period of abominable internal strife, and the nobility of Brittany hard at work rending the bosom of its fatherland and involuntarily rebelling against its master, all because of four or five hotheads. The king will not tolerate it; when the estates have adjourned, the parlement will prohibit [tax] collection; it in turn will be broken up or neutralized; the town taxes will not be collected and all the towns will be bankrupted, the other parlements will join in and take up the cause of Brittany and will suffer the same fate. What an upheaval in the kingdom! and this is what the enemies of order, the Jansenists and Molinistes,[1] men whose minds are dominated by partisan feelings, really want."

On December 9, he wrote [with regard to the resignation of the parlement], "Its letter is expected here, and my opinion will be that the king should reply to it in his own hand and send it letters-patent ordering it to resume its activities."

On January 16, 1765, he informed the Duke d'Aiguillon, "You will no doubt be obliged to announce to the members of the estates and of the parlement, that their perseverance in refusal will bring them, and the parlement, into the greatest danger; you can safely say this, for it is true and certain."

The Duke d'Aiguillon permits himself the liberty of transcribing here, from the letters of this minister, only the lines he needs to demonstrate what is essential to his case; namely, that the instruction for the dispersal and destruction of the court did not come from him. . . .

1. [The "Molinists" were followers of the Spanish theologian Miguel Molinos (1628-96) and professed a doctrine of religious quietism.—Ed.]

V

LEBRUN AND THE MODERNIZATION OF FRANCE'S GOVERNMENT

Introduction

In this chapter the reader will encounter two sources that he should ultimately discover to be of quite unequal value in interpreting the significance of the institutional revolution that developed in 1770-71 from the Duke d'Aiguillon's efforts to clear himself of charges of misrule in Brittany. A comparison of what can be learned from the memoirs of Bésenval and Lebrun should make clear how absolutely necessary it is for the historian to probe beneath the superficial level of anecdote if he wishes to understand the forces that shape great historical changes.

There is first a selection from the court *mémoires* of the Baron de Bésenval. These are an example of the kind of scandalmongering source that historians learn to distrust. The *mémoires* were disavowed by the family of the Baron, a prominent courtier, when they appeared fifteen years after his death; it is possible, in fact, that it was not Bésenval who wrote them. The reader can judge of their accuracy in detail from their account of the causes of the Brittany Affair. Nonetheless, the Bésenval *mémoires* can be taken as reflecting a common contemporary explanation of the events of 1770-71, one that the reader will want to evaluate in the light of the materials dealing with those events presented in the next

chapter. According to their author, the institutional changes of
1771 were the unplanned result of the self-serving intrigues of an
unholy trio opposed to the Duke de Choiseul: Chancellor Maupeou, Louis XV's last mistress Madame du Barry, and the Duke
d'Aiguillon. The reader may decide, as he reads the final chapter
of this book, that such intrigues did indeed play a part in Maupeou's violent assertion of royal authority over the privileged order
of the *noblesse de robe*. He may even conclude that so long as
random personal rivalries played *any* part in effecting change, the
crown was incapable of reforming the Old Regime, which was
consequently doomed.

But before deciding whether Maupeou was inspired to destroy
the parlements only by calculations of his own advantage, or
whether he had some grander design, it would be well to know
somewhat more about him than the Bésenval *mémoires* reveal. He
came himself from an old robe family; his father, René-Charles de
Maupeou (1688-1775), had been named first president of the
Parlement of Paris in 1743 and vice-chancellor in 1763. The elder
Maupeou had not been named chancellor only because the king
had been unwilling to take the grave steps required to dislodge the
previous incumbent, Lamoignon, from that ancient and tradition-
encrusted office at the head of the French judicial system. René-
Nicolas-Charles-Augustin de Maupeou (1714-92), with whom we
are concerned, had succeeded his father as first president in 1763.
Having shown great devotion to Choiseul, he succeeded Lamoignon as chancellor and "keeper of the seals" in 1768. In reading
the characterization of Maupeou by Lebrun, who knew him inti-
mately, the student should try to determine to what extent the
chancellor's ideas had been limited by this highly conventional
background.

In interpreting the events of 1770-71, however, the reader may
find that it is more important to understand Lebrun than Maupeou.
Charles-François Lebrun (1739-1824) had a career as a jurist
and government official that spanned some of the most tumultuous
years in French history. After visiting England in 1762, he studied

for the bar, and was appointed the legal tutor of the younger Maupeou's son. He thus became a close friend of the family and the chancellor's chief advisor. After 1768 it was in fact this young man of thirty who directed the chancellery; "What would Maupeou do," Louis XV was said to have remarked, "without Lebrun?" He was dismissed from office on the same day that Maupeou fell (August 24, 1774) and spent the years until 1789 in retirement on the country estate which his marriage to an heiress enabled him to buy.

After the outbreak of the Revolution, Lebrun took an active part, particularly by drafting fiscal legislation, in the Estates-General that became the Constituent Assembly after the victory of the third estate, but was arrested and imprisoned under the Jacobin Terror of 1793-94. Only the overthrow of Robespierre on 9 Thermidor saved him from the guillotine. He returned to political life after the Revolution had been purged of its most extreme elements under the Directory, and became third consul under General Napoleon Bonaparte after his *coup d'état* in 1799. Under the Consulate and the Empire Lebrun played an important role in constructing the standardized and centralized administrative, legal, and fiscal systems that even today remain as Napoleon's principal legacy to France. As a reward for his services he accepted a dukedom in 1808, although he had opposed Napoleon's creation of a new imperial nobility to replace the one the Revolution had abolished. Because Lebrun supported Napoleon during the Hundred Days in 1815, he was stricken from the list of peers by the restored monarchy, though his title was reinstated in 1819, five years before his death.

These details of Lebrun's career after the Revolution of 1789 are *not* extraneous to the story of the Brittany Affair and the crisis of the Old Regime. In fact, it is vital for the student to keep them in mind as he reads portions of Lebrun's autobiography and of his 1769 memorandum to Maupeou in this chapter, and the accounts by Lebrun and others of developments in France between 1768 and 1776 in the next chapter. For Lebrun was in

many ways typical of the men who made the French Revolution
of 1789, lost control of it at its height, but after 1799 helped
Napoleon to consolidate the changes that the Revolution had begun. He was untypical only because he had also held an influential
office *before* the Revolution. Therefore there are three essential
questions that the reader should ask himself as he studies the *dé-
nouement* of the Brittany Affair. The first is, to what extent was
Lebrun already trying, between 1768 and 1774, to use royal authority to effect those measures of modernization of France's
government and society that only a revolution fifteen years after he
left office finally carried out? The other two questions are related,
though the first is factual and the second speculative: why did
Lebrun and Maupeou fail? and, after their failure, did the destruction of the Old Regime by revolution become inevitable?
These questions should at least suggest that there were more complex forces at work in the last years of Louis XV's reign than
could be detected from reading the Bésenval *mémoires*.

In attempting to answer them, the student might begin by seeking the sources of Lebrun's ideas. Voltaire had begun the fashion
of contrasting France unfavorably with England with his *Lettres
philosophiques* (1734); could Lebrun have been similarly influenced by his trip across the Channel? What does he admire—
correctly or not—about English institutions and deplore about
French ones? Does his ideal political system have anything in common with Voltaire's? Do his aims of political modernization in fact
owe something to the *philosophes* despite his skepticism of their
activities, and how does he believe their efforts should be redi-
rected? Of what use does this young careerist commoner believe
the French third estate would be in effecting political change, and
how does he propose to make their weight felt? (With his knowledge of the behavior of the third estate in Brittany, the reader
might venture to judge whether Lebrun's political calculations in
this respect were realistic.)

When considering the memorandum Lebrun submitted to Maupeou in 1769, it is of course important to note the specific changes

he proposed. In the next chapter the reader will be studying the actual changes carried out in 1771, and will wish to determine not only to what extent they had been planned by Lebrun, but also in what respects they fell short of his total design. How does he analyze the political role of the parlements? What benefits both for France's government and for her society and economy does he expect from the revamping of the judicial system? Can the outlines of the Napoleonic state Lebrun eventually helped to build be detected in his proposals in 1769 for new legal codes and for a school of administration within his "supreme court"?

The broader ideas that inspired the specific proposals of the memorandum should not, however, be neglected. Like La Chalotais, Lebrun believed that the modernization of education was basic to the modernization of the state. The reader may wish to compare the educational prescriptions of the two men. Do these reflect their differing social positions and political orientations? Are the reforms sought by Lebrun conceived in a more democratic spirit than those of La Chalotais? What relationship did Lebrun expect to exist between a government dedicated to a new purpose and a newly enlightened people? The reader might find it helpful to ask himself how likely it was that the kinds of government and citizenship Lebrun envisioned could develop in a France ruled as the parlements declared it must be ruled. Were they any more likely to develop under a royal authority exerted in the manner it had been in the Brittany Affair? How then was such a state with such citizens to be realized, if many Frenchmen were eventually to agree with Lebrun that they were desirable?

The Frenchman whose agreement to his proposals Lebrun most needed in 1769 was, of course, the chancellor. Maupeou's comments after reading his young protégé's memorandum thus should be carefully studied for what they reveal about the possibility of change under the Old Regime and about Maupeou himself as an agent of change. Did he deny that Lebrun's proposals were desirable, or that they were practical? Who or what, according to Maupeou, could be expected to make their implementation impossible? Does this expectation suggest how the chancellor's approach to the problems of the regime differed from that of Lebrun?

Lebrun tells us that after this reception, he decided to confine himself to working for less sweeping changes. The final chapter will enable the reader to judge to what extent even piecemeal reform could be carried out under the Old Regime.

Selection from the Memoirs of the Baron de Bésenval

The Duke d'Aiguillon, in his youth, had served at the head of a regiment in the war against the King of Sardinia. At the conclusion of peace, following his inclination for public affairs, he asked to be employed by the government, instead of devoting himself to society, to women (for whom, however, he had a great deal of appetite), or to the life of Paris which is so seductive for a young man, and was employed in Brittany, of which he was given the command-in-chief. He soon revealed an obstinate, ambitious, evil, and above all vindictive character. War having again broken out, the English attempted a landing in Brittany, at Saint-Cast. M. d'Aiguillon, warned in time of this irruption, hastened there; but instead of placing himself at the head of his troops, he climbed up in a nearby windmill, from which he watched the battle and the repulse of the English. M. de la Chalotais, attorney-general of the Parlement of Rennes, was so imprudent as to comment in a letter: "Our commander-in-chief watched the battle from a windmill, in which he covered himself with flour instead of laurels." This got back to M. d'Aiguillon, who from that moment vowed the destruction of M. de la Chalotais and constantly searched for an opportunity to carry it out. This opportunity came; or he provided it himself, by charging M. de la Chalotais with sedition and other acts of grave import, at the time of the ferment he had himself aroused in Brittany by infringing upon the privileges of that province, and by the harsh and unjust manner in which he administered it. By means of one of those *lettres de cachet* so common during the reign of the late king, M. de la Chalotais was imprisoned in a castle, and a commission was named to try him. Either because no grounds could be found for condemning him, or because the public outcry intimidated the commission, exile and the loss of his office were for him the end of this affair.

As a result of the hatred which it aroused against M. d'Aiguillon, there were no limits to the things that were said about him. He was accused of everything, even of tampering with witnesses, poison, murder. Things went so far that he thought himself obliged to come to Versailles to ask for a trial to clear his name. M. de Choiseul, who still enjoyed unlimited influence, prevented his request from being granted, not for d'Aiguillon's own sake, since they were already on very bad terms, but in order that the king's orders, which M. d'Aiguillon would have been obliged to introduce as evidence in order to clear

Baron de Bésenval, *Mémoires* (Paris, 1805), II, 172-93.

his name, should not be brought into a court of law and divulged.

Since the rumors against him continued, M. d'Aiguillon kept asking to clear his name; and, finding that M. de Choiseul was falling into discredit, and aided by the Chancellor Maupeou, he succeeded in having the Parlement of Paris begin his trial. The king desired that this be done in his presence, and the parlement came to hold its sessions at Versailles. There were only two of them, after which the king commanded that the trial go no further, and forbade any further investigation. The parlement had been drunk with joy at trying a great lord, with the king presiding and ostentatiously permitting great freedom in the votes, and taking one side or another, and greeting by name the councilor who had raised a certain point: theatrics which will always turn the heads of second-rate people, who think that they are therefore playing a great role. The parlement, angry at M. d'Aiguillon who had offended it by personally attacking a magistrate [La Chalotais], hurt because the course of justice had been interrupted, and because the king had halted so swiftly a scene which flattered its pride; animated, moreover, by several other considerations, enacted a decree by which it declared M. d'Aiguillon to be of tarnished reputation, and, as such, not entitled to his seat as a peer, until a regular trial was held.

Chancellor Maupeou, who came from a robe family with not much of a reputation for probity, acted true to form. After he had become first president of the Parlement of Paris, M. de Choiseul had chosen him to be chancellor, in spite of all the warnings he received that he would soon repent of the choice, not only from the point of view of public affairs but also from that of his own interests, in thus elevating an unprincipled man capable of anything, who would soon become his most mortal enemy. Events swiftly bore out this prediction. M. de Maupeou, having everything to fear from the parlement which was planning to attack him and to denounce his management as first president (which indeed was not without blemish or reproach) declared openly against M. de Choiseul, rallied to M. d'Aiguillon and to Madame du Barry, who, having been unable to win over M. de Choiseul, went over completely to M. d'Aiguillon who controlled her.

M. de Choiseul, either for reasons of principle or for reasons of politics, defended the parlement and was on good terms with it. He is accused of having corrupted it to the greatest extent by lavishly spending money on it, in order to have registered the innumerable edicts under which the kingdom was crushed, in order to prevent the collapse of the finances, exhausted by the wars and depredations of the reign of Louis XV. To attack the parlement was thus to attack M. de Choiseul, who could not fail to come to its defense and thereby give his enemies a means to blacken his reputation with the king, who was weary of the eternal resistance of that company, as well as of the boldness and even insolence with which it had opposed his will. This reason alone would have been enough to decide M. de Maupeou and M. d'Aiguillon; but they had still more pressing motives. Maupeou feared that the parlement would bring charges against him; d'Aiguillon had a shady reputation and saw a possibility of clearing himself with a new trial at the first favorable moment; here were more than enough reasons for both to push things as far as they would go. This can be seen all the more clearly from the fact that M. de Choiseul had already been exiled to Chanteloup when the edict which brought about the catastrophe of the parlement appeared.

By this edict, which was issued December 7, 1770, the king destroyed all the present power of that company, placed a barrier against any further usurpations, and virtually limited it to the sole function of dispensing justice. If M. de Maupeou, the author of this edict, foresaw from the first all the consequences of such a step, it is undeniable that this plan was one of the boldest and vastest which a minister could conceive, and its principles, though they can be attacked, can also be defended. But the course of events, the slowness and uncertainty of decisions at various points, prove that M. de Maupeou, drunk with the power he had captured, restrained by no consideration, undertook this policy casually, prompted only by his hatred and thirst for vengeance, his sense of security and above all his ambition, hoping to seize control of all power, by making a despot of an old king sunk in debauchery, fatigued by the smallest amount of business, leaving it all to be directed by his ministers, and revolted by the additional trouble given him by the resistance of the parlements.

M. de Maupeou found it the easier to take such steps and risks because M. d'Aiguillon, a man of a more persevering and profound character, not yet having any marked influence, was only rising imperceptibly in his shadow, and consequently was closely tied and completely devoted to him. With his help, M. de Maupeou could be quite sure of managing the king as he chose, M. d'Aiguillon having entirely captivated Madame du Barry by a means which is infallible with women, if you know what I mean.

The edict of December 7, 1770, will always remain an event too memorable in France for there to be any need to give the details of its contents, which will be noted in all the annals of the nation. It caused the greatest excitement; everyone parliamentary, and everyone attached in some way to the parlements spoke out against it; the friends of M. de Choiseul, or, to use the expression of the time, the Choiseul party, made a great outcry; the women who had become cele- brated by openly resisting and reviling Madame du Barry did not miss such a good opportunity to support what they called the "fundamental constitutions of the state." In conversation, at suppers, people talked of nothing else; and these assemblies of high society and pleasure be- came little estates-general, in which the women, transformed for the nonce into lawgivers, recited maxims of public law and historical prece- dents, and established principles, with a confidence and boldness derived from their desire of dominating the scene and attracting attention, a desire reinforced by the importance and celebrity of the issue. . . .

As one might expect, the parlement combatted with all its power an edict so contrary to it. Without going into exact and continuous detail of everything which happened in this regard, it will be enough to say that there was remonstrance after remonstrance, in which eloquence, vehemence, and precedents were exhausted. Since the royal court re- mained unshaken, it was compelled finally to resort to a *lit de justice,* in which, despite the opposition of the parlement, of the princes, and of what were called the good peers, as well as of some of those to whom their offices gave a right to participate and vote, the edict was registered by force. With this operation completed, the parlement, as usual, employed its ordinary measures, and protested. But in view of the gravity of the situation, it employed its ultimate and strongest weapons, which had always worked so far; it remained, with all cham- bers assembled together; that is, . . . it refused to dispense justice.

With this step things had reached a point where a decisive choice had to be made. The uncertainty and slowness of the royal court to take this decision reveal, moreover, that it had engaged itself in this struggle irresponsibly, and that in beginning this great affair, it had not seen where it might lead, nor the alternatives suitable under various circumstances. Simply to exile the parlement only to let it return later was an outmoded policy which achieved nothing, and which ministers had only followed so as to be able to sacrifice the glory and the au- thority of the king less openly, and to give the impression that they were yielding to the public interest, to the cries of the people who soon become annoyed at the duration of the difficulties, and at seeing their businesses suffering from the interruption of justice. But in this par- ticular case, it was the interests and security of the chancellor and of M. d'Aiguillon which were compromised. Either these two personages would have to be brought down, or the parlement would have to be destroyed. But if they destroyed that company, it would be necessary to find another to take its place, and this was the difficulty. They had tried in vain with money and promises to detach some members of the parlement; if the avarice of some tempted them, they were restrained by the certainty of their dishonor if they went over to the king.

M. de Maupeou, embarrassed, thought for a moment that his schemes had been checked, when M. de Boyne came to his rescue, and found means to persuade the Great Council to replace the parlement. But since this tribunal did not have the necessary number of magistrates to make up a full parlement, anyone who wanted the vacant places was accepted. Ignorance of jurisprudence, vile ancestry, unspeakable reputation, none of these was a reason for exclusion. There was hardly any reason to expect any other sort of man, because anyone who accepted would be condemning himself to public scorn and hatred for sitting in the seats of judges who in the general opinion were being overwhelmed by royal oppression. The clergy, triumphant at finally seeing its enemy laid low, also worked with all their power to facilitate the actions of the chancellor; the Archbishop of Paris in particular distinguished himself by convincing several of his canons to take the place of councilors.

While all this was being arranged, the court not only made no reply to the remonstrances of the parlement, but also received very badly the delegations responsible for bringing them. It sent *lettres de jussion* ordering the resumption of service on three separate occasions, allowing between these the formally prescribed interval; these were of no avail: the parlement showed itself to be as unshakeable as the court, which finally took the decision to strike the great blow it had prepared with so much difficulty. That same night [January 19, 1771] the Grey and the Black Musketeers, who are commonly given this sort of detail, carried to each of the members of the parlement a *lettre de cachet* informing him of his exile, and of the place he should go to remain until further orders. Most of them were sent to their country estates; but those who had been the most mutinous, and who had stirred up the others, were relegated to the farthest corners of the kingdom, to isolated places with few attractions, where a stay would be very disagreeable.

Paris, which by its cries had prompted the parlement to an extreme resistance, went wild against this act of authority. It was far worse a few days later when the parlement, the court of *aides* and the Great Council were juridically abolished, and a new parlement was created from the debris of the Great Council and from the kind of men described above. Everyone lost his head, and even in the streets there were cries of injustice and tyranny. The women distinguished themselves especially. According to them, the monarchy was on the point of collapse; they spoke of the parlements as of victims being slaughtered on the altar of despotism, complaining less, perhaps, at the suppression of their offices, for which an offer was made to reimburse them, than at the exile, especially of those confined in unpleasant places. . . .

The common people and the *bourgeoisie,* although displeased, were not so violently so: regarding the parlements as the victims of their own selfish pretensions, they did not defend them as if it had been a matter of the public good. Nevertheless, the court seemed to fear revolts, and took some rather overdone precautions by placing posts of the Watch at the Palace of Justice and along the streets by which the chancellor and his following were to pass, when he went to install his new parlement. . . .

The proscription of the parlements was extended to the provinces. Almost all of them were destroyed; in their place were installed tribunals called "superior councils" composed of assessors of rather low quality, although nevertheless superior to the people who composed the new Parlement of Paris. In most cases the intendant of the province presided over these "superior councils". . . .

Selections from the Autobiography of Charles-François Lebrun

It was time for me to choose a profession, and I still could not decide; but finally I thought that I was destined for the bar; I would study law. The son of M. de Maupeou, the first president of the Parlement of Paris, who had already inherited the office of *président à mortier* from his father, was beginning his studies along with me. He needed an assistant for his work. M. Lorry, a professor then famous on the law faculty, spoke of me; and it is to him that I owe my acquaintance with M. de Maupeou.

The father of the first president was vice-chancellor and keeper of the seals; he was quite old; M. de Lamoignon, the titular chancellor, was likewise aged: the public had already marked out the president of the Parlement of Paris to succeed him.

This section and the following one have been translated and reprinted from Charles-François Lebrun, *Opinions, Rapports* . . . (Paris, 1829), 9-22, 171-88.

The vice-chancellor was no first-rate magistrate, and had grown feeble besides in his old age; but he had a most noble and most impressive aspect; his majestic air and his frequent happy inspirations compensated for his lack of the eloquence of other magistrates; besides, he was a most estimable man in his private life.

It was on his son that the government counted for hard work, mental capacity, and force of character. The son was neither a l'Hospital nor a d'Aguesseau. He had none of the qualities of some of his Lamoignon ancestors under Louis XIV, nor of Malesherbes in our times: that easiness of manners, that conviviality, that taste for letters and arts— qualities which made and will preserve their fame.

Indefatigable in his work, austere without being unpolished, careful with his money, but far from any thought or action which overstepped the boundary of delicacy in private affairs, his life was a continual bustle. He started at four in the morning at the Palais de Justice with reports, orders, appeals, often the tumult of the assemblies. Then home to more work: public and private audiences. In the evening came perhaps a short conversation with members of his family, but always about some serious affair, almost never literature. Scholars or *philosophes* came into contact with the first president only by accident. I did not know them myself except through their works; and I had neither the desire nor the opportunity to get acquainted with them. Even a vacation was just more business.

M. de Maupeou had succeeded M. Molé, a good man and a virtuous man, but hardly like the Molés in the days of the Fronde, in the first presidency. These were difficult times now; there was constant trouble in almost all the parlements, at Toulouse, at Grenoble, at Besançon, at Pau. There was trouble especially in Brittany where peculiar circumstances rendered the parlement more stubborn and dangerous. In the Parlement of Paris there was less excitement, but a fire smoldered beneath every inquiry.

In the affair of the Jesuits, the government had appealed to the peers in order that they might remove certain of their fellows from the power of the provincial parlements. These men, carrying the king's orders to the courts, had been detained by the very courts where they were fulfilling their missions. The government had hoped to create, in this way, a rivalry between the Parlement of Paris and the provincial parlements, thus breaking up the unity which had grown up between them. But the peers sided with the parlements; and a prince, who had already drawn great advantage from his dealings with the Parlement of Paris, sowed the seeds for new dealings.

A councilor of parlement, M. de L'Averdy, had been called to the ministry of finances; soon others who had influence with the parlements were called in. But they lost their influence as soon as they became the government's men.

In these circumstances, I thought that the calm spell would not last, that soon the joint meetings of chambers, judges' strikes, and perhaps mass exiles would start up again, and that consequently affairs would slow down and that a lawyer's business would suffer.

Besides big cases were rare and I wouldn't have wanted to waste myself on the little ones. I could have taken advantage of my position to attract clients, but this offended my sense of delicacy. A natural timidity, which has never allowed me to approach a rostrum without fright, made me feel that I would not succeed as an orator—besides the eloquence of the bar, modeled at the time on Gerbier, was not yet what I would have liked it to be.

Without deserting jurisprudence completely, I concentrated more on our public law and on the study of our history and its grandeurs. I had a colleague who had been a tutor for the Duke of Penthièvre, and whom this prince still consulted about his son's education. He asked me for a work on the history and government of England, but M. de Lamballe [the son] soon fled from his lessons and his life as well. I sometimes met at this same friend's the Abbé Mably.[1] I had read and liked his *Phocion;* as for his person, I found him to have a philosophical mien and a scholarly air which did not appeal to me. His book raised protest in the parlement and was menaced with denunciation and prosecution; I managed to help quiet the uproar. On my recommendation, the first president welcomed it with interest, promised his protection, and kept his word.

In 1765, without having desired it, without even having thought of it, I had been named [royal] censor. I seldom exercised this power of censorship. Still I recall a *Voyage à l'Île de France,* whose author I did not suspect, but who later wrote *Paul et Virginie* and the *Études de la Nature.*[2]

The *Testament de Voltaire* was brought to me. This was a joke which could hurt the old fellow of Ferney; I did not want to give my approval for it.

1. [Gabriel Bonnot de Mably (1709-85), historian and *philosophe,* is chiefly remembered today as a precursor of the nineteenth-century socialistic and communistic social theorists.—Ed.]
2. [The author was Jacques-Henri Bernardin de Saint-Pierre (1737-1814), whose works literary historians cite as foreshadowing the transition to Romanticism.—Ed.]

Thomas asked me to be his censor; I knew and respected his talents, but he was too much the *philosophe*. I did not want to enlist with the *philosophes;* I refused. I would have preferred to see them devote their energies to a field other than the one they had chosen. It seemed to me that the government could make them into useful auxiliaries in the fields of administration and internal politics, could direct their attacks against the barriers which separated province from province, against privileges which placed uneven burdens on the people, against number-less contradictory customary laws, against the diversity of legal systems, against courts which were distant and inaccessible to people bringing suit, against usurped jurisdictions, against that swarm of guilds which hindered industry and stopped its progress. In every part of France there were reforms to carry out, people to be enlightened; but what was needed was one single direction, one course and united action—and there was no such thing. In the different departments of the ministry reigned a continual flux of principles and systems.

Much was being written at the time on [religious] tolerance. Several works on this subject were sent to me, and I had to give my opinion; it was the same as it is today. Our conscience is free: our opinions, so long as they remain concealed within our minds, bow to no power. But when they break out they become an expression of doctrine and enter the domain of authority. If they are injurious to public morals, if they offend an established religion and threaten to overthrow it, they ought to be suppressed by the courts. And if they take on a hostile character, and break out in revolt, this means war, and one has no choice but to use force. This is what happens when political interests get mixed up with religious arguments; this is what happened in the time of Luther and Calvin: then there was civil war, and these wars ended in overthrow or in treaties. Henry IV did what was necessary under the circumstances: he granted political existence to the Protes-tants, he made concessions to them which, to a certain point, created a state within the state.

Richelieu repressed them; Louis XIV erased every last trace of their political existence. He decreed that there were no Protestants, just new [Catholic] converts. He banned the pastors; he had the churches de-stroyed; he thought he had annihilated the sect. But Protestants still existed, and in legal fiction these men were no longer citizens. The Catholic clergy, who issued the official documents of the state, did not recognize their births, their marriages, or their deaths; but finally the administration was forced to recognize the fact of their existence: it tolerated their gatherings, it tolerated their services, and the courts recognized marriages which the law did not. It was believed that the Protestants would become accustomed to this servitude; it was hoped that time would bring them again to the fold of the predominant religion—but a century of experience proved this a delusion. The Protestants were quiet, but they remained discontented, and consequently always potentially dangerous. The only solution was to make them full citizens, but the alarm of the clergy was feared, and this would also have destroyed all uniformity by creating for a few citizens a separate manner of registering births, deaths, marriages, and inheritances. The great name of Louis XIV dignified his errors; and there was no minister at that time who dared to propose such a measure to the King's Council. . . .

M. de Lamoignon was still in exile; his family, and especially M. de Malesherbes, desired his return to Paris; but to return he would have to give up his post and he was afraid that the vice-chancellor, whom he did not like, was earmarked as his successor; so he refused to resign. He had a bad leg; his doctor believed it to be the beginning of gangrene, and the old man believed it himself. People reassured him about his successor: so he gave for the son the resignation he had refused to the father.

When M. de Maupeou arrived at the Chancellery [in 1768], he certainly had the support of the most influential magistrates. The Duke de Choiseul ruled over the court at the time; he was less a favorite than a master. War and foreign affairs were in his hands; he dominated even more by his character than by his talents. His military reforms had made many discontented, his position and his power had made many enemies; but all bent beneath his will. The family alliance had connected Spain with France; he pampered Vienna, which responded in kind; in Russia there was great respect for his ability and capacity; he kept his eye on England, doubtless dreaming to avenge France's humiliations.

The Duke de Praslin, his relative, was minister of the navy. Less brilliant, more stable, he advised Choiseul while yielding to his influence. He rebuilt slowly, but he repaired the losses we had suffered with more dispatch and less cost than did the Duke de Choiseul in his two departments.

L'Averdy, the minister of finances, made a mess of a department he did not understand, and gained neither success nor confidence.

La Vrillière, the minister of the king's household, kept to his little circle, distributing *lettres de cachet,* bringing orders of exile to disgraced ministers. The king had found him in the ministry at the beginning of his reign; and he stayed put there during all the changes.

Bertin, who had been minister of finances, had become special minister of the fortune of the king which he separated carefully from state business; he paid for the king's fancies and was privy to his passing tastes.

These were the men, dressed in titles of state, who formed, with certain others, what was called the Privy Council, where matters of politics and foreign affairs were handled.

The chancellors and keepers of the seal did not participate in this council. Some of the predecessors of M. de Maupeou had taken part because they had first been ministers, and had kept their places there. Thus, under Louis XIV, Voisin, the minister of war who became chancellor, Machault, minister of finances and of the navy, Berryer who followed him and d'Aguesseau did not enter the council. M. de Torcy advised the latter to take part in politics and hinted that this would bring him a place; but d'Aguesseau was content to be minister of justice and never set his sights higher.

M. de Maupeou likewise kept within the narrow circle of his duties; the affairs of the magistracy kept him busy enough: he foresaw the storm which must come because of the new attitude of the parlements and especially because of the state of the finances.

We talked often. I spoke to him of England: I told him about the responsiveness of the organs of her government, about the security of her throne, about the ease of all great enterprises there, how the whole nation moved as a single man. No partial resistances—No bodies [*corps*] to disturb the ensemble of the system—How happy France would be with such a constitution! What might not one expect from this spirit which seemed to possess the whole society? There were no longer any of these great vassals who opposed their powers to the power of the monarchy, no more of the secondary powers with whom Henri IV and Louis XIII had had to negotiate. The principles of administration were starting to filter down to all of the classes; the third estate would support royal authority against the views and the interests of the nobility, the clergy, and the parlements.

With these ideas I drafted a memorandum in which I demonstrated that there was no possibility of government in France; that no true system of finances could be established; that no general legislation could be formulated, if the nation persisted in walking blindly in the footsteps of the past; that with all of these parlements divided in their views, but united in their resistance, the exercise of authority was no longer possible; that it was necessary to appeal to the nation without waiting for it to come over of its own will; that this was the direction in which public opinion was moving, that it would come to this sooner or later, perhaps under more difficult circumstances. I did not go into the constitution of the Estates-General. I believed that once the necessity of calling them was recognized, the best possible form to give them would be perceived by patriotism, intelligence, and interest of all.

The chancellor read the memorandum: "This is certainly a fine undertaking," he said to me, "But where are the means to carry it out? I'm no l'Hospital. I would have enough tenacity to pursue a plan from which I had some hope of success. But it is not enough for a minister to have character, he has to convince the other ministers, he has especially to convince the sovereign, he has to find in the sovereign enough constancy and firmness to support his projects.

"Unfortunately the Estates-General have not been convoked except in times of stress; composed of discordant elements, of ambitious and quarreling great lords, of a powerful clergy, of a very weak third estate, they have so far produced only unsatisfactory results. This is why sovereigns have feared and ministers opposed their convocation. They would rather deal with difficulties with which they are familiar than throw themselves into an unfathomable abyss. By his position a chancellor has nothing to fear in an assembly of estates; he only interprets the laws, he only recalls the courts to their duties: no manipulation of finances, no favors to distribute. It is different with the other ministers: they can be attacked from every side, they fall with the slightest breeze. If I were to take this memorandum to the council, everyone would rise up against me; I would be accused of betraying the throne, of being the accomplice or the dupe of the *philosophes;* they would send me home to my estate to learn something about government.

"Only a king of energetic character, covered with glory, controlling public opinion, could form and perhaps carry out such a plan. Such a king would find ministers ready to help him and a nation ready to follow him. Louis XV loves his people; but he is ruled by maxims left him by his ancestors and by fixed ideas that derive from his early education; innovations frighten him, obstacles discourage him, the strong moves which he has occasionally been persuaded to attempt have always ended in acts of weakness.

"But if the Estates-General could be convoked, and this led to a happy result, the difficulties would not be over yet. They would present their grievances and propose wise measures; it would then be necessary to convert these proposals into edicts, and present them to the parlements. The latter would discuss them; against every innovation they would invoke old principles and old customs. The *pays d'états* would demand their old constitutions; most of the provinces would claim historic rights and privileges. A great stir would be aroused with no result. Thus I am reduced to following in the footsteps of my predecessors, to modifying and correcting what I can in the department of justice, while awaiting a better day which for me will never come."

I took back my memorandum, and henceforth limited my ideas to more restricted topics.

The king's domains were composed of various territories, subject to diverse customs, and feudal dues varied with the customs: they were collected rigorously although they were adjusted with each individual lord. From this arose the most unfavorable arrangements in the tenure and the fiefs of the king. I thought that it would be equally advantageous to the king and to the public to reduce inheritance fees to a uniform tax, and to fix this tax so that it would be more advantageous to be a vassal or feudatory of the king, than to be a vassal or feudatory of an individual lord.

The king had his feudal right of pre-emption and a right of preference which he could cede to others. This double right frightened the buyers of properties which might be at the mercy of the royal domain or at the mercy of persons who had influence at the court: I would have wished at the least that the right of preference be suppressed.

With this done, acquisitions within the tenure of the king would have become more popular; but I had to make the idea seem attractive to the minister of finances who perhaps would have seen nothing in the plan but a decrease of production. It would have been necessary to overcome the resistance of the parlements, which would have been especially strong because their private interests would have been injured. Because almost all of them owned fiefs, the magistrates would have seen in a decrease of the king's feudal rights only the decrease of their revenues and would have disguised their private interests as the interest and untouchability of the crown domain.

The King of Sardinia had authorized in his estates the buying-up of feudal rights. M. de Maupeou tended to favor such a measure; but the buying up of these rights would have created new difficulties, and it might be contended that the sums derived from this operation would only go to waste in squandering and useless expenditures.

Legal studies had degenerated in almost all the universities. Pothier and a few other professors had kept them up at Orléans; they went on at some of the faculties in the south. I put forth reform proposals. I had a lengthy correspondence with Pothier, and following his ideas I drafted a project of law which events have made superfluous.

Seigneurial jurisdictions were a usurpation, and there were abuses in all of them; the chancellor would have liked to have abolished them. He would especially have liked to have evened out the districts of royal justice, distributing them in a more regular manner over the kingdom, and suppressing those which were unnecessary. I undertook this task with ardor.

Jurisprudence was not at all uniform in the different courts. D'Aguesseau had labored to establish this uniformity; but there remained much to do, and I was called to the job. It earned me, from 1770 on, a salary of 2,000 francs which I enjoyed until 1789. . . . .

Selections from a Memorandum Prepared in 1769 by Lebrun for Chancellor Maupeou

The dignity of the chancellor is nothing more than a vain title now that foreign policy on one hand and finance on the other have become the two pivots of all administration and governmental affairs.

The state has been swept aside by this double movement; and in a whole reign there is scarcely a moment of quiet when one can take a look at the civil constitution, at the internal organization of the monarchy, at manners and morals, and at the laws.

Circumstance and chance sometimes bring change, a few new modifications; but the foundations of the structure have never been examined; no one has ever tried to bind anew the links which ought to form the chain of society. The result of this is that this chain is often broken, its function left unfulfilled—thus, no common center, no united action, and consequently less real force, less public spirit, less patriotism.

EDUCATION

For a chancellor there are other duties and other spheres of activity than those to which he has been limited in recent times. Looking first at how the ancient legislators proceeded, at the foundation on which they built the edifice of government, one sees that the chain of society has always begun with education, that the principles of the constitution of society take root in childhood, become stronger as the child grows up, and blossom in the mature man. And this is the case not only in republics, but in monarchies and even the despotic state.

In France there is no civil education. Minds are cultivated but almost never are citizens trained. We never leave the hands of our teachers filled with the precepts, rules, and maxims of government by which we should live. Thus the nation has no fixed character; there are no general principles to which all minds can rally—only a vague taste for independence, freedom of opinion without any notion of the good and the bad which society can bring. Surrounded by all the benefits of administration, people only feel the burden which society imposes. Thus arises a murmur of discontent, always ready to erupt, and an eternal criticism which the government would heed if it were enlightened, but which leads instead to contempt and disdain because the government almost always acts absurdly. From this comes hatred of the instruments of public power and finally a constant contest of wills whose union would make the monarchy strong and prosperous.

The populace, almost always abandoned to itself, knows the government only as a regulating and repressive force. The zealous clergy inspires an obedience based upon the duties of religion, but rarely upon a settlement of self-interest and personal security. All that is seen of governmental authority is the hand that establishes it, that protects and avenges it: but authority should rather be seen as a beneficent knot, uniting all interests, and as a rampart defending them. Industriousness ought to be encouraged, and the miserable ought to be saved from their discouragement, which results more from their ignorance than from their wretchedness.

To remedy this failing in public instruction, we only need elementary books which can guide the first steps of youth. Such books would deal first with the elements of natural law, but in the simplest order and stated in terms capable of capturing the imagination of children. The instructors would put these principles into action: even the games of their pupils would demonstrate the bases of the moral and social order. Thus each child would form the habit of reflecting on his rights and his duties and fixing their limits, and of discerning the point at which individual interest, for its own security, ought to yield to the general interest.

The authority of institutions weighs upon children too heavily and without any intermediary. They obey out of a feeling of impotence and necessity, never from a feeling of suitability and order. The result is that to command and to obey are only expressions of tyranny and servitude for them; and once they accept this, their opinions on the nature of government and of the submission it requires are determined for the rest of their lives.

The education of several ancient peoples was much wiser. They put the pupils themselves between other pupils and the instructors. Children commanded other children under the eye of the teacher, whose task was to explain the commands and to encourage obedience. Thus the nascent society formed by itself; thus developed the feeling for and the logic of its ties. Because they were accustomed from the cradle to command and obey their equals, the citizens knew how to command without pride, and to obey without grumbling; and they exaggerated neither the rights of authority nor the misery of submission.

We are taught the exercise of private virtue; we ought to be trained in the exercise of public virtue as well. We ought to be moved by that enlightened benevolence which embraces a whole society, stimulates work and diligence while alleviating misery, and places in every worthy act a seed which reproduces and multiplies.

How the minds of children would be broadened, how their ideas would be extended, if useful and patriotic expenditures were substituted for these senseless expenditures which are lost in vain amusements! There would always be branches of industry to encourage, disasters to repair, some new trail to blaze, some experiment to try. We would need only to open this career to our teachers; they would know how to make it interesting for their pupils; and soon every educational institution would be known by its acts. The publicity they received every year would spread the enthusiasm. Children, accustomed from the start to seeing the true source of public prosperity and to considering it their own work, would support it with all the force of their self-respect, and would carry through their lives the imprint of their first habits and of their first principles.

As they grew older, they would be shown more extensively the nature of government, its organization, its rewards—everything that concerns public order, the interests and resources of the state, its commercial and diplomatic relations—that is, all except the secrets of domination. And all this would be presented in a clear, precise, and recognized work by the government.

These concepts would avoid any deviations, would keep imagination within definite limits, and the government would have neither abuses nor noisy ignorance to fear. Unjustified complaints would die within the narrow circle where they had been born; and a unity of sentiment would add all the energy of public opinion to all the power of authority.

As for the education of the populace, it would be necessary to adopt a very comprehensive plan which would relieve the government of that multitude of annoying details which leave it open to abuse and occasional intrigue. A bureau might be created in each diocese to supervise the education of children, to prevent and suppress begging, to direct useful public works and to keep workshops always open to employ the unfortunate; and finally to execute and justify to the administration and to the public any detentions requested by families or necessary for public order. This bureau, made up of the bishop of the diocese, of several other members of the clergy, of magistrates, of the most distinguished citizens, would keep in constant correspondence with each of the parishes of the diocese, would assess their needs, would direct the use of public charities, would supervise the schools and regulate the schoolwork; and along with instruction it would always provide work and means of subsistence. There is practically no child who is unemployable; and in this scheme each school would be a factory or a workshop. Thus a taste for work would be instilled in the children; there would be no more excuse for sending them away to beg for their bread; they would find it in the schools themselves.

All the infirm poor would stay in their parishes and would receive the necessary aid while remaining with their families; the able-bodied poor would obtain aid in an ever-open workshop without leaving their dioceses.

Mendicants, apprehended at every turn, confined to abodes designed uniquely for the poor, would be taken back to their dioceses at the expense of the diocese to which they belonged.

Every time that an order of detention was requested, the bureau would have to be consulted; only through its agency could individuals be arrested at the request of their relatives.

Vagabonds or presumed vagabonds arrested by the constabulary would be detained only after being examined by the bureau or by a commission of the bureau.

This scheme would take care of other necessary tasks which today burden the provincial intendants and are the bane of the administration.

No more of these vast depots for the poor which weigh down the public treasury and which, concentrated in a single town or region, constitute a privileged industry which ruins the others by the low price paid for labor; where a crowd of bad characters, thrown together, have nothing in common but vices; where the most honest administrator gets nothing for his trouble but abuse and ingratitude.

LAW STUDIES

In the midst of these general views the education proper for the magistracy ought to be discussed. The schools of law need to be revived; forgotten subjects must be renewed and revised in a manner appropriate to our legislation and our needs. Several schools must be suppressed which exist only by abuse, and whose scandalous leniency only serves to multiply those dangerous men who sow chicanery and new trials, and those useless men who vegetate beneath the shade of a title which they debase by their indolence and incapacity.

THE "SUPREME COURT" (HOW IT OUGHT TO BE DIVIDED)

Supreme justice is in the hands of the sovereign. It ought to reside in all its brilliance and purity at the foot of the throne. Thus, a tribunal is needed whose eminence could command the respect of the other tribunals; which would state the letter of the law when the others wandered from it, and which would also show its spirit and intent. This tribunal, among the perpetual changes of manners and customs, could indicate what changes in legislation were necessary, bring together its diverse parts, giving them a unity and harmony which would assure the confidence and veneration of the populace, and which would make them lasting.

Such a tribunal does not exist, and cannot exist except by means of a reorganization. The present council is composed almost entirely of old magistrates who have aged in the tasks of administration—who, in the course of their career, have forgotten or at least lost sight of the laws and their judicial manifestations—and of young men who, scarcely familiar with the first principles of law, strangers to our regulations and customs, all look to the moment when they can proceed from tedious individual discussions to the details of administration.

The "supreme court" could be formed only of magistrates whose whole life was devoted to the functions of the judiciary; who, after having distinguished themselves in the superior tribunals, would at last sit at the foot of the throne to judge the tribunals themselves. Limited to these functions, there would not be many of them and the royal finances would not be strained in repaying honorably their efforts.

Another council could be reserved for administrative matters. At its head would be men coming to the end of long careers as intendants; below them, those destined to enter this career. All administrative disputes would be brought to this tribunal. All purely administrative laws would be discussed there—those regulating the collection of taxes, those concerning internal and external commerce.

Men whom the sovereign would one day call to the most important posts would be formed in this school. From there they would go to work with the intendants to serve an apprenticeship of their functions, to study on the spot the needs and the resources of the different provinces. Thus would be established a chain of principles and a tradition of the true precepts of government. The men would change, but the spirit would perpetuate itself from epoch to epoch; and the administration would acquire a sort of consecrating immutability.

The Great Council would no longer be a tribunal of original jurisdiction but of judicial review, evocations, and special commissions which would constitute an important jurisdiction to embrace all areas, consequently forming magistrates fitted to serve on other tribunals.

PARLEMENTS

Several parlements cover too great an area; several, too restricted in one direction, spread out in the other, losing themselves in the bizarre divisions left over from feudalism. All are too large; all are burdened with a crowd of lesser officers who live off abuses and petty annoyances.

Bring the litigants closer to the judges, equalize the territory of the various tribunals, cut down their number so that all their members are continually occupied; specify definite limits for the inferior jurisdictions, and equalize them among themselves by exchanges and compensations; cut down everywhere on the number of public attorneys (*procureurs*) and bailiffs; these are all tasks which the chancellor ought to try to fulfill.

[There follow details on the resistance to be expected from the parlements, on the means to conquer this resistance, and on the creation of superior councils. The author then turns to the venality of offices, which he discusses in these terms:]

If bodies existed which could regard themselves as the recipients and proprietors of a portion of the royal authority; if these bodies, indestructible like the constitution of the state, could choose their members or only accept those whom they pleased; if all these members, linked already by common interest, were further linked by bonds of family and ancestry—would there not be a danger that a sort of oligarchy would soon arise, which at first would gain the support of the people to attack the sovereign, and after it had tied the hands of the sovereign, would fall upon the people with all its weight, oppressing them in every possible way? Guardians of civil rights, controlling life and honor—what resort would be left to the citizen to protect himself from oppression? There would be no more administration except that which was subject to these bodies, no more liberty, no more security except what they were willing to grant. It is the duty of the chancellor to combat this system, condemned by all the greatest and most virtuous men whom the magistracy has ever seen.

Venality was the fruit of public misfortunes. The funds that our kings drew from the sale of offices they should have drawn from the nation. The nation, thus, still really owes a debt and it is in its interests to pay off this debt.

A provisional tax, a contribution assessed to buy back the offices, but earmarked so that it would be impossible to use it for anything else, would certainly not frighten anyone. At least the sensible men whose opinion eventually becomes public opinion would have applauded this step.

Doubtless the reduction in the number of offices would diminish the yield of incidental revenues, but this loss would only be momentary. On the one hand, the superior councils could be subjected to some sort of tax; on the other hand, if the plan were executed in all its scope, the inferior jurisdictions where venality could be allowed to continue without great inconvenience would regain their former popularity, and offices which today are empty would finally have occupants.

But besides, the different branches of public revenue ought never to be regarded as isolated and unrelated. If the result of a new order of things were more activity in the provinces, more industry, better agriculture, more commerce—if a mass of individuals lost in the dust of the legal profession in petty procedural details, would engage in enterprises of all kinds—who would believe the sum of new wealth that this revolution would engender in the state? Who could estimate how much the other sources of revenue of His Majesty would grow? In any case it is certain that other sources of revenue nourish and stimulate one another, while venality dries up and devours these sources.

SEIGNEURIAL JUSTICE

Justice has become a part of private property. This is not the place to examine by what right the most important and most sacred branch of public power can have become the patrimony of a subject.

This is one of those abuses which time has consecrated and which, linked with the idea of property, could only be destroyed by undermining property.

But although justice is in the hands of individuals, the sovereign always has the power to modify its exercise, to prescribe its rules and its limits.

Our kings have sacrificed to the public interest the right to dismiss their officers; this same public interest demands the same sacrifice of the individual lords. A judge cannot be a servile tool to be engaged or dismissed at will; he cannot be just the first man to come along; he must have real competence, verified by a strict examination or derived from long practice at the bar, and guaranteed by a title. No judge should be dismissed. Every judge must have a law degree; every judge must be submitted to rigorous tests by the tribunal on which he is to serve; every judge must have exercised for five or six years the functions of a lawyer at the bar.

Doubtless these restrictions would strike a great blow at the swarms of seigneurial jurisdictions whose limited territory can give a judge neither real employment nor prestige. These jurisdictions would fade away by themselves; and without affecting their owners, their extinction would be one less affliction for the vassals.

CRIMINAL JUSTICE

Criminal justice can belong only to the sovereign; there is no excuse for the usurpation of this terrible and necessary right; these abuses have to be attacked head-on, and the inviolable rights of public power must be asserted.

By a further abuse this onerous right remains ineffective in the hands of the lords; thus ever more crimes are committed with impunity. We ought to work to bring this right back into the domain of the sovereign without offending anyone's ideas or rights. And this act of enlightened legislation could be presented to the justiciar-lords as a benefit. The usurpation would cease; there would remain only the memory, an insubstantial shadow which would fall effortlessly of its own accord if the government should ever believe it necessary to efface these vestiges of ancient barbarism.

CONFISCATION

The confiscation of the property of a convicted man is an atrocity stemming only from greed; it was born in Rome in the midst of the proscriptions; it was perpetuated by despotism; it has become part of our practices only to abuse and corrupt our morals. Although tempered today by the benevolence of the sovereign, it is still nothing but an instrument of vexation and plunder in the domain of the king. It breeds a race of informers; it debases the ministry with officers who, trusted with the interests of the crown, never look after any but their own.

A law which makes the offense of a single man into the crime of his whole family, which in punishing the offender wipes out all his posterity, is no law, it is madness. Such is the law of confiscations which disinherits an innocent son, which leaves him no patrimony but shame and censure, and forces him at last to flee a country where he is robbed by opinion of all the rights of honor and robbed by the law of all rights of property, a country which leaves him only a precarious and debasing existence.

The criminal code ought to be appreciated for that precision and energetic clarity which distinguished all of the codes of the good days of Louis XIV. It is radiant with all the splendor of the monarch from whom it emanated, and backed by the authority of the great men who had drafted and discussed its provisions. Today one can propose only with a sort of awe the modification of a few of its aspects.

It would seem suitable to suppress the jurisdiction of the military provosts, or at least limit it to the excesses committed by military personnel on march. Now that there are no more fortresses, now that the highways are open from one end of the kingdom to the other, now that commerce, industry, and the arts have tempered manners and morals, now that law enforcement has become more energetic and more rapid, France has no more need for the intervention of military power except to command respect for the laws and their agents. If there are extraordinary cases where authority must assert itself, authority is everywhere present, and has everywhere sufficient forces to repress and to punish. For these anticipated cases more abbreviated procedures could be established, which although not managed by the military, would nonetheless fill the guilty with terror and the innocent with confidence. When questions of jurisdiction were settled, the citizens would cease to be intimidated by a force which, intended to regulate and protect them, could still usurp the right to oppress them.

The greater part of the defects of which our criminal code is accused are the fault not of the criminal code itself but of the ignorance of the judges and of the general defects of our education. Most of the magistrates, rushed into their offices without a thorough study of the laws of nature and the first foundations of civil law, rely on unreliable guides: on routine and on the authority of former judgments and of jurists. It is from this double source that they draw these often erroneous precepts with which they fill what they call the gaps in the code; when they ought to be drawing only from reason and from the general principles of natural equity. Thus arises that fatal scorn in which the law is almost always held, but which is the fault only of the commentators who have obscured it. It would be a most useful enterprise to ban all the works of the criminalists and to set forth the elements of criminal jurisprudence which would serve as an introduction and a complement to the civil code, each of whose precepts would be sanctioned by a law. There, all the principles which ought to guide the judge would be expounded; there would be recalled the first laws which are born with man himself and which ought to be the basis of all positive laws and ought to clarify their application. Such a work would demand the participation of the most learned men and of the wisest magistrates.

As for the code itself, the quickest way to get rid of its imperfections would be to make trials public. But perhaps public trials would have their dangers for us: at least our customs seem still to be contrary to the restoration of this ancient practice. Still, immediately after the examination of each witness his name and his domicile ought to be made known to the accused. If some minor difficulties might result from this knowledge which today is concealed only from those deprived of all aid and support, the results of the ignorance to which the law condemns a man right up to the moment of confrontation are far more terrible. In the latter case he is startled and confused; his memory fails him; the facts are confounded in his mind; he cannot pull his thoughts together; he cannot understand the net of intrigue in which he is caught; he cannot distinguish in the stranger whose testimony is sending him to the scaffold the agent of an enemy who has sworn his ruin, or a rascal who has already brushed with the law and whose testimony the law ought to reject.

Counsel could not be given to the accused in the cases where the code refuses it to him; but after the confrontations he ought not to be refused a defense.

The public minister is his natural defender as well as his accuser; but these two roles combined in the same person inspire more terror than confidence. The most stoic and impassive mind can rarely resist forming a presupposition, born of public rumors and of that union of circumstances which rouses the first suspicions and provokes the accusation. Often the scales are tipped before the proof is complete and the magistrate is so carried away by a desire to avenge the crime that he can see nothing but guilt.

It is even more difficult for the judge himself to remain completely impartial until the evidence overwhelms him and necessitates conviction. In his examinations he acts with the suspicious spirit of an inquisitor; the uneasiness of the accused damages him in his eyes; and sometimes accumulated probabilities become for him convincing proof. To protect the citizen against these dangers, I would place, beside the magistrate whose duty is to condemn or absolve, a jurist whose unique duty would be to protect and defend the accused.

Obligated, like the judge himself, to inviolable secrecy, he would have the right to examine the proceedings, to assist in the report, and in between the report and the verdict, to set forth forcefully all that might disprove or mitigate the offense; and the text of this defense would be included in the record of the trial. Each year the bar would name one of its members to fill this august function; distinctions and, if necessary, remuneration would be attached to it.

Some may think perhaps that it would be more just and more humane to give the accused a counsel to aid him during the first stages of the trial. But perhaps others equally sage would think that this counsel would only hinder the proceedings, and would furnish the guilty with means to evade the vengeance of the laws, or at least retard punishment; and that a defender such as I propose would suffice both to hold the judges to the exact observation of the code, and to guard them against their own predispositions; and finally that, if the first judges resisted his defense, the court of appeals would have to weigh and discuss it again.

There is one law which does honor to the humanity of our neighbors and well merits to be inaugurated by the clemency of our sovereigns; this is the law stipulating that no condemnation involving physical punishment be executed before the verdict is put before the sovereign along with the reasons which might lead him to soften its rigor.

VI

THE DESTRUCTION OF THE PARLEMENTS AND THE ACCESSION OF LOUIS XVI, 1770–1776

Introduction

Between 1770 and 1776 the conflict that the reader has been studying since before the arrest of La Chalotais reached its crisis, a crisis that some historians believe was the decisive confrontation between the principle of royal authority and the principle of privilege—whether of a province or of a class—under the Old Regime. This crisis had two high points upon which the reader should focus his attention. The first came with what Voltaire called Maupeou's "revolution," and others called, with some exaggeration, his "destruction" of the parlements in 1771. The second high point, which since it reversed the "revolution" of 1771 might be called the moment of "counter-revolution," followed shortly after the death of Louis XV on May 11, 1774.

The reader might begin his study of the crisis by reconstructing the narrative as far as the issuance of the royal edict of February 23, 1771, comparing the account in Lebrun's autobiography with the documents promulgated by the contending parties and with Voltaire's private and public comments. The starting point is the opening of the Duke d'Aiguillon's trial before the Court of Peers (i.e. his fellow peers who sat in the Parlement of Paris) on April

4, 1770. After the duke's resignation as commander-in-chief in
Brittany in 1768, the crown had finally yielded, in July of 1769,
to Breton protests against the "baillage d'Aiguillon" by restoring
to their offices most of the judges of the former Parlement of
Brittany who had resigned in 1765. La Chalotais and his son, however, remained in exile. To obtain justice for them, their restored
colleagues launched a sweeping investigation of d'Aiguillon's administration, in the course of which it was alleged that d'Aiguillon
had bribed witnesses against La Chalotais and even plotted to
have him poisoned. It was to counter such charges that the duke
demanded a trial and had Linguet draw up the brief from which
excerpts have been provided in earlier chapters of this book.

As he continues his reading of Lebrun's autobiography, the
student already has a partial answer to the question of how the
Brittany Affair helped provoke Maupeou's "revolution" of 1771.
He knows that proving the guilt or innocence of d'Aiguillon, like
that of La Chalotais earlier, was a matter of political as well as
juridical concern. The quarrels of Rennes had already been trans-
muted into great constitutional issues when the duke went on trial.
Therefore Lebrun's account should be studied not for his explanation of the Brittany Affair but for what it reveals of his side of the
coming constitutional confrontation. How important, again, does
he show the incidents of court intrigue, on the one hand, and deliberate planning for reform, on the other, to have been in guiding
Maupeou's policy? Did the aftermath of the d'Aiguillon trial provide the chancellor with an excuse for acting, or did these events
compel him to act?

The ruthless and imperious Abbé Terray, appointed comptroller-
general in December 1769, has not always been highly regarded by
historians influenced by the scathing denunciations of contemporaries. It has sometimes been suggested, however, that Terray's
plans for fiscal reform represented the monarchy's last hope of
averting the bankruptcy that opened the way to revolution in 1789.
Does Lebrun's description of the Abbé's appointment suggest that
the crown was carefully preparing to deal with its chronic financial

problem by forcing a showdown with the parlements, the chief obstacle to tax reform? Were Terray, Maupeou, and d'Aiguillon a united "triumvirate" assembled to carry out such a policy, or were there divisions among them that reflected the varying paths they had followed to power and weakened them in the face of their adversaries?

One way to approach this question is to decide which side really initiated the see-saw procedural battle that began when the king closed d'Aiguillon's trial on June 27, 1770. Was Louis XV challenging the parlements by staking out an area within which his judicial authority was not to be questioned? Or was closing the proceedings against the former commander-in-chief again a clumsy tactical retreat from an embarrassing situation, in which witnesses before the highest court in France were testifying that the king himself had insisted on La Chalotais's conviction?

With the trial thus abruptly broken off, the reader has only the preceding chapters of this book to go on if he wishes to decide whether d'Aiguillon had been more or less guilty of malfeasance in office than La Chalotais had been. Does this lead the reader to sympathize with the contention of the Parlement of Paris, in its petition of July 2, that the trial must be reopened either to clear or to convict the duke? Or is justice for d'Aiguillon, the reputed enemy of the Breton nobility and friend of the Jesuits, the real motive for the protests of the Paris *noblesse de robe?* Does the language of the petition show the parlement to be on the attack once more, asserting a doctrine of its nature and function that the king had already rejected? How "humble and respectful" was its attitude? It is possible to answer this question by comparing the wording of the Edict for Regulation of December 1770 with Louis XV's speech at the "Session of the Scourging" four years earlier. Are the doctrines attacked in the edict familiar?

Since there would have been every reason, judging by previous performances, to suppose that the confrontation of 1770 would end as that of 1766 had done, it is a prime responsibility of the reader to decide to what extent this time the outcome was different, and why. Why does the list of officers of the parlements in 1772, given at the front of this book, change so drastically from the lists of previous years? Had the continuing echoes of the Brittany Affair proved the last straw for Louis XV and persuaded him to allow the chancellor to issue the edict of February 23, 1771? Had the curt dismissal of Choiseul on Christmas Eve of 1770 been a warning the parlements were foolish not to heed?

Both the extent and the form of Maupeou's changes in 1771 should be noted. Though the personnel of all the parlements was changed (seventy-five Breton magistrates, for example, were exiled) and venality of office was suppressed, only two sovereign courts, those of Rouen and Dijon, were actually abolished. Was the Duke de Croÿ therefore using too strong a word when he spoke of the "destruction" of the parlements? Particular attention should be paid to the last paragraph of the February edict. Does it suggest that there were traditions that even a king who derived his power from God alone dared not ignore? What was the purpose of creating "superior councils" (with salaried, non-hereditary judges) to hear cases within the sprawling jurisdiction of the former Parlement of Paris? Was this a device to make the blow the monarchy had inflicted upon the *noblesse de robe* more acceptable to public opinion, or was it a genuine attempt at reform (such as Lebrun favored) for the benefit of those Frenchmen who had previously been obliged to travel to Paris to seek a costly justice?

Whatever the intentions behind them, some idea of the impact upon public opinion of Maupeou's changes can be gained from Voltaire's writings and correspondence through the crisis. The extract from his *The ABC,* written in 1768, makes it evident, if further demonstration is needed, what his own reaction would be, and whether he believed France faced a greater danger from monarchical despotism or from judicial oligarchy. The inspiration for the appearance of the *History of the Parlement of Paris,* sections of which appear in the first chapter of this book, should now be clear. A guess might even be made as to which of its chapters disturbed Madame Denis, Voltaire's niece. But what were Voltaire's motives in actively backing Maupeou's "revolution," once it had actually begun, with pamphlets like *The Peoples to the Parlement?* His letters to the Duchess de Choiseul, in exile with her husband, offer one explanation; is it the true one? Or was Voltaire making a skillful effort to side with one of the court factions without losing touch with the other?

Perhaps the best way to analyze Voltaire's motives is to try to formulate just what his ideal of government—and the estimate of human capabilities that underlay it—really was. There are clues to both scattered throughout his correspondence, but his letter of April 29, 1771, to his nephew d'Hornoy, one of the councilors of the Parlement of Paris exiled in Maupeou's purge, is probably the most revealing. How does it help to explain the apparent paradox that Voltaire, who found so much to criticize in the Old Regime, nevertheless found much to praise in Louis XIV who had laid so many of that regime's foundations? Does it make that other paradox—that he, the anticlerical champion of the unjustly oppressed, backed Maupeou, whose other chief supporters were the so-called "devout" party, the friends of the Jesuits—seem less paradoxical?

Voltaire's letter to Maupeou himself suggests just how much he expected—whether realistically or not the reader must judge—from the assertion of enlightened and determined royal authority. Yet others of his letters—not to mention his pamphlet propaganda—attest to his continuing fears that Maupeou's assertion of that authority would not be sympathetically received either by French intellectuals or by the population at large. Condorcet's letter in defense of Voltaire's position shows that these fears were indeed realized. Condorcet's arguments may be found persuasive; it is important for the student to ask himself, however, whether Condorcet himself detested the parlements for the same reasons Voltaire did. Does he condemn them in terms Voltaire would not have used for reasons with which Voltaire would not have sympathized? When he has answered this question, the reader may see the necessity of posing another: if, as we know, Condorcet enthusiastically accepted the Revolution of 1789, would Voltaire, had he lived to see it, have done so?

The fact that Condorcet found it necessary to explain Voltaire's position makes it obvious, in any case, that many Frenchmen did not share Voltaire's enthusiasm for the Maupeou "revolution." Voltaire had a ready, and disparaging, explanation for this attitude of public opinon; is it an adequate explanation? To answer this question, the reader must really search his own mind to determine what his reaction to Maupeou's attack on the parlements is, and on what premises that reaction is based. Does the reader find himself in agreement with Condorcet's critical analysis of the parlement's motives in persisting in its attempts to try the Duke d'Aiguillon, or can he find a case to be made on some grounds—historical, political, or moral—in the parlement's favor? Voltaire declared that he would rather be in the grip of a lion than be gnawed to death by rats. Having seen both the lion and the rats at work throughout the Brittany Affair and its aftermath, the reader may feel that the lion was not so noble, even if the rats were as vicious, as Voltaire believed. But even if Voltaire's terms were correct, the reader may find rule by a lion or by rats an unappealing set of alternatives. Were these the only political alternatives available to eighteenth-century France (or any society, for that matter)?

The Duke de Croÿ's portrait of Louis XV may provide a clue to the explanation for the opposition to the Maupeou "revolution" that so annoyed Voltaire and Condorcet. The reader will have to decide whether some of the particular royal traits Croÿ describes actually negate his final verdict on the dead king. Would public awareness of these royal weaknesses explain why comparatively few Frenchmen were enthusiastic about the last episode of his reign? Does the character of Louis XV supply an argument for, or against, Voltaire's political philosophy? Croÿ's conversations at Versailles offer some additional evidence on why, in 1770-71, a new confrontation between the *noblesse de robe* and the monarchy did not end in stalemate as previous ones had done. Croÿ's misgivings about Maupeou's "revolution" and the fashion in which the king's ministers allayed them also suggest why that "revolution" was so much more limited than the one the young Lebrun had envisioned. (Croÿ's diary also raises a question which may tempt philosophers of history: would the Brittany Affair and thus Maupeou's attack on the parlements really "never have happened" had Croÿ agreed in 1762 to replace d'Aiguillon in the command of Brittany?)

Croÿ's description of the momentous events of August 24, 1774 —the second high point of this crisis of the Old Regime—also stresses mere chance as a causative factor. The reader will have to decide whether the decisions taken by the new king on that day were indeed an unpredictable accident, or whether they were the result of social and political realities of the Old Regime that not even the king could for long defy.

The effect of those decisions, in any event, was totally to reverse Maupeou's revolution. Eleven weeks after the chancellor's dismissal, on November 12, 1774, Louis XVI held a *lit de justice* before the judges of Paris whom he had recalled from exile. The former parlement was "recreated and re-established." Offices in it again became hereditary, and its jurisdiction reverted to the old boundaries. The "superior councils" were abolished. True, the king did insist on some changes: the *chambres des requêtes* were eliminated (one of them was restored less than a year later) and a place was found for Maupeou's judges in the *Grand Conseil,* where they were soon subjected to harassment by their triumphant rivals like everyone who had co-operated with the former chancellor. (Linguet, who had been unwilling to boycott the Maupeou parlement and had tried cases before it, was disbarred.) The effect of Louis XVI's solemn prohibition of remonstrances before registration was made, judges' strikes, and all the other tricks in the parlement's bag the reader will be able to gauge for himself from Voltaire's correspondence through 1776. Restoration of the Parlement of Paris was followed by restorations in the provinces. Thus it was that after all his tribulations, Attorney-General La Chalotais had the consolation of returning to Rennes in almost royal style, his coach preceded by two hundred jubilant Breton noblemen on horseback and followed by a long procession of the carriages of the aristocracy.

Further Selections from the Autobiography of Charles-François Lebrun

The troubles in Brittany still continued; the Duke d'Aiguillon had been in charge there for many years. This name, Aiguillon, stops me here; he has injured me, and I ought to be afraid to say it of him.

The Duke d'Aiguillon was intelligent, knowledgeable, restlessly active, and above all strong-willed—a forceful, peremptory, and stubborn will. One was either for him or against him; he did not forget his friends, but he forgot even less those he thought were not.

Often given difficult orders, he carried them out with more than precision. Under his regime, the Estates of Brittany were tumultuous; the members of the opposition were often called to the court, kept there for a long time, and sent away with harsh warnings.

Nor were *lettres de cachet* lacking. The Duke d'Aiguillon was a relative of M. de La Vrillière, who sent them out, and thus had only to ask for them.

In the parlement, as in the estates, there was resistance, and M. de La Chalotais, then attorney-general, was accused of being the leader. He had been active in the destruction of the Jesuits; his vigorous indictments—for which the Jansenists and the *philosophes* of Paris furnished the material—had gained him a great reputation; and this reputation had encouraged his opposition to the measures of the court.

With provincial frankness, in the liberty of conversation, he was free with his sarcasm at the expense of the government and at the expense of the Duke d'Aiguillon.

Parties had formed in Brittany; on one hand, the rigid Bretons, those who supported or thought they were supporting the interests of the province, and the ardent defenders of the parlement; on the other, the friends of royal authority and those who hoped for advancement. The members of the estates and the parlement were indicted; those who regretted the passing of the Jesuits, and in general all those who were religious but not Jansenist, grouped themselves around the authorities. Letters full of gross insults, in the vilest language, were sent to the minister. They were anonymous; but people thought or pretended they recognized the handwriting of M. de La Chalotais. Hate is credulous: M. d'Aiguillon and his party believed these rumors. La Chalotais was thrown into the Bastille; a commission was called to judge him. It was in this commission that M. de Calonne, who was minister of finance in the following reign, distinguished himself. The commission came to

C. F. Lebrun, *Opinions, Rapports* . . . (Paris, 1829), 22-42.

no decision; its members did not believe themselves impartial enough
to judge M. de La Chalotais.

When M. de Maupeou arrived at the Chancery [in 1768], Brittany
was without parlements. The magistrature was then re-established, M.
de La Chalotais was left in exile, and the Duke d'Aiguillon was dismissed. Furious at his disgrace, he thought only of how he could rise
out of it and avenge himself on M. de Choiseul, whom he deemed responsible, and who for his part regarded M. d'Aiguillon as an enemy.

Madame de Pompadour died in 1763. This left vacant a post of
honor; a king without a mistress was unthinkable. The place, although
it had been degraded because Mlle Poisson had been a commoner, was
still coveted as it had been in the days of de Mailly de Châteauroux.[1]
Louis, out of lassitude or indifference, would soon have forgotten his
loss. Everyone thought he would return to his family, and this was
doubtless his first thought and intention. He hoped to conquer his
weakness, or at least limit himself to his obscure, passing fancies; but
boredom pursued him ceaselessly; he had to have his little amusements.
He could not tolerate serious reflection and was disgusted by mimes.
Many beauties were available; he had the run of the court and of the
town. He fell for no one at first: a few minor affairs came to nothing
in the shade of the Parc-aux-Cerfs. Finally there came a great master
of corruption and intrigue, who undertook to give him a mistress.
From the depths of the gutter came suddenly a woman of charming
aspect, whom an adroit master had molded to all the arts of licence.
By what means this man had gotten close to the king, I do not know;
those who remembered the past said he was introduced by a great lord
ripened in the intrigues of the court, long privy to the weakness of his
master, and concerned with the fate of M. d'Aiguillon because of
family ties. In any case, it is certain that M. d'Aiguillon soon became
the counselor of the new mistress. Still, people tried to find other
support for her, and it was even hoped that she could gain M. de
Choiseul. He had come to power through the influence of Mme de
Pompadour, he had reigned with her, and it was believed that he would
like once more to have the support of the royal mistress. But M. de
Choiseul was unbending; if not from the austerity of virtue, it was from
indignation at the infamy and commonness of vice.

Others too complained softly; the devout at the court deplored the

1. [Madame de Pompadour had been Antoinette Poisson before becoming the
Marquise de Pompadour. Marie-Anne de Mailly-Nesles, Duchess de Châteauroux,
had been Louis XV's favorite in the 1740's.—Ed.]

weakness of the king, but who knows, perhaps the heavens permitted it to destroy the proud Aman and the *philosophes*.

Everything fell apart around M. de Choiseul, and his opponents soon took on the aspect of a party. I ask what Sully [2] would have done in such a situation. Doubtless he would have thrown himself at the feet of his master; he would have begged the king in the name of his honor, to protect him from disgrace and shame. If he could not have moved him, he would have gone silently, forgetting his pride, to bury himself at Rosny. M. de Choiseul thought otherwise and resolved to resist the storm which menaced him.

These times were among the saddest of my life. For a king of France to stoop so low; and at his age! And it was not the ardor of his temperament that swept him away; for I do not believe all these shameful stories spread by malicious courtiers. "Darmentières [Choiseul] is committing suicide" is about what the king said to his ministers at the time. "He is sacrificing himself to his name" (everyone smiled), "yes," he added, "when one marries at my age, those are just spadefuls of earth, thrown on one's head."

Louis clung to life, and was terrified of death; thus it is very probable that tales told about the secrets of his chambers were greatly exaggerated.

But what would be the attitude of the ministers? Would they lower themselves to be courtiers of the new mistress? I trembled at this idea.

The chancellor had not yet publicly bowed down to the idol; still M. d'Invau had put forth his projects for the finances. Before submitting them to the king in his council, he wanted to ask the opinion of the ministers; they were assembled. The comptroller-general elaborated his views; the chancellor combatted them forcefully, and the majority agreed with him. M. d'Invau shut his portfolio, said he had nothing more to propose, and resigned.

The king was informed of the result of the council and of the resignation of the comptroller-general. How would he be replaced? M. de Choiseul said he knew no one; that none of the candidates he had proposed to the king had yet been successful; that it was the chancellor who was familiar with the finances, and that he would have to be asked. The ministers retired and in the evening of that very day Mme du Barry visited the chancellor to offer him, on the part of the king, the portfolio of the finances.

2. [Maximilien de Béthune, Baron de Rosny and Duke de Sully (1560-1641) was the minister and friend of Henry IV.—Ed.]

When she had departed, the chancellor called me and told me of the proposition which had been made to him. "Of course you know," he added, "that a chancellor does not usually become comptroller-general and especially these days; but who else is there?" We considered the intendants; we could find no one. M. Turgot had a reputation, but more among the *philosophes* than among financiers. M. de Choiseul did not think he was of ministerial stature, and he belonged to the *économistes* who were still just a sect in the eyes of the court.

The Abbé Terray had the best mind in the parlement: this in itself was not enough to make him a minister of finances, but he had a sure touch, reliable judgment, capacity for work and extensive private means. Such a man, given the opportunity for real glory, would indubitably make a good minister. The chancellor could find no one better, and stopped there. The next day he presented himself to the king, explained to him the reasons which kept him from assuming the burden which the king wanted to impose on him, and suggested the Abbé Terray to him.

The Abbé Terray was named [December 22, 1769]. This choice displeased M. de Choiseul and his party. They decided to work at overthrowing the new minister.

The power to emit notes had been given to the treasurers of war, of the navy, of foreign affairs, in order to assure service. The notes were about to expire, but it was hoped that they would be renewed. The treasurers refused—the influence of the Duke de Choiseul was suspected.

The Abbé Terray did not hesitate to suspend the notes. "I suspend the 'assignations,'" he wrote to the Chancellor: *"Si fractus illabatur orbis, impavidum ferient ruinae."* And he paid for the services with the funds which were to have paid back the notes. . . .

Mme du Barry wanted to be presented at the court. The king feared a scandal; but she had her mind made up, and had to be obeyed. A woman was sought at the court who would be willing to perform this shameful function; the search was long and futile. Finally a woman of quality was found—newly arrived from the provinces, poor, and with children whose fortunes she wanted to assure. She undertook this shameful and cheerless mission [April 22, 1769] and was rewarded for it by a few favors accorded to her son and her daughter. It was a spectacle of ignominy which drew all the town and all the court.

The Duke de Choiseul, secretly undermined by the Duke d'Aiguillon, menaced by the king's mistress, still had great support and great hopes. . . .

M. de Choiseul had also great influence with most of the discontented princes of the court, with the parlements whose pretensions he had never injured, with the military whose present table of organization was his work, and with the *philosophes* whose voice then represented public opinion. Thus he imagined that he could ride out the storm.

M. d'Aiguillon advanced step by step to ingratiate himself with the king, and to give the impression that he was a favorite. He bought for a high price the post of commander of the light horsemen of the guard: it was said it had cost him twelve hundred thousand livres to obtain the resignation of the Duke de Chaulnes. All that remained was to dissipate the cloud which his command in Brittany had cast over him. He had an exonerating memorandum drawn up by Linguet, a man of talent, who had acquired some degree of celebrity at the time.

Armed with all the weapons which he believed necessary for his defense, he undertook to refute all the accusations leveled against him. The Countess of Forcalquier was his friend; and President de Fleury, a man well versed in these affairs, was the oracle and advisor of Mme de Forcalquier. Consulted by her about the position of the Duke d'Aiguillon, he deemed it necessary to carry the battle into the Court of Peers. The Duke of Fitz-James had avenged himself in this court for the attacks of the Parlement of Grenoble. The interests of the peerage were united with the interests of the Duke d'Aiguillon; many members of parlement, of the Great Chamber especially, favored him.

The chancellor at first opposed this step; he outlined the dangers involved in such an action. The mass of enemies whom the Duke d'Aiguillon had in Brittany would unite with his enemies at the court; then it would be necessary to justify not only the Duke d'Aiguillon, but also the authority whose instrument he had been. These observations passed unheeded. M. d'Aiguillon saw perhaps in the chancellor's opposition nothing but ill-will and hate: he was insistent. The will of the king, or rather the will of his mistress, had to be obeyed. The affair was brought to the Court of Peers [April 4, 1770].

The chancellor, in his speech at the opening of this assembly, traced the limits within which the case of the Duke d'Aiguillon ought to be kept. Had he betrayed the confidence of the king? Had he gone beyond his orders? Finally: had he turned to Brittany's misery an authority which had been given him only to insure the happiness of that province?

The trial began; witnesses were called from all corners of the province. They came armed with the *lettres de cachet* and king's orders with which he had plagued them. Passions were aroused; it was no longer just a matter of the duke's administration of the province; the government itself was being put on trial. Then it was realized that the royal authority was being compromised; it was decided that the trial would be halted, the minutes destroyed, and that absolute silence would be imposed [June 27, 1770].

This was done; the Parlement of Paris protested and released a decree [July 2] which held that this act could only be regarded as an act of annulment, and that the Duke d'Aiguillon was not yet cleared. Most of the other parlements adopted the same injunction. This co-operation revived the idea that all of the parlements formed one single parlement, and armed them against royal power.

Taxes were needed, and in this general mood struggles and united resistance seemed likely. The government resolved to anticipate them, to bring the parlements back to avowed monarchic principles, and to raise around them an impassable barrier. . . .

This was the state of affairs as the edict of December 1770 was prepared. This edict was not the work of the chancellor only. He was in agreement that it was necessary to set limits for the parlements which they were not to exceed; to forbid prohibitory decrees, judicial strikes, mass resignations, decrees adopted by one parlement from another; remonstrances before and after registration would always be permitted and always received. On these bases I prepared a projected edict; it was thought too weak; another was drafted by the Abbé Terray, and was adopted exactly as he had drawn it up, both the preamble and the articles.

No one imagined that such an edict would pass without opposition; there would certainly be stubborn resistance. But there were wise men in the parlement; the *Grand' Chambre* was full of magistrates grown old in office, beyond the heat of passions, no longer tormented by ambition. Content with their station in life, they thought of nothing but the trials and their vacations. Some were even assured of the favor of the court; all had the backing of their superiors in what they demanded for their children; they desired nothing beyond the serenity which they had achieved; the prestige which power always brings followed them everywhere. The agitation in the assemblies of the chamber was for them no more than an inopportune annoyance that distracted them from their affairs and from the things with which they were daily and uselessly occupied.

The chambers of inquiry [*enquêtes*] were made up of younger and more eager magistrates, hungry for fame; some aspired to higher positions and needed a stir to arrive there: there was no lack of examples to encourage their hopes. But there were many who did not have their sights set so high, who hoped for nothing more than to succeed quietly to the profits of the *Grand' Chambre*. Thus, there was hope that the edict would be registered in a *lit de justice,* that there would be nothing more than remonstrances which would gradually die out. It was even imagined that to weaken the edict, the parlements would solemnly recognize its principles, that they would formally agree to them and that then the government, disarmed by this public show, could withdraw with honor the edict, now rendered superfluous by the voluntary recognition of the parlement.

The edict was released; the first reaction was general stupor and consternation; then remonstrances were issued in the chambers. The parlement remained in session. The remonstrances had no effect; royal letters ordered registration; new remonstrances; more royal letters ordering both registration and resumption of services. There were no registrations; but the *Grand' Chambre* took up its functions again to judge a case involving Mme de Monaco, and through her the Prince de Condé. The assemblies of the chamber started up again; there was no new series of remonstrances.

Nevertheless, M. de Choiseul was disgraced; a stern *lettre de cachet,* the letter of an angry woman more than of a king, dismissed the minister, sending him to Chanteloup [December 24, 1770]. . . .

Foreign affairs was still unfilled; this was the department which the Duke d'Aiguillon desired; it was there that Mme du Barry wished to see him. For his part he would have liked all the offices that M. de Choiseul had given up but this had been forestalled by the nomination of M. de Montaymard [as minister of war]. The chancellor first recommended M. de Vergennes, the man who at the time had the greatest reputation of all our diplomats. But he was not able to exclude the Duke d'Aiguillon from the list of possibilities. The mistress had demanded it; the king resisted. He had a long-standing dislike for M. d'Aiguillon; he had reservations as to his character, and doubtless a bitter memory of the affair in Brittany; but how might he withstand the wishes of Mme du Barry? He put off his choice, and handled the department of foreign affairs himself, for a while with the help of the Abbé de La Ville.

It was thought that the disgrace of M. de Choiseul would change the mood of the parlement. But, although deprived of his support, the parlement still counted on the greater part of the princes, on the temper of public opinion, on the demands of the other parlements, and of the various courts of the kingdom. It would not yield; the chambers stayed in session. The third and the last orders to register the edict were given: they produced no result, and thus a *lit de justice* became necessary.

The discourse which the chancellor delivered on this occasion was my work, and the chancellor made no secret of this. It was a public success; someone wrote to the chancellor: "Why did you not let the fellow who wrote your discourse write the preamble of your edict?" It made me a reputation although I had no ambition. People wanted to meet me; I was forced to flee the clamor. People at the court sought to arouse my ambition, and proposed that I enter the council of the princes. I was given, without asking for it, a position as inspector of the domain of the crown.

After the *lit de justice* the parlement still stayed put; no more hearings, no more verdicts, just new remonstrances. Orders were given to the body as a whole to resume its functions; to no avail. Individual orders were given to each of the members; some presented themselves, but all declared that they could act only as a body.

Next came *lettres de cachet* and exiles, some of them very harsh. It was believed that this last measure would have some effect; but all accepted their exile despite its rigor; no one implored grace of the sovereign. No one offered to negotiate a truce. . . .

Thus, the parlement had to be replaced, and judges had to be found. First the councilors of state and the chiefs of requisitions were installed: they only staged a useless spectacle—neither lawyers nor public attorneys appeared, and justice remained mute. Nevertheless, superior councils were established at Lyon, at Blois, at Châlons, at Poitiers, in Artois [February 23, 1771]; this pleased the provinces. The towns where they were assigned received them with joy; Voltaire praised them in several pamphlets, thus losing favor with M. de Choiseul.

Magistrates to sit on these new councils were easily found in the provincial tribunals, and they were generally composed of respected and capable men. Many writers defended what the chancellor had done; I myself wrote and I also revised many works which were sent to us. We were waging this war of the pen with some success.

Nevertheless, the provincial parlements, the superior courts and a swarm of lesser tribunals took up arms, and remonstrances arrived from every corner of France. Among these remonstrances those of the *cour des aides* of Paris, drawn up by M. de Malesherbes, were especially telling. Your Majesty, he said, will never find anything but corrupted or corruptible men to replace the magistrates of this parlement. The phrase struck every one, and intimidated all who would have been tempted to resume their duties or to enter into the new magistracy.

The chancellor himself felt the blow; and the public believed his operation had failed.

The king still could not decide about the office of foreign affairs. M. d'Aiguillon believed I could convince the chancellor to put in a word for him. A certain M. de C***, like me an inspector-general of the domain of the crown, and the creature of M. d'Aiguillon, came every day to urge me to act. He would be minister, he told me, anyway; and if he were not obligated to the chancellor for the appointment, he would be his enemy. I could no nothing; I answered that the chancellor had done all he could do, that now one could only wait for the decision of the master. The king yielded out of laziness; M. d'Aiguillon was named; he remembered well that he did not owe his nomination to M. de Maupeou, and doubtless he did me the honor of thinking that I had played some part in this silence.

Still the attempt was made to form a parlement; the Great Council was left, a sovereign court which owed its existence to the Concordat. This court, often attacked by the parlements, was based on principles which conflicted with theirs, and had injuries to avenge. Pressure was put on those who had the most influence on the members of this tribunal, and a large part of them consented to replace the parlement. What magistrates of the Great Council could be assembled were not numerous enough to form a sufficiently impressive tribunal; the government called in the councilors of the *cour des aides* of Paris, the magistrates of Brittany who had attached themselves to the party of M. d'Aiguillon, magistrates of Besançon, of Pau, of the sovereign council of Alsace who had dissented from the opinions of these courts, members of several inferior tribunals, lawyers, and some ecclesiastics who had studied law and had made a reputation as enlightened men.

A leader had to be found for them who could add to their reliability, and this was a rather embarrassing problem. M. de Miromesnil, first president of the Parlement of Rouen, was approached and refused. M. de Montholon, first president at Metz, would have accepted, but he demanded too much in return. M. de B***, first president of a sovereign court, promised at first but went back on his word. Finally M. Berthier de Sauvigny, intendant of Paris and councilor of state, respected, wealthy and devoted, was asked. He accepted, was named, and the new parlement began to function.

The lawyers still would do no business: the state's attorneys were called to the bar; a few minor cases were pleaded by them in their own style. Finally the lawyers returned, and at their head Gerbier, the most eloquent among them.

Throughout these proceedings, M. de Maupeou maintained great coolness and courage.

Venality, suppressed in the Parlement of Paris, could no longer exist in the other parlements, and their internal state cried out for a general improvement; they were reformed, one after another. A great many of the lower tribunals had risen up in support of the parlements; they too had to be reintegrated into the general system. At last everything was back in operation; we believed we only had to wait for the consolidation which time would bring. I began to take up again the work with which I had previously been occupied: I investigated all that might pertain to the betterment of justice and of the laws. But an interlude was needed, and no respite was given. Soon the hand of M. d'Aiguillon was seen in the Parlement of Paris; a rivalry of influence arose: there was a party of the chancellor, and a party of the Duke d'Aiguillon. Then came a scandal which added to the pressure of opinion a new pressure.

Beaumarchais was in the midst of a trial in the *Grand' Chambre* against Count de La Blanche: the *rapporteur* was a M. Goesmann, former member of the sovereign council of Colmar.[3] Beaumarchais wanted to get at the man who was drafting the decision and paid a high price to obtain an audience with him. The *rapporteur* did not appear. Beaumarchais turned to the man's wife; she promised an audience and received jewels and money on this condition. There was no audience, Beaumarchais lost his case and asked for his jewels and money back. He made his demands public, thus arousing rumors at the Palace of Justice, and a great stir among the magistrates. Beaumarchais was accused of trying to corrupt a judge. He defended himself with the exceedingly witty *Mémoires* which still make for a great part of his renown. He was condemned, Mme Goesmann with him; the husband was declared innocent of the corruption of his wife. But the [new] parlement had been made to look foolish; this was a great stain on its reputation.

Furthermore, M. de Maupeou was put on the defensive—attacked by the old magistracy, by the friends of M. de Choiseul, by those around the Prince de Conti and the Duke d'Orléans, joined by the Duke d'Aiguillon. The latter did not want to overturn the new edifice, he only wanted to overthrow its architect. This state of war lasted until the death of Louis XV.

---

3. [Pierre-Augustin Caron de Beaumarchais (1732-99) later wrote *The Barber of Seville* and *The Marriage of Figaro;* the *rapporteur,* as the name suggests, was the judge responsible for reporting on the case before the court.—Ed.]

Letters-Patent of the King

Handed down at Versailles, June 27, 1770
Registered in Parlement
Louis, by the grace of God, King of France and of Navarre: To all
those who may see these letters; GREETINGS. The particular attention
which we owe to matters which might disturb public tranquillity had
convinced us not to allow our cousin, the Duke d'Aiguillon, to follow
up the complaint which he was to have presented to us last year; but
as our said cousin is now implicated in a trial begun in our Parlement
of Brittany, we have decided that the dignity vested in him requires
the convocation of the peers of our kingdom as he himself requested.
We have proposed to provide our cousin, the Duke d'Aiguillon, and
others who might be implicated in this trial with the most forceful
means possible of vindicating themselves. To this end, we have permitted our attorney-general to bring an indictment, and we have
ordered that for his plea the duke be informed of all the evidence
contained therein. Now that we have been informed of the testimony
we have recognized that some of the witnesses have entered evidence
irrelevant to the indictment entered by our attorney-general, and that
some have referred to the decrees of our council, have brought into
their testimony individual orders proceeding from us, and have attempted to compromise our ministers. We have thought that it is
impossible for us to let a trial continue which tended to submit to the
inspection of the courts the secrets of our administration, the execution
of our orders, and the particular use of an authority in the exercise of
which we are responsible only to ourselves. And however advantageous
it may be for our cousin the Duke d'Aiguillon, and for all those who
have been implicated along with him in the trial to vindicate themselves
according to the customary procedures, it is yet more important for
our authority not to suffer that persons whom we have honored with
our confidence and charged with the execution of our orders be compromised, investigated, or disturbed because of these very orders. Convinced that the conduct of our cousin the Duke d'Aiguillon and of
those implicated in the aforesaid investigations is irreproachable, we
have decided to make use of the plenitude of our sovereign authority.
And to efface the very memory of an investigation which could only
give rise to a dangerous ferment and revive the divisions which have
too long troubled our province of Brittany, we have decided that it is

Jules Flammermont, ed., *Remonstrances du Parlement de Paris au dix-huitième
siècle,* 3 vols. (Paris, 1888-98) is the source for this and the following selection.

in keeping with our wisdom to destroy all the proceedings up until this day, even the complaints entered by our cousin the Duke d'Aiguillon, [and] by our attorneys-general in our Parlement of Brittany. . . .

For these reasons and others which move us in our certain knowledge, full power and royal authority, we have annulled, and, by these acts signed by our hand, do annul: the four depositions of the investigation made in Brittany of February 9 of the present year; the indictment entered by our attorneys-general in our Parlement of Paris; the decree of last April 7 which implemented the said indictment, and which ordered that the evidence contained in it be investigated; the decrees of our Parlement of Paris of last May 9 and June 26 (the present month); along with the complaints entered by our cousin the Duke d'Aiguillon, [and] by our attorneys-general in our Parlement of Brittany. . . .

We desire that the aforesaid complaints, decree, investigation, and decrees be regarded as non-existent, and that all the proceedings remain quiet and dormant, imposing, as regards our attorney-general and all others, over the whole affair and its contingencies the most complete silence. WE ORDAIN to our beloved and faithful counselors and to those at our court, that they have these acts and all they contain read, published, and registered and that they maintain and observe them according to their form and spirit, ceasing in and halting all difficulties and hindrances, anything to the contrary notwithstanding. FOR SUCH IS OUR PLEASURE. In witness whereof we have affixed our seal to the aforementioned acts. Decreed at Versailles, the twenty-seventh day of the month of June, in the year of our Lord one thousand seven hundred seventy, in the fifty-fifth year of our reign. Signed, LOUIS. (And below) By the King. Signed, PHÉLIPPEAUX. And stamped with the great seal in yellow wax.

Read and published by the king in his *lit de justice;* and registered and heard, requiring the attorney-general of the king to execute them according to their form and spirit. In parlement, with the king holding his *lit de justice* at the château of Versailles, June 27, 1770. Signed YSABEAU.

Most Humble and Respectful Petition of the Parlement [of Paris] to the King

Concerning the letters-patent which annul the indictment entered by the attorney-general against the Duke d'Aiguillon . . . the decree rendered in the Court of Peers, the king presiding, which took action on said complaint, and ordered that its contents be investigated; the investigation which followed, etc.

Registered by the express command of the king in his *lit de justice* held at the château of Versailles on June 27, 1770.

Sire,

While all the orders of the state were applauding the return to normalcy and to justice, while all were overcome with admiration and filled with gratitude towards you, still they awaited with respect and with confidence the oracles of justice which it seemed ought to have been forthcoming from the solemn deliberations of your Court of Peers. Why have these so reasonable hopes been deceived? In a single moment they vanish; now an act of the most absolute authority, substituting whim for justice, violates the most precious of forms, nullifies the most eminent of rights, breaks the holiest of laws, and casts apprehension, terror and desolation over everyone. The princes of your blood, and the peers of your kingdom reclaim the exercise of their rights, the magistracy demands the free and customary course of justice, and the citizens of every order ask themselves tremblingly what has become of the rule of law.

Your parlement, Sire, cannot let you remain unaware for an instant of the terrible and sorrowful impression which this event has had upon all; and knowing your love for your people, your devotion to law and order, it is confident that, from your wisdom and your bounty, it can obtain the return to normalcy, when it has convinced Your Majesty of the falsity of the reasons for the decision which you have been prevailed upon to take, the irregularity of the instructions which you have been persuaded to give, and the frightful consequences which result.

Three reasons were apparently presented to Your Majesty to persuade you to hand down the letters published on the 27th of the past month: first the circumstance that, in the investigation ordered and carried out under the authority of your Court of Peers, the witnesses entered evidence which had nothing to do with the indictment; secondly, the fear of bringing to light secrets of the administration; finally the desire to restore order and tranquillity.

Only ignorance of the laws, of the forms, and of criminal jurisprudence, or deliberate neglect of the most obvious percepts, could have given rise to the first of these reasons. Those who presented them to Your Majesty must have known that in the investigations made at the request of a public minister, the public interest imposes on the investigating judge the duty to gather any evidence given by a witness which pertains to a public offense. They must have known that it is left to the wisdom and the prudence of the tribunals to separate out and discard all which does not deserve to be followed up in order to concentrate on things which it is important to go into more deeply; and that as regards the latter it is common practice that in addition the attorney-general of Your Majesty plead them. They must not have known, or must have hidden from you, that nothing is more common and usual in the ordinary course of justice than this. And this first reason totally disappears when one thinks that your Court of Peers could, themselves, in deciding on the basis of the investigation, have thrown out any matters which were completely irrelevant if there were any, and only concerned themselves with those which formed a *corpus delicti*.

But there seems to have been a fear that this supposedly irrelevant evidence might have led to the revelation of the secrets of the administration. How can this second reason be reconciled with the instructions given to your Court of Peers when, in its first meeting, your chancellor notified it of your intentions? Here is how he expressed it: "Accusations have been made against a peer of the kingdom, charged with the execution of the orders of His Majesty; the question is to determine whether a power given for the felicity of the people has become the instrument of their misery; if the confidence of the sovereign has been betrayed or abused. Never has a matter more important been submitted for the decision of the Court of Peers."

And today, Sire, any necessity there may have been to examine whether the use made of your orders and of your confidence corresponded to your views, has become a pretext to interrupt the course of the trial and to avoid the decision of your Court of Peers. Your parlement, Sire, leaves it to Your Majesty to weigh this manifest contradiction; it must deal with a matter more important. Could Your Majesty have been made suspicious of the deference, the respect and the submission of your Court of Peers, of a court made up of loyal magistrates, of the peers of your kingdom and of the princes of your blood? Was it not a personal insult to your foremost and faithful subjects to have aroused in Y. M. the fear that they were seeking to ferret out the inmost secrets of your administration? Would it not, on the contrary, have been better to have exposed to Your Majesty the sizable discrepancy which exists between the causes and reasons for your commands on one hand and the kind of execution which they are given, the uses to which they are put on the other; between the acts which emanate directly from your authority and the abuses which can arise in an administration of individuals, in which thousands of details necessarily escape Your Majesty's penetrating eye and cannot be regulated by you? It is to promote this confusion between objects so distinctly separate that people have succeeded in changing the decision which Your Majesty appeared to have taken last April 4. But you will perceive, Sire, by your superior acumen, the falsity of this second reason; you will perceive that things have not changed since then and consequently still call for perseverance in that resolution inspired by your wisdom and equity.

The desire to restore peace and tranquillity in your province of Brittany, a desire well becoming the paternal heart of Your Majesty, seems to be the third reason which sways you at this moment. But, Sire, permit your parlement to point out respectfully that Your Majesty has already found insufficient the means which today are suggested to you, and that after having recognized this, you took the opposite decision: to restore force to the laws and to rely upon normal judicial procedure. The nation applauded this decision with joy. Before you marched Justice, armed with her redoubtable torch, the truth appeared before your eyes in all of its splendor, a legal act, a solemn, authentic judgment, in conformity with the laws of the kingdom. An act against which it was impossible to protest, rendering due justice to all, would have molded irrevocably public opinion, and would everywhere have restored peace and quiet. It was with this prospect, perceived by your wisdom and prudence, that Your Majesty gave the order for the investigation begun in your Court of Peers; and now it is nullified! The least harm that can result will be that things remain in the state of violent crisis where they were before: convincing proof that the means employed to gain the results which Your Majesty desires are inadequate. But they are worse, Sire, they are contrary to all legal regulations.

The letters which have just been published present a vague and general provision for nullification which seems to apply most particularly to the results of the investigation carried out in your Court of Peers. It is, Sire, a familiar principle of judicial procedure that nullifications have to be formal; they have no effect unless they are preceded by your commands, and provisions are not sufficient in this respect. . . .

After having shown to you, Sire, the illegality of these letters and their contradiction to the ideas of wisdom and of equity which have important truth. These letters are obfuscating and underhanded, it is always moved you, it remains for your parlement to tell you a sad but only by false pretenses that they have taken advantage of your good faith. In actuality, Sire, Your Majesty has been told that the accused, "have always been of irreproachable conduct," nevertheless your parlement must inform you that, on the contrary, the investigations reveal indications of grave and full proof of several sorts of infractions. One single fact will place Your Majesty in a position to realize this: all that was contained in the investigations made in Brittany, all that consequently convinced you to receive the complaint of your attorney-general and to begin the criminal proceedings which concern us, has been verified in the new investigations. To it is joined new evidence of which much, having nothing to do with the administration, is relative only to the object of the complaint. Everywhere are seen the constant and intimate relations of the Duke d'Aiguillon with Audouart; the latter has been implicated by the testimony of a crowd of witnesses in the most culpable of intrigues, trying to force confessions, trying to bribe witnesses, demanding that people supply him with evidence, "immediately; true or otherwise" (these very words are part of the testimony; they send shivers up our spines), always speaking in the name of the Duke d'Aiguillon, always holding out the hope of favors or the terror of threats which only the Duke d'Aiguillon could bring about. Some of the persons, approached first by Audouart, were described as subsequently having had direct contact concerning the same matters with the Duke d'Aiguillon, who is also described as having menace on his lips and a reward in his hand. These practices are sometimes described as having been accompanied by the gravest of circumstances. Sometimes it seems as if they wanted to try to bribe servants; sometimes it seems as if they wanted to aggravate the discontent which subordinates might have had on certain subjects; sometimes, finally, it seems that they stirred up the complaints of obscure personages to whom (still more obscurely) they made loans and rendered monetary aid and other services. Other citizens, on the other hand, have delivered rigorous depositions against them; these persons maintain that it is easy to discern—according to some, by the evidence itself, according to others, by some judicial document, such as the interrogation which they were made to undergo—that they cannot be accused of any other crime than of having testified to the truth in the affair of the six accused magistrates, or of having carried out orders displeasing to the said Audouart in the course of their functions and in conformity with long-standing police regulations. New indications emerged from the evidence concerning the influencing of the votes of the magistrates. It appears that the hope for favors and rewards was not the only means employed, but that they went so far as to use the sordid aid of gold to corrupt them.

Finally, Sire, how can your parlement tell you? Five persons have testified that they knew of a clandestine trip taken by the Duke d'Aiguillon to Saint-Malo, during the time that criminal proceedings against the six magistrates were going on; and testimony already received from a witness bears this out: "The Duke d'Aiguillon asked two of the commissioners: 'But will you have enough to convict them? this evidence and this thing and that aren't sufficient.' To which one of the two commissioners answered: 'A magistrate may well refuse the king something once, twice, even three times; but when the king continues to ask his help he might as well give in. I had condemned M. de la Chalotais before arriving at St.-Malo, and I will condemn him before leaving!' "

Your parlement, Sire, will spare you the details of the diverse abuses in the day-to-day administration, which Your Majesty is necessarily obliged to entrust wholly to persons whom you honor and in whom you have confidence; but the simple sketch which your parlement has just placed before your eyes is enough, Sire, to prove to you, that, far from being described as maintaining irreproachable conduct, the accused [the Duke d'Aiguillon and others], already seriously incriminated by the decree of April 7, are even more incriminated by the investigations. Moreover, Sire, the nullity of the letters published in your *lit de justice,* is written in the very laws of your kingdom. Whatever twist people have tried to give them to delude your wisdom and to deceive your equity and your devotion to the regulations, these letters are at bottom nothing but disguised letters of abolition. The nature of things cannot be changed by changing their names. Letters which interrupt a criminal trial started and still unfinished in order to prevent its conclusion and to abolish or destroy (terms synonymous in their effects) what has already been done; such letters, Sire, we repeat, under whatever form they may be disguised, are letters of abolition. But letters of abolition can only be registered in view of the charges, and the laws leave to the judges the option either to go on from there and not to bother with them, or to appeal to the king in remonstrances. . . .

Several of the articles of the law of 1670 establish these precepts. . . .

Thus the letters of abolition which Your Majesty has been persuaded to have published in order to stop the unfinished trial of the Duke d'Aiguillon are null and void in the terms of the law as being incompatible with the charges, and no tribunal can ever recognize them as valid. These letters of abolition being null and void, the indictment remains in all its force. Under these circumstances, the Duke d'Aiguillon, charged and not acquitted, deprived of any means of vindication (which he could obtain only by continuation of the proceedings) cannot be allowed "to take part in the noble and vital functions of the peerage." Your Majesty brought this out yourself when in the letters-patent of last March 28, you declared that innocence and exemption from any suspicion was inseparable from membership in the Court of Peers. From this it follows necessarily that "the Duke d'Aiguillon cannot exercise the rights which gave him distinction, until he has cleared himself of all incriminating suspicion." Otherwise, Sire, how can public opinion, which yields to no command, be faced? It is written in all the laws of your kingdom, it is engraved in indelible characters in every generous and French heart, that every accused who obtains no judgment releasing him rests beneath the yoke of incrimination. There is, thus, Sire, only one way out for the Duke d'Aiguillon, and that is to obtain a judgment releasing him. Your parlement likes to think that the means to this would be easy for him; the laws which prescribe criminal proceedings present the accused with as many resources to acquit himself as to the accuser to convict him. Deign, Sire, to permit him to take advantage of the only suitable means of avenging his offended honor; your Court of Peers has taken the liberty to petition you for this. The votes of the members who make up this court are a very powerful motive of interest for the Duke d'Aiguillon; and for Your Majesty, Sire, a motive worthy of the justice and bounty of your heart, to return force to the laws by revoking the letters published on the 27th of last month.

To the interests of the Duke d'Aiguillon, deign, Sire, to add the interests of all your subjects; there is not one of them whom this recent event has not stricken with the greatest sorrow. Life is the possession of every man; honor is a possession yet dearer to the French. Now they see their honor attacked without hope of defense, they see their security impaired if criminal proceedings can be interrupted and terminated by act of a most arbitrary power, taking advantage of the good faith of the sovereign. The very prospect of this throws them into the profoundest consternation.

Finally, Sire, to the interests of justice and of the law, to the interests of the accused, compromised in incomplete trials, to the interests of all your subjects, are added on this occasion the interests of your own glory. Europe, watchful of anything which might concern one of her most powerful kings, all Europe has its eyes fixed on this great event, one of the most notable of the century, destined by its nature and by the circumstances which surround it to form an epoch in the history of your exploits. By destroying an act in which you were for a few moments misled, by letting judicial proceedings take their normal course, by rendering to each the justice he deserves in a solemn and legal act, teach all nations, Sire, that the French, besides so many other advantages, still enjoy the inestimable advantage of being governed by a monarch who is the friend of justice and of the law.

Decreed in parlement, by all the chambers assembled, on July 2, 1770.

Edict for Purposes of Regulation of the Month of December 1770

Louis, by the grace of God, King of France and of Navarre; to all present and all to come, greeting. The systematic mentality, as uncertain in its principles as it is bold in its enterprises, at the same time as it has caused grave damage to religion and morals, has not respected the sanctity of the deliberations of several of our judicial courts; we have seen them successively bring forth new ideas and advance principles which, at any other time and from any other body, they would have condemned as likely to trouble public order.

We have seen them turn several times to interruptions and cessations of service, by means of which, and by causing our subjects to suffer from delay of the justice for which they are responsible to us, and from misfortunes to which our affection for our peoples makes us very sensitive, they have hoped to force us to yield to their resistance.

On other occasions they have handed in resignations *en masse,* and, by a singular contradiction, they have disputed our right to accept these resignations.

Finally, they formed a confederation among themselves; they have considered themselves as forming but a single body and a single parlement, divided among several classes distributed among the various parts of our kingdom.

This innovation, first conceived and later dropped by our Parlement of Paris when it seemed useful to it to do so, still persists in our other parlements; it is expressed in their decrees and verdicts in terms of "classes," of "unity," of "indivisibility"; as if our courts could forget that several of them exist in provinces that do not form part of our kingdom, but that belong to us for particular reasons; that the establish-

This selection and the one following are taken from Jules Flammermont, *Le Chancelier Maupeou et les parlements* (Paris, 1883), 116-20, 277-79.

ment of each took place at a different date; that our predecessors, in creating them, formed them independently of each other, and created no precedent for relations among them; that they gave to each limits which we or our successors can extend or contract, when the interests of our peoples demand it; and that finally, beyond these limits, their decrees can only be executed by our orders.

If these errors were merely a momentary lapse of principles we would content ourselves with repeating the prohibition made in our session of March 3, 1766; but they are perpetuating themselves and each day sees a profusion of evil consequences.

The dispatches which our parlements are sending one to another, their mutual correspondence, and the thoughtless acceptance which some of them have made recently, without knowing the case, of the judgments of others, could lead them to more irregular acts, which would have to be severely punished if we did not avert them today by our prudence.

Although the system has not yet been pushed so far as to renew the decrees of union, which have been so strictly prohibited, is it not to be feared that if we let these principles develop further instead of destroying them, we would have to blame ourselves for the excesses in which our courts might one day indulge themselves by following them?

One of the most pernicious effects of this system of ideas is to persuade our parlements that their deliberations acquire more weight from it, and already several of them, thinking that they have become more powerful and independent, have laid down some maxims hitherto unknown: *they have called themselves the representatives of the nation, the indispensable interpreters of the public decisions of the kings, the watchmen over the administration of the public forces, and over the payment of the debts of the sovereign;* and soon, not allowing that our laws have any validity until, by a free deliberation, they have adopted and consecrated them, they will raise their authority as high as and even above our own, because they thereby reduce our legislative power to the simple function of proposing our desires to them, while reserving themselves the right to prevent their being carried out. . . .

We owe it to the good of our subjects, to the interests of the magistracy itself, even more than to the interest of our royal power, to halt the development of these dangerous innovations; but before prohibiting them by our edict, we desire to recall to our courts the principles from which they must never deviate.

We hold our crown only from God; the right to make the laws by which our subjects must be guided and governed belongs to us alone, without subordination or division; the function of our courts is to examine them, discuss them, and see that they are executed. . . .

It is by giving to our peoples the example of obedience that our legal officers will win respect for their function as magistrates, a function which they do not hold by virtue of any constitutional law, and which we alone bestow upon them by the offices which it pleases us to grant them. For these reasons and others inclining us to the same end, on the advice of our council, and by our infallible wisdom, full power, and royal authority, we have by the present perpetual and irrevocable edict pronounced, legislated, and commanded, we pronounce, legislate, and command, we desire and are pleased as follows:

ARTICLE ONE

We prohibit our courts of parlement from employing the terms "unity," "indivisibility," "classes" and other synonyms to signify and express that all together compose but one and the same parlement, divided into several classes.

We forbid them to send to our other parlements, except in the cases prescribed by our ordinances, any documents, titles, proceedings, memoirs, remonstrances, decrees, and sentences relative to cases tried before them, either on our orders or as a normal consequence of their jurisdiction.

As also we forbid them to deposit in their records, and to deliberate upon, the documents, titles, proceedings, memoirs, remonstrances, decrees, or sentences drawn up or handed down by other parlements, commanding them to send to us such documents: all on pain of the loss and deprivation of their offices.

ARTICLE TWO

We desire that, in accordance with the ordinances, the officers of our courts dispense to our subjects, in our name, the justice we owe them, and that they do this without any other interruptions than are authorized by the same ordinances; consequently we forbid them to cease service, either as a result of their own deliberations, or by interrupting it in fact by assembling all chambers together, during the session, except in cases of absolute necessity, recognized as such by the first president to whom we leave the decision; and this on pain of the loss and deprivation of their offices.

We prohibit them, under the same penalties, from giving combined or previously arranged resignations, or resignations resulting from a common deliberation or oath.

Not preventing them, however, from assembling when the *Grand' Chambre* is not sitting, as often and for as long a time as the cases with which they are occupied shall require.

ARTICLE THREE

We again permit them, before the registration of our edicts, declarations or letters-patent, to make to us such remonstrances or representations as seem to them suitable for the good of our peoples and the good of our service, while enjoining them to exclude anything which would not accord with the respect which they owe us.

When, after having heard them as often as we judge necessary to learn their comments and judge of their importance, we persevere in our will and have had registered, in our presence or in the presence of the bearers of our orders, the said edicts, declarations, and letters-patent, we forbid them to hand down any decrees which might tend to prevent, to impede, or to delay the execution of the said edicts.

Similarly we prohibit any person who shall have presided over the sessions, the officer who brought the said edicts for registry, and all others to sign any record of such decrees of parlement; we prohibit all recorders, clerks, or other subordinate officials from drawing up and authorizing any communication or publication of such decrees; we prohibit all bailiffs, sergeants, troopers of the constabulary who might be so ordered, to proclaim or execute such decrees; all this on pain of loss and privation of their offices, and of being prosecuted and punished as for disobedience of our orders.

Thus we entrust to our beloved and faithful councilors, the persons holding our court of Parlement in Paris, this our present edict to be read, published and registered, and its contents to be kept and observed according to its form and text. For such is our pleasure, and in order that it may remain firm and unaltered forever, we have affixed to it our seal.

Excerpts from the Royal Edict of February 23, 1771, Creating "Superior Councils"

. . . It is with the most painful regret that we have seen the officers of our Parlement of Paris abandon themselves to a disobedience equally condemned by the laws, by their oaths of office, and by the necessities of the public interest, that we have seen them making into a principle the arbitrary suspension of their functions, and finally openly arrogating to themselves the right to prevent the execution of our royal will. In order to invest their pretensions with specious pretexts, they have tried to alarm our subjects with claims that there is a threat to their rank, to their property, and even to the laws which establish the succession to the throne, as if a disciplinary rule could be extended to threaten these sacred things, to these institutions which we are rightfully unable to change, and the stability of which will always be guaranteed by the inseparable link which binds us to our peoples. We have long postponed the exercise of our authority in the hope that reflection would restore the officers of parlement to a proper conception of their duty; but even our indulgence has only served to increase their resistance and to increase the number of irregular actions which have finally forced us to choose between punishing them and sacrificing the most essential rights of our crown. Obliged thereafter to provide judges for our subjects, we have had recourse at first to the officers of our council, whose talents, intelligence, zeal, and service have always justified our confidence; but, having provided for the needs of the moment, we have looked farther ahead, and we have felt that the interests of our peoples, the good of the judicial system and our very glory required in these circumstances the reform of the abuses existing in the administration of justice. We have recognized that the venality of offices, introduced by the misfortunes of ages past, was an obstacle to the choice of our judicial officers and often excluded from the magistracy those who deserved most, by virtue of their talents and merit, to belong to it; that we owed to our subjects a swift, pure, and cost-free justice and that the slightest tinge of private interest could not but offend the delicacy of magistrates responsible for maintaining the inviolable rights of honor and property; that the excessive size of the district of our Parlement of Paris was infinitely harmful to those bringing suits, who were obliged to leave their families behind in order to come and seek a slow and costly justice; that already exhausted by the expenses of their trips and travels, their ruin was completed by the length and multiplicity of the proceedings and they were often forced to abandon the most legitimate claims; finally we have considered that the custom which forces lords [*seigneurs*] to bear the costs of the prosecution of crimes committed within the bounds of their jurisdiction was a very heavy burden upon them and sometimes a reason for allowing the criminal to escape.

In consequence we have decided to establish in various provinces superior tribunals, whose offices will be given by us without cost to officers chosen on the basis of their talents, experience, and ability, who will receive no other pay than their salaries. By bringing closer together in this way the judges and the plaintiffs, we shall facilitate access to the courts; we shall make them more useful and more beloved by the people by simplifying the forms and diminishing the costs of lawsuits. Finally we shall assure the tranquillity of our subjects, the maintenance of public order and the punishment of crimes by showing to the lords possessed of high justice their personal advantage in the prosecution of the guilty, and by furnishing them with the means to compensate themselves for the costs of criminal trials. If to carry out these intentions we have been forced to contract the jurisdiction of our Parlement of Paris, we have made it our responsibility to preserve for it all its rights and prerogatives. As the depositary of the laws, responsible for promulgating them, for executing them, for making their defects known to us and for informing us of the needs of our peoples; final judge of all the questions which involve our crown and the rights of peers and of the peerage, it will continue to enjoy the most precious sort of prestige, which is conferred by virtue, intelligence, zeal, and impartiality.

Selection from Voltaire's **The ABC, or Dialogues among A, B, C**

FIRST CONVERSATION

On Hobbes, Grotius, and Montesquieu
. . . B.   Montesquieu, at the beginning of his Second Book (chapter 1) defines a despotic government in this fashion: "One single man, without laws or rules, runs everything according to his own will and caprice."

Oeuvres complètes de Voltaire (Paris, 1877-85), XXVII, 323-25.

Now it is not true that such a government exists, and it seems to me quite untrue to say that it could exist. The *Koran* and its approved commentaries are the laws of the Muslims; all monarchs of that religion swear on the *Koran* to observe these laws. The ancient body of fighting men and the men of the law have immense privileges; and when the sultans sought to violate those privileges, they were all strangled, or at least solemnly deposed.

I have never been to China, but I have talked to more than twenty people who have, and I think I have read all the authors who have referred to that country; I know, with much more certainty than Rollin knew ancient history, by the unanimous reports of our missionaries of different sects, that China is governed by laws, and not by a single arbitrary will; I know that in Peking there are six supreme tribunals with forty-four other tribunals under their jurisdiction; I know that the remonstrances that these six supreme tribunals send to the Emperor have the force of law; I know that no porter or charcoal-burner in the farthest reaches of the Empire is executed unless his trial is reviewed by the Supreme Tribunal in Peking which reports it to the Emperor. Is that an arbitrary and tyrannical government? . . .

Despotism is nothing but the abuse of monarchy, a corrupt form of a good government. I would as much equate tyrants with kings as I would equate highwaymen with public bodies.

A.   You have not mentioned the sale of judicial offices, that fine traffic in laws which in the whole world is known only to the French. They must be the greatest businessmen in the universe, for they even buy and sell the right to judge men. What the hell! if I had had the honor to have been born in Picardy or Champagne, and to be even the seventh son of a tax-farmer or an army contractor, I could become, by paying twelve or fifteen thousand écus, the absolute master of the lives and fortunes of my fellow citizens! According to the etiquette of my colleagues, I would be called *monsieur,* but I would address the litigants, were they Châtillons and Montmorencys, merely by their last names, and I would be the tutor of kings for my money. It's an excellent deal. Moreover, I would have the pleasure of ordering to be burned by the man whom Jean-Jacques Rousseau wants to make the Dauphin's father-in-law all the books that displeased me.[1] That is a great privilege.

B.   It is true that Montesquieu was weak enough to say that venality of offices is *good in monarchical states.* What do you expect? he was *président à mortier* in the provinces. I have never seen a mortar-board,

1. See *Émile,* book V. [Voltaire's note.]

but I imagine that it is a superb ornament. It is difficult even for the most philosophical of minds to be unaffected by self-interest. If a grocer spoke of legislation, he would try to have everyone buy cinnamon and nutmeg. . . .

Selections from the Correspondence of Voltaire, 1769-1771

From Marie Louise Denis

March 8, 1769, from Paris

. . . Marin is tremendously busy. It appears that the chancellor wishes to resume control of the book-trade. He confers often with him on this subject, and the chancellor after conferring with Marin has memoranda prepared on everything they say. It would be very good for literature if the chancellor resumed control of the book-trade, although M. de Sartine is a fine man he does not want to take any risks, since he is far more attached to his position than to letters. The chancellor is intelligent, has no desire to climb higher, perhaps he would steer the ship more easily.

I take advantage of Perachon who has come to Paris and who is going straight back to Versoy to write you openly. What are your intentions concerning the trip you were expecting to make to Paris? Only you can know if M. the Duke de Choiseul approves. . . . M. de Choiseul is so simple and frank, he knows so well that you are the greatest genius of France, that if you want to make the trip you should ask him frankly if it would be agreeable to him and if he advises you to do it. I am quite sure that he would be flattered by that mark of your confidence and by advising you he would, so to speak, be obliged to support you. I am very eager for this trip, you would make a lot of people happy and would have some very brilliant moments. On the other hand you would have to give up your favorite passion, that of writing. The parlement is your enemy. What will astonish you is that M. de Choiseul favors the parlement. He supports them at every opportunity. This may be inconceivable, but it is true. Perhaps this is a good thing for us, because he would be in a better

In this section, five letters have been translated and reprinted with the permission of the editor and publisher from Theodore Besterman, ed., *Voltaire's Correspondence*, 107 vols. (Geneva, 1953-65): the two letters from Madame Denis (LXXII, 240-44); and Voltaire's letters to Gabriel Cramer, to d'Hornoy, and to Joseph Vasselier (LXXVIII, 66-67; LXXIX, 42-43; LXXX, 116). The other letters are taken from the *Oeuvres complètes de Voltaire*, XLVI-XLVII.

position to restrain that body if they should want to do you harm. . . .

If your intention is to come this autumn, my dear friend, I offer you my apartment which would suit you well. . . . Who knows. If you want to answer me about all this, address your letter to M. Marin. He told me again today that his are never opened. M. de Choiseul is still in the same position, but he has gained some time and that means a lot. He has time to take a new line. The lady [Mme du Barry] has not yet been presented and the king has delayed nine or ten ladies who were supposed to be. Yet people think that she will be. She is said to be gay and kindhearted. If there were not whispers about her perhaps there would be no difficulty, but. . . . Actually I hope that the Duke [de Choiseul] will get on good terms with her. The king still has pains in his arm, he cannot raise it, he cannot sign anything. His fall was more serious than people thought. It is too bad that they were not able to bleed him. Since he cannot ride horseback it is feared that this may injure his health. I told you that he had taken over the apartment of Madame to enlarge his own and that of Mme du Barry. He still loves her with the same passion.

Moreover, my dear friend, the finances are in a frightful state. People talk of nothing but a general bankruptcy. Far from selling one's lands, one should buy some. Unlucky he who has none. It is now the only form of wealth on which people can count. . . .

To M. the Marshal, Duke de Richelieu

Ferney, July 10 [1769]

The oldest and most faithful of your servants importunes you, Monseigneur, only on occasions that furnish some excuse. You must be overwhelmed with letters and requests. It is always to the dean of our Academy that I write and not to the governor, to the first gentleman of the chamber.

Do you remember the *Mémoires de Maintenon* written by La Beaumelle and several other brochures of the same sort that calumnied the greatest houses of the kingdom, beginning with the royal family? You deigned to tell me what you thought of them. A rather curious book written in that style has appeared abroad—the *History of the Parlement*.[1] I have nothing to say against the first volume of the work; it makes it clear that the parlement draws all its dignity from the peers. I have always been of that view. There are, however, anecdotes in the first volume that I cannot judge: it would be necessary to have con-

1. [Selections from the *History of the Parlement* are reprinted in this book, above, pp. 52-64, and below, pp. 320-22.—Ed.]

sulted the record office. I doubt that La Beaumelle had the ability to dig in those archives and it is this that makes me suspend any guess about the author's name.

As for the second volume, I find it not only false but excessively indecent and I have said this quite frankly. The author, whoever he is, is trying to pass his work off as mine. I am accustomed to these impostures, but this one mortifies me. I belong to a body of which you are the principal member and the king the protector. It is just fine when they impute lame verse and languishing prose to my old age. But certainly there are, in that second volume, impertinent expressions that would displease the king, if he were not too great to be at all informed about these stupidities. In the state of indignation that I enter when such a work is imputed to me, I can only declare that the author is very ill-advised, that he is an impudent person and that I disapprove of his work which is full of errors. . . .

From Marie-Louise Denis

August 10 [1769], from Paris

I take advantage, my dear friend, of the departure of M. des Franges to write to you frankly. Everything is still as it has been at court. There are two parties, the king's and the minister's. These two great interests will not be reconciled, but the Duke [de Choiseul] will not tolerate this for very much longer.

The king loves Mme du Barry passionately. However, there are still only five ladies who are willing to receive her, and among the men M. de Soubise, the chancellor, M. the Count de Maillebois whom she has restored to good standing with the king, the Marshal [Richelieu], the whole clique, all the discontented and all the enemies of the Duke, which adds up to a great number of people. . . .

I do not doubt that without that wretched chapter all the nobility of France and the ministry would have placed you on a pinnacle for writing the history of the parlement. Can't you change that chapter? Could you not send me a manuscript of it by way of M. Lefevre? By the way, my dear friend, do not refer to him by name in your letters. I received one through the mail in which you referred to him by name. You would ruin him, and he is perhaps one of the men most useful to you in the kingdom.

I am quite certain that the parlement will do nothing. But let us change that chapter, while there are still only thirty copies in Paris. Consider that the men of letters were the people most upset by it. In general this book is perhaps one of those which will do you the most honor. The blemish must be removed. People say that that chapter is not fit to be in such a praiseworthy book as this, that it is a continual satire and that you attack too many people in it. Pardon me for saying this, you should know this, only great interest and friendship can warn you.

We are saying that the book was printed in England because Marc Michel, seeing that his edition could not come into Paris, distributed it all in London, and that people returning from England are bringing it back and that it is only available there. As for the parlement they are angry, but they will not dare do anything, you may be sure. If the book is more widely circulated, perhaps they will order it burned. This would be a very small misfortune about which I hope you would not concern yourself.

Far from being afraid, I think, my dear friend, that now would be the time for you to come to Paris. Try, see what you think. I have asked a gentleman who does not yet wish to tell you his name, to get Mme du Barry to speak of you to the king, telling him that she is very anxious to meet you. We shall see what the king answers. *M. de Choiseul must not know about this.* I will have an answer in a week at the latest. If the answer is favorable, and you have that woman close to the king on your side, and with the Choiseuls liking you, I think you would have no reason to hesitate.

Remember first of all that the court, the city, and the Palace of Justice are firmly convinced that you are the author of the history of the parlement, that the court and the city are delighted with it, that the Palace is angry, that is, the parlement, for the rest of the robe is enchanted with it. But everyone would like to tear out that wretched chapter. I even think that there would be some people who would bring you their copy in order to have you give them a new one.

You have no idea how much the court and the city wish that you would send a disavowal of that work. M. de Pralin has said it ten times to the angels, M. de Sartine and M. Bertin have sent me word. Everyone was firmly convinced that it was by you, and wanted to cover for you. Everyone said to himself, it is by him like the history of Louis XIV, but we must say that it isn't. When one is regarded in that light by the public, there is never anything to be feared.

I shall be able to inform you in a week of the reply of the king. I shall appeal to M. de Vime, Mme du Bari and Mme de Long, you should appeal to M. Talon and M. de Choiseuille, my brother-in-law. Take careful note of this, dear friend, I beg you. When we have that answer give careful thought to it. I am not advising you to do anything, I simply am bringing you up to date on everything, while leaving you a loose rein. The public has a great desire to see you, and the cream of the public will be delighted. Do what you please, what influences me is that you will be able to shake off your solitude for a while, and I would be glad of that. I forgot to tell you that if you come, you should say that it is *only for three months*. I offer you my apartment which is very convenient. You should take it, you would find a home all ready for you. Since you will be receiving all of France, you must have a decent place to do it. . . .

Farewell, my dear friend, I am collapsing from fatigue. Remember that you must *bring Mme du Barry into agreement with M. de Choiseul.* If you succeed in that people will be able to say that you are a great courtier. I don't seem able to finish this letter. Think carefully when you have the answer of M. de Vime and Mme de Long, and be confident that there is nothing I would not do to try to make you happy, and to prove to you how tender and inviolable are my feelings for you.

To M. Marin

January 27 [1771]

If I had access to monsieur the chancellor as you do, I should like, my dear correspondent, to know if it is really true that the poor people of the provinces will no longer be compelled to go plead their cases one hundred and fifty leagues from their homes and if a new code, which we need so badly, is being prepared. At the same time, a civic crown of laurels will have to be prepared for monsieur the chancellor. . . .

Do you think that we shall have a minister of foreign affairs? Is M. the Duke d'Aiguillon still to be named? It is possible for someone to be very tainted by the parlement and yet serve the king very well. But the important point is that there be rejoicing at Paris. I always say: O Welches![2] enjoy your pleasures and all will go well. But in order to have pleasures, one must have money, and it is reported that M. the Abbé Terray is not coming up with any.

To Gabriel Cramer

[*Ca.* February 1771]

My nephew d'Hornoy is in a submerged village called Sancoins, six leagues from Nevers, surrounded by ducks and geese who cackle the praises of the chancellor. Every councilor is at a village where he is learning agriculture. The first president is at Corbeil which is really a

2. [Germanic name, derived from the Latin *Gallus,* for the Celtic peoples of Gaul, northern Spain, and Wales; by extension, as a name applied by foreigners, a pejorative synonym for the French.—Ed.]

town. The fees have been confiscated to the profit of the lord king. People were horrified in Paris at noon; they were dancing by 8 o'clock in the evening. . . .

You ask for a new chapter of the parlement. No doubt one is necessary; but we must await the outcome of the catastrophe just begun. . . .

To M. de Veymerange

February 25 [1771]

. . . I am informed from Lyon that monsieur the chancellor has already named eleven councilors of the supreme council that he intends to establish at Lyon. If this is true, it is one of the greatest services that he can render to the state, and he shall be blessed forever. Was it not horrible to be obliged to go spend oneself into ruin on appeal, one hundred leagues from home, before a tribunal which understands nothing of commerce, and has no idea how silk is spun? M. the Chancellor appears to be a man of very enlightened and determined mind; if he holds firm he will cover himself with glory; if he weakens he will always have enemies to combat. . . .

To M. the Marquis de Florian

February 25 [1771]

. ∴ . I do not know how the affair of the parlement will end, but I would certainly not hesitate to say that corporations [*les compagnies*] make greater mistakes than individuals because, since no one is speaking on his own responsibility, all of them become rasher. It has always seemed absurd to me to want to indict a peer of the realm, when the king in his council has declared that that peer acted only on his orders and served him very well. Basically, what this amounts to is trying to put the king himself on trial; moreover, it is to declare oneself to be both plaintiff and judge, and as I see it totally to disregard one's responsibilities.

I admit also that the blood of the Chevalier de la Barre and of the Count de Lally still troubles me. Happily d'Hornoy's hands are not soaked in it, but are those who were responsible for these cruelties which outraged Europe to be pitied because they are in the country? I have been living in the country for seventeen years, even though I have never murdered anybody. . . .

To M. Tabareau

March 4 [1771]

I admit to M. Tabareau and to M. Vasselier that I am delighted by the edict and the speech of monsieur the chancellor. I think that the king will be better loved because of it, and that M. de Maupeou will cover himself with glory. However, it is reported that on the day of the publication of this edict, all the shares dropped at Paris. It seems to me that they should have risen; but jurisprudence is not finance. But be the stock of the Indian Company high or low, it does not alter the fact that monsieur the chancellor has rendered the kingdom the most important service. . . .

To Alexandre-Marie-François de Paule de Dompierre d'Hornoy
                                        Ferney, April 29, 1771
I believe that you are now, my dear nephew, at your estate of Hornoy. You are just making your entrance into the world that I shall soon leave. Your future can only be fortunate, while I have none. You have endured only some small and honorable misfortunes, while I have lost my health and my sight. I bear life and death with patience. Endure in the same way, my dear friend, the little troubles that you have encountered at the beginning of your career.

You will have to admit, just between us, that your body went too far. You must admit that by obstinately seeking to taint a peer of the realm whose entire conduct had been approved by the king, you were seeking to taint the king himself.

You must admit that what was said of the litigants could be said of certain corporations,
        The spirit of defiance is in that family [3]
This is the cause of this great excitement in Paris and in the provinces. My dear friend, this disease too shall pass, like everything else.

Do you wish me to speak frankly to you? We are not worthy of being free. If you read the history of France carefully, you will see that the corporations, from the Sorbonne to the Jesuits, have committed nothing but stupidities. We are pretty children who must be led.

I do not think that the king can back off after the steps that he has taken. Such weakness and thoughtlessness would cost him the respect of Europe forever.

Take the trouble to read the document in the hand of Louis XIV which is in the royal library and which I quoted from in my history of the century. "It is possible to avoid taking a decision, but when one has his mind fixed on something, and feels that he sees the right course of action, one must take that course and hold it; it is because I did this that I succeeded in everything that I undertook."

It is thus very probable, my dear nephew, that the king will perse-

3. [Racine, *Les Plaideurs,* II. v.—Ed.]

vere in his measures, for if the government were to weaken, it would be lost.

I am sure that the friendship between my two nephews will not be altered. You know that the Abbé Mignot has always had the same point of view. He cannot be blamed for upholding a position which he believes to be a good one. Each of you is very virtuous according to his lights; thus you will always be friends.

When you are seized with the desire to have what in France is called an office, which in the final analysis offers only a superficial advantage, it will not be difficult to get one. From my point of view, and I think from yours, it is of no particular importance to be announced in someone's house as monsieur the grand audiencer or monsieur the grand master of waters and forests. The English are wiser than we are, in writing to them one does not even say Monsieur Jakson, member of parliament. We are full of illusions, but with an honest fortune and a wife still more honest who loves one with all her heart, one can be as happy as the feebleness of human nature allows.

Pardon an old man for rambling on. . . .

To M. de Maupeou, Chancellor of France

Ferney, May 9 [1771]

Monseigneur,

Will a useless old man be permitted to dare to introduce to you a young lawyer whose family has exercised that honorable profession for more than two hundred years in Franche-Comté? He is one of your greatest admirers, and very capable of useful service.

The case that he has taken, which M. Chéry is defending in His Majesty's council, is certainly deserving of receiving your judgment. The question is whether twelve or fifteen thousand people of Franche-Comté will have the good fortune to be the subjects of the king, or slaves of the canons of Saint-Claude. They are offering in evidence their charters, which place them on the same footing as other Frenchmen; the canons have on their side only a usurpation that has been clearly demonstrated.

There is reason to think, Monseigneur, that among the services you are rendering to the king and to France by reforming the laws, the abolition of serfdom will be included, and that all the king's subjects will owe you their enjoyment of the rights that nature has given them. I respect your great labors too much to abuse your patience any further. Permit me to express with my admiration the profound respect with which I have the honor to be, etc.

To Madame the Duchess de Choiseul

Ferney, May 13 [1771]

Madame,

. . . Only permit me to tell you, Madame, that my last sentiments will be the gratitude I owe you, my admiration for your character and that of Barmécide [the Duke de Choiseul], and my respect and inviolable attachment for both of you. That is my profession of faith and nothing will make me change it. I will die as faithful to the faith I've sworn you as I will to my just hatred for the men who have persecuted me as much as they were able and who would still persecute me if they were the masters. Surely I shouldn't like those men who were likely to do me a bad turn in January, those who shed innocent blood, those who brought barbarism to the center of gentility, those who, solely concerned with their stupid vanity, allowed their cruelty to operate without scruple, now by immolating Calas on the wheel, now by causing the death of a young gentleman who expired in the torments after torture, and who hardly deserved six months at St.-Lazare and would have been worth more than all of them put together. They have defied all of a Europe revolted by their inhumanity. They dragged a lieutenant-general around in a tumbril with a gag in his mouth, and although I confess that this man was justly hated, his innocence was demonstrated to me by the very documents of the trial. I could cite twenty barbarities equal to these and render them execrable for posterity. I would rather die in the canton of Zug or among the Samoyeds than be subject to compatriots such as these. I might easily have become their colleague once, but I would never have thought as they think.

I open to you, Madame, a heart that can conceal nothing and which is a hundred times more touched by your kindness than it is ulcerated by their atrocious injustices and their insupportable despotism.

I don't flatter myself, Madame, by thinking that the circumstances which you and I are in permit you to write to me. It is true that if you have your granddaughter send me a few words I will die more content. But if you remain silent I will be no less at your feet and I will be no less devoted with a gratitude that is as lively as it is respectful.

To Madame the Duchess de Choiseul

May 15 [1771]

Allow me, Madame, to add a little codicil to my Testament and to explain to you the New Year's gifts they wanted to give me in the month of January this year.

M. Séguier, after the reception given him by the public at the *Académie française,* took a trip. He came to my home and told me that several councilors of the parlement were pressuring him to bring charges against the history of that body, printed, it is said, two years ago; that he could not in the end refrain from fulfilling his office; that if he did not bring the charges, these councilors would do it themselves and that this could go quite far.

In the presence of M. Hennin, minister to Geneva, and of my niece, I replied that this affair had absolutely nothing to do with me; that I had no part in this history; that, moreover, I regarded it as very veracious; and that, if it were possible for a company to have gratitude, the parlement owed thanks to the writer who had treated them with extreme kindness.

That, Madame, is my completed confession. If you give me absolution, I'll not die for fifteen days; if you refuse it, I'll die within four, but if I don't die adoring you, I'd believe myself to be more damned than Beelzebub.

THE OLD HERMIT

To M. the Marshal Duke de Richelieu

May 20 [1771]

If my hero cannot predict how this brawl will end, it is not likely that a blind old man can foresee what the viceroy of Aquitaine cannot. I only think, at a quick glance, that our nation has always been irresponsible, and sometimes very cruel; that it has never been able to govern itself, and that it is not really very deserving of being free. I shall also add that despite my great taste for liberty I would prefer living under the claws of a lion to being continually exposed to the teeth of a thousand rats who were my equals.

I have been sent a much larger second edition of the pamphlet *The People to the Parlements.* Monseigneur will permit me to report this to him. It is producing some effect in the provinces; that does not mean that it will be a success in Paris; and yet all its facts are true.

I am very grateful to the author for having so boldly praised M. the Duke de Choiseul; he has the greatest obligations to that minister.

M. the Duke de Choiseul has favored his colony and has accorded astonishing privileges to his little estate; he has at once granted him all the favors which this solitary individual has asked for the benefit of other people; offices, money, privileges, he held nothing back; and the last favor he granted was a commission as brigadier for one of the nephews of the solitary one. The latter would therefore be the most ungrateful and unworthy of men, if he did not show a gratitude in proportion to so many benefactions. Woe to him who would condemn him for having fulfilled his duty! Certainly my hero will not be the one to advise ingratitude. One brave knight may be on the opposite side from another brave knight; but each should be just toward the other. I am like Atticus caught between Caesar and Pompey. The solitary one has listened only to his own heart; he is firmly convinced that the former Parlement of Paris was as much in the wrong as at the time of the Fronde; moreover, he cannot have any affection for the murderers of Calas, or of poor Lally, or of the Chevalier de la Barre. The jurisconsults of Europe, and especially the celebrated Marquis Beccaria, have never described their sentences as being anything but murders.

The solitary one has in the new parlement, a nephew [Abbé Mignot] dean of the clerical councilors, who think entirely as he does.

The solitary one flatters himself that monsieur the chancellor, who thus far has fully approved his sentiments and conduct, will find it proper that while honoring the truth he also honors his obligations to M. the Duke de Choiseul.

The solitary one regards the new institutions established by monsieur the chancellor as the greatest service that could be rendered to France. He has seen only too often the misfortunes caused by the overextension of the district of the Parlement of Paris. He feels that the princes and the peers will have much more influence over the new parlement, which will be less numerous. He thinks that all the lords of high justice should thank monsieur the chancellor for the rights he is giving them. He believes that the head of the judiciary is almost the only one whose eloquence is the very opposite of pedantry, and he is full of esteem for him, without knowing anything or wanting to know anything about the private quarrels that may have divided the court.

The solitary one even implores monseigneur the Marshal de Richelieu to be kind enough, if he has an opportunity, to emphasize to monsieur the chancellor the candor and disinterest that are set forth in this letter, and that cannot be doubted. Monsieur the chancellor has been kind enough to write to him.

It sometimes happens, in such cases, that an individual alienates both of the parties who are at odds; but in the long run, frankness and purity of motives always win out.

I also dare to think that in the long run the new system will win out, because it is for the good of France.

What alarms the provinces the most, is the fear of new taxes, and the painful realization that after nine years of peace the finances of the kingdom are in such a deplorable state, while thirty or so financiers, who have made immense fortunes, insult the poverty of the state with their private splendor.

I have said to my hero everything that lay upon my heart; I add very seriously that my greatest disappointment is to die without the consolation of once more paying him my respects; but the present circumstances do not permit it, and my unhappy condition absolutely deprives me of what I am most eager for. . . .

This is too much prose; I really beg your pardon. Accept my most tender respect, and all the sentiments that attach me inviolably to you for as long as I shall live.

To M. the Count d'Argental

July 1 [1771]

I no longer write; in a short time I have become incapable of everything; I have fallen down very heavily, after performing a few more tricks of hocus-pocus. . . .

I thank most deeply Mme d'Argental for sending to Mme Corbi the imprecations against the cannibals in robes who so often stained themselves with innocent blood, and whose destruction people are stupid enough to regret. It was typical of our nation of baboons to look upon our murderers as our defenders. We are flies who are taking the side of the spiders.

I know very well that there is wrong on both sides; it could not be otherwise in a country without principles or rules.

It is said that the fortunes of individuals will be affected by the general confusion; it is indeed inevitable, and I am expecting it. My colony will be destroyed, my investments lost, all my beautiful illusions dissipated. . . .

What else shall I say from the end of my desert to my angels? that there are two solitary people who are attached to them more tenderly than ever, for all their life.

To Joseph Vasselier

Ferney, November 9, 1771

Behold now, my dear correspondent, the whole revolution very peacefully concluded. Behold M. the chancellor covered with glory. If M. the Abbé Terray can do as much for the finances, people will no longer look back with nostalgia to the reign of Henri IV. . . .

Letter of Condorcet

[Antoine de Caritat, Marquis de Condorcet (1743-94), mathematician, economist, *philosophe*, admirer and biographer of Voltaire, played an important role during the French Revolution, which he welcomed as a landmark in what he believed to be the continuous progress of the human race toward ultimate perfection. He wrote his *Sketch of a Historical Description of the Progress of the Human Spirit* while in hiding after his moderate faction had been proscribed by the Mountain in 1793, and is thought to have taken poison after his capture to escape the guillotine.]

To Amélie Suard

[June-July 1771]

. . . It is because Voltaire is still alive that it would have been right to praise him, and I shall not pardon the men of letters who have abandoned a great genius, the implacable foe of tyranny and superstition, in order to admire the clumsy prose of the remonstrances, and to feel sorry for murderers. For any thinking man can find no other name for the Pasquiers, the St.-Fargeaus, and the judges of la Barre, Mauriceau, Lally, etc., etc. People should reflect also that the parlement, by sharing the legislative power with the king while keeping the administration of justice, was tending to introduce the most tyrannical sort of government, as Montesquieu said and as all the *philosophes* said up until last January. Anyone who lives, as Voltaire and I do, in the provinces, knows how harmful the justice of the parlement was to the people, with what impunity it let its subordinates commit robbery, what a disgusting indulgence it had for the business agents of the princes and the great. Anyone like us knows that it is only for these things that the parlements enjoy the zeal of their subordinates and the sympathy of powerful people. I recall that the Parlement of Paris approved the St. Bartholomew's by a decree; that it opposed to the edicts of pacification of l'Hôpital the same resistance it opposes to M. Maupeou; that the Parlement of Provence by a decree caused forty-two villages to be sacked and ten thousand Vaudois massacred; that the Parlement of Toulouse caused two hundred Protestants to be executed in one day; that the Parlement of Paris had the Maréchale

Translated and reprinted with the permission of the editor and publisher from Besterman, ed., *Voltaire's Correspondence*, LXXIX, 160-62.

d'Ancre hanged because her doctor prescribed chicken broth for her, the priest Petit because he had composed a song about an adventure that had occurred long ago in Syria, and the dreamer Morin because he said that he was a prophet; that it banned the teaching of anything contrary to the ridiculous philosophy of the schools, forbade the *Encyclopédie,* prevented the edict on exports which was enriching the provinces, and prohibited vaccination. I have not forgotten that the Abbé de Prade was sentenced because of his connections with the publishers of the *Encyclopédie,* that M. Helvétius was forced by them into a humiliating recantation, that they sentenced Rousseau, condemned to the galleys those who sold the books of the *philosophes,* and that these same *philosophes* were treated by them as a public pestilence; that these Pasquiers recently have wept with rage because in the preamble of his edict, M. de Maupeou accused them of being *philosophes,* apparently to make fun of them. I notice that these same men who did not [prosecute] the Duke d'Olonne, who was accused of murder, have ferociously prosecuted the Duke d'Eguillon, and that this single difference proves that the interests of the people mean nothing to them and that their concern is all for themselves. Having said all this I think that M. de Voltaire can be excused for having sworn eternal hatred of the parlement and for regarding its destruction as a good thing and its re-establishment as the worst of evils. . . . As for the praises that he bestows on M. de Maupeou, I think that he is praising an operation that he believes to be useful in itself, and that everybody agreed was so, until just recently we have been informed that it had been very desirable that the people could not obtain justice, or defend their property without spending more than they possessed. This new discovery made by the men of the parlement has appeared brilliant to many of our great lords and princes, who have often had reason to know how useful it was, since they owe it their peaceful enjoyment of innumerable usurpations. . . . But what Voltaire could foresee even less is the zeal with which men of letters are crying out in favor of the old parlement, with the same enthusiasm with which they cried out against it a year ago. I do not know how to explain this change, except to say that they have been seized by a desire for martyrdom, and that, thoroughly convinced of the intention of the parlement to persecute them, they aspire to its re-establishment as the first Christians aspired to persecution.

You understand that M. de Voltaire, who has never been so heroic, and who, following the example of the great St. Cyprian, contented himself with exhorting his people from the desert to defy persecution, has no desire to see the ministers and auxiliaries of justice re-established in their right to murder the *philosophes* legally, nor to be prosecuted criminally himself as guilty of blasphemy toward God and the honorable Denis Pasquier. This, Madame, is what I think can be said in the defense of M. de Voltaire. . . .

Selection from Voltaire's **The People to the Parlement**

Respectable organs of the laws, created to follow them and not to make them, listen to the king and deign also to hear the people.

If the English nation today debates its rights in the Estates-General of England which are called Parliament, permit us to represent our rights to you, tribunals named parlements which are *not* the estates.

You are men, you possess all that is in man's nature: the sentiment of honor, jealousy of your rights, *esprit de corps,* love of power. All of you claim the respect owed your useful labors. Suffer, therefore, that other bodies, superior to you, should have the same sentiments, or, if you wish, the same passions.

"Within the august palace and almost at the foot of the throne of our kings, there has arisen, under the name of Council, a sovereign tribunal where judgments are remade and justices are judged. It is there that weak innocence comes to shield itself from the ignorance or the malice of the magistrates who prosecute it. From there are launched the thunderbolts which, consuming iniquity, go forth even to the most distant tribunals. It is there that contested jurisdictions are determined. And there that the first and universal magistrate, from the height of his dignity, in the midst of judges of consummate probity and experience, watches over the whole realm of justice and over the good or bad conduct of those who exercise it."

That is how the orator Flechier spoke in the *Oraison funèbre* of Chancellor Le Tellier.

Since you are so often citing Massillon's *Sermons* and even the *Politics of Holy Scripture* (a work unworthy of the great Bossuet), we can also cite an eloquent man. But if we go on citing all the time nothing will ever be proved.

[*Oeuvres complètes de Voltaire,* XXVIII, 413-20. One of seven brochures written by Voltaire on this subject, *Les Peuples aux parlements* was first published in 1771 in a collection of pamphlets called *Recueil de toutes les pièces intéressantes publiées en France relativement aux troubles des parlements* by Chancellor Maupeou, who altered Voltaire's text only to the extent of toning down two flattering references to Choiseul.—Ed.]

The Council of State certainly existed before you did. You have been established to render justice according to the laws emanating from the king in his Council of State. You know that. This is the origin of all jurisprudence in the nation.

We won't repeat to you that the registrations that can be made in the register of the Council of State were admitted to the register of the Parlement of Paris only for the sake of convenience and following the example of the Clerk Montluc who kept a register for his own personal use.

Such a custom is undoubtedly not a fundamental law, unless the practice of getting married at Versailles rather than at Blois, of being crowned in the Cathedral of Reims rather than in that of Paris, of being buried at Saint-Denis rather than at Saint-Martin, is regarded as a fundamental law.

Custom is not law. Here we're only repeating what you have taught us.

A depositary of laws is without doubt necessary. But a quarrel between the depositaries of the laws and the King's Council which has lasted since Francis I and which has produced such bloody consequences is not necessary.

You love justice and the fatherland. Among you there are a great number of enlightened, wise, and equitable men. Are there fewer of these in the Council of State?

The difference between this supreme tribunal and your tribunals is that the council, which alone is as old as the monarchy, having been placed next to the throne is the center where all the affairs of the kingdom converge. It sees all the districts while you can perceive only a part of them. Food is lacking in a province. It knows which other province will be able to help out; what factory is useful in one city and harmful in another; what canton has suffered from seasonal irregularity and what aid must be brought to it; what contagious disease menaces a country and how its course can be stopped. In everything it acts as you would act in its place. It thinks as you would think. . . .

Let us give thanks for the six established councils which will prevent the ruin of six hundred families which were formerly dragged a hundred leagues and even five hundred to the foot of a tribunal ignorant of their customs.

They tell us that these establishments, so long wished for, and today so criticized, will cost too much money. They will cost ten times less than the transportation of prisoners which has exhausted the domain.

They ring the tocsin to alarm us. They keep repeating that we are going to be slaves from the moment that judges will no longer receive *épices*. Tremble, they tell us, it's going to rain taxes when the Parlement of Paris will no longer judge cases from Châlons-sur-Marne. . . .

Finally, they repeat that finances are in disarray. Is it then the fault of the new parlement and the six provincial councils that the kingdom has been exhausted by an unfortunate war, if we have lost Canada, if our fleets have been destroyed, if our commerce has been ruined? Certainly, no parlement could have either prevented or repaired such losses. Economy alone can close our wounds. Louis XV loves the memory of Henri IV. His Council of Finance loves the memory of the Duke de Sully: let us hope, and in revering our monarch, in saying: Long live the King! let us say: Long live liberty and property!

Selections from the Diary of the Duke de Croÿ

On December 12 [1771] I finished my work and, since my rheumatism was causing me great pain, I took medicine on the thirteenth, which made me feel a little better, and enabled me to go to Versailles on the fourteenth, with a great amount of business put well in order.

I can do nothing better than to report the conversation I had on the fifteenth, on the subject of the destruction of all the parlements of the kingdom, with the chancellor [Maupeou] and especially with M. Bertin, a minister who had always had a confidence in me of which he had given proof in seeking to have me named, against my will, to the command of Brittany, a long time ago, and all this might not have happened if I had accepted.

When I said to M. Bertin that he would not himself have believed, three years ago, that everything could have gone so smoothly, he said to me that indeed he would not have believed it, but that one side or the other had had to carry out a revolution, either a slow underhanded one or a sudden and striking one; that the parlement had been carrying on a slow underhanded one for the last ten years.

I agreed that the parlements had gone too far, and had displayed a spirit of selfish partisanship which was concerned only with increasing their own authority. He interrupted me and said "It was more than that! It was like a conspiracy and a general association, or like a very fanatical sect which wanted to destroy the monarchical system, in

Translated and reprinted with the publisher's permission from the *Journal inédit du Duc de Croÿ*, 3 vols., edited by the Vicomte de Grouchy and Paul Cottin (Paris: E. Flammarion, 1906-7), II, 509-11; III, 108-11, 135-37.

order to transform it into an aristocracy which would be in the hands of their own guild. That is, it was a total, concealed revolution, for which the plans were well advanced. Therefore, there were no two ways about it, since they could not be reprimanded or broken one by one: it was all or nothing, since, in the end, somebody has to come out on top!"

I warmly approved this summation, but I told him that I had just had a very interesting conversation with the chancellor, in which, after having praised him for the firmness and resolution he had shown in the affair, if it turned out well, I had forcefully pointed out to him that he had rendered the king the service of making him again the master, of giving him the last word, even of making him a monarch again, but that he had made him a monarch so absolute that there were no more limits upon him; that therefore he must never cease to impress upon the king, as well as on those who influenced him, the extent of the danger, and that if it were a good thing that all authority emanated from one point, everything would be lost if that authority were abused, and how difficult it was for one individual to attain that degree of perfection; [I told M. Bertin that Maupeou] had agreed and had assured me that he also did not wish authority to be abused, but that it was restrained by sufficient restrictions, as he had planned.

In reply, M. Bertin told me that this was the point, but that one individual—whom nothing inclined to rivalry or jealousies, being above all that, having ordinarily been well brought up, or being on especial guard against them—was always a better basis of authority than a guild [*compagnie*], or than a multitude driven by envy and by the bad characters in it rather than by the wise, who did not shout as loudly as the others, or who did not dare be wise, because of their human respect for the guild; that the edict does not say that the Parlement of Paris is compelled to register before making remonstrances, but afterwards, and even, if it is worth the trouble, after the *lit de justice;* that if those who persuade the king to make a law make it a bad law, the parlement, not out of vanity, partisanship, or irresponsibility, but reasonably, should refuse to register and make remonstrances; that these are not prohibited, are not even limited; that the parlement should make them modestly but firmly, reiterate them, try to temper them, but that in the end after twenty-three well-founded remonstrances, if an attempt is made to force the issue, they should say, not threateningly, nor otherwise, but simply and constantly, that neither their duty nor their conscience permits them to register; that, if they are sent *lettres de jussion,* if the thing goes that far, they should say the same thing; that then the king's only recourse is a *lit de justice,* and that since he is the monarch, he has the last word; that then the parlement, registering on his express order, should give in and throw up no more obstacles, because the king, being the monarch, and especially when the whole thing has been trashed out, must have the last word.

But he added that these were limitations, long and multiple limitations, which led the master and his council to weigh the issue carefully; that it was essential that neither side gave way to ill-humor or stubbornness; that the time provided by this process for examination tends to eliminate these by preventing a first flare-up; and thus, that it was a regulated and mixed monarchy, with a master who must weigh each step carefully, but must finally decide and have the last word as a monarch.

I agreed, on the whole, and only insisted that holding the *lit de justice* at Versailles made it too convenient; that the trouble of going into Paris for purposes which only revealed to the king sadness in people's faces, inclined him to take a second look at the law in question.

In sum, it may all be reduced to the fact that the king, in his council, may be the master, but with sufficient limitations and delays to prevent him from doing evil things. Therefore it results that one must do justice to the chancellor; that if, in the end, he composes the [new] Parlement of Paris of good men, he has left it sufficient powers; and that, if they are intelligent enough to use them properly, wisely and firmly, they will still play a very fine part. And taking everything into account, and since there are drawbacks to any system, anarchy or a disorderly assembly being not the least of these, everything may still go well under this system.

REFLECTIONS ON LOUIS XV AT HIS DEATH, MAY 11, 1774

As for his character, he had some excellent traits, and, on the whole, more good ones than bad ones. He had a good memory and unique presence and precision of mind. He never told lies and throughout his life always thought carefully. He was mild-mannered, an excellent father and relative, and the most honest individual in the world. He was learned in the sciences, especially so in astronomy, physics, chemistry, and botany, but always very modest about it. In general, his modesty was a virtue pushed to such an extreme as to become a vice.

Though he always saw things more clearly than others, he always thought he was wrong. I so often heard him say "I would have thought thus and such (and he was correct) but I am told the opposite, so I must be mistaken!—That is not my concern, I have no right to do that!" And he was more inclined to forego than to assert his rights.

He never said anything vicious or cruel deliberately, and if he often said to somebody "You'll soon be dead!" or something like that, it was just a childish bad joke, and he did not mean to say something cruel. He had a habit of speaking lugubriously, by inclination. If he did not have a great deal of wit by modern standards, he had a singularly clear mind and the best and most righteous good sense possible. That is why he never allowed one minister to become more important than another, and spoke with each only about the affairs which concerned him.

I have often been a witness to the fact that he was very brave, but his bravery was too modest. He would perhaps have been a great general, if he had thus judged himself and decided to be one, since he saw and evaluated things clearly, but he did not like war, because it is an affliction, and he had none of the vanity which creates a taste for action. Finally, as I have said so often in my *Mémoires,* his greatest failing was not to make his own decisions, and always, out of modesty, to turn to the opinions of others, even though he saw the issue more clearly than they did. Louis XIV was too haughty, but he was not haughty enough.

Except for his extreme modesty, his principal and only vice was women. He was the handsomest man of his century, very well-built, and as soon as the queen, for reasons of false religion, forsook his bed, and because she was too old for him, and he had enjoyed mistresses, the libertines of high rank and great wit who unceasingly surrounded him, and who alone, in their joking tone, could talk to him, persuaded him that this was a necessary vice and especially that the sovereigns of every age have permitted it to themselves. Thus, he became callous on the subject and thought that, if one repented on his deathbed and received the sacraments, it did not amount to much of a sin.

Therefore he let himself be mastered by women, and, something which will ever remain the chief black mark on his record, he thought that only his mistresses loved him enough to tell him the truth. . . . For that reason, he let himself be led by them, a fact which contributed to ruining the public finances and caused most of the harm of his reign. Finally the last choice of mistress [Mme du Barry] that he made rightly left him covered with opprobrium. It was a great shame that with so many good qualities, he abandoned himself to this dangerous vice, the riskiest vice for kings, whose passions are continually flattered, and who are always lonely and miserable even in the midst of a fawning crowd.

When he had reached the point at which he only continued out of habit (for it was all a matter of habit) with Mme de Pompadour, to titillate his senses he was unceasingly given new objects, even though he continued to live, out of habit, with the official mistress, in whose lodgings he often found it convenient to relax. He had two useful valets in particular who procured him the means of enjoying himself and it is thought that he certainly had affairs with ninety different beauties, though this did not separate him from the little household of his ordinary mistress, who had far too much influence on pardons, on the selection and dismissal of ministers, and it was she who decided all the favors of his reign.

These are some most unfortunate shadows in a portrait which should have been beautiful, and they did great harm to religion, especially at the end of his reign, when the libertines became much more open.

The way in which the taxes were multiplied time and again, both by the inevitable increases in his family and the luxury which pervaded everything, and by the considerable abuses produced by the expenses of his mistresses, and above all the scandal, which is always displeasing to the populace, made him most unpopular at the end. Thus, the people of Versailles showed no interest in his illness and death. It was the same with the people of Paris, except for the last two days, when the sort of full reparation for his sins, which his confessor obliged the grand almoner to make, became known, a reparation which the king had really approved. If he had changed his ways and his mode of life, all the hearts of the populace would gladly have restored him the name of "Louis the Well-Beloved" which had been given him . . . but which had not been heard in a long time.

Because of the danger of infection from the contagious disease of which he died, there was, exceptionally, no autopsy. . . . For the same reason, he could not be embalmed. He was put in quicklime, in a leaden coffin, and, for this reason, it was decided that there would be no lying-in-state, either at Versailles or in the Louvre, and he was taken without ceremony, and as it were incognito, to Saint-Denis. He was carried there on the night of May 12, with only three carriages and a hundred guards and pages bearing torches.

At the death of Louis XIV, there was virtual rejoicing, but at the death of Louis XV nothing happened, and the event seemed to have made no impression. And yet these were the two longest reigns of the monarchy, and in the latter, even Vienna was made to tremble. [Louis XV] acquired Lorraine, and personally conquered the Low Countries, though he restored them afterwards. It was under his reign that, in general, all the great highways and communications of the kingdom were built. He had, on the whole, three glorious wars and, the rest of the time, France enjoyed the most perfect internal tranquillity. Some very great events like the destruction of all the parlements and that of the Jesuits, and many other things, brought about great changes without revolution, and, except for the increases in taxation and the rise in the price of grain, never, surely, was France on a firmer basis or enjoying so much repose as during his reign. Thus, during its course, the population increased by three million souls and agriculture was doubled; these are some very large objects for consideration by which one may judge.

. . . .

August 24 [1774], Saint Louis's eve, was one of the most memorable and important days there has ever been, a day most decisive for the organization of the state and for the fate of the new reign, and the only thing which brought it about was the choice that Madame Adelaide had caused to be made, at the outset, of M. de Maurepas, as well as the queen's sympathy for the Choiseul faction. People may talk about the laws of the state, people may say that it was inevitable that such a thing should happen, but the truth of the matter is just as I have expressed it, since, if M. de Maurepas had not returned to the government, and if the queen had not come to hate the chancellor [Maupeou] because of her sympathy for the Choiseul faction, which led him [Maurepas] to be chosen, all the rest would not have come to pass, especially since it was contrary to the inclinations of the master [Louis XVI].

On this great day, the comptroller-general, the Abbé Terray, without being exiled, was forced to hand in his resignation, and to go to his property at La Motte. The chancellor was rather harshly exiled to his estate of Roncherolles in Normandy. He left at eight o'clock in the morning. He had not been willing to resign, but his exile and expulsion with a stroke of the pen meant the victory of the former parlement, of the Duke d'Orléans, and the loss of royal authority. Many things which had been created because of a long series of events were destroyed without reason or purpose, by a stroke of the pen.

M. de Miromesnil, a former member of parlement, and first president of the Parlement of Rouen, was named keeper of the seals, and thus acting chancellor. . . .

M. Turgot, who had had the navy for a month, was made comptroller-general. . . .

To give a better image to all this, and to announce measures of apparent reorganization and economy, the reform of one of the king's equipages was made public . . . a matter of 200,000 francs.

Here certainly were a great number of big changes coming all at once, and with no compelling reason for them! For the king would only have had to continue to do as he had done at first, to forbid people to speak of [changes] and to institute reorganization and economies everywhere, and there would have been no more talk about it. It must be observed that this was the same king who, as dauphin, had said to the chancellor, at the time that the parlement was destroyed, that he [Maupeou] had just put the crown on the king's head again, and it was thought that he had repeated this phrase to him since he had become king; here are events which make clear how unstable human affairs really are! It is possible that despotism might have been pushed too far, and have become very dangerous, but this was not in the apparent character of the [new] king, and to act as he was now doing was to plunge himself into infinite new difficulties. In sum, the principles and the so-called fundamental laws of the state were shaken up and reversed.

As for the comptroller-general, he had done a great deal of harm with his taxes, but he had saved the revenues of the state. When he had come to office he had found them five or six years in arrears, the expenses regularly exceeding the revenues by more than fifteen millions. He had increased receipts by about twenty-four millions, and, unlike the others, far from constituting the income from loans, he had paid back a great many and had given the king a plan by which, in two years, with everything paid off, there would remain an income of at least sixteen million a year, even though the building program would be continued. No doubt his rule was harsh, but he and the chancellor were two of the brightest men around, and the latter was one of the greatest geniuses ever seen. He had some great defects of character, but also very great talents. . . .

These new measures [in 1774] put into office everything which was directly opposed to the king's first principles, some famous *encyclopédistes,* especially M. Turgot, and all this resulted from no other cause than the unexpected return of M. de Maurepas to the ministry. He changed everything, being the first person to whom the king listened.

If he had listened to someone else who had thought differently, everything would have been different. On such chances depend the affairs of this mortal world!

By all this, the party of the Duke d'Orléans and of the Choiseuls regained control. . . .

The worst of it was that one could see that, despite his innumerable good qualities and a great deal of good sense and even precision of mind, the king was going to allow himself to be led, would not learn to govern or to do his own work, and that, in many respects, it looked as if absolutely nothing would be different from the time of the late king. . . .

Such was this most memorable day, which led one to fear that the king would allow himself to be led, and that, though he was very well intentioned and capable of learning, he would lean on the opinion of others like his grandfather [Louis XV], and, although there may be perceptible advantages to arresting a dangerous despotism, one judged that these new measures were going to revive many old quarrels which had abated, and re-create factions who would cause difficulties. One feared the systematic mentality of M. Turgot and of the *encyclopédistes* who, by weakening the king's religious principles, could reinforce the idea of religious toleration which was already widespread, and feared also that, if the king gave himself up to amusements and did not learn to draw up a fixed plan and follow it, a general indifference would come to prevail which would not restore to the kingdom the force and vigor it needed.

For the rest, everyone judged the measures pretty much according to his own convictions. The men of the parlements jumped for joy; their opponents groaned, and one would have to await the outcome to decide on the effects; but I was pained because I did not perceive, in the whole business, any evidence of a firm plan for the economy, for the relief of the people, or for the re-establishment of the great objectives which were being forgotten.

Selections from Voltaire's Letters, 1774-1776

To Alexandre-Marie-François de Paule de Dompierre d'Hornoy
September 5, 1774

My dear friend, you were not expecting the trip to Roncherolles. It is said that this Roncherolles is hardly better constructed than Sancoins. Fortune with a turn of her wheel sends us where she will. I was just about to obtain what I wanted. The Referendary had taken responsibility for everything, was arranging everything, and St. Bartholomew's Day overturned everything. It only remains for me to ask your pardon for having been liked a little bit by him who had done you harm.

I doubt very much that you will come to Ferney to philosophize on the end of autumn. I foresee that you will prefer your business to my pleasure. I only see things from a long way off with a poor telescope. But people who are a little bit in the know assure me that the plan is to make a new parlement into which neither the murderers of the Chevalier de la Barre nor the slaves of the priests will be admitted. I wish that a corporation would be created of which the big Abbé and you were the principal members. All these beautiful plans appear to me to be difficult to carry out. To re-establish the former parlement, restore to it the whole extent of its district, besmirch it again by the sale of offices, seems to me an even more difficult enterprise. It is a chaos which requires more than six days to make a regular piece of work out of it. The first Zoroaster who spoke of the creation of the world in six gahambars composed these gahambars of three hundred and sixty days, and still God had a great deal of trouble (or so it is said) to render his work free of defects.

I hope that M. de Maurepas and M. Turgot will work swiftly enough to arrange the whole job during the vacation. But after all, the wheel of fortune turns so rapidly nowadays that parlements can be constructed and reconstructed as quickly as grapes are harvested. Perhaps you will be sitting again on your *fleurs de lys,* with what is called the mob of *enquêtes,* by Saint Martin's Day, and a beautiful red mass will be said for you. If you do not have the pleasure of hearing that mass, you will at least have the pleasure of hoping for it from one day to the next, and you will not absent yourself from Paris. If my skeleton could move itself, I would come to see you, but the only trip I shall probably

The letter to Vasselier and the two to d'Hornoy in this section have been translated and reprinted with the permission of the editor and publisher from Besterman, ed., *Voltaire's Correspondence,* LXXXIX, 8-9, 32-33, 173. The remaining letters have been taken from the *Oeuvres complètes de Voltaire,* XLIX.

take is the one to that other world where there is neither a parlement, nor a chancellor, nor an Abbé Terray, nor a comic opera. . . .

Is it true that twenty-five exiles have already been recalled? That is already a great deal of ground covered. It is pleasant to have suffered ostracism and to return in triumph. Great events are pleasant; they shake the soul, which loves to be moved. Tranquillity is deadening. People in this world are like people at the opera; they want changes of the scenery. Be an actor in the new play. You will always be a very good actor, and I shall applaud you from afar. I embrace you tenderly from my bed where my body is in pain and where my soul is tranquil.

To Madame the Marquise du Deffant

Ferney, September 7, 1774

Never have I had more themes to write to you, Madame. Did you know that it was that rascal Vadé, the author of several beggars' operas, who in a bar at la Courtille gave the late king the title of the "Well-beloved"? and who perfumed all the almanacs and notices with it? Do you remember that the cries of fanatics and men of parlement inflamed the brain of the miserable Damiens and provoked an attack on the well-beloved king by the hand of that pig, as insane as he was guilty? Now you see the memory of the well-beloved king attacked by that same people who were ready to raise altars to him because he parted for two weeks from Mme de Châteauroux.

It is this people that makes novenas to Sainte Geneviève, and that makes a mockery every year of Jesus and his mother by Christmases full of filth. It is the same that was responsible for the Fronde and Saint Bartholomew's, and that for a long time booed *Britannicus, Armide,* and *Athalie.* Perhaps no one is more crazy and feeble-minded than the Welches but people who try to please them.

Perhaps it is astonishing that it is intended to sacrifice the new parlement, which has done nothing but obey the king, to the old one, which did nothing but defy him. Perhaps a great many honest people would be disgusted to see returning to their places those who with the dagger of justice murdered the brave and unfortunate Count de Lally, who had the cowardly barbarism to conduct him to the place of execution in a tumbril of garbage with a gag in his mouth; those who soiled their hands with the blood of a child of seventeen in person, and with the blood of another child of sixteen in effigy; those who ordered their hands cut off and their tongues pulled out; those who condemned them to ordinary and extraordinary interrogation and to be burned over a slow fire on a pyre composed of two cords of wood, all for having passed a procession of capuchin monks in the street without saluting it, or for reciting Piron's *Ode to Priapus* when this Piron, parenthetically, was drawing a pension of twelve hundred livres from the royal purse. The people who are occupied with the music of Glück and with their suppers never think about all these horrors; they would go gaily to the Opera and to their little houses over the corpses of the people who were slaughtered on the days of Saint Bartholomew and of the battle of the Saint-Antoine suburb.

There are other people who take all these events seriously, and who groan at them. I like to laugh as much as anybody else, and I have laughed only too much; but I also like to weep over Jerusalem. I console and reassure myself with the opinion I have of M. de Maurepas and M. Turgot. They are both very intelligent, and above all far removed from a superstitious and fanatical outlook. M. de Maurepas, at an age of close to seventy-four, must not and cannot have any desire but to distinguish his career by examples of equity and moderation.

M. Turgot was born wise and just; he is hardworking and studious. If anyone can re-establish the finances, it is he. . . . This is the fashion in which I ramble on at the age of eighty. . . . Farewell, Madame; enjoy all the spectacles of the court and the city, and deign sometimes to remember the sick old man.

To Alexandre-Marie-François de Paule de Dompierre d'Hornoy
                                            Ferney, October 2, 1774
Either I am mistaken, my dear friend, or you know more than you are telling. You say nothing to me about Blois and Châlons which are being returned to your district, or about M. d'Ormesson whom you are being given as first president, or about the sixty preliminary articles. Perhaps this news is false, or perhaps it has been decided to make you all these propositions and leave your vicars in place if you refuse the offers of the court. All I know is that I love you; but I do not at all like the mentality that for such a long time animated your body [*corps*] and especially its persecution of men of letters. Your colleagues should have been taught that the senate of Rome never limited freedom of thought.

The murder in juridical form of La Barre still makes Europe tremble. If your parlement returns I hope that you will do more than anyone to cure it of its fanaticism, and to make it more worthy of a colleague like you. It is shameful and horrible that there is more humanity and wisdom at Petersburg and at Berlin than at Paris. Your parlement is reproached for its eternal mischievous prank of seeking to embarrass the ministry, of trying to make itself necessary by often pointless opposition, of having stirred up an underground war within the nation from the time of Henri IV until the reign of Louis XV (except for the beautiful years of Louis XIV). But as for me, I reproach it with the Maréchale d'Ancre, L'Anglade, Le Brun, La Barre, Lally, and I would even wish that in expiation for these horrors it would forever disqualify itself from judging what it cannot understand, and would not concern itself with rendering decrees on philosophy or smallpox. There is enough grandeur to be had from judging one's fellow citizens, without clinging to the desire to tarnish that very grandeur by judging what is beyond one's competence.

That is my feeling. Decide whether I am wrong or right, and in either case pardon me for my opinion. . . .

To Joseph Vasselier

[December 19, 1774]

The sick old man commends to the kindness of Monsieur Vasselier the enclosed letters.

He sends him also a fishing-lure of the Colony for Dijon.

If Monsieur Vasselier encounters the slightest difficulty, he should return the fishing-lure to us.

It is very astonishing that the Parlement of Paris should begin by making remonstrances to the king who revived it, it is as if Lazarus were to make complaints to Jesus Christ.

To M. the Count d'Argental

April 19 [1776]

My dear angel, the big Abbé Mignot has brought me some very consoling letters from you. I had great need of them when he arrived; for all my ills had me in their grip again. Your letters always salve my wounds; but I must admit that the cuts are a bit deep. Everything that you say about the fathers of the country is well thought-out, very just, very true. You have every reason to be of the opinion of the Pont-Neuf, who says in the song:

> O the sorry fathers!
> Oh! joy!
> O the sorry fathers!

But, sorry fathers though they are, did they any the less shed the blood of the Chevalier de La Barre and of the Count de Lally? Have they any the less persecuted the men of letters who were stupid enough to take their side. Have they any the less declared themselves against the good the king is doing? Have they sought any less to cause trouble for the ministry? Are they any the less to be dreaded by individuals? Do they plot any less with that same clergy they have prosecuted with such determination? Do they oppress any less whoever is not a relative or a friend of their big shots? Do they give any less the appearance of having religion? Do they any the less force people who think to leave their district? Have they any the less prosecuted M. de Boncerf, first clerk of M. Turgot, and are they not still prosecuting him, without naming him, in the decree that they handed down the day after the *lit de justice?* If they are kings of France, one must then leave France, and prepare oneself a refuge elsewhere. No one is sure of his life. They will take their revenge on the first person who comes along for the disgrace they brought upon themselves under Louis XV, and they will embarrass Louis XVI as much as they can. The king will defend himself well; but his subjects can only defend themselves by running away.

I confess to you, my dear angel, that all this poisons the last days of my life. . . .

Always live happy, my dear angel, and I shall be less sad.

                                                                        VOLTAIRE

Selection from Voltaire's **History of the Parlement of Paris**

CHAPTER LXIX. THE PARLEMENT DISCONTENTS THE KING AND PART OF THE NATION. ITS DECISIONS AGAINST THE CHEVALIER DE LA BARRE AND GENERAL LALLY

Who could have believed then that in a short while the parlement would suffer the fate of the Jesuits? For several years it had been trying the king's patience and it did not gain the good will of the public by the torture of the Chevalier de La Barre and General Lally.

This body displeased the government much more by its perpetual struggle against the king's edicts than by its cruelties toward a few citizens. It seemed in fact to take the people's side but it hampered

Oeuvres complètes de Voltaire, XVI. This chapter was added in the edition of 1775 to the text of the original edition of 1769, reproduced in part in Chapter I of this book.

administration and it always appeared to seek to establish its authority on the ruins of the supreme power.

It united, in fact, with the other parlements and claimed to form with them but one body of which it was the principal member. They all then called themselves *classes of parlement:* the one in Paris was the first class. Each class remonstrated on edicts and did not register them. They were even some of these bodies that juridically prosecuted the provincial commanders-in-chief sent to them on the king's authority to force registration. A few classes issued warrants of arrest against these officers. If these decrees had been executed there would have been quite a strange result. The costs of justice are paid from funds derived from the royal domain. Thus, the king would have paid money from his own lands for the decisions rendered by those who were disobeying him against his principal officers who had executed his orders.

This astonishing anarchy could not continue: the crown had to regain its authority or the parlements had to prevail.

In such critical circumstances what was needed was an enterprising and audacious chancellor. He was found. The entire judicial system in the kingdom had to be changed and it was changed.

The king began by attempting to win over the Parlement of Paris. He had the parlement come to a *lit de justice* held at Versailles (September 7, 1770) in the presence of the princes, the peers, and the high officers of the crown. There he forbade the parlement ever to use the terms *unity, indivisibility,* and *classes:*

> To send to other parlements memoirs other than those that are specified by the ordinances;
> To cease its services, except in the cases provided for by the same ordinances;
> To hand in their resignations in a body;
> To ever render a decision that slows up registrations; . . .

The parlement still withholding its services under this solemn edict, the king had letters of royal command brought to them. They disobeyed. New letters of royal command, new disobedience. Finally, the monarch, pushed to the limit, made a last attempt. On January 20 (1771) at four in the morning, the king sent out musketeers who brought each member a paper to sign. The paper contained only an order to declare whether they would obey or refuse. Several wished to interpret the king's will. The musketeers told them that they had orders to disregard commentaries; what was necessary was a *yes* or a *no*.

Forty members signed the *yes*. The others did not. The *yeses* having gone to the parlement the next day with their comrades, begged their pardon for accepting and then signed *no*. All of them were exiled.

Justice continued to be administered by councilors of state and *maîtres des requêtes,* as it had been in 1753. But this was only provisional. Soon a useful solution was drawn from the chaos.

First the king yielded to the wishes of the people who for centuries had complained about two grievances, one of which was ruinous, the other both shameful and costly.

The first was the excessively extended jurisdiction of the Parlement of Paris. This required citizens to come a hundred and fifty leagues to spend before the court amounts that often exceeded the capital [involved in the case]. The second was venality of judicial offices, a venality that had introduced the heavy tax of *épices.*

To reform these two abuses six new parlements were instituted on February 23, 1771, under the name of superior councils. They were enjoined to dispense justice free of charge. These councils were established in Arras, Blois, Châlons, Clermont, Lyon, and Poitiers. Afterwards, others were added to replace a few parlements that were suppressed in the provinces.

Above all it was necessary to form a new Parlement at Paris which would be paid by the king. Its members would not buy their places and would exact nothing from litigants. Its establishment took place on April 13. The shame of venality with which Francis I and Chancellor Duprat had unfortunately soiled France was washed off by Louis XV and by the efforts of Chancellor Maupeou. . . . In the end all the parlements were reformed and it was hoped, but in vain, that a reform of jurisprudence would follow.

The death of Louis XV, in 1774, gave rise to a new administration. Louis XVI, his successor, re-established the parlement with some necessary modifications; these modifications honored the king who ordained them, the minister who drew them up, and the parlement which conformed to them. And France saw the dawn of a wise and happy reign.[1]

1. [Voltaire omitted this final paragraph from the edition of the *History* published in 1777, a year before his death.—Ed.]

BIBLIOGRAPHICAL NOTE

The following brief compilation, limited largely to readily accessible titles in English, conveys hardly any idea of the vast wealth of historical literature on the period of the Brittany Affair. A recent comprehensive bibliography for the late eighteenth century will be found in Jacques Godechot's volume in the "Nouvelle Clio" series, entitled *Les Révolutions 1770–1799* (Paris, 1965).

Students who wish further to explore the last century of the *Ancien Régime* might begin with the incisive treatment in Alfred Cobban's *History of Modern France,* vol. I: *Old Regime and Revolution 1715– 1799* (London, 1957). A fascinating and indispensable manual is John Lough, *An Introduction to Eighteenth Century France* (London, 1960). To compare developments elsewhere in Europe, Leo Gershoy's volume, in the "Rise of Modern Europe" series edited by William L. Langer, *From Despotism to Revolution* (New York, 1944) is still valuable. But the most significant recent interpretation has been provided by Robert R. Palmer in *The Age of Democratic Revolution,* 2 vols. (Princeton, 1959–64).

For the seventeenth-century background, John Lough's *An Introduction to Seventeenth-Century France* (London, 1954) is quite as valuable as his volume already cited. The reign of the Grand Monarch is more lightly, but deftly treated in W. H. Lewis, *The Splendid Century* (Garden City, 1953).

The French Revolution may be the one historical episode about which the most has been written, but the most stimulating analysis, though corrected in detail by a century of research, is still Alexis de Tocqueville's *The Old Regime and the French Revolution,* available in an English translation by Stuart Gilbert (Garden City, 1955). Georges Lefebvre's *The Coming of the French Revolution* (Princeton, 1947) has more recently become a classic. For the course of events between 1789 and 1794, Norman Hampson, *A Social History of the French Revolution* (London, 1963) is a balanced, up-to-date treatment. The outlines of the state that finally emerged are sketched in R. B. Holtman, *The Napoleonic Revolution* (Philadelphia, 1967). An overview of French civilization from the sixteenth century through the Napoleonic years, outdated in some respects but still suggestive, is A. L. Guerard, *France in the Classical Age* (New York and Evanston, 1965).

The intellectual history of the eighteenth century is surveyed in Kingsley Martin, *French Liberal Thought in the Eighteenth Century* (London, 1954) and in George R. Havens, *The Age of Ideas* (New York, 1955). A subtler analysis is to be found in Ernst Cassirer, *The Philosophy of the Enlightenment* (Princeton, 1951). On Voltaire, the sparkling yet thorough study by Peter Gay, *Voltaire's Politics* (New York, 1965), should be consulted.

A most stimulating application by a historian of the concept of "modernization" is found in C. E. Black, *The Dynamics of Modernization: A Study in Comparative History* (New York, 1967).

Finally, mention should be made for readers of French of the exhaustive monograph of H. Fréville, *L'Intendance de Bretagne 1689–1790,* 3 vols. (Rennes, 1953), one of those studies of the particular from which much of general interest can be gleaned.